D1029866

ACADEMIC CAPITALISM AND THE NEW ECONOMY

Sheila Slaughter
and Gary Rhoades

ACADEMIC CAPITALISM and the NEW ECONOMY

Markets, State, and Higher Education

The Johns Hopkins University Press
BALTIMORE AND LONDON

Printed in the United States of America on acid-free paper

9 8 7 6 5 4 3 2 1

The Johns Hopkins University Press
2715 North Charles Street
Baltimore, Maryland 21218-4363
www.press.jhu.edu

Library of Congress Cataloging-in-Publication Data

Slaughter, Sheila.
Academic capitalism and the new economy : markets, state, and higher education / Sheila Slaughter and Gary Rhoades.
p. cm.
Includes bibliographical references (p.) and index.
ISBN 0-8018-7949-3 (hardcover : alk. paper)
1. Education, Higher—Economic aspects—United States. 2. Industry and education—United States. 3. Universities and colleges—United States—Sociological aspects. I. Rhoades, Gary. II. Title.
LC67.62.S62 2004
338.4'337873—dc22

2003024783

A catalog record for this book is available from the British Library.

To Larry L. Leslie
Scholar and colleague, and much more

CONTENTS

FIGURES AND TABLES

Figures

Tables

ACKNOWLEDGMENTS

The writing of this book benefited from the support and input of many agencies, organizations, and colleagues. Much of the data and analysis received substantial support from the National Science Foundation, which funded the following research: "Universities in the information age" (SDEST); "Creating flexible structures of academic work" (STS); "Steps toward resolving ambiguities in university-industry relationships" (SBR); "Academic science policy and the Clinton administration" (EVS); "Protecting the public's trust: A search for balance among benefits and conflict of interest in university-industry relations" (SBER-RST); and "The effects of research related activities on undergraduate education" (SBR). We are especially grateful to supportive program officers Rachelle Hollander and Len Lederman and to the colleagues with whom we conducted these studies and with whom we wrote articles that contributed to this book—Larry L. Leslie, Ron Oaxaca, Samantha King, Teresa Campbell, Jen Croissant, and Andrea Hoplight Tapia. We thank other colleagues with whom we co-authored articles that inform this book: Cynthia Archerd, Ben Baez, Rachel Hendrickson, Margaret Holleman, Chris Maitland, Brian Pusser, Barbara Sporn, Scott Thomas, and Cindy Volk. Additionally, we deeply appreciate the insights and criticism of colleagues who read chapters of this book or articles that contributed to this book: Debbie Anderson, Ernie Benjamin, John Cheslock, Joan Hirt, Ken Koput, Rob Rhoads, and Doug Woodard. Over eighteen years Doug has raised a range of issues about the role of student services in the academic capitalist knowledge/learning regime and reminded us that colleges and universities must attend to undergraduate education and student development. To our new colleague, Jenny Lee, our thanks for pushing us to more explicitly place ourselves in relation to the academic capitalist knowledge/learning regime.

In addition to these principal investigators, we thank the many graduate students who worked on these grants. Thanks also to Sheila's Academic Capitalism seminar in spring 2003 who sharpened our thinking and writing: Tamara DeStefanis, Teri Knutson-Woods, George McClelland, Jeff Orgera, Marcus Machado, Charles Rice, Vernon Smith, Glen Williams, and Greg Wilson. Special thanks to Amy Metcalfe, who participated in all the above activities, was a dedicated research assistant, and helped us realize the possibilities of intermediating organizations.

The database of collective bargaining agreements (the Higher Education Contract Analysis System), which enabled us to explore the policy dimensions of academic capitalism in the new economy in community colleges and comprehensive universities, was developed and made available through the good work and generosity of the National Education Association and the American Federation of Teachers. We particularly thank Christine Maitland and Rachel Hendrickson at the NEA. We appreciate as well the feedback and support of Larry Gold at the AFT.

Further, we also owe a debt to each other. Over the course of seventeen years of conversations and exchanges ranging over political economy, professions, policy, and organizations in higher education, and much more, we have challenged and stretched each other in ways that have enhanced and brought out the best in our work and lives.

Finally, we dedicate this book to Larry L. Leslie, whom we could not pull away from the joys of retirement, poker, hiking, and county politics to co-author this volume. In more ways than we can enumerate, Larry has influenced our work and shaped the very special Center for the Study of Higher Education in which our work has thrived. His contributions, for each of us, in distinctive but profound ways, go well beyond the boundaries of simple colleagueship. To Sheila Slaughter, who is S2, he is L3, and a partner nonpareil who grounds her in the realities of hiking, camping, hunting, and country western dancing. To Gary Rhoades, whose unparalleled partner is his wife, Janet, centering him in the realities of an eternal Enchanted April, and of being a dad making Knots in a Counting Rope with Elizabeth and Olivia, Larry is and always will be, simply and affectionately, Chief.

ACADEMIC CAPITALISM AND THE NEW ECONOMY

1

THE THEORY OF ACADEMIC CAPITALISM

At the turn of the twenty-first century, the rise of the "new," global knowledge or information society calls for a fresh account of the relations between higher education institutions and society.[1] Our analysis of these relations has led us to develop a theory of academic capitalism which explains the process of college and university integration into the new economy. The theory does not see the process as inexorable; it could be resisted, or, more likely, alternative processes of integration could be developed. Nor does the theory see the university as being "corporatized" or subverted by external actors. Instead, the theory of academic capitalism sees groups of actors—faculty, students, administrators, and academic professionals—as using a variety of state resources to create new circuits of knowledge that link higher education institutions to the new economy. These actors also use state resources to enable interstitial organizations to emerge that bring the corporate sector inside the university, to develop new networks that intermediate between private and public sector, and to expand managerial capacity to supervise new flows of external resources, investment in research infrastructure for the new economy, and investment in infrastructure to market institutions, products, and services to students. Expanded managerial capacity is also directed toward restructuring faculty work to lower instructional costs (although not costs generally).

The theory of academic capitalism moves beyond thinking of the student as consumer to considering the institution as marketer. When students choose colleges, institutions advertise education as a service and a life style. Colleges and universities compete vigorously to market their institutions to high-ability students able to assume high debt loads. Student consumers choose (frequently private) colleges and universities that they calculate are likely to bring a return on educational investment and increasingly choose majors linked to the new

1. We use the terms *knowledge society, information society,* and *new economy* interchangeably throughout this volume.

economy, such as business, communications, media arts. Once students have enrolled, their status shifts from consumers to captive markets, and colleges and universities offer them goods bearing the institutions' trademarked symbols, images, and names at university profit centers such as unions and malls. College and universities also regard their student bodies as negotiable, to be traded with corporations for external resources through all-sports contracts, test bed contracts, single product contracts, and direct marketing contracts. When students graduate, colleges and universities present them to employers as output/product, a contribution to the new economy, and simultaneously define students as alumni and potential donors. Student identities are flexible, defined and redefined by institutional market behaviors.

We open this book with an account of a research effort at Texas A&M University called the Missyplicty project. It was funded by John Sperling, who founded the University of Phoenix and is currently president of the Apollo Group, of which Phoenix is a part. Although we do not analyze for-profit higher education institutions in our book, we think the example of the University of Phoenix is useful because public and nonprofit private colleges and universities engage markets in ways that are very similar to the approach Phoenix takes. Sperling used his profits from for-profit education to clone his dog, Missy. The Missyplicity project captures many of the promises, pitfalls, ironies, and contradictions that characterize the changing relations of colleges and universities to the new economy. The project was made possible by profits from for-profit higher education for adults, which depends on treating education as an alienable service rather than as a public good, and relies on mechanisms such as copyrighting and commercialization of instruction via part-time faculty and on-line education. The Missyplicity project illustrates non-profit universities' involvement with private patrons, intellectual property, and new economy start-up companies, dramatically revealing a number of the themes of an academic capitalist knowledge/learning regime.

> Welcome to the home page for the Missyplicity Project, which aims to clone a dog for the first time in history—a specific dog named Missy. Missy is a beloved pet, getting on in years, whose wealthy owners wish to reproduce her—or at least create a genetic duplicate (which we all know is not the same thing).
>
> The Missyplicity Project is funded and managed by Genetic Savings & Clone, a gene bank and cloning company with offices in College Station Texas and Sausalito, California . . . The Missyplicity Project is being executed by a team of world-class scientists and technicians headquartered at Texas A&M University [TAMU], in College Station, Texas. Several senior scientists from other major universities and institutions have also been recruited . . . the senior team members [are]:

> Dr. Mark Westhusin, TAMU—Principal Investigator, Nuclear Transfer Specialist
> Dr. Duane Kraemer, TAMU—Embryo Transfer
> Dr. Robert Burghardt, TAMU—Tissue Culturing, Analysis, and Cryopreservation
> Dr. Lisa Howe, TAMU—Animal Tissue Collection.

> GSC's [Genetic Service and Clone] service is gene banking: Cellular DNA is first extracted from your animal by your own veterinarian using materials supplied by GSC, then the samples are shipped to GSC via BioBox™, grown in culture in GSC's laboratories for up to one month, then finally cryopreserved in liquid nitrogen.

> Anyone can order GSC services, either online or by calling 866–9CLONES . . . Standard service is for live, healthy animals . . . The price for Standard service orders is $895 each, plus shipping . . . Emergency service is for terminal or recently deceased animals (up to one week post-mortem depending on storage conditions, though the sooner the better) . . . The price for Emergency service orders is $1395 each, plus shipping . . . The annual maintenance fee for Standard jobs is $100 per year, versus $150 for Emergency jobs (which involve twice as much tissue). The first year's maintenance is included in the initial service fee for both grades. (Genetic Savings and Clone 2003)

> The company [Genetic Savings and Clone] has also tried to shield the identity of its main financial donor, the source of $5.5 million in cash and credit for the young company and $3.5 million to its Texas A&M research effort. But documents point to billionaire John Sperling . . . founder of the University of Phoenix, the nation's largest for-profit university . . . A privately held company, GS&C's equity is held by its anonymous investor [later identified as Sperling], Hawthorne [the CEO], researcher Dr. Mark Westhusin of Texas A&M and three other Missyplicity scientists . . . According to Texas A&M, the money and Missy's cell samples were donated with the explicit purpose of cloning Missy. (Krieger 2001)

> Texas A&M began a white-tail deer cloning project last fall . . . The information gathered from the cloning project could be used to produce larger bucks with bigger antlers that would appeal to Texas hunters. "We want to know how much the antler growth is dependent on genetics," Westhusin (associate professor of the Veterinary Medicine Department) said . . . Dr. Billy Higginbotham, professor and extension wildlife and fisheries specialist for A&M [said] . . . "Hunting as an industry in Texas provides 31,711 jobs, salaries and wages of over $864 million, and generates $93 million in state sales tax revenue." (Baker 2003)

Billionaire John Sperling provided the impetus for the Missyplicity project. Sperling made his money through the University of Phoenix, a for-profit higher education system. University of Phoenix, Inc., became a subsidiary of a larger enterprise run by Sperling, the Apollo Group, which also included the Institute for Professional Development, The College for Financial Planning Institutes Corporation, and Western International University, Inc. (Apollo Group 2002). The Apollo Group is an example of the trade in services characteristic of the new economy. In the new economy, knowledge is a critical raw material to be mined and extracted from any unprotected site; patented, copyrighted, trademarked, or held as a trade secret; then sold in the marketplace for a profit. The University of Phoenix uses all these mechanisms to protect its intellectual property.

Sperling makes the case that public and nonprofit private universities receive about "60 percent of their operating expenses from direct and indirect public subsidy [while] the University of Phoenix has managed to secure market share and make a profit wherever it operates—and has done so with no public subsidy" (Sperling and Tucker 1997, p. x). Sperling states that public and nonprofit universities have "capital-intensive input standards and operationally inefficient structures" and are protected by "extensive regulation by federal and state agencies and by the federally authorized private accrediting associations" (p. 52). Although Sperling claims that his operation has been able to make a profit without public subsidy, his businesses, like many in the new economy, depend upon government shifting resources from public welfare functions to production functions, sometimes directly, often indirectly. For example, the University of Phoenix receives substantial indirect federal subsidy. As the Apollo Group's annual report notes, "Many of our students participate in government sponsored financial aid programs under Title IV of the Higher Education Act of 1965, as amended. These financial programs generally consist of guaranteed student loans and direct grants to the student" (p. 15). Federal financial aid is available to students at for-profit institutions because their leaders were active lobbyists for the deregulation and reregulation of aid programs. Phoenix has no libraries of its own, instead relying on students' use of public libraries and publicly subsidized college and university libraries to cut costs. In the new economy, market and market-like activities are foregrounded, while the state and the many subsidies it provides are backgrounded.

Public and nonprofit or private institutions of higher education use the same mechanisms as Phoenix—extended managerial capacity, part-time faculty, copyright, and information technology—to create profit centers. These profit centers do not accrue revenue for stockholders, but they do generate (nontaxed) external monies that are used to cross-subsidize other institutional activities, which often involve investment in infrastructure to integrate colleges and universities with the new economy. Like Phoenix, public and nonprofit private higher education institutions rely heavily on public funding, expending taxpayer dollars in pursuit of external revenues from corporations. Again like Phoenix, such institutions are increasingly targeting applicants who will pay full tuition or differential tuition, rather than seeking out underserved, often minority eighteen year olds. Public and nonprofit institutions increasingly engage in market and marketlike activities.

Sperling, drawing on his profits from the Apollo Group, provided Texas A&M University (TAMU) with private grants ($3.5 million) for cloning Missy, but he also conceived of cloning his beloved pet as a business opportunity. Simultaneously, Sperling put up venture capital ($5.5 million) for a publicly traded business, Genetics Savings and Clone, which depended on science that was in progress at TAMU. Four TAMU veterinary science faculty became Sperling's business partners, trading their expertise for equity shares in Genetic Savings and Clone. Although it is not clear from the newspaper accounts whether TAMU, as an institution, held an equity position in Genetics Saving and Clone, TAMU actively lobbied to have the state of Texas change laws that prevented institutions from holding equity shares in corporations based on faculty discoveries (Schmidt 2002).

In the Missyplicity case, we see faculty housed in public institutions not as undergoing corporatization but as seeking profits from corporations. Institutions not only are acted on by corporations external to them but actively seek to lobby state legislatures in order to change regulations so that colleges and universities have more opportunity to engage in market and marketlike behaviors. Generally, college and university involvement in entrepreneurial activity is portrayed as win-win. Faculty equity holding in corporations based on their research is seen as an incentive for professors to move technology to the market. Colleges and universities are viewed as playing an important part in state economic growth, contributing to general prosperity.

However, the faculty at TAMU were able to participate in the Missyplicity project only because of their previous education and training, which was heavily state subsidized. Sperling sought out TAMU veterinary scientists for his project because they had successfully cloned several animal species, including a calf named Second Chance. Much of this cloning research had been federally funded. Thus, the Missyplicity project drew on taxpayer-funded, state-subsidized educational and research talent. The project also drew heavily on the legitimacy provided by TAMU scientists to convince pet owners to fast-freeze their pets' bodily fluids at $895–$1,395, depending on the pet's state of decrepitude.

Although the Missyplicty project was represented as the altruistic act of a dog owner trying to replicate his beloved pet, the cloning technologies involved are part of a multimillion-dollar animal models market. Designer animals—such as mice in which nonprofit university researchers have inserted human genes—are especially valued for disease research and sometimes cost more than $2,000 for a breeding pair. Genetic Savings & Clone, working on more complex cats and dogs, had "to pay to use other companies' patented cloning techniques," but, according to Charles Long, the general manager, "we hope to change the process so significantly that we wouldn't be bound by other patents, and we'd have our own . . . that someone else might license . . . That's the position you want to get yourself in—to get others to pay" (Monro 2002, p. 1).

Although the Missyplicity project used private funds, it built on taxpayer-funded research in biotechnology. While most taxpayers are unlikely to purchase cloning services, they already purchase medicines based on patented cell lines and research animals, such as oncomouse, developed at Harvard and marketed by Dupont for the study of cancer. Taxpayers pay for the federal research that professors perform in universities, they effectively subsidize the corporations that partner with universities to develop technologies based on federal research, and they pay again when they purchase various high-priced pharmaceuticals.

The TAMU researchers successfully cloned a cat, named CC (Carbon Copy), but not a dog, which is more reproductively complex. Although CC was genetically identical to the calico cat from which it was cloned, CC looked like a striped tabby rather than a calico, alarming pet owners who sought at least facsimiles, if not eternal life. Sperling—who wanted dogs not cats, let alone cats that were not carbon copies—withdrew his funding from TAMU, although he continued to fund Genetic Savings and Clone. Although TAMU researchers were not successful in cloning Missy, they still held equity in Genetics Saving and Clone. They were not chastened by their inability to meet their sponsor's goals. Instead, they have turned to deer cloning in hopes of producing bucks with bigger antlers for the Texas hunting "industry," a bigger buck for the bang. In many regards, faculty at TAMU functioned as state-subsidized entrepreneurs who risked little by partnering with Genetic Savings and Clone. Although they were not able to clone Missy, they kept their positions and their salaries, and moved on to another entrepreneurial project.

Our analysis of the Missyplicity project highlights a number of themes relevant to this book. Among them are the growth of market and marketlike activity in the sciences and engineering, as captured by patenting, and the recent aggressive commercialization of instruction, as practiced by University of Phoenix and as captured by copyrighting in public and private higher education. Market and marketlike activities are no longer confined to the sciences and engineering; they permeate the higher learning. Faculty and institutions are not merely acted on by external organizations, such as corporations and the state; they are also actors who form boundary-spanning organizations and networks to integrate with the new economy. Although the rhetoric surrounding entrepreneurial faculty and institutional activity highlights the close connection to the market, the state plays an important role in subsidizing the emerging academic capitalist knowledge/learning regime. Projects like Missyplicity, which depend heavily on the work of previously accomplished, state-subsidized science even though entrepreneurial funds pay for the immediate research work, raise questions about opportunity costs. Does the citizenry of Texas or the United States want their tax dollars to support any work corporations or entrepreneurs choose to do, or would they rather see public funds for research applied to corporate ventures with a more socially redeeming purpose, such as fighting AIDS or educating children more effectively? The Missyplicity project raises questions about the terms of the academy's engagement with the new economy; we explore these questions in this book.

In the remainder of this chapter, we review the 1990s scholarship on higher education and research, noting what distinguishes our book from previous literature. We then point to the ways in which our book builds on and is different from *Academic Capitalism: Politics, Policies and the Entrepreneurial University* (1997). Following this brief literature review, we present a theory of academic capitalism that explains the processes by which colleges and universities are integrating with the new economy, shifting from a public good knowledge/learning regime to an academic capitalist knowledge/learning regime. We conclude with an overview of the book's content.

More Academic Capitalism and the Higher Education and Research Literature

In the 1990s, a substantial literature on how to change higher education emerged: Leslie and Fretwell's *Wise Moves in Hard Times: Creating and Managing Resilient Colleges and Universities* (1996), and Tierney's *The Responsive University: Restructuring for High Performance* (1998) and *Building the Responsive Campus: Creating High Performance Colleges and Universities* (1999). The premise underlying this work is that colleges and universities are difficult to change and that whatever changes take place are largely located on the margins of a relatively unchanging core.[2] For the most part, this literature deals with undergraduate education.

At the same time, a literature developed around the research function and research universities that saw higher education as undergoing a great deal of change. For example, Etzkowitz, Webster, and Healey (1998, p. 1) talk of a "second [academic] revolution" that involves "the translation of research into products and into new enterprises." However, the scholarly work that deals with

2. Exceptions are Francis and Hampton 1999, who point to significant ways in which public research universities have been responsive to market pressures.

research focuses mainly on patents and various forms of university-industry-government partnerships. It does not address college and university commodification and commercialization of a wide range of copyrightable educational products and services, often directed toward undergraduates or niche graduate student markets. For example, Geiger (1993), when speaking to "the university's embrace of commercial endeavors" during the 1980s, refers to research activities. A similar focus on research is evident in critiques of industry-university connections, whether they argue that industry is in some sense taking over the academy, as does Soley in *Leasing the Ivory Tower: The Corporate Takeover of Academia* (1995), or that universities are too eager to sell out to corporations, as does Bowie in *University-Business Partnerships: An Assessment* (1994; see also Feller 1997).

In contrast, our book looks at undergraduate and research/graduate education and at copyrights and trademarks as well as patents, focusing on generation of external resources from market activities that turn on the selling of products, processes, and services. We see significant changes occurring across research/graduate and undergraduate education and in professional schools, as well as in science and engineering. We conceptualize these changes as a shift from a public good knowledge/learning regime to an academic capitalist knowledge/learning regime. The changes we discuss encompass instruction as well as research, involve administrative and trustee activities, and attend as much to student consumption as student learning.

A second point that distinguishes our work from that of others is our attention to networks of actors that link universities to each other, to corporations, and to various state agencies. Most of the literature on change in higher education focuses on individual organizations. Dramatic case studies, such as those by Clark (1970, 1998), tell stories about organizational transformations in the culture and practices of individual colleges and universities, exploring, for example, how campuses develop entrepreneurial culture. The organization has been the focus of recent work that specifies culturally contingent aspects of successful change (Kezar and Eckel 2002). However, the larger environment and particularly the organizational networks of which most organizations are a part remain relatively unexamined.

Rather than simply focusing on individual organizations, the literature often anthropomorphizes the organization as suggested by the titles of some of the books on organizational change discussed earlier: the "learning college," the "responsive university." Such metaphors convey a sense that the organization is bounded and is a single entity. The referent, after all, is "the" organization, with clearly defined boundaries. There is little, if any, consideration of subunits and groups within the organization, or of their multiple connections with various units and groups outside the organization.

The prevailing models for analyzing higher education organizations are grounded in a presumption that higher education is distinct from the state and from the market. In comparative scholarship, scholars work out of a triangle model (Clark 1983) that categorizes systems in terms of the influence of the state, the market, and the academic profession on higher education organizations. In studies of governance in U.S. higher education, scholars explore dimensions of substantive and procedural autonomy from the state, building on Berdahl's (1971) classic work. The academic discourse tends to privilege the market in a laissez-faire sense. Academic managers seek to situate higher education enterprises as farther and separate from "the state" and closer and connected to "the market."

When the literature does look beyond "the" organization (Gibbons et al. 1994; Council on Competitiveness 1996; Stokes 1997; Branscomb 1997a, 1997b; Feldman et al. 2002a), it focuses on how universities interact with corporations and, less frequently, state agencies. However, this literature still sees universities, corporations, and the state as having relatively clear boundaries, and for the most part does not look at networks. (For an exception, see Powell 1990.) Even Etzkowitz, Webster, and Healey (1998), who offer a biological "triple helix" model in which the strands are the entwined relations of university-industry-government, still treat the strands as separate and distinct, although they foreground universities and industry and background the state.

In contrast to literatures that focus on "the" organization or on research relations between universities and industry, construed as separate organizational spheres, we look at networks of actors that cross boundaries among universities and colleges, business and nonprofit organizations, and state(s).

In much of the literature the interests of the organization are equated with the interests of its managers. For instance, a key to change is generally thought to be an organizational leader who initiates and supports the new development.[3] By contrast, we focus on a wider range of academic actors, examining changes in the academic profession and the structure of faculty employment, as well as on the emergence of groups of other professionals involved in com-

3. See Shaw and London 2001 for an exception with regard to community colleges; they map out cases in which the core faculty and core culture affect the activities of the organization in fundamental ways.

modifying and commercializing intellectual products.[4] Presently we see academics becoming increasingly managed professionals (Rhoades 1998a), who are governed by central administrators and nonfaculty managerial professionals (Rhoades 1998b; Rhoades and Sporn 2002), ranging from technology transfer and chief information officers to university attorneys, who are increasingly central players in the academic enterprise. In our view, the ascendance of the academic capitalist knowledge/learning regime requires us to rethink the centrality and dominance of the academic profession.

The Scope and Analytical Focus of *Academic Capitalism and the New Economy*

Academic Capitalism and the New Economy differs not only from the literature on higher education and research; it also differs from its predecessor, *Academic Capitalism* (1997). An important difference between the books lies in their substantive focus in terms of countries and institutions. *Academic Capitalism* (1997) examined public research universities in four countries—Australia, Canada, the United States, and the United Kingdom. In this book, we concentrate on the United States and on the nonprofit higher education institutions in the U.S. system, from public and private research universities to community colleges.[5] We offer a fuller and more focused picture of academic capitalism in the United States that encompasses the varied institutional settings in which market and marketlike practices are pursued.

In expanding the institutional scope of our study, we have also expanded our analytical interests. *Academic Capitalism* (1997) concentrated on technology transfer. In this book, we follow through on and update the earlier analysis of patenting and technology transfer. In addition, we address the intensified commercialization of instruction, educational materials, and software/courseware in relation to changes in copyright policies nationally and at the institutional level. Copyright represents an area of market and marketlike activities by institutions, faculty, and students that touches a much broader range of places and

4. For us, a central part of academic capitalism is a reversal of Jencks and Riesman's *Academic Revolution* (1968). Jencks and Riesman were conceptualizing the ascendancy of the national academic profession in the post–World War II era, which was supported by federal research and grounded in meritocracy. Etzkowitz, Webster, and Healey 1998, in referring to a second academic revolution, misread Jencks and Riesman's work, attributing the first academic revolution to the late nineteenth and early twentieth century and the introduction of the research mission.

5. We do not focus on the for-profit sector of higher education, which in proportional terms remains quite small; in our view, this sector could be seen as an important indicator of academic capitalism and its relation to the new economy, but it merits a separate study.

players than does patenting; it involves the commodification of higher education not just in technoscience fields in research universities but in virtually all fields and classrooms in all types of institutions. For example, we consider the intellectual property policies of less prestigious institutions, including unionized ones (see Rhoades 1998a), which address the ownership, commercialization, and use of educational materials produced in community colleges and comprehensive masters and doctoral degree-granting universities.

Much of the policy and scholarly attention in the realm of copyright has concentrated on distance education, on the development of videotaped and on-line courses and programs delivered to students off campus (e.g., see Noble 2001). Those are important developments and areas of intensified activity, nationally and internationally, and we analyze some of these activities. However, we are also interested in copyright as it relates to educational materials, courses, and programs delivered on campus in traditional classrooms but mediated in various ways by technology, whether through new projection technologies in the classroom, or software platforms for organizing syllabi, chat rooms, readings, and focused questions for orienting students to the readings.

Academic Capitalism and the New Economy has a somewhat different conceptual focus than *Academic Capitalism* (1997). This difference is partly a function of changing authors. Initially, *Academic Capitalism and the New Economy* was to be written by Slaughter, Leslie, and Rhoades. However, Leslie retired, and, when asked if he would continue to participate, replied, ever the economist, that he could not see the marginal utility, either to his career or any personal utility function, of yet another book. Partly the new conceptual focus stems from profound changes in U.S. higher education that occurred in the 1990s as colleges and universities aggressively pursued the market behaviors outlined in *Academic Capitalism* (1997). Previously Slaughter and Leslie (1997, p. 210) drew conclusions regarding the "encroachment of the profit motive into the academy." We now point to the internal embeddedness of profit-oriented activities as a point of reorganization (and new investment) by higher education institutions to develop their own capacity (and to hire new types of professionals) to market products created by faculty and develop commercializable products outside of (though connected to) conventional academic structures and individual faculty members.

In this book, we do not feature resource dependency theory. Although we continue to define academic capitalism as the pursuit of market and marketlike activities to generate external revenues, our current analysis focuses on the blurring of boundaries among markets, states, and higher education. A premise of resource dependency theory, as of much organization theory, is that there is a relatively clear boundary between the organization and its environment. Resource dependency theory predicts that the organization, which is the object of study, will take on and reflect the organizational characteristics of the principal external resource providers in its environment, a conception that requires the focal organization to be distinct and separate from organizations in its resource environment. In contrast, we see the academic capitalist knowledge/learning regime as characterized by the development of new networks of actors who develop organizations that span and blur the boundaries between public and private sectors. We have come to see colleges and universities (and academic managers, professors, and other professionals within them) as actors initiating academic capitalism, not just as players being "corporatized."

However, we do see the changing resource mix as promoting an academic capitalist knowledge/learning regime with regard to state funds, federal monies, and tuition dollars. Fiscal crises combined with rising tuition have created a climate that emphasizes the importance of new sources of external revenues. Periodic state fiscal crises, marked by budget shortfalls and clawbacks from the higher education sector, give legitimacy to notions of resource shortages. Even though such shortages do not occur regularly or predictably and seldom affect all institutions, they nonetheless reinforce faculty and administrators' beliefs that increases in external resource flows are necessary to sustain the academic enterprise. The growth of the academic enterprise, especially in science and engineering fields, means that even though federal funds continue to grow in absolute terms, these monies do not meet the expectations for generous funding to which scientists and engineers have been accustomed (Greenberg 2001). The (somewhat) slow rate of increase in federal research funding intensifies competition among scientists and engineers in federal grant and contract markets. Although a great deal of attention has been paid to patents and university-industry-government partnerships, the external revenue stream to which institutions have turned most frequently is student tuition. The greatest increase in shares of institutional funds has come through raising tuition, which has heightened students' and parents' consumer consciousness about what they expect in terms of their educational experience and in terms of returns on investment in their human capital. These changed expectations reshape student identity from that of learner to that of consumer.

We do not follow up the important analysis of revenue and expenditure trends in *Academic Capitalism* (1997) because these have been mapped out by others. As Francis and Hampton (1999) show, the trends delineated in *Academic Capitalism* continued in the 1990s. That ongoing pattern is evident in Figure 1.1.

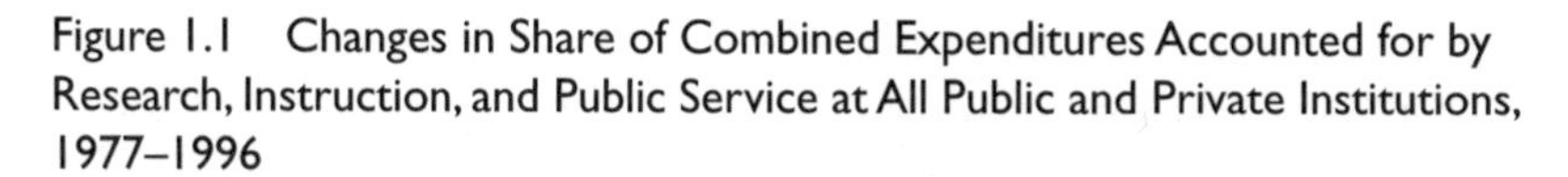

Figure 1.1 Changes in Share of Combined Expenditures Accounted for by Research, Instruction, and Public Service at All Public and Private Institutions, 1977–1996

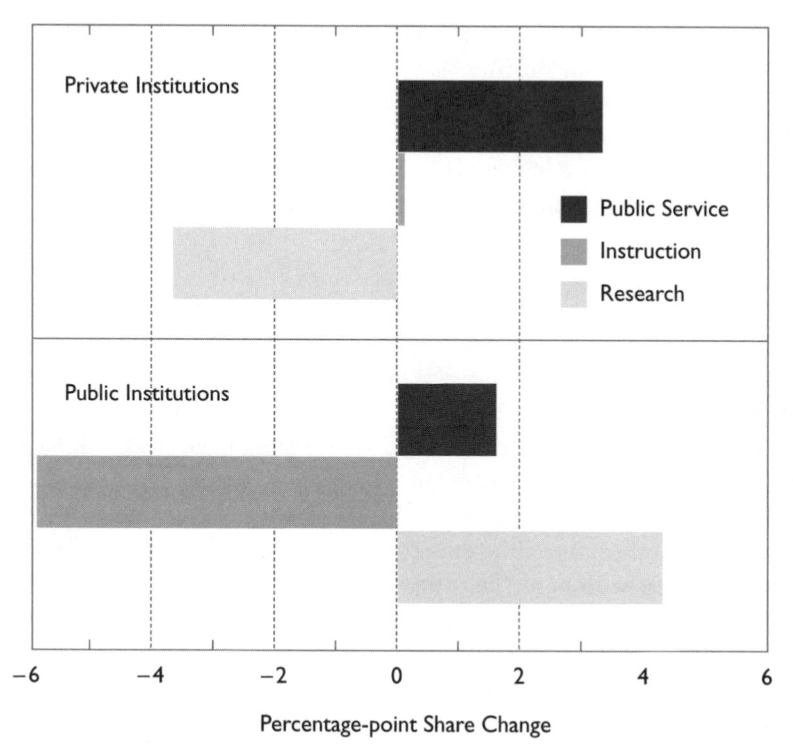

Source: National Science Board, Science and Engineering Indicators, 2002. Arlington, VA: National Science Foundation, 2002 (NSB-02-1).

For the late 1970s and 1980s *Academic Capitalism* (1997) documented smaller shares of college and university revenues coming from the state and a lesser share of institutional expenditures in higher education going to instruction. This continued in the 1990s. Although in the national aggregated data, this appears as a gradual, incremental trend, we believe that at the level of colleges and universities, shifting resource dependencies are more often experienced as periodic episodes of crisis during which institutions go through restructuring processes.[6] For many universities, for example, one such period was the early

6. We make this argument only for the United States. In other countries, for example, Brazil, state fiscal crisis may be a continuing condition that brings about the rise of alternative institutions—in the Brazilian case, private tuition-based higher education.

1990s. Many institutions are again in the midst of such a process, after several years of having been spared, in relative terms, fiscal stringency. Although we do not see resource dependency as causal, we think that it plays an important part in the development of the academic capitalist knowledge/learning regime. The slow and continued decrease in state block grants as a share of annual operating revenues of public universities, marked by periodic, intense fiscal crises, has played an important part in legitimating academic capitalism. However, during the periods in which states recovered and increased budgets (although not shares), university pursuit of market activity nonetheless increased.

The Theory of Academic Capitalism

Unlike in *Academic Capitalism* (1997), in this book we offer a theory of academic capitalism. This theory explains the processes by which universities integrate with the new economy. In constructing our theory, we draw on the work of Foucault (1977, 1980), Mann (1986), and Castells (1996, 2000). Although these theorists see the centrality of knowledge, organizations, and networks to the economy, generally—and, in Castells's case, to the new economy, specifically—none of them directly addresses universities or the part played by universities in the new economy, other than Castells's brief mention of universities as "milieus of innovation." We acknowledge our intellectual debt to these theorists, as well as to many others, for ideas and concepts that helped us, but we have crafted a theory of our own.

In the last quarter of the nineteenth century, universities integrated with the industrial economy, shifting from a focus on theology, moral philosophy, and the education of gentlemen, overseen by the clergy, to science-based disciplines ranging from chemistry and engineering to the social sciences. Land-grant institutions played an important role by contributing to the industrialization of agriculture (Williams 1961). Many of these new fields of knowledge were concerned with the development and management of science-based, mass-production industries and the establishment of states' ground rules for capitalism. Although jurisdiction over new fields was contested, professionals exercised an increasing amount of oversight. While a handful of moral philosophers and university presidents resisted colleges and universities' integration with the industrial economy, the majority of professors and scholars participated in the stabilization and expansion of professional careers rooted in university education.

Generally, the superiority of scientific knowledge over theology—the triumph of a more perfect knowledge—was offered as the theoretical explanation for the institutionalization of the new knowledge in universities. This explanation allowed professors and professionals to keep a (shifting and tenuous) distance between the university and industry, which provided the wealth that made the modern university possible, and between the university and the state, which often provided the proximate resources for higher education. Professors and higher education interests certainly served the industrial economy and the state, but in doing so they arguably gained some power by claiming a social contract with society in return for disinterested, nonpartisan research (Silva and Slaughter 1984).[7]

At the turn of the twenty-first century, we cannot ignore corporations and the state because knowledge is not easily separable from the new economy. In the information society, knowledge is raw material to be converted to products, processes, or service. Because universities are seen as a major source of alienable knowledge, they are in the process of establishing new relations with the global economy. Autonomy, the preferred but perhaps always fictive position of universities with regard to capital and the state, becomes less possible.[8]

The theory of academic capitalism focuses on networks—new circuits of knowledge, interstitial organizational emergence, networks that intermediate between public and private sector, extended managerial capacity—that link institutions as well as faculty, administrators, academic professionals and students to the new economy. New investment, marketing and consumption behaviors on the part of members of the university community also link them to the new economy. Together these mechanisms and behaviors constitute an academic capitalist knowledge/learning regime.

The New Economy

Although the new economy is central to the rise of the academic capitalist knowledge regime, it is not causal. Universities are difficult to separate from the new economy because they contribute richly to its development. The new economy treats advanced knowledge as raw material that can be claimed through legal devices, owned, and marketed as products or services. As such, universities

7. We apologize for this extremely compressed account of the relationship between universities, corporations, the state, and professional associations in the last quarter of the nineteenth century. For a deeper understanding, see Haskell 1977, Bledstein 1977, Furner 1975, Ross 1991, Silva and Slaughter 1984, Slaughter 1997, Perkin 1989, Geiger 1993, Ben-David 1984, Barrow 1990, and Veysey 1965.

8. We see organized professors, in learned associations such as the American Economic Association and cross-disciplinary organizations such as the American Association of University Professors, as tacitly agreeing to curb the revolutionary potential of new knowledge in return for academic freedom. This freedom is a somewhat circumscribed right, which allows professors to use their expertise only if they serve the existing order. See Slaughter 1981, 1988, and Barrow 1990.

are sites where knowledge is rendered alienable in multiple ways, a number of which we describe in the course of this volume.

In considering the new economy, we are not so much concerned with causality or characteristics, which have been discussed at length by scholars from various disciplines (Barnet and Cavenaugh 1994; Bell 1973; Carnoy 1993; Castells 1993, 1996, 1997, 1998, 2000; Chomsky 1994; Cohen 1993; Cohen and Zysman 1987; Greider 1997; Harrison and Bluestone 1990; Jessop 1993; Kuttner 1997; Reich 1991; Sassen 1991; Slaughter and Leslie 1997), as with the implications of the new economy for academe. We see the salient characteristics of the new economy for colleges and universities as being its global scope, its treatment of knowledge as raw material, its non-Fordist production processes, and its need for educated workers and consumers.

Global Scope

Unlike *Academic Capitalism* (1997), we do not focus on the global dimensions of higher education in this book. Although we recognize its growing importance, we think that concentration on the global dimensions of colleges and universities can occlude our view of the many new mechanisms, organizations, networks, and market practices that connect higher education to the new economy in any one country. Indeed, the proliferation and complexity of these processes is so great we sometimes think we have barely scratched the surface of the country we know best, the United States. In the future, we plan to follow the mechanisms, organizations, networks, and practices we identify into the global arena, but to do so now would call for another volume.

Nonetheless, globalization is a central feature of the new economy. The global nature of the new economy disperses manufacturing around the world. Transnational corporations with headquarters in the United States or the European Union have moved many manufacturing plants to nations with lower labor costs. Simultaneously, countries such as Japan, Korea, and segments of countries such as China and Mexico have developed their own manufacturing capacity for products such as appliances, automobiles, and computers. The success of competitor countries has turned the United States toward high technology products and services, where it has a global advantage, at least in part because of its research universities. The dispersal of manufacturing has precipitated greater reliance on information technologies to manage far-flung operations, stimulating research in information technology, including infrastructure, and especially distance learning.

U.S. universities also have globalized, although their globalization processes have been distinct from corporations. Scholars traditionally have participated in international learned networks. The growth of the Internet and the World Wide Web, which originated in academe, has intensified the global dimension of scholarship. As the cost of research has risen, federal policy has promoted international cooperation to reduce costs (Greenberg 2001). As the numbers of U.S. students interested in science and engineering careers has decreased, universities have recruited international students to the point where roughly half of all graduate students in science and engineering are foreign nationals, constituting a global labor force within U.S. universities. Schools ranging from community colleges to universities recruit international students and offer off-shore distance education programs. University and corporate globalization processes tend to converge around markets for knowledge-intensive new economy products, a number of which are licensed to corporations by universities.

Knowledge as Raw Material

Corporations in the new economy treat advanced knowledge as a raw material that can be claimed through legal devices, owned, and marketed as a product or service. The knowledge is often heavily technologized and/or digitized. Biotechnology and information technology are key examples and illustrate the importance of universities as knowledge sites. Corporations protect knowledge through patents, copyrights, and trademarks. Corporations have moved beyond protecting individual pieces of intellectual property, such as books, and have started to copyright education programs and services. The rise of for-profit education, perhaps most successfully exemplified by the University of Phoenix, strongly suggests that education can be treated like any other service.

Like corporations, colleges and universities have begun to treat knowledge as a raw material. Prior to 1981, fewer than 250 patents were issued to universities per year. In 1999, colleges and universities filed 5,545 patents (COGR 1999). In 1978, several universities permitted acquisition of equity in companies licensing their technology; by 2000, 70 percent of a sample of sixty-seven research universities had participated in at least one equity deal (Feldman et al. 2002a). In the past five years (1997–2002), approximately half of the states have adjusted their conflict of interest laws so that universities, as represented by administrators, and faculty, as inventors and advisors, can hold equity positions in private corporations even when those corporations do business with universities (Schmidt 2002). Many universities developed copyright policies, particularly in the period 1983–1993. Universities and colleges have also developed their own distance education services, for example, Columbia University's Fathom and University of Maryland University College, which are sold to nontraditional markets and serve as profit centers for these universities.

Non-Fordist Manufacturing

The new economy does not rely on mass production to the same degree as the industrial economy. Corporate leaders in the new economy have downsized middle management and developed new manufacturing processes that heavily utilize computers (CAD/CAM) and feature just-in-time manufacturing processes. These processes call for smaller numbers of educated workers who are supplemented by larger numbers of part-time or contingent workers who labor for relatively short periods of time and then disperse: the flexible work force. Although Fordist / mass production manufacturing continues, it has grown primarily in countries outside the United States that have appropriately educated but low-wage workers.

Corporate leaders also have begun to "unbundle" work. For example, rather than having customer service for products tied to product manufacturing or even sales, service is separated and often outsourced. Information technology services are often offered over the web or the telephone, and the person who walks the customer through the steps needed to repair a device is often based in another country. (However, in an inversion of globalization, the identity of the repair person is often masked. Indian call operators for a variety of computer products go to "call colleges" where they acquire American names and identities.)

Like their corporate counterparts, university managers have reconfigured their labor force. They too are concerned with developing a flexible work force, which they see as necessary to restructure colleges and universities to integrate with the new economy. In academe, flexibility is attained by increasing the numbers of part-time or contingent faculty. Part-time teachers increased from 22 percent of the labor force in 1970 to approximately 50 percent in 1997 (Benjamin 2002).

Again like their corporate counterparts, university managers also have begun to "unbundle" work. Unbundling of professorial work is most dramatic with regard to on-line education and distance education, for which curricula are often written by specialists and delivered by adjuncts. As with many market practices, unbundling varies somewhat by type of institution. In some community colleges, a very small number of faculty serve as full-time managers of part-time, low-cost faculty who provide some face-to-face interaction with students as well as internet contact. In universities, faculty involved with general education courses often become content providers who are members of teams of academic professionals who are specialists in multimedia, pedagogy, and web design. Other faculty functions that have been unbundled are advising, counseling, and some forms of mentoring, which have been turned over to academic professionals in student personnel services. Full-time faculty, whose salaries constitute the largest item in annual operating budgets, therefore have their work concentrated on the classroom and/or the laboratory.

Ironically, academic managers have adopted some techniques that their corporate counterparts have moved away from (or moved overseas). For example, academic managers have expanded middle management. A growing number of middle managers supervise the mass production of education through the use of information technologies such as Blackboard or WebCt. These programs create educational platforms in which all faculty must participate, standardizing teaching and making education modules interchangeable. A combination of partial automation and managerial oversight may be necessary for quality assurance as colleges and universities increase numbers of part-time faculty.

Educated Workers and Technology Savvy Consumers

Corporations in the new economy require educated workers and technology-savvy consumers. Corporations need well-educated workers in business related areas—science, engineering, medicine, law—to create and protect knowledge-based products, processes, and services. At the undergraduate level, business has become the core curricula: the majority of all courses taken in four-year schools are in business fields (Adelman 1999). Universities have restructured their curricula in these areas through complex processes that we describe in this volume.

College and universities have a (somewhat) hidden extracurricular course of instruction in consumption capitalism and as a milieu of use for technologically sophisticated corporate products.[9] Universities instruct students in consumption capital before they enter through their own complex and subtle, irregularly discounted pricing structures. Once they are on campus, students have greatly increased opportunities for consumption, ranging from luxury dormitories to minimalls in student unions. Colleges and universities have formal agreements with corporations in which they serve as test beds for new products, often in information technology lines. Corporations and universities form strategic alliances in which universities serve as test beds for new products, offering a milieu impossible to duplicate in a laboratory. Often students and faculty participate in modifying or improving the products, the benefits of which are captured by both the university and corporations in terms of use and by the corporation in terms of economic return. Informally, "wired" campuses

9. Castells uses the term *milieu of innovation* in reference to universities. We think they may serve an equally important new economy function (product instruction) as milieus of use.

create opportunities for students to play with information technology and thus are sites where desire and consumption are fused, creating technology-savvy consumers whose purchases fuel the new economy.

Although colleges and universities work closely with corporations, they have not simply replicated corporate processes. Unlike corporations, whose products know no borders but whose workers are restricted by national boundaries, universities have a global graduate student body that performs essential research work. Furthermore, although we are not focusing on the altruistic endeavors of colleges and universities, certain segments (such as some humanities programs) within these complex, multimission institutions do not endeavor to capture external resources. However, many higher education actors have created new circuits of knowledge, interstitial organizations, and boundary-spanning networks that link them to the new economy. Nonetheless, colleges and universities remain distinct from corporations.

The Neoliberal State

Corporations work closely with the neoliberal state to construct the new economy. The neoliberal state focuses not on social welfare for the citizenry as a whole but on enabling individuals as economic actors. To that end, neoliberal states move resources away from social welfare functions toward production functions. For example, since the 1980s, the U.S. Congress has formed a competitiveness coalition that has passed numerous laws enabling the development of civilian technology for global markets (Slaughter and Rhoades 1996, forthcoming). Although this legislation was initially aimed at small corporations deemed engines of economic growth, large corporations with global reach often have been the beneficiaries. The neoliberal state redefined government, privatizing, commercializing, deregulating, and reregulating state functions to promote the new economy in global markets. While universities were not primary players in creating the neoliberal state, they often endorsed initiatives, directly or indirectly. For example, university managers lobbied for Bayh-Dole (1980), a law that allowed universities to own and profit from federally funded research performed by faculty. Student loans offer another example. Although university managers always ask Congress for greater amounts of student aid, when it has not been forthcoming as grants, they have endorsed expanded student loan programs, which has hastened and strengthened the redefinition of students as consumers rather than learners.

The neoliberal state has participated in creating global governing structures, especially those related to protection of trade and intellectual property. The Uruguay Round of the General Agreement on Tariffs and Trade (GATT) of

1986 stood for vigorous patent enforcement around the globe. The Trade-Related Aspects of Intellectual Property Rights (TRIPs) were also initiated in the 1986 GATT. TRIPs played a major role in extending copyright fifty years beyond the life of the author of a work. The World Trade Organization (WTO) brokered the General Agreement on Trade and Services (GATS), which regulates global trade in educational services. The U.S. Department of Commerce, along with several other countries, has recently put forward negotiating proposals for GATS to treat education like any other service that is traded in the global market place. The proposal is limited to higher (tertiary) education, adult education, training services, and educational testing (Sauve 2002). The neoliberal state has developed new legislation and regulations to cover knowledge-based products, processes, and services in the new economy, extending global protection to commercial endeavors of corporations and universities.

The neoliberal state has also promoted privatization, commercialization, deregulation, and reregulation within the United States. Colleges and universities that pursue an academic capitalist knowledge/learning regime have benefited from these processes. Commercialization has been legislated in a number of instances. Bayh-Dole (1980) commercialized and privatized federal research, allowing universities and corporations to claim ownership of patents taken out on products and processes discovered during the course of federally funded research. At the federal level, the purpose of Bayh-Dole (1980) was commercialization. Many states have legal requirements that faculty disclose patentable discoveries to ensure that colleges and universities have the opportunity to review them for commercial potential (Chew 1992). The deregulation and accompanying reregulation of federal communications law promoted low-cost corporate ownership of the airwaves, creating commercial opportunities for broader bandwidth that colleges and universities have exploited through product development via Internet2.

The neoliberal state has reinterpreted labor law to increase workplace flexibility in corporations and universities. Beginning with Ronald Reagan and the air traffic controllers, the government has discouraged unionization on the part of state workers. Presidential candidates routinely speak against white collar unionization, usually targeting teachers, who comprise the largest union in the nation.

The several states also enact neoliberal legislation and administrative policies that allow corporations and universities to use "flexible" or part-time workers. The states have also altered accreditation practices. They accredit for-profits, such as University of Phoenix. In so doing, they accept hiring practices that decenter full-time faculty—the states affirm lack of faculty involvement in shared governance as well as universities with no libraries and little face-to-face instruction. The neoliberal state, like the new economy, has put in place rules and regulations that valorize "virtual" instruction. The state itself has become a flexible employer, outsourcing, relying on temporary workers, and reducing health care benefits.

The National Labor Relations Board has taken an increasingly conservative stance toward labor law and disputes in the corporate sector, and unionization is down. However, professionals employed by state and nonprofit organizations are turning to unions for protection, suggesting that highly educated workers with a guild tradition may be able to use unions to buffer the workplace fragmentation that characterizes the neoliberal state. Public sector faculty unionization has increased for part-timers as well as full-timers. The National Labor Relations Board has supported part-time faculty organization, as it has graduate student unionization in private as well as public higher education. Protections found in the Keynesian welfare/warfare state can still be invoked and activated.

The neoliberal state began to turn students into consumers as early as 1972, when Congress shifted higher education funding from institutions to students. Combined with rising tuition, the shift from grants to loans over the course of the past thirty years has confirmed students' identity as consumers of higher education. The neoliberal state also prefers relatively well-to-do students with legislation such as the Middle Income Assistance Act (1978) and the 1997 Tax Relief Act that enables high-achieving students from middle- and upper-middle-class families to use nonpayment of tax to pay for shares of tuition at costly institutions.

In many ways, the new economy depends on the neoliberal state for ground rules that create and sustain a global playing field. Colleges and universities, often arms of the state, benefit from (and sometimes participate in lobbying for) neoliberal initiatives to the degree that they are committed to an academic capitalist knowledge/learning regime. Those colleges and universities unable or unwilling to integrate with the new economy have difficulty accessing new programs and opportunities. Similarly, programs, departments, or colleges that resist, ignore, or are unable to intersect the new economy within institutions that are generally pursuing an academic capitalist knowledge/learning regime rarely share in its rewards and incentives.

Circuits of Knowledge

Knowledge no longer moves primarily within scientific/professional/scholarly networks. Teaching is no longer the province of faculty members who work with students in classrooms, connected to wider realms of knowledge through their departments and disciplinary associations. Courseware like BlackBoard and WebCT link faculty to electronic platforms that standardize teaching across colleges and universities, creating new circuits of knowledge that are more accountable to administrators than disciplinary associations. University-industry-government partnerships are another obvious example of new circuits of knowledge. University research is judged not only by peers but also by patent officials, who award ownership based on who is first to reduce to practice, and by corporations, which judge knowledge on its commercial potential.

Although peer review is still important within scholarly disciplines, universities as institutions no longer judge their own performance. Instead, outside organizations like *U.S. News and World Report* rate college and university performance, judging their worth to the student/parent consumer. To some degree, such outsiders have replaced accrediting associations, creating new circuits of knowledge that move outside the educational profession, fusing education with consumption. Institutions compete for position, as concerned to maintain place in these venues as in ratings of the disciplines by scholarly peers (Ehrenberg 2000). When *U.S. News and World Report* develops new rating categories, such as the degree to which campuses are "wired" or the "port to pillow ratio" for information technology in dormitories, colleges and universities compete for high rank, even though the relation between expenses for new infrastructure to educational outcomes is not examined.

Peer review, the cornerstone of the academic profession, is no longer conducted solely by university members. The refereeing or review of scholarly papers by experts has come to include degree holders who work in industry as well as academics. The number of scholars from industry sitting on National Science Foundation (NSF) peer review programs has risen substantially (Slaughter and Rhoades 1996). Although the industrial scholars may well be as competent as academics, the shift illustrates the new circuits of knowledge created under an academic capitalist knowledge/learning regime.

Interstitial Organizational Emergence

A number of new organizations have emerged from the interstices of established colleges and universities to manage new activities related to generation of external revenues. Many of these organizations are boundary spanning, bringing universities, corporations, and the state closer together. For example, technology licensing offices equipped to manage intellectual property have burgeoned. Economic development offices have grown to oversee the linking of areas in which universities have research strength to efforts by the states to build their economies. Trademark licensing offices have emerged in an increasing number of universities. Fund-raising officials are no longer confined to university foundations; they are now frequently located in colleges and even in departments. University, colleges, and departments are developing educational profit centers that market instructional programs that are not part of the official curricula to niche markets.

Intermediating Networks

Actors and organizations that participate in an academic capitalist knowledge/learning regime are arrayed in networks that intermediate between public, nonprofit and private sectors (Metcalfe, in progress). Intermediating organizations have proliferated in the past twenty-five years. Examples of such organizations are the Business Higher Education Forum (Slaughter 1990), the University-Industry-Government Research Roundtable, Internet2, Educause, and the League for Innovation. These organizations bring together different sectors interested in solving common problems that often stem from opportunities created by the new economy. In corporatist fashion, representatives of the different sectors attempt to arrive at solutions before approaching the policy or legislative process. Networks of intermediating organizations allow representatives of public, nonprofit, and private institutions to work on concrete problems, often redrawing (but not erasing) the boundaries between public and private. For example, in the 1980s, the Business Higher Education Forum, an organization of corporate and university CEOs, made the case for individual education accounts (IEAs), to which workers could make tax-free contributions from which they could then withdraw funds to pay for retraining to retool for another of the multiple careers occasioned by the rapidly changing new economy (Slaughter 1990). Corporations envisioned IEAs as a mechanism for perpetual worker retraining, and, given the educational demands of the new economy, community colleges could design certification programs, four-year colleges could offer off-curricula programs able to act as profit centers, and universities could develop masters of science degrees that were essentially professional retraining or professional development courses. Legislation similar to the IEA was passed as part of the Taxpayer Relief Act of 1997 (see chapter 2). The network of business and university leaders redrew traditional educational boundaries, taking advantage of new markets in ways that served the new economy, and providing directly for education of corporate workers at state and worker expense.

Extended Managerial Capacity

New circuits of knowledge, interstitial organizational emergence, and intermediating networks to some degree called for extended managerial capacity on the part of colleges and universities. With trustees' and university presidents' approval, managers increased their capacity to engage the market, redrawing the boundaries between universities and the corporate sector. Although we use patents and copyright to exemplify extended managerial capacity, the concept is also demonstrated in trademark licensing programs, economic development offices, distance-education profit centers, foundations, and other organizations.

In the 1980s, technology transfer officials engaged the market by licensing patented technology to corporations in return for royalties. In the 1990s, many universities began to take equity in start-up companies based on intellectual property discovered by faculty members. In effect, university managers acted as venture capitalists, picking technologies they thought would be winners in the new economy. By the end of the 1990s, university managers were involved in the market in terms of licensing income, usually received in the form of royalties from sales; milestone payments, which were made when particular research results were reached; equity interest, which could include publicly tradable shares, privately held shares, or options to acquire shares; material transfer agreements; tangible property sales (cell lines, software, compositions of matter); and trade secrets. A few universities permitted profit-making corporations in which faculty and/or administrators participated in corporations in which they held stock as consultants, employees, members, or chairs of boards of directors.

Copyright policies were developed primarily in the 1980s and 1990s. Although a number of institutions "allowed" faculty members to personally own their scholarly and creative works, universities increasingly claimed materials that were "work for hire," which included all work by academic professionals, or work directly commissioned by universities—for example, general education syllabi—or that made substantial use of university resources, which faculty often did when developing digitized courseware. The educational materials covered included video recordings, study guides, tests, syllabi, bibliographies, texts, films, film strips, charts, transparencies, other visual aids, programmed instructional materials, live video and audio broadcasts, and computer software including programs, program descriptions, and documentation of integrated circuit and databases. Some university managers who negotiated with corporations over copyrighted products, processes, and services were located in technology licensing and transfer offices. Sometimes these offices were expanded to become intellectual property offices or technology transfer and creative works offices. These offices oversee the business aspects of commercializing intellectual properties and managing copyright issues or of developing enterprise centers to further build up and market copyrightable educational materials. Extended managerial capacity is less developed with regard to copyrights than it is for patents because institutional copyright policies and offices are a more recent phenomenon.

Market Behaviors

New circuits of knowledge, interstitial organizational emergence, intermediating organizations, and expanded managerial capacity create networks through which college and universities connect to the new economy. Colleges and universities also engage in an array of miscellaneous market and marketlike behaviors that cut across colleges and universities, attaching a price to things that were once free or charging more for items or services that were once subsidized or provided at cost. For example, most universities now charge, whether outright or through fees, for parking, use of student recreation facilities, and use of computer facilities. Historically, subsidized meal services were located in dormitories and provided low-cost food for students. Now food services are outsourced to fast-food companies such as McDonald's and Domino's and are part of food courts located in student unions, which serve as minimalls and profit centers. Although market and marketlike behaviors are defined by competition for external resources, they are also associated with a host of ancillary behaviors, such as advertising and marketing. Enrollment management offices spend large sums on advertising, designing view books and other materials that represent the educational life style of the institution and then mailing them to affluent zip codes or to students who scored well on standardized tests. Trademark licensing officials work with "athleisure"-wear corporations to cross-license products that are sold in bookstores, where students are captive markets. Market and marketlike behaviors, as well as ancillary practices such as advertising, have permeated the fabric of colleges and universities, contributing to an academic capitalist knowledge/learning regime.

Although colleges and universities are integrating with the new economy and adopting many practices found in the corporate sector, they are not becoming corporations. Colleges and universities very clearly do not want to lose state and federal subsidies, or, in the case of research universities, to pay taxes, to be held to corporate accounting standards, to be held accountable for risks they take with state and donor money, and to relinquish, if they are public, eleventh-amendment protection and be liable for mistakes and various forms of malpractice. However, colleges and universities are participating in redrawing the boundaries between public and private sector, and they favor boundaries that allow them to participate in a wide variety of market activities that enable them to generate external revenues. Corporations participate in this redrawing because the new boundaries move research closer to the market, allowing universities to act as industrial laboratories and subsidizing the cost of product development. Similarly, many of the new forms of education prepare nontraditional student markets to use new economy products or prepare them for entry-level work, socializing the cost of education.

These boundaries between private and public are fluid: colleges and universities, corporations, and the state (of which public universities are a part) are in constant negotiation. Contradictions and ironies are rife. For example, for-profit tertiary education makes money for corporations that provide educational services but may conflict with corporations that prefer state subsidy of worker training. Corporations worked with universities to support Bayh-Dole (1980), which privatized federal research, but are unhappy with universities' aggressive claims to intellectual property and litigate regularly against them about ownership of broad patents that underlie a variety of pharmaceutical products. The "firewall" that once separated public and private sectors has become increasingly permeable.

Professional Strategies

As colleges and universities integrate with the new economy, professional groups within them have to develop strategies for how they will position themselves. Departments and fields that are close to markets—for example, biotechnology, medical substances and devices, or information technology—have some built-in advantages, given the importance of these fields to the new economy. However, the proximity of a department or program to the market does not always predict how it will fare in terms of institutional resource allocation or ability to generate external revenues. For example, a number of fine arts colleges, traditionally not conceptualized as close to the market, have redefined themselves so that they train art students in graphic design, digital animation, and web design, therefore connecting directly to the new economy. Some departments find niche markets that allow them to generate external revenues. For example, some classics departments augment their budgets by sponsoring revenue-generating educational trips to Greece and Rome, while some anthropology departments offer tours of prehistoric sites, charging for the tour and the pleasure of digging. Some departments in education sell tests and measurements copyrighted by their faculty. Often the external revenues brought in by these market revenues allow such departments to continue to deliver the standard of education they think appropriate to their fields, while colleges and universities generally invest in other areas, such as information technology infrastructure or advertising for high-end, high-scoring student markets.

Faculty are no longer the only important group of professionals within universities. Academic professionals have also organized themselves—in groups like the Association of University Technology Managers, Association of Collegiate Licensing Administrators, Association of University Marketing Professionals, and many others. In many cases, they were able to crystallize as professional groups because they responded to opportunities offered by the new economy. Lacking the prerogatives accorded to faculty, these new groups of professionals may be more strategic, aggressive, and flexible than faculty in responding to the opportunity structures associated with the new economy.

Shifting Knowledge/Learning Regimes

Overall, we conceptualize colleges and universities as shifting from a public good knowledge/learning regime to an academic capitalist knowledge/learning regime. The public good knowledge regime was characterized by valuing knowledge as a public good to which the citizenry has claims.[10] Mertonian norms—such as communalism, universality, the free flow of knowledge, and organized skepticism—were associated with the public good model. The public good knowledge/learning regime paid heed to academic freedom, which honored professors' right to follow research where it led and gave professors rights to dispose of discoveries as they saw fit (Merton 1942). The cornerstone of the public good knowledge regime was basic science that led to the discovery of new knowledge within the academic disciplines, serendipitously leading to public benefits. Mertonian values are often associated with the Vannevar Bush model, in which basic science that pushes back the frontiers of knowledge was necessarily performed in universities (Bush 1945). The discoveries of basic science always preceded development, which occurred in federal laboratories and sometimes in corporations. It often involved building and testing costly prototypes. Application followed development and almost always took place in corporations. The public good model assumed a relatively strong separation between public and private sectors.

10. This model decentered an earlier model, embedded in land-grant universities, which saw research as a public service, offered directly to citizens of a state, a concept which is perhaps best captured by *The Wisconsin Idea* (McCarthy 1912).

However, returning to the public good knowledge/learning regime would be problematic because it had an unacknowledged side. In the 1945–1980 period, much scientific and engineering research depended on Department of Defense funding for weapons of mass destruction. The first university-industry-government partnerships were with military contractors such as General Electric and Westinghouse who build nuclear reactors as part of the Atoms for Peace program. Much scientific and engineering research was classified, and the need for secrecy fueled movements like McCarthyism, which created an unfavorable climate for academic freedom.

The academic capitalism knowledge regime values knowledge privatization and profit taking in which institutions, inventor faculty, and corporations have claims that come before those of the public. Public interest in science goods are subsumed in the increased growth expected from a strong knowledge economy. Rather than a single, nonexclusively licensed, widely distributed product—for example, vitamin D irradiated milk—serving the public good, the exclusive licensing of many products to private firms contributes to economic growth that benefits the whole society. Knowledge is construed as a private good, valued for creating streams of high-technology products that generate profit as they flow through global markets. Professors are obligated to disclose discoveries to their institutions, which have the authority to determine how knowledge shall be used. The cornerstones of the academic capitalism model are basic science for use and basic technology, models that make the case that science is embedded in commercial possibility (Stokes 1997; Branscomb 1997a, 1997b). These models see little separation between science and commercial activity. Discovery is valued because it leads to high-technology products for a knowledge economy.

Academic capitalism also has an unacknowledged side. The benefits of economic growth do not always fall evenly on the population. Treating knowledge as a private good may make much of it inaccessible, perhaps constraining discovery and innovation. Conferring decision-making power on institutions rather than faculty may impinge upon academic freedom. Basic science for use and basic technology may provide narrow forms of discovery and education that do not sit well with concepts of public good. An academic capitalist knowledge/learning regime may undermine public support for higher education.

Although we see the academic capitalist knowledge/learning regime as ascendant and have sharply delineated the boundaries between the two models for analytical purposes, academic capitalism has not replaced the public good knowledge regime. The two coexist, intersect, and overlap. For example, securing entrepreneurial revenue streams, a focus of the academic capitalist knowledge/learning regime, has become more important but has not replaced the research prestige associated with the public good knowledge regime. However, the two intersect at points where money for research, as is often the case in biotechnology, becomes entrepreneurial funding. Research universities continue to emphasize doctoral education, associated with the public good knowledge regime and research prestige, but also increasingly emphasize (terminal) professional masters' degrees that are associated with the new economy and the academic capitalist knowledge/learning regime. Community colleges continue to promote transfer and associate degree programs but also have a growing emphasis on certificates and contract education, which connect students to the new economy without degrees. Because the burden of our book is depicting and explaining the academic capitalist knowledge/learning regime, we concentrate heavily on demarcating it from the public good and previous knowledge regimes, but we understand that the regimes coexist.

Overview of the Book

Chapter 2 asks how selected federal legislation enables an academic capitalist knowledge/learning regime. Building on our earlier studies that focused on how federal legislation promoted competitiveness research and development policy (Slaughter and Rhoades 1996, forthcoming), we have broadened our legislative selection to include copyright and trademarks as well as student financial aid. The implications of each piece of legislation for academic capitalism are presented. Because we are concerned with politics as well as policy, we analyze the congressional voting patterns on the selected legislation, for which we found broad, durable bipartisan support.

Building on our work on Arizona patent policies (Slaughter and Rhoades 1993), chapter 3 asks how state, state system, and institutional patent policies create opportunities for more academic capitalism. We analyze state system and institutional policies in six states—California, Florida, Missouri, New York, Texas, and Utah—from 1980 through 2002. The patent policies reveal a shift from a public good to an academic capitalist knowledge/learning regime. The change is most apparent in colleges and universities' greatly expanded managerial capacity, which allows them to engage the new economy.

Chapter 4 asks how these policies play out in the lives of students and faculty. We draw on work regarding federal appellate court cases in the 1990s involving patents and students (Baez and Slaughter 2001). We analyze three cases that suggest that students who participate in the academic capitalist knowledge/learning regime by working on patents learn that they are valued more as intellectual workers than students, which leads them to become market actors

(Slaughter et al. 2002; Slaughter and Archerd, forthcoming). Building on work from the 1990s on university-industry relations (Campbell and Slaughter 1999a, 1999b), we analyzed thirty-eight interviews with faculty involved with business to see how they negotiate the market. We found them uncertain about the boundaries between public and private spheres, enticed by market opportunities, and plagued by conflict of interest issues.

Chapter 5 parallels chapter 4, asking how state and state system copyright policies create opportunities for academic capitalism. Chapter 5 uses data from the same states and over the same time period as chapter 4. We are particularly interested in the expansion of market activity beyond the research domain. We find that copyright policies create commercial opportunities in almost all fields, enabling "instructional capitalism" (Anderson 2001).

Chapter 6 builds on previous work on union contracts (Rhoades 1998a). It raises two broad questions. First, what do faculty negotiating union contracts want with regard to ownership of courseware, teaching materials, and digitized intellectual property? The data are drawn from a national data set containing union contracts, and position papers developed by the American Association of University Professors (AAUP), the American Federation of Teachers (AFT), and the National Education Association (NEA). We find that faculty seek ownership of copyrights for both market benefits and quality control. Our second question builds on recent work on information technology (Croissant, Rhoades, and Tapia, forthcoming) and asks how technologies that promote digitized copyrights shape social relations within universities. We find that university learning centers staffed by managerial professionals facilitate faculty use of technology to develop digitized products, but use of campus resources enhances university rather than faculty claims to ownership.

Chapter 7 asks to what degree the academic capitalist knowledge/learning regime has penetrated to the academic heartland (Clark 1998). Building on previous work on the relation between teaching, research, and market activities (Leslie, Rhoades, and Oaxaca 1999), we examine entrepreneurial practices in 135 science, engineering, and social science departments in eleven public research universities. We find that departments pursue educational entrepreneurial activities as well as research. However, faculty often resist managerial direction altogether or pursue entrepreneurial activities of their own.

Chapter 8 asks how college and university presidents contribute to an academic capitalist knowledge/learning regime. We use the case of Internet2, an organization of presidents, to explore the question, drawing on the voluminous material provided by its website. We find that presidents work with corporate leaders and leaders of various government agencies to build the telecommunications infrastructure for the new economy. Universities and corporations follow an intellectual property framework that allows each to profit from products and processes derived from publicly funded research and development discovered while building Internet infrastructure. Administrative academic capitalism has its own circuits of knowledge, related to but distinct from those of faculty.

In chapter 9 we ask how university trustees are networked and how the network contributes to the academic capitalist knowledge/learning regime. We conduct a network analysis of the boards of trustees of the top ten private and top ten public universities that receive the most NSF funding (Pusser, Slaughter, and Thomas 2002). We analyze the interlocks created by trustees who sit on corporations in the NSF Research 500 and at the top thirty capitalized public corporations in the United States. We discover that the private boards are very tightly interlocked and speculate that the trustees' networks articulate universities with the new economy.

Chapter 10, coauthored with our colleague Samantha J. King, raises questions about students as captive markets. Using cultural studies theories about branding and image, we examine eight all-school sports contracts with Nike, Adidas, and Reebok. We also look at university trademark licensing of institutional names, logos, and mascots. We find that athletic shoe companies seek out universities to market their brands; they in turn find universities eager to sell their sports programs as an advertising milieu. In the 1990s, universities developed trademark programs that marketed products with institutional names, logos, and mascots to students almost as aggressively as did shoe companies. Indeed, athletic shoe companies and universities often cross-licensed products.

Chapter 11 addresses the relationship of institutions to students in the context of the academic capitalist knowledge/learning regime, drawing mostly on secondary materials. We ask how the pursuit of academic capitalism leads institutions to maximize tuition revenues and minimize student aid expenditures in recruiting their freshmen classes. We also ask to what extent pursuit of external revenues leads institutions to market their educational services to student populations outside historic catchment areas. In answering these questions, we draw on scholarship that advances conceptions of information and consumption (but not consumer) oriented capitalism. Our analysis is informed by sociological scholarship on social stratification and higher education in the United States.

Chapter 12 revisits the theory of academic capitalism, placing earlier chapters in broader context. We also explore the contradictions, ironies, and inconsistencies of an academic capitalist knowledge/learning regime. We conclude by examining alternatives.

Looking to the Past, or Pointing out Alternative Futures?

Our book is focused on what we see as an ascendant tendency and orientation of colleges and universities to engage in market behaviors in the pursuit of revenues that involve developing new organizational infrastructures, fostering new professions and structures of professional employment, and forming new intersectoral networks that affect the very identity of higher education institutions and their relations with faculty, staff, and students. From our tracking of this path of more academic capitalism, some readers might infer that we are looking back to some imagined past of professorial and managerial commitment that valued the public good more than institutional gain. They would be wrong. We neither look to nor pine away for the past, nor do we suffer any illusions about its problems. The not-too-distant past in higher education (like the continued present) featured fundamental social inequities, significant constraints on the free pursuit of knowledge, a linking of the research enterprise to the purposes and mechanisms of the cold war, and a commitment to knowledge that served a relative few at the cost of many. When we were born, the doors of many colleges and universities were closed, effectively and legally, to women and students of color. Our youth was spent in the midst of a cold war that created an icy climate for ideas and beliefs that were critical of the capitalist economy or that called for economic democracy; it also served as a rationale for much secrecy in academic science in the form of classified research. It has only been in the past three decades that a systematic questioning of the classical knowledge canon and an opening up to new forms of scholarship and knowledge has emerged. We do not wish to return to the past.

We are social scientists, trying to grapple with changes in the organization, structure of work, and orientation of higher education institutions. We understand that the academic profession and colleges and universities have long been involved with the world of commerce. One of our dissertations was about how social scientists professionalized by serving corporate and political power (Slaughter 1975). However, we see the current pattern of what we are calling more academic capitalism as distinctive. Just as in academic science and technology policy we see the ascendance of a "competitiveness coalition" in policy networks, gaining prominence in relation to (but coexisting with) the cold war coalition of previous decades (Slaughter and Rhoades 1996). So in the policies and practices of colleges and universities we see the ascendance of an academic capitalist knowledge/learning regime, gaining prominence in relation to (but coexisting with) the public good knowledge/learning regime of previous decades. Such changes are consequential for society in terms of access to higher education, knowledge production in academia, and higher education's performance of and balance between various cultural, economic, educational, political, and social functions.

Having proposed an ascendant pattern in higher education, we are well aware that other patterns of practice persist. Indeed, we see our activities and ourselves as being linked to a network of actors and structures providing social critique and seeking social justice in higher education and society. However, we understand that we are complicit in academic capitalism, even as we analyze it, given that our book creates our careers, allowing us to intersect opportunity structures and revenue streams offered by the new economy.

2

THE POLICY CLIMATE FOR ACADEMIC CAPITALISM

In this chapter, we review national and international legislation, treaties, and trade agreements that create opportunities for academic capitalism in post-secondary education. The period of study is from 1980 to 2000, but we focus on the 1990s. We follow legislation, treaties, and trade agreements that affect two policy areas, student financial aid and research.

Student financial aid began the process of marketization in 1972, when the Higher Education Act of 1965 was amended to give aid to students rather than institutions. Basic Educational Opportunity Grants, later known as Pell grants, became vouchers, which students used in partial payment for education at institutions of their choice. The shift initiated a degree of marketlike competition among institutions for federally subsidized student tuition dollars. Grants and loans were gradually expanded from covering full-time, traditional age students attending public and nonprofit, private colleges and universities to supporting students at proprietary institutions. In the late 1980s and early 1990s, the proprietary institutions' default rates were so great that their federal student aid was cut back. Beginning in the late 1990s, proprietary institutions recast as for-profits, such as the University of Phoenix, were again able to draw heavily on federal grants and loans for nontraditional students attending part-time and on-line.[1] Nonprofit public and private colleges and universities began to emulate programs such as those offered by Phoenix. Many of the students who currently benefit from the expanded federal student financial aid are employed adults in need of retraining or professional development. The dynamic new economy calls for workers to change jobs frequently. Increasingly, workers use tertiary education to train and retrain through certificate and associate degrees, or to retool and upgrade through four-year degrees.

1. We are aware that there are caps on the number of hours that students can take on-line and as part-timers, and are also aware of the lobbying efforts by for-profits to remove these caps. We discuss this in more detail later in the chapter.

In the research policy area, there are two streams of policy shaping legislation. The first deals with research and graduate students, the second with intellectual property. Historically, these two policy streams were separate, but research and intellectual property became more closely related as the academic capitalism knowledge/learning regime gained strength. Beginning in the 1980s the intellectual property stream was fed by legislation designed to stimulate U.S. economic competitiveness, and it initially intersected academe through the Bayh-Dole Act (1980), which gave universities and other researchers patents on intellectual property derived from academic research funded by the federal government. As the information economy grew, the intellectual property stream swelled, offering extended copyright protection not only to printed matter but also to all digitized products, which had important implications for distance education, professors' courseware, academic libraries, and student learning. All the legislation that enabled competitiveness policy (Slaughter and Rhoades 1996, forthcoming) offered opportunity structures to higher education actors who created networks that integrated with the new economy, intensifying the academic capitalism knowledge/learning regime.

Researchers who write about these policy areas are often members of different knowledge and policy communities. Scholars who write about financial aid and undergraduate students are part of the higher education community and write for journals such as the *Journal of Higher Education,* the *Review of Higher Education, Research in Higher Education,* and sometimes *Economics of Education.* They are members of organizations such as the Association for the Study of Higher Education, the American Educational Research Association-Division J, and the Association for Institutional Research. For the most part, they specialize in fields such as higher education finance, economics of higher education, or economics of education. With regard to state and national policy, they are concerned with how undergraduate financial aid influences student access and persistence.

Generally, scholars who write about research policy are part of the science and technology policy community. They write for journals such as *Research Policy, Science and Technology Policy, Science Technology and Human Values,* and a number of others. The national organizations to which they belong are often tied to the American Association for the Advancement of Science and the "Academy complex."[2] These scholars are often physical and biological scientists, math-

2. The National Academy of Science, along with its component organizations, the National Research Council, the Institute of Medicine, and the National Academy of Engineering, and their various directorates, are often referred to as "the Academy complex."

ematicians, and engineers concerned with policies that shape federal support for those areas of science, or economists interested in innovation processes and economic development. Scholars who study intellectual property are often attorneys, research managers, or technology transfer officers. They belong to organizations such as the Association of College and University Attorneys and the Association of University Technology Transfer Managers. Their work appears in journals such as *Research Management* and the *Journal of the Association of University Technology Managers.* For the most part, they are concerned with how to better exploit and develop intellectual property at the institutional level.

Although the knowledge communities of these groups of researchers differ, they have a common object of inquiry: higher education institutions. The separation of these knowledge communities is unfortunate because it obscures important trends. For example, the commercialization of research, whether through patents or copyrights, complements and reinforces market and marketlike student financial aid activity. This marketlike and commercial activity stimulates generation of external revenues or fees for services in areas such as economic development, trademark licensing, fund-raising, and many areas of student services, such as union food courts, outdoor adventures, sports and fitness training, and career counseling. Together, these activities shift institutions to an academic capitalist knowledge/learning regime, which sees the economy rather than the polity as central to the citizenry's well-being. This approach affects the kinds of students, types of education, and types of research that we fund.

Theory

Student financial aid scholars have analyzed the move from grants to loans, which shifts the burden of payment from the state to students or their parents, as a change of great magnitude in higher education (Kimberling 1995; Hannah 1996; Hearn 1998). Science and technology policy scholars have sought to describe and theorize fundamental changes occurring in academic science and technology using the metaphors of "Mode 1 and Mode 2" (Gibbons et al. 1994), "triple helixes" (Etzkowitz and Leydesdorff 1996), or "academic capitalism" (Slaughter and Leslie 1997). Whether describing student financial aid or research policy, scholars from both communities see great changes during the years 1980–2002.

We draw on Foucault's (1977, 1980) concept of "disciplinary regimes" to help us understand these changes. This notion refers to broad changes in the ways in which power/knowledge moves through society. Foucault saw the (French) nineteenth- and twentieth-century knowledge regime as moving away from "blood" and the power of the aristocracy toward the professions, the state, and intellectual elites. He focused on the power of professionals who shaped a new knowledge regime through the "pleasures of analysis," which were discursive, calibrating, and norming. Nineteenth- and twentieth-century professionals portrayed themselves as independent but were supported by the state in many ways, ranging from licensure to the funding of organizations—such as schools, prisons, and hospitals—which enabled professional careers. We believe that in the twenty-first century knowledge/power regimes have shifted again, and now professionals, who still portray themselves as independent, are aligning themselves with the market and corporate elites, backgrounding the state and the public domain (Brint 1994). Professionals, including faculty, are building new networks that connect them with the new economy, spanning boundaries between public, nonprofit, and market organizations. In so doing, they are restructuring universities to accommodate an academic capitalist knowledge/learning regime.

Although we admire Foucault's analysis, which sees power as more dispersed throughout society than do most theorists and which is attentive to the power of professionals, we see economic structures of power, such as business networks, as *primus inter pares* in the power game (Useem 1984). We also see party politics, a traditional and concentrated site of power, as an essential element of policy.

Economic structures of power, such as business networks, play an important part in shifting knowledge/learning regimes (Useem 1984). Organizations such as the Committee on Economic Development (CED), a nonprofit business policy organization, played a major role in setting tuition policy. The rise of an information economy has increased the interdependence of universities and business networks in terms of research and education. Members of networks of firms in knowledge areas critical to the new economy—for example, information and electronics, medical devices and substances, biotechnology—serve on boards of trustees of universities that are integrating with the new economy (Pusser, Slaughter, and Thomas 2003). These dense networks of corporate and university CEOs stand behind the congressional competitiveness coalition and play an active role in agenda-setting policy organizations that influence higher education (Slaughter 1990; Slaughter and Rhoades 1996, forthcoming).[3]

Whether partisan or bipartisan, congressional coalitions are essential to deliver votes for loan-based student financial aid as well as legislation that creates opportunities for privatizing and protecting intellectual property, whether

3. In this chapter, we do not explore networks of boards of directors of firms and universities because we are concentrating on the political side of the political economy, but we take up the economic side in chapter 9, in which we explore interlocks between members of boards of directors of Fortune 500 corporations and research universities.

through patents or copyrights. The scholarly communities that study higher education and research policy have somewhat different approaches to the study of politics. Higher education policy scholars have studied "policy arenas," focusing narrowly on proximate actors—congresspersons, legislative aids, and heads of higher education associations (Gladieux and Wolanin 1976; Hannah 1996). However, focus on a small policy arena often obscures the larger political dynamics that shape policy. For example, the policy arena perspective led Gladieux and Wolanin to interpret the 1972 amendments to the Higher Education Act as a lobbying failure on the part of the "1 Dupont Circle" higher education associations. They missed the market implications of Pell grants. Our approach, following Domhoff (1967, 1980, 1990, 1996), Domhoff and Dye (1987), and Mann (1986), looks at broader networks of actors, often comprised of heads of firms and higher education leaders, allowing us to identify influential organizations that play a part in shaping tuition policy. For example, we see the marketization and "choice" agendas of the CED as strongly influencing the 1972 higher education amendments.

Historically, research policy scholars have downplayed politics, perhaps to distance themselves from their dependence on parties and platforms, focusing instead on presidential leadership and the administrative branch of government (Greenberg 1967; Herken 1992). However, we think understanding political coalitions and congressional voting patterns is essential to understanding the stability and durability of entrepreneurial research. Thus, we are "bringing" politics "back in" (Evans, Rueschemeyer, and Skocpol 1985) by examining the composition and strength of congressional voting coalitions on legislation related to research that created opportunity structures for networks of actors interested in developing an academic capitalist knowledge/learning regime.

Method

We begin with brief historical accounts of student financial aid policy and research policy. We then identify legislation, treaties, and trade agreements that shape opportunities for the academic capitalism knowledge/learning regime and briefly analyze the implications of these policies for colleges and universities. We conclude by analyzing the roll-call votes in Congress, looking to see if there is stable and predictable support for academic capitalism. Legislation was identified through a variety of sources, including the American Association for the Advancement of Science's *Science and Technology Policy News*, the *Chronicle of Higher Education*, Daniel Greenberg's *Science and Government Report*, the *Journal of the Association of University Technology Managers*, as well as other journals and scholarly works.

Enabling an academic capitalist knowledge/learning regime depends to some degree on stable, national political coalitions that reliably enact supportive legislation. We infer political coalitions from congressional voting behavior, using roll-call records of the selected federal legislation, treaties, and trade agreements. We recapitulate and expand our earlier analysis (Slaughter and Rhoades 1996), which covered the period 1980–1993, and then extend it to the present. The research questions we seek to answer are: What federal policies and legislation stimulated the academic capitalism knowledge/learning regime? How do these policies link colleges and universities to the new economy? How solid is the national political coalition that supports the academic capitalism knowledge/learning regime? Is there evidence of a congressional and legislative commitment to an academic capitalism knowledge/learning regime?

Although we make the case that academic capitalism has been instituted during the past two decades, this knowledge/learning regime is far from hegemonic. It coexists uneasily with others, for example, the liberal education regime and the military-industrial research regime (Slaughter and Rhoades 1996, forthcoming). The academic capitalist model is also contested by numerous groups, ranging from professors committed to freeware to fundamentalists who are opposed to traffic in human materials. Examples of such opposition are the ban on fetal tissue research, which halted the opening of new areas of academic medicine with commercial potential, and the proposed ban on human cloning.

Although federal legislation creates opportunities for academic capitalism, it is far from causal. The individual states often develop policies that precede and influence federal legislation. Colleges and universities have been active participants in the process. In a number of instances in the 1970s and 1980s, administrators and professors worked in coalitions to skillfully build public/private partnerships that drew together powerful corporate partners, legislators, and the heads of federal mission agencies to orchestrate support to leverage public policy and funds for an academic capitalist knowledge/learning regime. These endeavors were new only in that they moved far beyond the "Dupont Circle" policy arena (Bailey 1975; King 1975) and the "Academy complex." In the 1990s these partnerships expanded to cover global digital infrastructure, educational trade in services, and all forms of intellectual property, including trade marking.

Student Financial Aid Legislation

Generally, we see federal financial aid legislation as segmenting student markets in higher education, directing different types of aid to very different kinds of students.[4] Some programs and appropriation patterns encourage upper-middle-class as well as high-achieving students from other social strata to attend costly, elite, (increasingly) private institutions. Others encourage large numbers of adult learners to upgrade their educations in order to master skills appropriate to the new economy through two-year and four-year programs, sometimes with substantial distance education components and often through for-profit higher education. The first type of aid serves well-to-do parents who vote and seek privilege for their children. Many of these students enter the new economy in managerial positions that put them on the fast track for promotions and rewarding careers. The second type of aid serves corporations that need employees who can operate in a knowledge economy as well as students who seek entry-level jobs or modest career advancement in the information society.

A big step toward market segmentation occurred in the early 1970s when federal legislation shifted from supplying institutional student aid, making students consumers. In the early 1970s, the CED was very interested in higher education because elite private-sector universities were losing students to public universities as a result of the widening tuition gap between the two (Domhoff 1967). The CED was founded in the 1940s to shape policy in the postwar era and had approximately 200 members, most of whom were CEOs of large corporations—many of which were financial institutions, arguably predecessors of the new economy—or presidents of universities (CED 1973). Many CED members had attended elite private colleges and universities and saw private education as embodying different ideals than did more utilitarian public institutions. Presciently, CED leaders valorized the private sector as a site of market value as well as educational currency, certain that students and their parents would choose private higher education if they could afford it.[5] Ironically, the market value of private higher education could only be realized through public subsidy.

4. Generally, the states, which have greatly increased their student aid programs, have increased merit scholarships, which tend to benefit the well-to-do. In other words, state policies have generally followed much the same direction as federal. See Heller 2000.

5. Student aid to private higher education was complicated because of the range of private institutions. Most of the CED members had attended elite schools, but most private higher education was not elite. The division is somewhat like that between monopoly and competitive capitalism (O'Connor 1973), in which monopoly sector corporations, like elite institutions of higher education, are able to mobilize state support to build their institutions and capture markets, while competitive sector corporations, like most private institutions of higher education, have to engage in more laissez-fare competition for markets. Even though elite institutions of higher education benefited most, most private institutions were willing to support a market approach because without public subsidy they were in danger of going under. Public institutions, especially the elite, also supported the market approach because it enlarged their student market and tuition revenues (so long as the marginal return for adding students was rising).

The CED, together with a number of foundations, particularly the Carnegie Institute, worked assiduously for marketization of higher education, using discourse about student choice. Federal financial aid placed in the hands of students rather than institutions was the mechanism. Student choice in this context preferred private colleges and universities because the (public) grants to private nonprofit schools were larger than those to public schools. The CED also pushed strongly for all postsecondary students, whether enrolled in public or private institutions, to pay for one-third to one-half of their education costs. If public higher education students paid more, then the high-tuition private sector would remain competitive. Moreover, increasing tuition to cover a greater share of the cost of public higher education reduced the cost to the state, always an interest of taxpaying businesses.

Since 1972, federal student financial aid in grant form diminished relative to the cost of higher education, while the supply of loan money expanded rapidly. "Most of the absolute growth in aid totals has come from the growth of the dollar volume of federal loans. The figure reveals that student financial aid in the United States is increasingly composed of federally supported loan aid. That aid moved from around 20% of all aid in 1963–64 to a low of 17% in 1975–76, then rose to a high of 55% in 1994–95" (Hearn 1998, p. 51). In 2000–2001, loans accounted for 58 percent of total aid (College Board 2001).

Federal legislation supported marketlike competition for students among higher education institutions on the grounds that greater efficiency would lead to cost reductions. Ironically, as the market model became entrenched, costs escalated (Ehrenberg 2000). Rather than a Fordist market for mass-produced higher education that lowered costs for all, higher education markets became increasingly segmented. Although costs went up in all market segments, niche markets developed in which a small number of (largely upper- and upper-middle-class) students competed for ever more expensive places at a relatively small number of (elite and increasingly private) institutions. Federal loan programs enabled middle- and upper-middle-class students, especially those attending high-cost elite private institutions, to meet higher tuition costs. In effect, federal loans subsidized markets in students by providing relatively privileged students the funds to choose high-tuition institutions.[6]

By the 1980s and 1990s, higher education was construed less as a necessary public or social good and more as an individual or private good, justifying "user

6. The Middle Income Assistance Act of 1978 provided grant aid to a greater number of middle-income students and took the $25,000 limit off the Guaranteed Student Loan. The Middle Income Assistance Act was an anomalous moment in student financial aid's movement toward a greater reliance on loans, and by the 1980s it proved too broad a welfare benefit for the neoliberal state. For details, see Hearn (1998).

pays" policies (Leslie and Brinkman 1988). Although loan programs for upper-middle-class students were not directed toward the new economy, they in effect privatized the cost of college attendance, following general policy trends that were part of the emergence of the neoliberal state. As all students paid a greater share of their tuition and fees, the costs to working adults who returned to school to improve their positions in the new economy were normalized, even though those students paid a greater share of their income for tuition than did well-to-do traditional age students (Heller 2000).

As the shift from grants to loans benefited families and students confident of their ability to repay, some programs in the Taxpayer Relief Act of 1997 benefited families with money to protect. The Taxpayer Relief Act included several programs: Hope scholarships, the tax credit for lifelong learning, tax-sheltered college savings accounts, and penalty-free IRA withdrawals for college expenses. The Hope scholarship provided a $1,500 nonrefundable tax credit for the first two years of college that phased out for individuals earning $40,000 to $50,000 per year or couples earning $80,000 to $100,000 per year. The penalty-free IRA withdrawals do not count withdrawals from IRA accounts as gross income so long as they pay for college expenses. Additionally, families may shelter up to $500 per year for each child; these savings are taxed as an IRA so long as the funds are spent on college expenses. This program was capped for families earning $150,000 to $160,000 per year.

These programs contribute to competition among institutions for preferred student customers or clients. As Hoxby (1997) has noted, higher education has become an increasingly integrated and competitive market, especially for the elite private nonprofit sector. As a result, colleges and universities have responded by "differentiating themselves vertically [by specializing in a certain quality of student and level of admissions selectivity] and horizontally" (by finding a market niche—for instance, serving local managers who wish to pursue an MBA in the evening) (1997, p. 60). The set of programs established by the 1997 Taxpayer Relief Act enables high-achieving students from middle- and upper-middle-class families to use nonpayment of taxes to pay for shares of tuition. The subsidies provided by tax credits are not trivial. "The package of tax credits and tax deductions has been estimated to cost $39 billion in the first five years, making it slightly larger than the Pell Grant program, the primary federal grant program for low income youth" (Kane 1999, p. 22). The increased ability of these well-to-do and/or market-knowledgeable and academically able students to pay makes them preferred customers for elite institutions.

Despite the market rhetoric, these students are more than consumers. They are also "inputs" and "outputs." High-quality students (high scorers on standardized tests) strengthen the market positions of the colleges or universities that enroll them (Rothschild and White 1995). The higher the scores of incoming students, the higher the prestige of the institution. Greater prestige attracts more applicants. The greater the number of applicants, the more the institution is able to turn down and thus the greater the exclusivity and prestige of the institution. These same students are also "outputs" or products; the success of graduates signals the success of the school. The multiple functions of students (consumers, inputs, outputs, or products) fashions a virtual circle of competition in which students and institutions in the same (elite) market segments compete ever more vigorously with and for each other, contributing to the instantiation of an academic capitalism knowledge/learning regime.

The 1997 Taxpayer Relief Act applied primarily to nonprofit institutions of higher education, whether public or private. However, some programs benefited working adults seeking further education to better compete in the new economy. The tax credit for lifelong learning offered a nonrefundable tax credit for undergraduate and graduate education that was worth up to 29 percent of up to $5,000 per year spent on tuition and fees through 2002, and 20 percent of up to $10,000 per year after that, with the same income caps as the Hope scholarship. In many ways, this was the Business-Higher Education Forum's Individual Education Account (IEA, see chapter 1) come to life. The tax credit for lifelong learning expanded markets for for-profits like the University of Phoenix, itself a new economy corporation, which required attending students to have jobs. The tax credit created increasing numbers of public institutions, such as the University of Maryland University College, that emulated for-profits by serving working adults retooling for the new economy.

The 1998 Higher Education Act contained a number of special provisions to aid for-profit higher education. The law made it easier for such institutions to appeal federal penalties stemming from their students' defaults on loans. Given that for-profits have an excessively high default rate, this was an important provision. Additionally, the law no longer required unannounced accreditation visits, allowing for-profit postsecondary education to prepare for inspections by making sure students were in class. Most importantly, the law no longer treated for-profits as a separate category; they were redefined as institutions of higher education. This allowed them to share in federal aid. Their students were twice as likely to receive federal aid as students at nonprofits, and at the two-year level, their students received more federal aid than comparable students in public institutions. The 1998 Higher Education Act further signaled federal government support for for-profits by creating within the Department of Education a special liaison for proprietary schools, a privilege previously held only by historically black tertiary education institutions and community colleges (Crew

2002). Currently, for-profits are lobbying to change financial aid requirements that require institutions to register their students for at least twelve hours of instruction, offer less than 50 percent of their courses via distance education, and prohibit bonuses or incentives to admissions officers for enrolling students (Crew 2002). For-profits are also asking the Department of Education to revise rules that require 10 percent of their revenues to come from sources other than federal aid; in other words, for-profits envision themselves as able to run on students' Pell grants alone, especially if students are able to receive federal aid for low-cost education delivered by adjuncts and taken one course at a time, on-line.

Changes in student aid legislation over the past thirty years have contributed to the academic capitalist knowledge/learning regime by marketizing higher education. The legislation made students (partially) state-subsidized consumers in quasi markets for higher education. According to the rhetoric surrounding marketization, markets empowered students by making them consumers through allowing them to use their grant or loan to discipline markets to better serve them. However, higher education markets seem to work like all others. Far from being perfectly competitive (Leslie and Johnson 1974), offering goods and services at the lowest price to any buyer, markets tend to favor the middle and upper middle classes. Just as housing markets prefer middle-class customers with high credit ratings who are unlikely to be loan risks, and then indirectly subsidize them through mortgage tax deductions, so markets in higher education prefer students (and families) who are confident they can repay loans and are indirectly subsidized through parental tax relief and higher grant/loan aid attached to private institutions. Ironically, market legislation, which defines higher education as a private benefit captured by individuals, prefers the middle and upper middle classes.

Student aid legislation has also contributed to market segmentation. While middle- and upper-middle-class students became preferred customers, lower-middle-class students and working adults entered two-year colleges, four-year college programs with substantial distance education components, and for-profit institutions of higher education. Given that many do not complete two-year college programs, they learn a modicum of skills through just-in-time education that channels them into entry-level jobs in the new economy. Working adults in four-year programs often receive college degrees for what amounts to retraining or professional development, allowing them to upgrade skills to better serve the needs of the new economy corporations where they are employed. Although these students do not receive dramatic returns on their investment in human capital, they are often satisfied because they do better than if they had not acquired some college education or a degree.

The student aid legislation was the first federal legislation to explicitly use market discourse. In some ways the market rhetoric was as much a trope for partial privatization as for marketization in that the neoliberal state moved to a high-tuition, low-aid position (Griswold and Marine 1996; Hearn 1998). The legislation followed the general direction of neoliberal policy, moving away from treating public benefits as social goods for the citizenry as a whole and toward making the user pay more. Public funds were shifted toward production functions by making aid available for working adults reeducating themselves for knowledge economy jobs. That well-to-do users paid (relatively) less than others also reflected trends characteristic of the new economy and the neoliberal state.

Research Policy

By and large, science and technology scholars discuss policy but not politics. Science and technology (S&T) policy scholars often approach policy through "social contract" discourse (Guston and Kenniston 1994; Mukerji 1989). This discourse serves a relatively small group of research universities, scientific associations, and organizations that are highly unified in pressing for more research and development (R&D) funding (Greenberg 2001). These research universities receive the bulk of federal R&D funds. *Social contract* is shorthand for the complex negotiations between these universities and society, a rhetorical strategy that enables scientists and engineers or their representatives to draw on Lockean natural rights / social contract discourse to obligate and direct the power of the state. The social contract discourse is simultaneously an analytical concept and a (depoliticized) discourse that asserts professional and scientific rights even as it masks complex, power-laced relations between science and society. The social contract model makes the case that society, through federal funding for various mission agencies, should fund academic science and engineering, in return for which professors provide basic research, which is the "seed corn" for further scientific discovery as well as technologies that will be developed into products and processes for markets.

The social contract model was perhaps most powerfully developed by Vannevar Bush, an MIT engineering professor, president of the Carnegie Institute, and wartime director of the Office of Scientific Research and Development. Immediately after World War II, Bush argued for federal funding for science through grants to academic scientists and engineers, indirectly (but very deliberately) funding (elite) universities, whose faculty would push back the "endless frontier" of science through heroic discovery. In this narrative, science as an endeavor was serendipitous (a euphemistic way of saying unaccountable), and only scientists were able to follow where it led; therefore, university scientists had to be funded through a peer review process (Slaughter 1993). Such funding was justifiable because science, although serendipitous, ultimately offered society the fruits of research through a rich cornucopia of new technologies. These benefits were realized when university professors handed off their discoveries to federal laboratories for development to a prototype stage, after which industry applied the science in new products and processes. In effect, Vannevar Bush proposed a division of scientific labor in which the government agreed to fund some science done in universities (basic), some done in government laboratories (development), and some done in corporations (applied). He advocated an agency like the National Science Foundation (NSF), which would be the balance wheel for federal mission agencies, insuring that necessary research was funded.

However, the majority of funding for science and engineering in the 1950s and 1960s came from the Department of Defense (DOD), for weapons and missiles; from the Department of Energy, for various forms of nuclear energy, including weapons of mass destruction; and the National Aeronautics and Space Administration, for demonstrating cold war superiority of U.S. science and engineering. The defense mission agencies adapted the rhetoric of pure research and labeled as basic a large part of the funds they allocated for science performed by professors in universities. Professors often preferred DOD funds to others because they were usually long-term, ample, and not micromanaged (Foreman 1987; Slaughter 1990). Ironically, the "social contract" between university science and society, of which research was the cornerstone, was built on military funding that flowed from the cold war.

The political coalition that funded basic science was the same one that funded the cold war. The cold war was supported by conservative, Southern, anti–civil rights or Bourbon Democrats as well as by some Northern Democrats, and most Republicans. This coalition delivered almost twenty years of ever increasing funding for academic research. When the coalition fell apart due to disputes over the Vietnam War, academic science funding fell into disarray from which it did not recover until the 1980s (Dickson 1984).

During the 1980s, neither Ronald Reagan nor George H. W. Bush promoted policies aimed at increasing U.S. competitiveness in global markets. Indeed, Reagan led the largest military build up in the post–World War II era, which included enormous amounts of money for research (Knight 1987). However, Congress, which supported the military-industry research regime, simultaneously began to support civilian technology. Civilian technology R&D was not in and of itself the focus of congressional attention. Rather, Congress funded "competitiveness legislation" aimed at supporting U.S. industry's quest for greater shares of a growing global market. That part of competitiveness legislation which addressed civilian technology R&D usually promoted technology transfer from federal laboratories and universities to industry, and a variety of university-industry-government partnerships as well as enhanced protection of intellectual property.

The emergence of a congressional competitiveness coalition stemmed from a number of related factors: increased competition in global markets, a drop in U.S. productivity, a disagreement among U.S. industrial leaders over the nature of R&D funding, the restructuring of defense industries, the rise of an information economy, and the end of the cold war. In the 1970s and 1980s, Europe and Japan dramatically increased productivity, gaining greater shares in global markets, while U.S. productivity fell drastically from the 1970s until the late 1980s (Carnoy 1993; Castells 1993; Cohen 1993). U.S. industrial leaders, long accustomed to R&D filtered through the military, began to have second thoughts. Some favored continued support for the military-industrial-academic model. Others, influenced by Japanese and German success in global markets, wanted federal R&D for science and technology geared to civilian rather than military standards, and much greater attention given to the transfer of civilian technology to commercial products for global markets. Simultaneously, the end of the Vietnam War and the lack of an imminent enemy led government and business to restructure defense industries. Between 1975 and 1985 the number of defense prime contractors declined from fifteen to five (Markusen and Yudken 1992; Slaughter and Rhoades 1996). Companies such as Hewlett-Packard and Ford, long stalwarts of military industries, cut their defense divisions. When the Berlin Wall came down in 1989 and the cold war fizzled out on other fronts, government support of military R&D continued to diminish. At the same time, information assumed greater economic importance, given the growth of the Internet, electronically linked global stock exchanges, and digitization of an increasing number of products that could move over electronic superhighways and grids.

These factors—increased global competition, U.S. productivity declines, divisions among industrial leaders over R&D strategies, the restructuring of defense industries, the end of the cold war, and the rise of the information economy—called into question the "social contract" between science and society. In the 1990s, science and technology policy analysts attributed the recovery of U.S. productivity to competitiveness policy legislation enacted in the 1980s. Various science and technology policy groups began to criticize the "old" or "Vannevar Bush" model of economic innovation in which basic research necessarily precedes applied science. They labeled the Bush model as a "linear sequential view of innovation [that] is simplistic and misleading" and dependent on the Department of Defense (National Academy of Sciences 1995, p. 5). Instead, science and technology policy organizations began to offer what they saw as a more complex model of the role of science in economic innovation, which was referred to variously as "basic science for use" (Stokes 1997) or "basic technology" (Branscomb 1997a, 1997b), in which entrepreneurial science was privileged and in which basic science did not necessarily precede applied.[7]

The National Institutes of Health, not the Department of Defense, was the federal agency that exemplified the basic-science-for-use model. The federal government invested heavily in medical and health research in the National Institutes of Health in the 1980s and 1990s, far surpassing other mission agencies. Medical substances and devices, along with biotechnology, became key industries in the new economy.[8] Intellectual property discovered by faculty working on National Institutes of Health grants was protected through patents (i.e., pharmaceuticals) and copyrights (diagnostic programs), not through classified research, which had been the practice of the Department of Defense.

The Bill Clinton administration was most aggressive in developing programs based on competitiveness policy legislation. As the cold war ended, it attempted to use the "peace dividend" to finance civilian competitiveness programs, many of which were located in the Department of Commerce, under the National Institute of Standards and Technology. Among these were the Advanced Technology Program, the Technology Reinvestment Program, the Environmental Technology Initiative, the Manufacturing Extension Partnership, the Partnership for a New Generation of Vehicles, and the Small Business and Innovation Research (Vonortas 2000). Although Clinton took an active leadership role, he was strongly supported by the New Democrats and a substantial number of Republicans, as our analysis of congressional voting behavior demonstrates.

7. The policy savants were far from the first to question the Vannevar Bush model of science. The challenge to the Bush model began during the Vietnam war when critics such as Noam Chomsky, Daniel Greenberg, Seymour Melman, David Noble, and others began to stress that the foundation of basic science was the military-industrial-university complex. Beginning in the 1970s, a new field, science and technology studies, began to challenge this Bush model from another angle. They made the case that closely observing science showed a very different pattern in which people, politics, and money played parts that were ineluctably intertwined with science (Knorr-Cetina 1981; Latour 1987; Mulkay 1979; Busch, Lacy, Burkhardt, and Lacy 1991), although neither money nor party politics were foregrounded.

8. We are not making the case that federal investment had to precede development of medical substances and devices as key industries in the new economy. We see causality in this case as a chicken-and-egg question. We also want to point out that approximately half of the money invested in biotechnology research is from private sources, a remarkable percentage, given that private sources generally fund only about 10 percent of research (U.S. Congress 1991).

From 1995–1998, the Republic revolution, led by Representative "Newt" Gingrich disrupted the bipartisan competitiveness coalition. Gingrich also wanted a science policy for the new economy but one that was distinct from the Democrats'. He was against management by the central government ("picking winners and losers") and "corporate welfare" (Slaughter and Rhoades 2003). The Republican revolution eliminated some of Clinton's programs, such as the Technology Reinvestment Program, which, under the rubric of dual use, had extended strategic alliances between universities and industry to include the military. The Republican revolution weakened other civilian technology programs, for example, the DOD Advanced Technology Research Projects Agency (ARPA) and the Advanced Technology Program (Vonortas 2000). However, the Technology Reinvestment Program "was reincarnated as 'dual use' programs in the research agencies of the armed services, buried deeper in the bureaucracy to reduce visibility and controversy" (Etzkowitz and Gulbrandsen 1999, p. 57). The legislation that enabled the Advanced Technology Program was not revoked, and military commitment to economic security augurs well for continued program funding. Even the revolutionary Republicans supported legislation that strengthened intellectual property rights, such as the 1995 Digital Performance Right in Sound Recordings Act. In 1996, the Republicans supported the Telecommunications Act, which had been developed by Al Gore as part of the Clinton administration's competitiveness policy (Hundt 2000). By 1998, the Republicans were regularly negotiating and passing competitiveness policy measures and legislation that had important consequences for academic capitalism. Particularly important were the Next Generation Internet Act and the Digital Millennium Copyright Act (DMCA).

Federal Legislation Related to Research and Intellectual Property

In this section we identify selected legislation and briefly describe some of the opportunities it created. Competitiveness legislation and technology transfer dominated the 1980s. In the early 1990s legislation related to computing opened up prospects for which copyright was important, leading to the DMCA and the Teach Act, which have implications for teaching and learning as well as research. Legislation that improved trademark protection had implications for university trademark licensing programs.

Prior to the Bayh-Dole Act, federal policy placed in the public domain discoveries made with federal grant funds. Universities were able to secure patents on federally funded research only when the government, through a long and cumbersome application process, granted special approval. Only a small number of universities engaged in patenting prior to 1980, when the Bayh-Dole Act directly signaled the inclusion of universities in profit taking. It allowed universities and small businesses to retain title to inventions made with federal research and development monies. In the words of Congress, "It is the policy and objective of the Congress . . . to promote collaboration between commercial concerns and nonprofit organizations, including universities" (Bayh-Dole Act 1980 [Legal Information Institute 2003]). Bayh-Dole "explicitly recognized technology transfer to the private sector as a desirable outcome of federally financed research, and endorsed the principle that exclusive licensing of publicly funded technology was sometimes necessary to achieve that objective" (Jaffe 2000).[9]

The Bayh-Dole Act changed the relationship between university managers and faculty in several important ways. As potential patent holders, university trustees and administrators could see all research generated by faculty as relatively easily protected intellectual property. Faculty too could better conceptualize their discoveries as products or processes, private, valuable, licensable, not necessarily as knowledge to share publicly with a community of scholars (Rhoades and Slaughter 1991a, 1991b). The Bayh-Dole Act gave new and concrete meaning to the phrase "commodification of knowledge." The act streamlined universities' participation in the marketplace.

Although Bayh-Dole had great consequences for universities, it was an early piece of competitiveness policy legislation aimed primarily at stimulating economic recovery. Its main objective was support for small businesses, which the Reagan administration had deemed engines of economic growth. In 1983, however, through executive order, Reagan extended Bayh-Dole's coverage to include large corporations. After 1983, any entity performing federally funded R&D could patent and own discoveries made in the course of research, a shift that

9. An earlier piece of legislation that contributed to an academic capitalist knowledge/learning regime was the Plant Variety Protection Act of 1971. Its implications were not fully realized until the 1980s when biotechnology assumed great economic importance. The Plant Variety Protection Act extended property rights to breeders for sexually propagated plants. Under the1930 Plant Patent Act, only asexually produced plants had been protected (Busch, Lacy, Burkhardt, and Lacy 1991). The Plant Variety Protection Act, together with case law and administrative law, extended industrial patents to all plant varieties and hybrids. The 1980 Supreme Court decision *Diamond v. Chakrabarty* (447 US 202) allowed the patenting of "novel life forms." Based on that decision, the U.S. Board of Patent Appeals in *Ex parte Hibberd* (1985), allowed very broad plant patenting, including genetically engineered plants. Taken together with the Bayh-Dole Act (1980), these legal developments allowed universities to hold patents on a variety of lucrative life forms. Indeed, academic advances in rDNA techniques developed sophisticated genetic mapping that allowed patent owners to offer compelling proof of patent infringement, further strengthening intellectual property rights, thus increasing academe's stake and investment in it (Busch, Lacy, Burkhardt, and Lacy 1991).

contributed to the privatization and commercialization of research across all categories of performers, including large corporations.

Competitiveness legislation blurred the boundaries between public and private sectors. Several technology transfer acts, beginning with the Stevenson-Wydler Act (1980), pioneered the legal and administrative mechanisms for transfers between public and private entities. These acts were aimed primarily at the federal laboratories but also touched on universities. For example, in the Federal Technology Transfer Act of 1986, federal laboratories could enter into cooperative research and development agreements with "other federal agencies, state or local governments, industrial organizations, public and private foundations, and nonprofit organizations, *including universities* [emphasis ours]" (Federal Technology Transfer Act of 1986, 100 STAT. 1785). Although universities were not a main target of Stevenson-Wydler, the technology transfer acts were important in incorporating universities into the competitiveness agenda because they pioneered the legal structures that shaped collaborative research agreements between public nonprofit organizations and private sector corporations. Collaborative Research and Development Agreements (CRADAs) permitted private corporations to select marketable products and processes from inventories of federal laboratories' intellectual property and work in collaboration with federal scientists to bring the product or process to market. In return, federal laboratories received a share of the profits through license or royalty agreements. Universities emulated CRADAs, developing directories of the problems on which scientists and engineers were working, and sharing the directories with the business community in hopes of promoting collaboration. Like the Bayh-Dole Act, the several technology transfer acts changed common understandings of what public and nonprofit meant. Also like Bayh-Dole, Stevenson-Wydler authorized segments of public and nonprofit organizations to participate in the market, dissolving the boundaries between university and society, and allowing interpenetration in areas of market potential.

The Federal Courts Improvements Act (1982) created a new Court Of Appeals for the Federal Circuit (CAFC), which handled appeals from district courts, thereby ending "forum shopping" in intellectual property cases, creating a more uniform approach to patents. The new court led the way for a greatly strengthened approach to intellectual property. "Before 1980, a district court finding that a patent was valid and infringed was upheld on appeal 62% of the time; between 1982 and 1990 this percentage rose to 90%" (Jaffe 2000). The CAFC led the patent office to offer broader protections through patents. "There are now patents for genetically engineered bacteria, genetically altered mice, particular gene sequences, surgical methods, computer software, financial products, and methods for conducting auctions on the Worldwide Web. For each of these, there would have been prior to 1980 at least serious doubt as to whether or not they would be deemed by the PTO and the courts to fall within the realm of patentable subject matter" (Jaffe 2000).

University administrators and faculty members were well aware that strengthened intellectual property protection made patentable knowledge more valuable. The Small Business Innovation Development Act (1982) mandated that federal agencies with annual expenditures over $100 million devote 1.25 percent of their budgets to research performed by small businesses, on the grounds that they were critical to economic recovery. Universities strongly opposed this legislation, making the case that it diverted the mission agencies from funding university research (Slaughter 1990). Ironically, as universities became more deeply involved in academic capitalism, they increasingly took equity positions in small enterprises started by their faculty, often with funding provided by the Small Business Innovation Development Act (Etzkowitz and Gulbrandsen 1999).

The Orphan Drug Act (1983) provided incentives for developing drugs for rare diseases affecting human populations of under 200,000. This act encouraged biotechnology firms, which drew heavily from academically based, federally funded R&D, whether through university spin-off companies or through licensing, to pursue (through tax incentives and market monopolies) niche markets for vaccines and diagnostics for diseases, such as Huntington's chorea, that struck relatively small groups. Such companies received a 50 percent tax credit for the cost of conducting clinical trials, often performed by universities, as well as a seven-year right to exclusivity in marketing the product (U.S. Congress 1991). A number of universities profited from the sales of such drugs, as did UCLA and the University of California System, for example, which drew external revenues from the sale of human growth hormone, produced and marketed through Lilly.

The 1984 National Cooperative Research Act afforded special antitrust status to R&D joint ventures and consortia. This act was crucial to university-industry collaborations. Previously, the courts had ruled that collaborations at the enterprise level were inappropriate, barring joint R&D efforts by firms in the same industries on the grounds that these constituted restraint of trade. The National Cooperative Research Act made an exception enabling broad government-industry-university funding of R&D, such as occurred with Sematech. In short order, there were over one hundred such ventures (NSF 1989). The National Cooperative Research Act also figured in business leaders' strategy to overhaul national antitrust policy, promoting cooperation at home and competition abroad (Dickson 1984; Fligstein 1990). While universities could participate in the opportunities created by this legislation, they were not its target. They benefited from it in so far as they were willing to embrace the competitiveness R&D agenda.

The passage of the Trademark Clarification Act (PL 98-620) in 1984 further expanded the rights of universities by removing certain Bayh-Dole restrictions regarding the kinds of inventions that universities could own and the right of universities to assign their property rights to other parties (Jaffe 2000).The Trademark Clarification Act also strengthened the ability of colleges and universities to protect their names, logos, and mascots. In the late 1980s and 1990s, this gave rise to extensive trademark licensing programs on the part of some universities.

The Drug Export Amendments Act of 1986 allowed drugs not yet approved by the Food and Drug Administration (FDA) for use in the United States to be exported to twenty-one foreign countries that had regulatory mechanisms. Prior to 1986, if U.S. companies with new drugs wanted to reach foreign markets with more rapid regulatory processes than the United States, they had to forfeit proprietary rights in the technology to their multinational partners in those countries in order to gain market access (U.S. Congress 1991). Like the Orphan Drug Act of 1983, the Drug Export Amendments Act created a supportive climate for the development of biotechnology, a dynamic sector among burgeoning university-industry relationships.

At the federal level, the Federal Technology Transfer Act of 1986 and Executive Order 12591 (April 10, 1987) required government research agencies engaged in extensive biotechnology work to establish close collaboration with private companies. This promoted privatization of public research and created rules and precedents that universities followed. Universities were also often involved in trilateral research agreements with federal laboratories and private corporations.

The 1988 Omnibus Trade and Competitiveness Act (PL 100-418) stressed the growing importance of intellectual property in world markets. This act stipulated that anyone who sold or used a product in the United States or who imported without authority a product made by a process under patent protection by the United States was liable as an infringer. Like much of the competitiveness R&D policy legislation, the 1988 act increased protection of intellectual property and heightened penalties for violation, again stressing knowledge as commodity.

The National Competitiveness Technology Transfer Act extended opportunities for federal laboratories to enter into CRADAs with universities and private industry. It also allowed information and innovations developed through cooperative arrangements to be protected from disclosure. This greatly extended intellectual property protection, freeing public universities from freedom of information regulations with regard to cooperative arrangements and contracts with industry.

The Defense Appropriations Act of 1993 provided for the Technology Reinvestment Program, which was headed by the Advanced Research Projects Agency (ARPA) but spread across the military services, the Departments of Commerce, Energy, and Transportation, NASA, and the NSF. Its mission was to merge defense and commercial industrial bases so that the DOD could have access to low-cost critical technologies. The program included "Manufacturing Education and Training projects [that] combine university and industry expertise to formulate new programs of education in the science of manufacturing" (DOD 1994, p. 71). Although this legislation was repealed by the revolutionary Republicans, cross-agency programs continued that encouraged competitiveness of which entrepreneurial science was a component.

Federal research policy treated R&D very well during the period 1980–2000. Despite faculty, university, and "academy complex" claims to the contrary, federal research funding for academic R&D grew steadily, expanding academic research and funding graduate education in science and technology. The federal budget for academic R&D rose every year from 1968–1998. It increased in all categories (basic, applied, development) with the exception of a dip in the early 1990s for basic research. The R&D budget increased from 2.32 percent of the gross domestic product (GDP) in 1981 to 2.67 percent in 1998, an increase of tens of billions of dollars (Greenberg 2001, Tables 1–3). However, these funds were not allocated in the same fields as in the 1960s and 1970s. Rather than physics, which was associated with nuclear energy and weapons of mass destruction and was funded by DOE and DOD, the National Institutes of Health (NIH) received the greatest increase in research money. In the 1980s and 1990s, programs on nuclear engineering closed while biotechnology programs proliferated.

Although NIH biotechnology funds expanded rapidly, private funds increased even faster, constituting half of biotechnology funding by 1990 (U.S. Congress 1991). The commercial funding of biotechnology often leveraged federally funded academic research, tilting the whole field toward the market. NSF funding for engineering experiment stations and funding for various computing and Internet infrastructure programs often had commercial components that also tilted academic research toward the market.

Most of the legislation analyzed thus far was not directed specifically at universities and colleges. Rather, it was aimed at increasing U.S. business competitiveness in growing global markets. Although universities were not the focus of this legislation, they restructured to intersect the new policy thrust. Networks within universities—administrators, faculty, and support professionals—began developing intellectual property policy, technology transfer, and economic development offices, bringing their institutions into closer alignment with the new economy.

Legislation Related to Copyright and Competitiveness

As patent legislation was strengthened, so was copyright legislation. The federal government initiated legislation for research that supported the infrastructure for an information economy—for example, the High Performance Computing Act of 1991 and the Next Generation Internet Act of 1998 (Table 2.1). New copyright legislation was enacted in the 1990s as digital technologies and telecommunications grew rapidly. The new laws strongly emphasized protection of digital forms of creative expression, including new forms of intellectual property such as courseware, multimedia, electronic databases, and tele-immersion, and extended copyright protection as well. Information assumed a greater role in the "new" global economy, particularly with regard to exports. When export of copyrighted products, processes, and services increased, U.S. copyright policy became enmeshed in global trade and international copyright agreements. These had important implications for academic capitalism at home because the agreements began to treat intellectual products like all other goods and education as a service able to be traded in international markets.

As new forms of intellectual property were protected, they presented new possibilities that drew together networks of actors within universities who worked to develop new products or services that utilized them. The most obvious such service was distance education. Digitized courseware, whether used for distance education or to supplement traditional print media on campus, was increasingly covered by copyright. The networks of actors involved in distance education often spanned the boundaries between public, nonprofit, and profit-taking organizations, frequently partnering with corporations in educational enterprises (Schiller 1998), thereby moving universities into an academic capitalist knowledge/learning regime.

The 1976 Copyright Act laid the ground, perhaps unwittingly, for the changes that occurred in the 1990s. Unlike the 1909 Copyright Act, the 1976 act did not include a specific "teacher's exception" in the work-for-hire doctrine. Despite this change, faculty continued to behave according to custom and tradition, acting as though they owned their copyrightable intellectual property. Initially, universities did not challenge them, perhaps because the economic incentives were not great enough.

Table 2.1 Selected Legislation Enabling a Competitive Research and Development Policy

1970	PL 91-577	Plant Variety Protection Act
1976	PL 94-553	Copyright Act
1980	PL 96-480	Stevenson-Wydler Technology Innovation Act
1980	PL 96-517	Bayh-Dole Act
1982	PL 97-219	Small Business Innovation Development Act
1982	PL 97-164	Federal Courts Improvement Act
1983	PL 97-414	Orphan Drug Act
1984	PL 98-462	National Cooperative Research Act
1984	PL 98-620	Trademark Clarification Act
1984	PL 98-551	Orphan Drug Act, Amended
1985	PL 99-91	Orphan Drug Act, Amended
1986	PL 99-502	Federal Technology Transfer Act
1986	PL 99-660	Drug Export Amendments Act
1988	PL 100-418	Omnibus Trade and Competitiveness Act
1989	PL 101-189	National Competitiveness Technology Transfer Act
1991	PL 102-194	High-Performance Computing Act
1991	PL 102-245	American Technology Preeminence Act
1993	PL 102-396	Defense Appropriations Act, Technology Reinvestment Program
1993	PL 103-42	National Cooperative Research and Production Act
1995	PL 104-39	Digital Performance Right in Sound Recordings Act
1995	PL 104-113	National Technology Transfer and Advancement Act
1997	PL 105-34	Taxpayer Relief Act
1997	PL 105-115	Food and Drug Administration Modernization Act
1998	PL 105-244	Higher Education Act, Re-authorization
1998	PL 105-304	Digital Millennium Copyright Act
1998	PL 105-305	Next Generation Internet Research Act
2002	PL 107-273	Technology, Education and Copyright Harmonization (TEACH) Act

In the 1990s, a series of laws developed to deal with technological change in telecommunications and digital industries that made digital intellectual property increasingly valuable. The 1995 Digital Performance Right in Sound Recordings Act created a new property right that gave a limited public performance right in digital transmission sound recordings, such as streaming audio technologies and web casting (U.S. Copyright Office Summary 1998). Technological developments together with the Internet created the possibility of music on demand, downloaded from the Internet. The Digital Performance Right in Sound Recordings Act makes this illegal, increasing the protections around sound recordings and contributing to the overall alienability and value of intellectual property (Chung 1997). The Telecommunications Act of 1996 dramatically altered the industry regulatory framework. Prior to 1996, the 1934 Communications Act, as implemented through the Federal Communications Commission (FCC), authorized separate monopolies: broadcast, cable, wire, wireless, and satellite. The 1996 Telecommunications Act deregulated these various industries, creating a competitive climate that favored growth of the Internet, World Wide Web, and e-business, all of which utilized previously separated communications media in new patterns. Deregulation of telecommunications created numerous possibilities for an academic capitalism knowledge/learning regime, ranging from software to distance education.

The Next Generation Internet Act (1998), tied into the development of Internet2, contributed to infrastructure that greatly increased the speed and broadened the bandwidth on the information super highway. Universities were simultaneously participants in developing new nodes on the information superhighway and beneficiaries of new technologies. The legislation also committed universities to commercialization in that Internet2, a university-led initiative that worked in tandem with the Next Generation Internet, expected to derive intellectual property and profits from joint corporate-university technical breakthroughs in the course of development research. This infrastructure greatly enhanced the economic value of distance education and other forms of digital intellectual property.

The Digital Millennium Copyright Act (DMCA) of 1998 protects digital property by prohibiting unauthorized access to a copyrighted work as well as unauthorized copying of a copyrighted work. The DMCA is far-reaching and covers an array of technologies, from web casting to hyperlinks, online directories, search engines, and the content of the materials made available by these technologies. Not only are citizens penalized for unauthorized access, devices and services that circumvent copyright are also prohibited. The law very deliberately seeks to develop electronic commerce and associated technologies by strengthening protections of all forms of digital property.

There are some exceptions, the broadest being for law enforcement and intelligence. The other exceptions are quite narrow. For example, the exception for nonprofit libraries, archives, and educational institutions allows them to "circumvent solely for the purpose of making a good faith determination as to whether they wish to obtain authorized access to the work." All encryption research, including academic, is severely constrained in that it is permitted only "in order to identify the flaws and vulnerabilities of encryption technologies." Reverse engineering, which historically was not protected by copyright, is now allowed only when someone has legally "obtained the right to use a copy of a computer program for the sole purpose of identifying and analyzing elements of the program necessary to achieve interoperability with other programs." Colleges and universities can lose these limited exceptions if faculty or graduate student "employees" distribute cached materials outside of a limited time period or if an institution receives more than two notifications of faculty or graduate student infringement in a three-year period. Moreover, the institution has the obligation to provide all its users with "information materials describing and promoting compliance with copyright law" (U.S. Copyright Office Summary 1998). Such strengthening of protection makes all digital property more valuable, more vulnerable to privatization, and less likely to be publicly available to research and teaching communities.

In order to facilitate development of digital technology and commerce, the liability of on-line service providers is limited so that they are not responsible for the behavior of their clients. Universities and colleges, which often act as on-line service providers for their student, faculty, and staff communities, thus have limited liability. But there is a Catch-22. If infringing activity is identified, the university has to control it by blocking or taking down the material. To accomplish this, the institution must designate an official to receive and act on claims of infringement. In other words, universities and colleges are obligated to police their students, faculty, and staff, should the owner of a copyright so request.

The DMCA has a special section on distance education. Generally, the DMCA seems to take the position that purchasing or licensing digital materials should be a cost born by distance educators, as is the case with hardware and software. Currently, exemptions for educational use of digital products are only for traditional classrooms that offer "systematic instructional activity by a non-profit educational institution or governmental body" or for students who are in situations that make them unable to access such classrooms (U.S. Copyright Office Summary 1998). In other words, there is no exemption for distance education networks not tied into conventional instruction. Fair use offers an exemption that might apply to distance education, but there is not yet a body of case law that clarifies how this would work. Moreover, if a U.S. educational institution transmits courses to students in other countries, the law is not clear as to which will apply, U.S. law or the law of the country receiving the transmission.

As it currently stands, the DMCA offers traditional colleges and universities an advantage in developing distance education. They are best able to make use of such educational exemptions as exist because of the physical classroom requirement. They also benefit because for-profit distance education organizations are currently unable to access federal financial aid for their students. (However, the Department of Education has provisionally agreed to a change in these regulations, which will provide federal aid for students taking for-profit distance education courses.) Traditional colleges and universities have every incentive to try to capture a sizeable market share of distance education before for-profit competition explodes.

The Technology, Education, and Copyright Harmonization (TEACH) Act was passed in 2002. TEACH attempted to modify DMCA provisions that constrained the delivery of distance education. TEACH also allows educators greater freedom with regard to copyrighted materials. For example, the new law allows display and performance of most works, unlike the DMCA, which limited broad classes of work, particularly those that had entertainment as well as instructional value. The DMCA confined free use of copyrighted materials to classrooms; TEACH allows institutions to reach students through distance education at any location. Unlike DMCA, TEACH also lets students retain material for a short time. Further, TEACH permits digitization of analog works but only if the work is not available in digital form (University of Texas System 2002; Crew 2002).

However, TEACH also has many restrictions. Copyrighted material used in distance education must be part of "systematic mediated instructional activity," supervised by an instructor, directly related to the teaching plan, and technologically limited (protected) to enrolled students. It must provide information about copyright protections attached to the works; the works may not be retained by students, and dissemination cannot interfere with technological protections embedded in the works (University of Texas System 2002). TEACH assigns responsibility for monitoring and policing copyright to universities, steering them in the direction of developing and disseminating copyright policies and staffing copyright offices. The act applies only to accredited nonprofit institutions, which must institute copyright policies that provide informational materials about copyright to faculty, students, and staff.

Generally, the TEACH provisions are designed to permit use of digitized products and processes in distance education but protect the material and property of copyright holders, especially for commercial developers of educational materials. The involvement of the institution to some degree reflects Bayh-Dole, which required a responsible person at the institution to oversee the act. The "person" often developed into an office, as may be the case with regard to TEACH, which calls for an information technology official to oversee implementation of provisions. In a process of organizational learning, information technology officials may model after technology transfer officials and create offices that could ultimately oversee institutional management of faculty copyrights (see chapter 4). The responsibilities assigned to the institution make faculty members less liable for violations but call for administrative intrusion into the teaching process.

International Treaties and Trade Agreements that Stimulate Academic Capitalism

Beginning in the 1980s, the United States began to take a much more aggressive position on global protection of intellectual property. Until this point, world trade in intellectual property had been governed by agreements forged in the last quarter of the nineteenth century: the Paris Convention (1883) covering various industrial property rights and the Berne Convention (1886) covering copyrights (Maskus 2000). Recently, the United States took action on bilateral trade agreements, regional trade agreements (North American Free Trade Agreement), and Trade-Related Aspects of Intellectual Property Rights (TRIPs), which were initiated during the Uruguay round of General Agreement of Tariffs and Trade (GATT) in 1986. After prolonged negotiations, all of the agreements gained greatly strengthened intellectual property protection. Among the more important changes TRIPs inaugurated was extending the length of copyright to fifty years beyond the life of an author. Given that U.S. copyright law initially construed copyright as an incentive to authors to produce creative works, the extension of copyright to the estate of the author signals information economy commitment to strengthened intellectual property protections.

Although databases are neither creative nor original, TRIPs, now the U.S. standard for copyrights, mandates that computer software and data compilations be protected as literary works (Busch 2000; Maskus 2000). TRIPs also calls for a fifty-year minimum term of protection for performers and producers of recorded music. The U.S. team was often the lead negotiator for enhanced copyright protection, even though the positions it took were often at odds with U.S. law. After successfully arguing for greater international copyright protection, representatives of the United States then argued to Congress that U.S. law had to be changed to comply with global standards. Among the laws changed to meet TRIPs mandates were the 1995 Digital Performance Right in Sound Recordings Act and the 1998 Digital Millennium Copyright Act.

Trademark protection was enhanced by two laws in the late 1990s. The Anticounterfeiting Consumer Protection Act of 1996 criminalized unauthorized (royalty-less) use of protected images, which include university names, logos, and mascots. Universities were able to use this legislation to obtain court orders authorizing the seizure of goods bearing counterfeits of their marks. The 1999 Anticybersquatting Consumer Protection Act extended such protection into cyberspace (Bearby and Siegal 2002).

Copyright protection assumed importance because of the rapid expansion of the information economy. Academic research was important to that expansion in terms of developments in computer hardware as well as software operation systems, much of which was protected by patents. Other types of software, ranging from instructional packages for distance education to sophisticated statistical analysis packages, developed their own markets and were more and more aggressively protected by copyright. As courseware and other traditional teaching materials, including syllabi and course notes, were digitized and put on the web, they too were copyrighted, often by the universities at which the faculty who created the materials were employed. Changes in copyright law opened opportunities for academic capitalism to spread rapidly beyond researchers in the physical and life sciences, who had been involved in the patent phase of the academic capitalism knowledge regime. Faculty from all fields were involved with copyright as it applied to student instruction, making academic capitalism not just a knowledge regime but also a knowledge/learning regime.

The World Trade Organization (WTO) General Agreement on Trade and Services (GATS) refers to trade in services rather than goods, which are covered by GATT. The United States is very interested in trade in educational services because it leads global imports and exports of students. Exports are the sector in which the majority of commercial activity occurs. U.S. export earnings from foreign students as a percentage of total export earnings from services was 3.5 percent or U.S. $10.28 billion in 2000 (Larsen and Vincent-Lacrin 2002). In 2002, the U.S. Department of Commerce, along with several other countries, put forward negotiating proposals for GATS consideration. They deal only with higher (tertiary) education, adult education, training services, and educational testing (Sauve 2002).

Two of the four GATS modes of supply, both important for commercialization, are heavily involved in current U.S. negotiations. Mode 1 (not to be confused with Gibbons's Modes I and II), which includes distance education, virtual education, educational software, and corporate training through the Internet, is a small but rapidly growing market. Mode 3, commercial presence, involves the equivalent of foreign direct investment in higher education. Both modes of supply can be provided by public universities, which are considered private when they are so engaged, and corporate vocational providers, such as McDonald's and Motorola Universities and Microsoft's Certified Technical Education Centers. Sylvan Learning Systems, "which has recently acquired private universities and business schools in Mexico, Spain, Chile, France and Switzerland," as well as the University of Phoenix, which has subsidiaries in Canada and Puerto Rico, provide examples of Mode 3 for-profit institutions (Larsen and Vincent-Lacrin, p. 22).

Through the Department of Commerce, the United States has developed a proposal to eliminate a number of barriers to educational trade in services among WTO signatories and has submitted them to GATS. Among the many barriers the United States wants eliminated are prohibitions on higher educational and educational training services by foreign entities, obstacles to establishing educational facilities, lack of foreign degree recognition, requirements for local partners, restrictions on electronic transmissions of course material, tax treatments that discriminate against foreign suppliers, and excessive fees and taxes imposed on licensing or royalty payments.

WTO countries do not have to accept the U.S. negotiating position. Higher education is defined as a public service, which is "any service which is supplied neither on a commercial basis, nor in competition with one or more service suppliers" (WTO 2003). However, the status of higher education is somewhat ambiguous in that public sector higher education provides some services through commercial arms—for example, New York University's School of Continuing and Professional Education, University of Maryland University College, or eCornell—and competes with commercial higher education offerings. Public or nonprofit higher education that offers education in foreign countries, whether Mode 1 or 3, is treated as private higher education. In global trade arrangements, these institutions in effect become commercial, committing home institutions more firmly to an international academic capitalism knowledge/learning regime.

GATT and GATS are part of multilateral trade agreements directed toward liberalization of world trade. Although WTO countries do not have to participate in these agreements because higher education is currently considered a public service, the United States, along with several other English-speaking nations, has taken a commercial approach to trade in tertiary educational services (Larsen and Vincent-Lacrin 2002). This approach commits institutions commercializing at home to a deeper degree of commercialization abroad, recursively strengthening an academic capitalism knowledge/learning regime.

Research policy initially intersected the market through Bayh-Dole (1980) and was characterized by patenting in the 1980s. In the 1990s, developments in information technology and legislative changes such as the 1996 Telecommunications Act, together with broader copyright protections, stimulated universities' market involvement in a wide array of instructional commodities. Trademark legislation from the 1980s through the late 1990s enabled colleges and universities to profit from their names, symbols, images, and mascots. Together these clusters of legislation created opportunities for higher education to invest itself in an academic capitalist knowledge/learning regime.

Congressional Voting Patterns

Table 2.2 shows the degree to which support for selected legislation enabling an academic capitalist knowledge regime was partisan. Of the twenty-nine laws shown, the House passed voice votes for sixteen. Voice votes are taken for various reasons, including members' wish to have no record of their vote or because consensus is so strong that a roll-call vote is inefficient. Given the overall strength in favor of most votes in the House, the consensus explanation is more

Table 2.2 Votes on Competitive Research and Development Policy

Legislation	House of Representatives						Senate					
	Bill #	Vote #	Dem	Rep	Indp	Total	Bill #	Vote #	Dem	Rep	Indp	Total
PL 91-577		NA	Voice	Voice	Voice	Voice	S 3070	NA	Voice	Voice	Voice	Voice
PL 94-553	HR 2223	800	*	*	*	316-7-107	S 22	40	61-0-1	35-0-2	1-0-0	97-0-3
PL 96-480		NA	Voice	Voice	Voice	Voice	S 1250	NA	Voice	Voice	Voice	Voice
PL 96-517	HR 6933	NA	Voice	Voice	Voice	Voice		NA	Voice	Voice	Voice	Voice
PL 97-164	HR 4482	310	*	*	*	321-76	S 1700	NA	Voice	Voice	Voice	Voice
PL 97-219	HR 4326	167	195-30	158-27	0	353-57	S 881	461	40-0	50-0	0	90-0
PL 97-414	HR 5238	NA	Voice	Voice	Voice	Voice		NA	Voice	Voice	Voice	Voice
PL 98-462	HR 5041	110	255-0	162-0	0	417-0	S 1841	209	43-0	54-0	0	97-0
PL 98-551		NA	Voice	Voice	Voice	Voice	S 771	NA	Voice	Voice	Voice	Voice
PL 98-620	HR 6163	NA	Voice	Voice	Voice	Voice		NA	Voice	Voice	Voice	Voice
PL 99-91	HR 2290	164	238-0-13	175-0-7	0-0-0	413-0-20	S 1147	NA	Voice	Voice	Voice	Voice
PL 99-502	HR 3773	439	227-0	159-0	0	386-0		NA	Voice	Voice	Voice	Voice
PL 99-660	HR 4326	NA	Voice	Voice	Voice	Voice	S 1744	NA	Voice	Voice	Voice	Voice
PL 100-418	HR 4848	231	243-4	133-41	0	376-45		288	50-1	35-10	0	85-11
PL 101-189	HR 2461	185	*	*	*	261-162	S 1352	NA	Voice	Voice	Voice	Voice
PL 102-194	HR 656	NA	Voice	Voice	Voice	Voice	S 272	NA	Voice	Voice	Voice	Voice
PL 102-245	HR 1989	3	236-1-31	155-0-11	1-0-0	392-1-42	S 1034	NA	Voice	Voice	Voice	Voice
PL 102-396	HR 5504	266	204-52-12	124-41-1	0-1-0	328-94-13		229	49-5-3	37-5-1	0-0-0	86-10-4
PL 103-42	HR 1313	NA	Voice	Voice	Voice	Voice	S 574	NA	Voice	Voice	Voice	Voice
PL 104-39	HR 1506	NA	Voice	Voice	Voice	Voice	S 227	NA	Voice	Voice	Voice	Voice
PL 104-113	HR 2196	NA	Voice	Voice	Voice	Voice	S 1164	NA	Voice	Voice	Voice	Voice
PL 104-153	HR 2511	NA	Voice	Voice	Voice	Voice	S 1136	NA	Voice	Voice	Voice	Voice
PL 105-34	HR 2014	245	27-177-2	226-1-1	0-1-0	253-179-3	S 949	211	37-8-0	55-0-0	0-0-0	92-8-0
PL 105-115	HR 1411	NA	Voice	Voice	Voice	Voice	S 830	256	43-2-0	55-0-0	0-0-0	98-2-0
PL 105-244	HR 6	135	198-0-7	215-4-7	1-0-0	414-4-14	S 1882	195	44-0-1	52-1-2	0-0-0	96-1-3
PL 105-304	HR 2281	NA	Voice	Voice	Voice	Voice	S 2037	137	45-0-0	54-0-1	0-0-0	99-0-1
PL 105-305	HR 3332	NA	Voice	Voice	Voice	Voice	S 1609	NA	Voice	Voice	Voice	Voice
PL 106-113	HR 3194	562	6-201-4	210-8-4	0-1-0	216-210-8	S 1948	NA	Voice	Voice	Voice	Voice
PL 107-273	HR 2215	NA	Voice	Voice	Voice	Voice		NA	Voice	Voice	Voice	Voice

Note: Vote format: Yae-Nay-Nonvoting

* Party breakdown not available

likely. All but three of the laws had the support of 70 percent or more of the congresspersons.

Democrats very likely opposed the 1989 National Competitiveness Technology Transfer Act because it was included as Section 3131 et seq. of the DOD Authorization Act for fiscal year 1990, which increased defense funding, a policy to which the Democrats, proposing a peace dividend, were opposed. The 1997 Taxpayer Relief Act was part of wider tax relief bill more aligned with Republican than Democratic Party politics; it was understandably opposed by a substantial number of Democrats. The 1999 Anticybersquatting Consumer Protection Act was designed to protect corporations' "domain names when they are identical or confusingly similar to trademarks with bad faith intent to profit from the goodwill of trademarks" (Wertheim 2000). Critics of the law, among which were many Democrats, feared it would stamp out parody and social commentary, diminishing free speech.

The coalition that supported the selected federal legislation enabling an academic capitalist knowledge/learning regime was even stronger in the Senate. Nineteen of the twenty-nine votes were voice votes. No more than fourteen senators opposed any piece of legislation on which a roll-call vote was taken. These congressional votes were taken during a period when acrimony between the parties was increasing, suggesting the strength of the coalition.

The political coalitions for student aid as well as science and technology depended on centrist Democrats, often identified by their participation in the Democratic Leadership Caucus, and centrist Republicans. These congresspersons generally supported neoliberal policies that funded segments of the state that supported the private sector, and undercut policies that supported welfare functions of the state. This legislation did not dictate an academic capitalism knowledge/learning regime. Other than student aid, it was often not concerned with academe. However, it created opportunities for academic capitalism on which new networks of administrators, faculty, and students acted.

The congressional voting pattern on selected federal legislation that we have reviewed is important because it indicates that there is a coalition that creates opportunities for the academic capitalist knowledge/learning regime. The coalition is broad, stable, and durable. Indeed, this coalition has endured as long as the cold war coalition that supported the military-industrial-academic complex. In order for the academic capitalist knowledge/learning regime to be altered, new political coalitions would have to emerge and the legislation that has reregulated U.S. higher education would have to be dismantled.

Conclusion

We make the case that a knowledge/learning regime shift has occurred. Foucault (1977) used the concept of "disciplinary regimes" to refer to broad changes in the way power/knowledge moves through society. His use of the term *disciplinary* referred to means of obtaining obedience from the citizenry rather than to fields of study, although according to Foucault the learned disciplines also disciplined. He began with the aristocracy, whose power was drawn from blood and who used bloody methods—for example, public drawing and quartering—as a text to instruct the citizenry about the penalties of disobedience. Foucault saw the aristocracy's disciplinary regime as superceded by that of intellectuals and professionals, often associated with or attached to the state.[10] The powers of intellectuals and professionals were discursive, depending on surveilling, calibrating, and norming all aspects of human behavior, suppressing deviance by foregrounding and naturalizing the "normal." We see this regime as being overlaid by an academic capitalism knowledge/learning regime.

At the turn of the last century, professionals wanted to be neither proletarians nor bourgeoisie (Perkin 1989). They tried to open up space between workers and capital. They did this by aligning with the state, which supported education, certified professionals, and opened up careers for them in organizations ranging from hospitals and universities to prisons and social welfare agencies. The tacit social contract between professionals and society read that professionals received monopolies of expertise for altruistically serving the public good (Silva and Slaughter 1984). Because they were outside of the market economy they were neither compensated as highly as capitalists nor treated like wage labor. Professionals aligned with the state underlined their altruistic purpose by developing discourse about the public good. However, in the 1960s and 1970s many "altruistic" professionals transformed themselves into expert professionals, downplaying the public dimensions of their knowledge, maximizing their profits, and moving closer to the technoscience core of the economy (Brint 1994).

Although scholars who write about professions usually do not deal with professors, professors are perhaps the paramount professionals because it is they who train and certify all others. We see professors as following the course of expert professionals outside the academy but as doing so somewhat later, in the 1980s and 1990s rather than the 1960s and 1970s. Because professors were based

10. Although Foucault recognized the power of the bourgeoisie and capital, he did not dwell upon it nor upon the relationship of professionals to the business class.

in nonprofit institutions, whether private or public, they were unable to move easily toward the market until the legislative and regulatory climate we have described in this chapter presented opportunities.

Many institutions took advantage of the opportunities presented by federal legislation by generating external revenues.[11] Resource dependence is one form of discipline, but, as Foucault points out, there are others. Academic capitalism disciplines through economic incentives or the promise of economic incentives. It pulls some professors out of the orbit of the associations of learned disciplines and closer to the private economic sector, where they function as somewhat atomized scientific/entrepreneurial actors with highly specialized, commodifiable expertise. The university, through its administrators, moves to represent the faculty to external entities interested in various entrepreneurial activities and partnerships, in part because associations of learned disciplines and faculty senates do not. However, university administrators could not take on such roles unless faculty were "disciplined" through the intrinsic power of money, a value in and of itself under late capitalism. Very often faculty initially seek money for their programs or fields but discover that the enticements of the new economy are many and reward individuals rather than collectives of professionals. Administrators who do not benefit directly from patent and copyright royalties nonetheless benefit indirectly because success in entrepreneurial activity signals competence to other universities and increases their career opportunities. College and universities did experience resource dependency, most often in the form of periodic but very intense state fiscal crises (e.g., in 1983, 1993, 2003), which pushed actors into networks that articulated with the market. However, the economic opportunities offered by the legislation we have described strongly pulled networks of actors toward the market.

Faculty and universities did not have to respond to these opportunities, and many, perhaps most, have not. However, networks of faculty and administrators were constituted that actively intersected the openings created by legislative opportunities. Initially, they directed their energy to patentable intellectual property. Over time, as the intellectual property regime for U.S. business became more protective (Coriat and Orsi 2002), especially with regard to copyright, networks of faculty and administrators became involved with "instructional capitalism" (Anderson 2001) via distance education and courseware.

11. By profit taking we mean generating revenue streams through commerce, whether from licenses or royalties on patents, copyrights, or trademarks and other forms of intellectual property, university industry partnerships, strategic alliances, all sport contracts, and other forms of contracting out. We understand that these profits are not redistributed to owners or shareholders but are used for education and research.

The student aid legislation "disciplined" working adults so that they used grants, loans, and tax relief to recast themselves as employees suitable for the new economy. The state and working adults themselves paid for education, allowing new economy corporations to subsidize some costs of production. Yet not all student aid legislation served working adults. The legislation segmented student markets. Student financial aid continued to modestly serve low-income students attending two- or four-year schools, but steered larger grants, generous loan packages, and tax relief to a relatively small segment of students who attend costly, elite private institutions.

The markets to which colleges and universities turned were heavily state subsidized. Most colleges and nonresearch universities competed for students and their financial aid dollars, whether in the form of federally funded grants or subsidized loans. Universities competed in federal research markets, which expanded steadily and significantly over the twenty-year period under study.

Analyzing the two major arenas of federal higher education policy—research policy and student financial aid—together rather than separately allows us to see how they influence each other, moving higher education in new directions. Student financial aid introduced and legitimated market ideas in the 1970s, giving rise to a competitiveness discourse for higher education. When competitiveness legislation aimed at increasing U.S. productivity and global market shares developed in the 1980s, the higher education community was familiar with the discourse from its experience with student financial aid. The step from markets in students to markets for faculty intellectual property was not a big one. Universities and colleges used organizational strategies developed in one set of market endeavors in others. As enrollment management offices were developed to make competition for students more efficient and successful, so technology transfer and licensing offices were developed to exploit intellectual property. When the revenue-generating possibilities of copyrights became apparent, universities wrote copyright policies and began hiring staff to manage intellectual properties. As more digitized products were copyrighted, the possibilities of instructional capitalism began to be explored in terms of distance education and a wide variety of on-campus multimedia learning experiences. The external and internal segmentation of student markets, made possible in part by instructional capitalism, heightened the opportunities for differential tuition in niche markets for distance education students and for high-demand internal programs, allowing an academic capitalism knowledge/learner regime to diffuse throughout the instructional process.

3

PATENT POLICIES
Legislative Change and Commercial Expansion

THE PURPOSE OF THIS chapter is to illustrate, problematize, and analyze the ways in which the legislative changes reviewed in chapter 2 intersect state and higher education system policies, as well as college and university policies. These intersections and incorporations are reinforced by legal and administrative practices, as suggested by our use of case law and the administrative practices to which case law sometimes refers. The academic capitalism knowledge/learning regime is not abstract: it is embedded in higher education practice and culture.

We begin by examining a patent case that reveals how the shift in knowledge regimes (described through changes in federal law in the previous chapter) plays out in terms of states, universities, faculty, and students. After deconstructing *Moore v. The Regents of the University of California* (1988), which we call the hairy-cell leukemia case, in order to illustrate the players and the stakes in an academic capitalist knowledge/learning regime, we analyze patent policies in six states so as to understand how mechanisms promoting academic capitalism change over time. We start our analysis in the 1970s and conclude with current policies, focusing on the range of patent parameters among states, state systems, and institutions. Theoretically, we draw on science and technology studies, with its emphasis on technology and normative change, narrativity, and social construction under late capitalism to approach the hairy-cell leukemia case. Our analysis of state system and institutional patent policies is informed by theories that deal with the norms and values of science and engineering and how they interact with changes in knowledge regimes.

The Hairy-Cell Leukemia Case

> In 1976, plaintiff and appellant [John Moore] sought medical treatment at the Medical Center of the University of California, Los Angeles (UCLA) for a condition known as hairy-cell leukemia. He was seen by Dr. David W. Golde, who confirmed the

> diagnosis. Without plaintiff's [Moore] knowledge or consent, Dr. Golde and Shirley G. Quan, a UCLA employee, determined that plaintiff's [Moore's] cells were unique. Through the science of genetic engineering, these defendants developed a cell-line from plaintiff's cells which is capable of producing pharmaceutical products of enormous therapeutic and commercial value. The Regents, Golde and Quan patented the cell-line along with methods of producing many products therefrom. In addition, these defendants entered into a series of commercial agreements for rights to the cell-line and its products with Sandoz Pharmaceuticals Corporation (Sandoz) and Genetics Institute, Inc. (Genetics). The market potential of products from plaintiff's cell-line was predicted to be approximately $3 billion by 1990. Hundreds of thousands of dollars have already been paid under these agreements to the developers. Without informing plaintiff [Moore], and in pursuit of their research efforts, Golde and UCLA continued to monitor him and take tissue samples from him for almost seven years following the removal of his spleen.
> (*Moore v. The Regents of the University of California* 1988)

The hairy-cell leukemia case is a story about patenting in universities. The case involves many of the actors in patent dramas: faculty, managerial professionals, regents, corporations, and the public, in the form of the plaintiff. Although there are a number of ways to approach this rich and multifaceted case, we see it as a story about knowledge regime change captured in the very different tales told by the California Court of Appeals (1988) and in the California Supreme Court (1990). The 1988 story was firmly rooted in a public service knowledge regime. The 1990 story repudiated the public service knowledge regime and instead gave voice to a narrative that endorsed an academic capitalism knowledge regime as an essential component of late capitalism.

In the 1988 story told by the court of appeals, Moore, the patient and plaintiff, was the innocent, and Dr. Golde, the physician researcher, and Quan, his research associate, were the villains, aided and abetted by UCLA and the regents of the University of California. Moore was innocent because he was unknowing. He thought his many treatments, which included removal of his spleen, were performed to cure his diagnosed hairy-cell leukemia. However, Golde and his research associate knew prior to initiating Moore's treatment that "certain blood products and blood components were of great value in a number of commercial and scientific efforts, and that a steady and abundant natural source of these substances in a human being would be highly desirable" (*Moore v. The Regents of the University of California* 1988). The vampire imagery used by the court is unmistakable. Moore, unknowing and innocent, is drained of his vital fluids by vampire scientists, who must draw sustenance from him to thrive unnaturally. The sustenance the scientists draw is economic, allowing them abnormal profits. Such imagery, of course, underlines the monstrosity of the scientists.

Golde and Quan were well aware that Moore's blood and bodily substances would provide them "with competitive, commercial, and scientific advantages" (1988). They disclosed their discovery to UCLA and the regents, although discovery may be a misnomer because they did not so much find something new as identify that which was already present, the unique properties in Moore's cells. The technology transfer office, the agent of UCLA and the regents, assisted Golde and Quan in securing a patent, ironically named the Mo cell line after the unwitting donor, and then brokered the patent to various pharmaceutical companies, two (Sandoz and Genetics, Inc.) of which took up licenses. Golde never told Moore, even when directly asked, that his "blood and bodily substances" were of great commercial value. When Moore discovered that his physician and the regents of the University of California had developed and marketed a cell line from his "blood and bodily substances," Moore sued, on the grounds that his physician had not acted in his best interests, had not disclosed relevant facts to him, and had unfairly profited from him.

The California Court of Appeals criticized the regents for using the rhetoric of freedom and altruism even as they profited from their exclusive right to license the cell line in question. The court knew that genetic engineering had initiated a revolution that made it possible for "John Moore's mere cells" to "become the foundation of a multi-billion dollar industry from which patent holders could reap fortunes." The court believed that Moore had the right to ownership of his own cells and found it ironic that the regents claimed Moore could not own his own tissue but they could. The court was not sympathetic to the regents' argument that Golde and Quan's culturing of the cells so increased the value of Moore's blood and bodily substances that this process negated his property rights to them. The court portrayed the regents as Janus-faced, on the one hand arguing for "unencumbered access to human tissue" as "essential to progress and public health" and on the other denying an individual a right to his own body parts because that would "inhibit research that could potentially benefit humanity" (1988).

In note 15, the court of appeals made clear that it was reading the case from a public service knowledge regime perspective. It cited Leon Wofsy, an immunologist at the University of California, Berkeley, who said: "The business of business is to make money and the mode is secrecy, a proprietary control of information and the fruits of research. The motive force of the university is the pursuit of knowledge and the mode is open exchange of ideas and unrestricted publication of the results of research." The court also drew on medical ethicists in formulating its opinion, pointing out that ethicists "supported the idea that a physician should not be involved with both the research and the therapy of the patient at the same time" (1988). The court realized that public policy would have to decide whether it would support a "gift-based" notion of academic science embedded in a public service knowledge regime or a "free-market" in academic science, but the court supported science once removed from the market.

The court of appeals took its decision, saying: "This appeal raises fundamental questions concerning a patient's right to the control of his or her own body, and whether the commercial exploitation of a patient's cells by medical care providers, without the patient's consent, gives rise to action for damages" (1988). The court ruled that Moore had action for damages with regard to the various defendants. It suggested that Dr. Golde and the regents were the appropriate targets for future litigation on Moore's part by portraying the commercial firms involved, Sandoz and Genetics, Inc., as very distant from Moore's treatment, and, by implication, not as culpable as the professor/physician and the regents.

The California Board of Regents appealed the decision to the California Supreme Court. That they appealed indicates that by the late 1980s, the regents, as a public body, were committed to moving toward an academic capitalist knowledge regime and were willing to put their considerable resources into legal battles to defend intellectual property owned by universities in the system. The shift from a public service knowledge regime to an academic capitalist knowledge regime was not the product of disembodied, inexorable, and incremental forces; rather, it was managed by many groups of skillful strategists, of which the California Board of Regents was one.

In the 1990 story told by the California Supreme Court, Moore was treated as a nuisance rather than an innocent victim. While Golde was specifically chastised for overstepping ethical boundaries, the court made clear that researchers generally were properly involved in patenting. Had Golde disclosed to Moore, all would have been well because "enforcement of physicians' disclosure obligations protects patients directly, without hindering the socially useful activities of innocent researchers." In this version of the story, researchers were categorically innocent, not patients. The California Supreme Court took the position that many medical researchers used human tissue, which contributed to the booming biotechnology industry in the United States. Were the court to decide in favor of Moore, it would "threaten to destroy the economic incentive to conduct important medical research." UCLA and the regents of the University of California were doing their job, transferring university science to the new economy. The court moved to "resolve disputes between specimen sources and specimen users [in ways that were not] detrimental to both academic researchers and the infant biotechnology industry, particularly when rights are asserted long after the specimen was obtained" (*Moore v. The Regents of the University of*

California 1990). Ironically, the court allowed Moore, now redefined as a specimen source, to pursue Golde for not properly disclosing his intent to commercialize, but undercut whatever claims Moore could make by denying his rights to his body parts as property.

In addition to deciding property rights, the California Supreme Court redefined some of the actors' responsibilities so they fit more compatibly with an academic capitalist knowledge regime. The regents were distanced from Golde's dealings with Moore on the grounds that he was never their patient, thus they had no knowledge of the patient-client relationship. This absolved the regents from responsibility for monitoring and enforcing ethics issues with regard to physician-client relationships in university hospitals, freeing them from legal liability and opening up new opportunities for regents to pursue profits based in academic knowledge. To some degree, this was in keeping with historical practice. Professors and physicians traditionally assumed the responsibility for policing themselves as a mark of professionalism. However, the supreme court did not address the inconsistency of the regents as the formal owners of faculty intellectual property, entitled to 50 percent of the profits but not legally responsible for their employees' patient-client relationships.

The hairy-cell leukemia case was unusual because it was a tort, which meant it was heard in state rather than federal court, the usual venue for intellectual property cases. However, the case is not unusual in what it tells us about the commitment of public university trustees to using the law to protect their intellectual property. Public universities developed strategies that turned on the use of the Eleventh Amendment, which says that a citizen of one state cannot sue another state, nor can foreign citizens sue any of the states. California, through its university system, was one of the states that aggressively used the Eleventh Amendment.

Over time, universities were able to expand their Eleventh Amendment protections. In 1982, three University of California, San Francisco, researchers patented a method for producing the human growth hormone (HGH) using recombinant DNA technology. The University of California system gave Eli Lilly an exclusive license on the patent and told Genentech, a competitor of Lilly that also produced HGH, that it was infringing. Genentech brought suit in federal court in Indiana, where Lilly was located, while the University of California system brought suit against Genentech in the northern district of California, its preferred litigation site (Polse 2001). The university system and Lilly engaged in litigation against Genentech on Eleventh Amendment grounds over the venue of the case for approximately seventeen years. When Congress passed 1992 amendments to both the Copyright and Trademark Acts to eliminate state immunity from lawsuits in federal courts, it looked like universities would lose Eleventh Amendment protection. However, the U.S. Supreme Court ruled the congressional amendments unconstitutional. The Rehnquist Court, a very strong defender of states' rights, interpreted the Eleventh Amendment to expand state immunity, taking the position that "federal courts cannot hear suits against unconsenting states regardless of the plaintiff's citizenships" (Polse 2001, p. 3). As Polse wrote in regard to the Genentech case:

> [The Rehnquist Court has] materially altered the landscape for businesses that compete with or wish to license technology from state research universities. Under the Court's current interpretation, the Eleventh Amendment allows the university to dictate when and in what court its patents may be challenged. Moreover, if a state university researcher infringes patents on the way to developing a non-infringing product, the patentee has no effective method for protecting her federal intellectual property rights. The Court's decisions came at a time when state universities are rapidly expanding their acquisition and enforcement of intellectual property rights. Ironically, federal research grants help fund much of the research that leads to the inventions the universities are seeking to patent (2001, p. 14).

The legal strategies of boards of regents in public universities came together with a conservative U.S. Supreme Court, indicating how the federal policies discussed in the previous chapter complement other modalities of power and work to instantiate an academic capitalist knowledge regime. Universities were not passive participants in this process. The boards of regents or trustees of at least three state university systems (California, Florida, and Texas) litigated tenaciously to advance their intellectual property rights through Eleventh Amendment protection.

Biotechnology was a new and powerful technology that raised issues that cut across previously separate spheres. As the California Supreme Court noted in 1990, the context in which courts had previously addressed human ownership was slavery, which, after protracted struggle, was prohibited. What were courts to do with the issue of ownership of body parts of a living donor? The very different stories told by the California Court of Appeals in 1988 and the California Supreme Court two years later show how biotechnology was open to social construction when it first emerged from university laboratories (Latour and Woolgar 1979; Bijker, Pinch, and Hughes 1989). In 1988 the appeals court drew on narratives from academe about the public good. In 1990, the state supreme court told a story characteristic of the new economy, competitiveness, and the centrality of science and intellectual property to a global economy. The 1990 story, which embodied an academic capitalist knowledge regime, was promoted and defended by faculty vested in intellectual property, by university trustees and their administrative apparatus (legal counsel, technology transfer officials), and by corporations that produced and marketed intellectual property. The state, as represented by the university and the legal system, was more attentive to the market, as represented by the corporations to which the University of California system had licensed its technology, than to patients or the public good (Haraway 1990, 1996).

State System and Institutional Patent Policies

In this section, we try to show how the hairy-cell leukemia case became possible by illustrating the policy process by which states, state university systems, and institutions developed laws, policies, rules, and regulations that promoted patenting. Patent policies are a way to track the degree to which universities are involved in an academic capitalism knowledge regime. We look at state system and institutional copyright policies for six states to see if they indicate a shift from a public good to an academic capitalist knowledge regime. The questions we are particularly interested in answering are: What values are embedded or explicit in these policies? Have they changed over time? What is the direction of the changes? What do they tell us about the relation between market, state and higher education, and how these are valued? Generally, we make the case that an academic public good knowledge regime (Figure 3.1) is shifting to an academic capitalist knowledge regime (Figure 3.2).

Theory

There are several strands in the U.S. literature on the norms and values of science. The first, which we will call the Mertonian strand, looks at values associated with science and scientists, sometimes not differentiating clearly between the two. The second, which we call the critical, challenges the Mertonian. The third social constructionist strand also challenges the Mertonian, but from a different perspective than the critical. The fourth, or university-industry collaboration strand, takes the position that science is not value-free but that it can accommodate both academic and market values. The fifth strand, which we call the commons strand, approaches science and values from the point of view of the public good. The five are closely related, and, some, particularly the commons strand, are currently counterpoising traditional academic values with market values. Very few deal with organizations (such as the university) that sustain science, with how the state and private sector interact with organizations that sustain science, and with how values are embodied in these organizational relations.

Figure 3.1 Public Good Model of Research

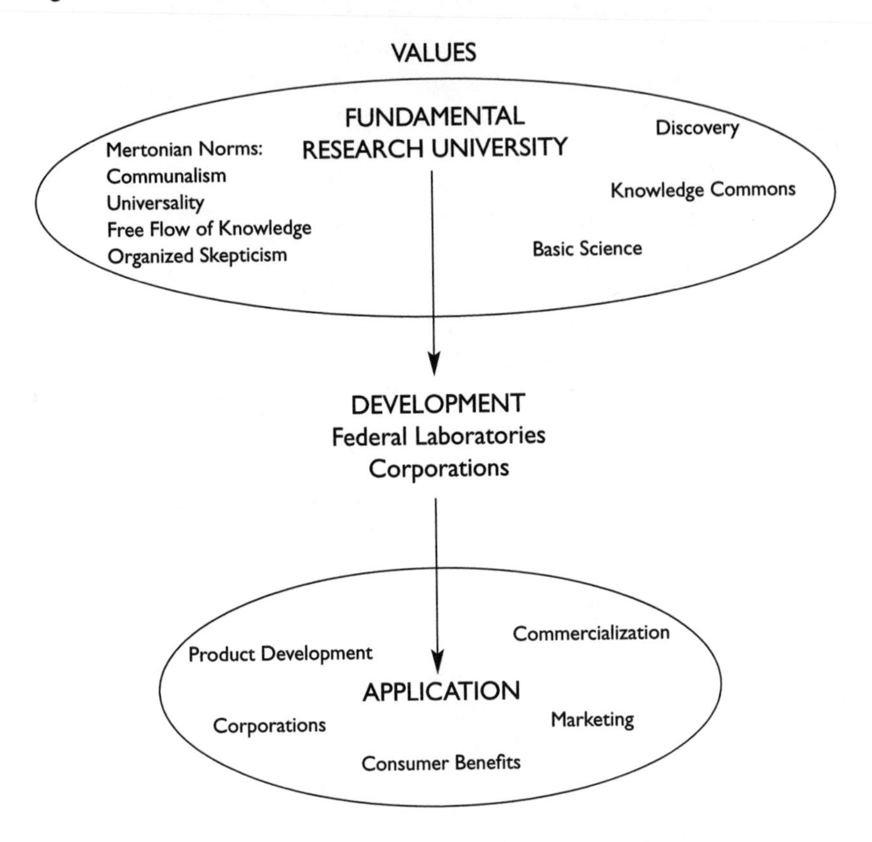

The norms and values of science are taken to include not only the physical and biological sciences but also the social sciences and any other field that claims to have science at its core, which includes most areas of study in the university. Merton (1942) is generally regarded as offering an early and enduring formulation of scientific norms and values with his conception of science as open, communistic (later changed to communal), universal, disinterested, and characterized by a skeptical habit of mind. Openness spoke to the nonsecret character of science. Communistic or communal meant noncommercial. Universal referred to the idea that there was no national cast to science and that knowledge flowed freely across borders. Disinterestedness addressed the objective nonpartisan stance of the scientist toward knowledge. Maintaining a skeptical habit of mind challenged scientists to always question results. (There is more than a little irony in Merton's conceptualization of disinterested science,

Figure 3.2 Academic Capitalism Research Regime

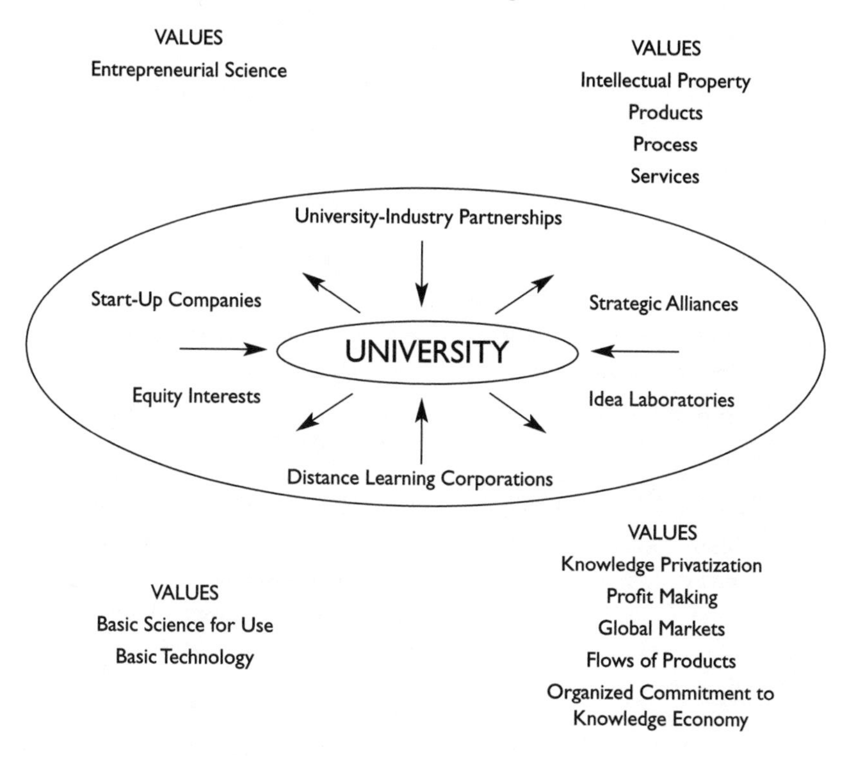

in that he associated science with democracy and wrote to challenge the rise of nationalistic, Fascistic Nazi science. Even as he envisioned democratic science as open, the advent of World War II, which spurred him to write, gave rise to secret or classified science, justified in terms of national security.) In the 1950s, and 1960s, Merton's values were compressed into "basic" or "fundamental" science, and the value of science was that it was "value-free" or "objective." These properties were often conceived as embedded in science itself and separate from the scientist, who nonetheless was value-free and objective because "he" served science. In the Mertonian model, which was closely aligned with the Vannevar Bush model, academic science stood alone, not tied to the state or corporations. A necessary condition of excellent science was university autonomy. Basic science, done in universities and unfettered by the state or commerce, preceded development, often accomplished in federal laboratories, which was then followed by application, which occurred in corporations. Independence from state and market was essential for excellent science.

The second or critical strand sees science as historically and presently serving corporate America and the military-industrial complex. Critics of corporate America and Marxists, neo-Marxists, and post-Marxists have seen close connections between science and business, with the result that science often served commercial values (Veblen 1918; Noble 1976; Soley 1995). Opponents of the Vietnam War saw science as the servant of war, the capitalist state, and the imperial ambitions of U.S. leaders (Foreman 1987; Leslie 1993). Strand two deidealizes science and is concerned with explaining how a nonautonomous and nonideal science gained funding, power, and authority through its links to corporations and the state, whether the military- or medical-industrial complex, and posits dehumanizing imperial and/or capitalist values as dominating science.

The third, or social constructionist, strand also deidealizes science, but from a materialist rather than a Marxist perspective. This view deidealizes science by explaining how science is done, from construction of scientific facts to organization of resources for research. Social constructionists challenge the notion that science is separate from the scientist or that it embodies pure and noble ideas (Latour and Woolgar 1979; Dasgupta and David 1987). Much social constructionist work focuses on laboratory life and the values and practices that animate and characterize it, such as competition for discovery, status, and resources; as of yet science and technology studies scholars have largely overlooked the institutional context of colleges and universities.

However, some have developed actor-network theory, exploring the agency of individual actors and groups, who through various complex networks are engaged in the social construction of practice, reality, and policy (Callon 1986; Latour 1987; Law and Callon 1992; Mulcahy 1999). Just as scientific facts are deidealized through the analysis of their social construction, so too the changing policies and structures within which science is enacted are deidealized by analyzing their social construction according to the interests and interpretations of particular actors. Related constructs such as the social worlds approach (Clarke and Fujimura 1992) and boundary organizations (see the Autumn 2001 issue of *Science, Technology and Human Values*) note the changing boundaries and network dimensions of organizations but leave the values effects to the contingencies of microlevel interactions and negotiations, and do not look at larger structures of power embedded in the political economy of higher education (Kleinman 1998).

The fourth strand of values literature is currently reframing market and academic values so they are not in opposition. Both policy makers (Council on Competitiveness 1996) and social scientists (who are sometimes policy makers as well) argue that the connection between science and business should not necessarily be viewed critically (Stokes 1997; Branscomb et al. 1997a, 1997b; Etzkowitz, Webster, and Healy 1998; Mowery and Ziedonis 2002). They stress three points in making their case. First, science has always been involved with the economy through application/use; second, science is a crucial component of the new/information/knowledge economy; and third, science can accommodate market and academic values. The third strand takes the insights of the second strand, which challenges an idealized science, and reframes the ends of science not as serving the (unspecified) public good but rather as serving (unspecified) economic prosperity, redefined as the public good, which more easily enables the coexistence of market and academic values. Indeed, the market capabilities of higher education are highly valued. In this conception, academic science is closely related to the market, but the state is backgrounded even though it supplies resources for partnerships between higher education and the market.

The fifth strand of values literature approaches science from a different direction, that of the public good. Scholars like Heller and Eisenberg (1998) and Bollier (2002a) make the case that science is an "intellectual commons" that must not be appropriated by the corporate or economic sector because to do is against the interest of the public good or commonweal. The intellectual commons is a nonmarket space that is used for the well being of society in much the same way that open pasturage was shared by medieval communities. As the aristocracy enclosed common land in England, Scotland, and other parts of the world, so the intellectual commons is now being appropriated by global corporations. The intellectual commons is sustained by an academic "gift economy" which is open, free, nonalienable (and very Mertonian). These very properties allow science to flourish. To enclose the intellectual commons is to destroy it, wreaking havoc on the very system that created the science and technology that gave rise to the new/knowledge/information economy. Corporate values are understood as opposed to the public good because they stress profit for individual firms rather then the well being of society as a whole.

The first and fourth literatures concentrate on science and technology rather than universities as organizations. (They sometimes address what makes university-industry collaborations work, but the focus is generally on the partnership rather than the university.) If they address policy or the state, it is almost always federal policy and a (mythic) state that honors the autonomy of science by giving money without strings attached. Strands one and four are concerned with explaining and interpreting what values make (U.S.) science excellent (the best in the world), and raising funds to support U.S. science. These two issues are not seen as contradictory, even from a values perspective. In both strands, the values elucidated by the scholar in post hoc fashion are offered as the explanation for excellent science. As theory, strands one and three purport to interpret and explain why U.S. science is excellent, and predict that dire consequences will come from lack of funding, although strand one calls for funding an idealized basic science, and strand three calls for funding an idealized entrepreneurial science.

The fifth or intellectual commons strand, like the first and third strands, is concerned with explaining why science is excellent. It argues that the intellectual commons and academic gift economy are at the core of excellent science, and predicts that if they are destroyed by corporate predation, science itself, as well as the public good, will be irreparably harmed. The intellectual commons is presented as a form of social organization, but it is an undefined space in terms of organizations and law. It draws authority from its connection to the public good, but the public good has always been an amorphous concept in that it purports to include everyone—or at least promises the greatest good for the greatest number—and an unspecified public good is very difficult to defend in an era that celebrates individual rights.

Most of the values literature does not look directly at values formation; instead, it seems to assume socialization through scientific apprenticeship (strands one, three, and four) or to assume that values are defined by external resource holders (neo- and post-Marxist, strand two) or are narrowly limited to the laboratory and scientific organizations (social constructionist, strand three). Yet there is a subtext in the values literature that suggests that the organization of science and its location in relation to markets and the state is very important. The Mertonian/Bush strand insists on an autonomous science, separate from the state (development) or markets (application). The various Marxisms suggest that science and scientific values are very strongly shaped by interactions with the imperial state and the defense economy. The social constructionists concentrate on the micropolitical level, suggesting that the effect of social structures and organizational arrangements in science and technology are contingent on the local activities of various social groups and individual actors, specific to the particular value choices and decisions in question. The intellectual commons theorists suggest that invisible organizations, such as the commons and the gift economy, are key organizational parameters for excellent science.

We too think organizations and policy play a powerful intermediary part in values formation. However, we think these organizations are often outside scientific departments and disciplinary associations. For example, we see universities and state agencies as influencing scientific values through their formation of intellectual property policies. They intermediate between scientists in their laboratories, associations, federal granting agencies, and the world of use, property, and market actors, shaping values and concepts of excellence by the way that they shape incentives and opportunities, permit close relations between market, state, and higher education, and create new venues for assessment and judgment that are outside the peer review system.

Data and Method

We concentrate on states even though patents, copyrights, and trademarks are the province of the federal government because the states have authority for shaping institutional policy for public universities and colleges; that authority is sometimes delegated to state systems of higher education, sometimes to the institutions themselves. State systems and public institutions of higher education are arms of the state and have the authority to specify the treatment of intellectual property within these systems or institutions (Chew 1992). State and institutional policy sometimes precede and always interpret and implement federal policies and statutes.

That state policies are fertile grounds for investigating knowledge regime shifts and the changes in values and practices associated with such shifts is suggested by statistics on university intellectual property activity. Partly in response to the Bayh-Dole Act (1980), which allowed colleges and universities to own patents discovered by faculty working on federal research grants, state systems and/or universities and colleges initiated or began to develop and change their intellectual property policies. Prior to 1981, fewer than 250 patents were issued to universities per year. Between fiscal year 1991 and fiscal year 1999, annual college and university invention disclosures increased 63 percent (to 12,324). New patents filed increased 77 percent (to 5,545), and new licenses and options executed increased by 129 percent (to 3,914) (COGR 1999). In 1978, several universities permitted acquisition of equity in companies licensing their technology; by 2000, 70 percent of a sample of sixty-seven research universities had participated in at least one equity deal (Feldman et al. 2002a).

As universities' intellectual property activity and potential have grown, states have expanded their policies, some of which have changed dramatically the way intellectual property is handled. For example, from 1997 to 2002, approximately half of the states adjusted their conflict of interest laws so that universities (as represented by administrators) and faculty (as inventors and advisors) can hold equity positions in private corporations even when those corporations do business with universities (Schmidt 2002). This is a major shift in the pattern of state conflict of interest laws, breaching the historic firewall between public and private sectors.

Table 3.1 Summary of Institutions in Study and Technology Transfer Activities, Fiscal Year 2000

State	Institution	Tech Trans FTE	Research Funding Related to Licenses/ Options	License Income Received	Income: Cashed-in Equity	U.S. Patents Issued	Licensing/ Options Generating More than $1M	Start-Ups Initiated	Start-Ups in which Institution Holds Equity
CA	U of California System	105	$9,136,852	$267,765,000	$2,150,000	324	10	26	6
	Stanford U	23	$0	$36,944,000	$10,267,083	98	6	8	8
	San Diego State U	1	$0	$99,881	$0	1	0	2	2
FL	U of Florida	14	$383,667	$26,274,999	$0	56	3	6	3
	U of Miami	5	$2,643,103	$603,753	$0	2	0	0	0
	U of South Florida	5	$700,000	$892,526	$0	20	0	3	3
MO	Southeast Missouri State U					Not in sample			
	Washington U	14	NA	$8,488,984	$1,659,807	59	0	1	1
	U of Missouri System	6	$544,659	$1,568,903	$0	12	1	0	0
NY	City U of New York					Not in sample			
	State U of New York Research Foundation	17	$2,701,363	$16,523,098	$128,969	72	1	4	1
	New York U	10	$4,704,266	$8,484,044	$1,091,388	25	1	7	2
TX	U of Texas at Austin	8	$1,524,477	$1,513,838	$0	28	0	5	2
	U of North Texas HSC Fort Worth	2	$1,200,000	$0	$0	3	0	2	1
	Rice U	2	$0	$80,713	$0	2	0	1	1
UT	Utah State U	3	$80,000	$206,748	$0	5	0	1	0
	U of Utah	11	$3,280,684	$4,554,318	$1,444,688	28	1	10	4
	Brigham Young U	6	$314,730	$5,072,274	$1,589,425	5	0	0	0

Source: AUTM Survey, FY 2000

We analyzed institutional and system patent policies in California, Florida, Missouri, New York, Texas, and Utah. In each state we looked at a flagship and a state comprehensive institution. In some states, the policies covered systems or segments of systems. In California, the University of California system (research universities) had a single patent policy as was the case in Texas. The City University of New York (CUNY) and State University of New York (SUNY) systems had separate policies. Other systems—Utah, Missouri, Florida—had institutional policies. The six states provide geographical representation and a range of patenting behaviors. To see if there was variation between public and private universities, we also included a private university in each of the states (Stanford, Miami University, Washington University, New York University, Rice, and Brigham Young). Where possible, we used historical as well as current data.

Table 3.1 describes the patent activity in the six states. Public nonresearch universities had the fewest technology transfer officers, the least research funding related to licenses and options, the least license income received, the fewest patents, the fewest number of licenses generating more than $1 million, and the fewest start-ups. Generally, the public research universities performed more strongly than the private, except in Missouri, where Washington University of St. Louis did better than the University of Missouri system on all measures for which there were data. However, some of the public research university results pertain to systems—California, Missouri, the University of Texas, and SUNY—and it is probably unfair to compare them to the single private research universities in their states. Stanford, for example, may have performed as well as any one of the institutions in the University of California system. As Table 3.1 indicates, our sample covers institutions and systems with a wide range of patent activity. Of the eighteen institutions or systems, only five receive more than $6 million in licensing royalties and only one more than $2 million in cashed-in equity, but all had patent policies.

The questions we are particularly interested in answering are: What values are embedded or explicit in these policies? Have they changed over time? What is the direction of the change? What does organizational change tell us about the relation between market, state, and higher education?

To test the two knowledge regime models (public good and academic capitalism), we developed the following categories for analysis: patent policies, royalty splits, policy coverage, exceptions, managerial market capacity, and public good. Patent policies specify the types of intellectual property covered. The inclusion of more and more types of intellectual property suggests movement from one knowledge regime to another. Royalty splits tell us about incentives for faculty and institutions to participate in generating intellectual property; change signals shifts in intellectual property regimes. Policy coverage—additions of new categories of university members—that becomes more inclusive does the same. Elimination of exceptions to institutional ownership of patents—for example, faculty being able to claim patents if any university resources were used in research—also is indicative of a shift. A highly developed capacity for market activity points to erosion of the separation between markets, state, and higher education posited in the Mertonian/Bush model and preferred in the commons/public good model. For example, elaboration of rules, regulations, and offices to facilitate faculty and university market activities—for example, rules governing start-up companies—is an indication of a shift to an academic capitalism knowledge regime. Finally, the public good category refers to policies and statements within policies that give voice to or create rules that foster public good knowledge regimes (e.g., by mentioning the public interest), which include Mertonian norms.

We review changes in state university system intellectual property policies and the policies of individual institutions. The period of change considered is variable, given that states introduced intellectual property policies and changes at different times. We compare additions and deletions across time, focusing on the substance of the changes in the categories described above.

Patterns of Policy Initiation

Historical data was difficult to obtain. Frequently, university archives are not well organized. Archivists are overburdened and unable to search files. Several institutions—the University of Florida and New York University—had patent policies prior to the 1960s (Table 3.2), and we suspect that the University of California system and Stanford did as well. The two earliest initiators of patenting activity used outside patent management firms. The University of Florida, which in the 1940s focused research on agricultural materials, had a contract with Research Corporation, and New York University had one with University Patents. These two nonprofit firms handled patents for most colleges and universities in the United States until the 1970s, in large part because most universities did not aggressively pursue patents. Many of the initiating dates for patent policies in Table 3.2 probably refer to the year in which the system or institution developed its own office for handling patents rather than to the date of the institutions' initial patent policy. As Table 3.2 shows, most systems or institutions developed offices and patent policies during the early 1970s to the mid-1980s.

Over time, as the "Copyright Policy" and "Other" columns in Table 3.2 indicate, more and more systems and institutions protected more and more types of intellectual property. The majority of copyright policies were established from 1983 to 1993. From the early 1980s onward, other types of intellectual

Table 3.2 Patents, Copyrights, and Other Intellectual Property

	Patent Policy	Copyright Policy	Other
1943	U of Florida		
1956	New York U		
1963	U of California System		
1970	U of Utah		
1971	Washington U U of Missouri, Columbia		
1972		New York U	
1976	U of Miami	U of Miami	
1979	State U of New York		
1980	Stanford U		
1983	Southeast Missouri State U	Southeast Missouri State U	Stanford: tangible research property, i.e., micro-organisms, computer chips
1984			U Mo: educ. materials
1985	U of Texas System City U of New York		
1986		City U of New York	
1987		U of Texas System	
1989	U of South Florida	U of South Florida	NYU: computer software
1990		State U of New York	
1992		U of California System	
1996			U Mo: plant varieties Stanford: patentable software, trade secrets & marks, distance learning
1998			SUNY: computer software Wa U: all technical data, material transfer agreements, mask work, tangible property trade secret
1999			Rice: computer software trade secrets
2001		U of Utah	
2002		U of Missouri	U Tx (Austin): educ. materials, data

property were protected: tangible research property (microorganisms, computer chips), computer software, education materials, plant varieties, technical data, mask work, and trade secrets. With the exception of copyright, private universities specified other types of intellectual property to a greater degree than did public universities. System and institutional claims to copyright, treated in chapter 4, will likely affect the largest numbers of faculty members because the copyright policies essentially make courseware and teaching materials that depend on university resources the property of the system or institution. Prior to the 1970s a small number of systems and institutions had patent policies; none specified other types of intellectual property. The specification of more kinds of intellectual activity as alienable and appropriable by faculty, institutions, and systems shows movement from a public good to an academic capitalist knowledge regime.

At least eight systems or institutions developed patent policies prior to Bayh-Dole (1980), indicating, as a several scholars have suggested (Mowery 2002), that the legislation in and of itself did not initiate an academic capitalist knowledge regime. The development of the University of Florida patent policy suggests the relation between university activity, state law, and Bayh-Dole. Although the University of Florida had a patent policy long before 1980, the 1993 patent document noted that Public Law 96–517, the Patent and Trademark Amendments Act of 1980, more commonly known as Bayh-Dole, "clearly sets forth, as the objective of Congress, the utilization of the patent system as a vehicle to 'effectuate the transfer of government-funded inventions to the public'" (University of Florida 1993, p. 1). In other words, the Florida patent policy read Bayh-Dole as encouraging patent activity on the part of universities. After Bayh-Dole, the State of Florida, via Statute 240.229, claimed "a discovery or invention which is made in the field in which the investigator is employed by the University or by using University funds, facilities, equipment, personnel or proprietary technological information" as the property of the university, to be shared with the inventor (University of Florida 1993, p. 2). University activity, federal law, and state law interacted to form a dense web of regulation and surveillance over faculty research in science and technology. With regard to intellectual property, systems and universities were not so much acted upon as actors eager to embrace the market. Overall, the data suggests colleges and universities took an entrepreneurial posture toward intellectual property prior to the development of federal legislation. Federal legislation intersected state system and institutional policies, enhancing the opportunities for academic capitalism.

Royalties as Incentives

The various patent policies offered a wide range of royalty splits among faculty, department and/or college, and university. All were sufficient to provide strong incentives to patent. The greatest incentives were for the faculty, who were able to put the income in their bank accounts, as compared to all others, who had to use the revenue stream generated by patents for institutional purposes.

The institution with the most generous policy was Southeast Missouri State, which allowed university employees and students to retain in full all copyright and patent privileges resulting from their usual intellectual endeavor, a position an institution that did not generate much intellectual property could afford to take. The University of Texas, the University of Missouri–Columbia, and New York University, split royalties with faculty fifty-fifty. Private universities tended to be less generous than public, with many offering faculty one-third of the income from their licenses, the faculty's program or department one-third, and the universities one-third. When policies were changed over time, as was the case with the University of California, the University of Florida, Washington University, and Rice, they usually gave faculty a lower percentage. The University of California changed most dramatically, dropping the faculty share from 50 to 35 percent. Utah was unique in offering faculty a large incentive if they took the initiative for commercializing, which meant filing the patent and finding a commercial partner. Utah gave these enterprising faculty 65 percent of royalties, in 1984 reimbursing them up to $5,000 for filing and locating a business partner; in 1993, they took the cap off the reimbursement (University of Utah 2003).

Most institutions took costs for patenting and legal fees out of faculty royalties. For example, in 1997, the University of California took out 15 percent for administration and also deducted costs for patent litigation prior to giving faculty their 35 percent. The university could withhold distribution and impound royalties until litigation, "actual or imminent," was resolved (University of California patent policy 1997a, p. 4). Given that the California system engaged in more patent litigation than any other university system, patent protection could easily absorb a great deal of any single inventor's royalty income. As noted earlier, the California system had engaged in approximately seventeen years of litigation with Genentech and Eli Lilly over the human growth hormone patent. Stanford gave faculty 33 percent, less 15 percent for administration, and less direct expenses. The University of Miami held all royalties until costs were covered, then gave inventor faculty a $1,000 bonus, after which they received one-third of royalty income. Although the royalty division was quite varied, with various restrictions and extra charges, patent income was a powerful incentive for faculty to participate in academic capitalism.

Some institutions specified how the university's share of the royalties would be divided. Most common was to apportion one-tenth to one-third of institutional royalties to the faculty member's program or department and college and give the rest to the institution. When systems and institutions specified how their share of royalty income would be used, which most did not, they spoke generally about support for research and educational programs. The University of California system was the exception. In 1985, it agreed to "give first consideration" to "support of research" when disposing of its 50 percent of net income from patents. What type of research was unspecified. In 1997, the system's institutions' patent income was directed toward technology transfer activities and improving "inventions not earning income" (University of California 1997a). In this system, applied or entrepreneurial research trumped any other kind when it came to disposal of patent income.

Royalty income from patents and licensing was discretionary income for state systems and institutions and, as such, provided a powerful incentive for administrators whose pay and career opportunities depended on maintaining or improving the national position of their institutions. It offered a potential solution to the slow increases in block grants and for making up periodic short falls in state budgets. However, Association of University Technology Managers (AUTM) data indicates that returns from patenting and licensing are very uneven. Some institutions reap great rewards, but most do not (AUTM 2002). Indeed, some institutions lose money due to the costs of technology licensing offices, litigation, and bad investments.

Although private universities did not experience the same loss of block grants as public institutions, patent income still provides a strong incentive for senior administrators at private institutions. Increased patent income was a visible external revenue stream that signaled administrative competence to other research universities. Senior administrators then became desirable job candidates, advancing their careers.

In sum, royalties served as incentives for a number of campus groups. Faculty had the potential to multiply their salaries many times over. Senior administrators who increased royalty revenue streams to their institutions were able to generate discretionary funds and signal their competitiveness to the national university community. Successful technology licensing officials and other support personnel created their careers and, since a number of offices were self-supporting, in some instances funded their own salaries.

Policy Coverage

Categories of persons covered by patent policies were elaborated over the years. The exceptions were the early adopters of patent policies. For example, the University of California system's policy applied to all in 1963 and still does. However, a number of institutions specified a narrow range of community members when they first wrote policies and later clarified. In 1971 Washington University's patent policy covered only "inventors." In 1998, it was revised to include "faculty, staff, graduate students, post-doctoral fellows, and non-employees who participate in research projects at the University" (Washington University in St. Louis 1998a). Similarly, in 1985, the University of Texas system policy applied to all employees, anyone using university facilities, post- and predoctoral students. In 1992, this was expanded to include candidates for the MA and PhD degrees and, in 2002, to cover part-time and visiting faculty and undergraduates. By the mid-1980s research universities initiating policies began to use comprehensive language, as did the CUNY system, which covered "principal investigators, project directors, faculty, staff and all others who produce inventions in the course of or related to activities on grants or contracts administered by the Research Foundation or supported in any way be the University through funds, facilities or equipment" (CUNY 1985). Intellectual labor is complex in that work may be less than full-time, is often collaborative, and faculty, such as visiting professors, may have allegiances elsewhere. The aim of systems and institutions to control intellectual property generally called forth greater and greater degrees of specificity over time. Even undergraduate students were increasingly included in patent policy coverage, with the University of Texas system being the extreme, treating them like all employees, regardless of whether they received wages or salaries. Ironically, universities and colleges sometimes simultaneously treat students as clients or customers and as a captive market from which they can appropriate intellectual property.

Several universities—the University of California system schools and Stanford among them—instituted mandatory signing of the patent policy agreements by employees. Mandatory signing ensured that no employee could plead ignorance of university or system claims, as had happened at several other institutions. For example, the professor who invented and patented Retin-A had worked for the University of Pennsylvania since the 1940s and pleaded ignorance of changes in patent policy. (Although the professor donated a percentage of his royalties to Penn, the university nonetheless brought suit against him, and the court found for Penn.) The trend toward elaboration of persons covered by system and institutional patent policies suggests a shift from an intellectual property regime in which patents were not central to an academic capitalist knowledge regime where ownership of intellectual property is very important.

Exceptions

Several court cases, the first of which occurred in the 1950s, made clear that universities were the owners of intellectual property invented by faculty (Chew 1992). However, faculty continued to assert claims to inventions by taking the position that if they made a discovery outside of their university work, they were the rightful owners. Qualitative studies of faculty who participated in technology transfer noted that they used metaphors such as "I thought of it in the shower" to indicate their distance from the university when they wanted to assert ownership of an invention (Slaughter and Rhoades 1990).

In the 1980s, as intellectual property assumed more salience for universities, institutions began to specify patent policies so that it was more difficult for faculty to make any claims to ownership. Universities began to list the exceptions to institutional ownership, which grew fewer and fewer. The University of California system was most aggressive, allowing no exceptions. Two universities excepted discoveries made during consulting, although one later reversed this. Two others acknowledged sponsors' rights, and one mentioned federal march-in rights. Generally, faculty could claim intellectual property only if they had used their own time and resources and had not used institutional facilities. Several institutions were more specific. The University of Miami said faculty could not claim any intellectual property if it was related to the line of research they pursued at the university. In 1999, Stanford added a section to its policy that offered "practical considerations" about what these sorts of restrictions meant for faculty. To claim patentable discoveries and inventions, faculty had to prove they had not made "more than incidental use of university resources." These were specified in such a way that researchers who depended on anything other than routinely "available office equipment and commercially-available software" or library materials "generally available in non-Stanford locations" were regarded as making substantial use of Stanford resources. Since most science researchers used specialized university equipment, they were unlikely to be able to claim patents. Stanford took the position that its employees could not use university resources for "non-university purposes, including outside consulting activities or other activities in pursuit of personal gain" (Stanford University 1999). Thus, in the mid-1970s through the 1990s, universities specified more and more clearly the conditions for exceptions to patent policies. This suggests the movement from a research regime that did not focus closely on intellectual property to one that did.

Expanded Market Capacity

We take rules and regulation created to specify system, institutional, and individual engagement with profit taking in commercial markets to describe academic capitalism. We are aware that all the systems and institutions we consider are nonprofit. The rules and regulations express a conundrum. They prescribe how profit-taking activity shall occur in a formally nonprofit organization. Of particular interest are organizational structures, oversight, forms of market involvement, and degree of faculty and administrator involvement in firms. Because of the escalation over the course of time of printed material relating to regulations on academic capitalism in the six states under study, we consider only one system and two institutions: the University of California system, the University of Utah, and Washington University in St. Louis. These represent the range of practices of the institutions in our sample that have ambitious intellectual property programs.

The University of California System

Organization. During the 1980s, the rules, regulations, and offices dealing with academic capitalism proliferated. In 1985, the University of California had a Patent, Trademark, and Copyright Office that handled intellectual property. By 1997, that office had changed into the Office of Technology Transfer.

Oversight. In 1985, the University of California (UC) system had an Intellectual Property Advisory Council that advised the president on patent management. This committee was chaired by the senior vice-president of academic affairs, who evaluated inventions and discoveries, negotiated patent and equity agreements as well as licenses and license option agreements, and negotiated prospective rights with research sponsors and federal agencies. In 1997, however, the senior vice-president for business and finance fulfilled these functions. The committee that advised the senior vice-president changed as well: it was the Technology Transfer Advisory Committee. Although the provost, senior vice-president of academic affairs, and head of the faculty senate were members of the new committee, the movement of the committee from the academic side to the business side represented a boundary shift. Academic affairs took a back seat to commerce when intellectual property was involved.

Forms of Market Involvement. The revised 1997 patent policy noted an equity policy, specifying a form of market involvement other than licensing. The 1997 patent policy referred readers to the 1996 Policy on Accepting Equity When Licensing University Technology. This policy was elaborated in 2002 in Bulletin G-44. Together these documents addressed some of the ways in which system officials should conduct themselves as academic capitalists.

The UC system equity policy began by making the case that applied science could best benefit the general public through an active technology licensing program. The UC system sought licensees who were able to pay the costs of patenting, developing and protecting patents, and ensuring fulfillment of regulatory requirements. Generally, the companies best able to meet such requirements were large corporations. However, small or start-up companies often pioneered new technologies. To meet its financial concerns, the UC system accepted equity in these small companies under certain circumstances.

The UC system claimed it selected technology to license on the basis of "principles of openness, objectivity and fairness in decision-making, and pre-eminence of the education, research, and public service missions of the University over financial or individual personal gain," as specified in the University Guidelines on University-Industry Relations, the Conflict of Interest Policy, and the University Policy on Integrity in Research. While the 1996 Policy on Accepting Equity firmly put education, research, and public service at the forefront, and fulfillment of university missions over financial or individual gain, the various sets of related policies on which this dictum was based suggest that business principles were often more important than academic considerations and that when universities engaged in academic capitalism, conflicts of interest and threats to the integrity of research were rife.

Degree of Faculty and Administrator Involvement in Firms. According to Bulletin G-44 (University of California 2002), neither administrators nor faculty could hold positions on the board of directors of companies in which it held equity, or exercise voting rights. However, faculty could hold observer rights for board meetings and participate on scientific boards of the licensee. Given these privileges, the prohibition against voting did not necessarily prevent faculty from wielding extensive influence in companies, especially small companies, given their stature as inventors of the licensed technology. Whether employee-inventors could hold management positions in corporations in which they held equity was not addressed. University investigators were able to perform clinical trials for companies in which the university held equity, provided review committees assessed "real or perceived" conflict of interest. The equity policy apparently assumed that when faculty performed clinical trials for companies in which the university held equity, it was not a prima facie conflict of interest.

As AUTM data show, a large number of university-held patents are licensed to start-up corporations or small corporations (AUTM 2002). However, these small companies are usually purchased by large corporations when their technology proves marketable (Kenney 1986). The UC system profited when a large corporation purchased the small innovator corporation and its equity was liquidated for substantially more than the university had invested. By taking equity in lieu of payment for a license, the UC system in effect used state money to provide venture capital to small and start-up corporations. By choosing corporations to subvent, the UC system was a market actor that influenced the cutting edge of U.S. technology.

The UC system generally did not hold more than a 10 percent share of equity, and it took all equity, including the inventor's share, in its name. Decisions about equity were made "upon sound business judgment and publicly available information" (University of California 2002). Equity income was treated the same way as was royalty income in the patent policy. As always, exceptions to any policies could be made, subject to scrutiny by review committees, and given presidential approval.

Bulletin G-44, which provided guidelines for accepting and managing equity, said that the university would manage equity in a "businesslike manner." In this document, business principles and research principles at best coexisted uneasily and sometimes came into sharp conflict. When making decisions about converting stocks to cash and exercising options, the university would give "no consideration to unpublished University research programs related to the technology or to company information uniquely available [through] technology program activities." While this was portrayed as "sound business practice" that dictated that the university should work through "publicly available information," it meant that the university could be aware that a better technology was available or that the technology to be licensed had severe problems, yet not acknowledge this information. Given that universities, by definition, harbor a great deal of unpublished knowledge, the decision to abide by public information cut off the business arm of the university from the scientific, allowing business to occur without science informing it. Similarly, the treasurer was directed to evaluate technologies in which the university might take an equity position "in terms of the financial return to the University, not in terms of the status of nor the need for support of the subject invention" (University of California 2002). Following this guideline, the university might reject an equity position in a company that wanted to build and rent a high-energy physics testing facility or in a company proposing an HIV vaccine. While such decisions might not involve monetary conflict of interest, they did clash with traditional conceptions of university research, in which prestige was maximized and science was finally justified in terms of its service to humanity.

Another business practice that impinged on research was "pipelining." This refers to granting a license in a new technology that was related to an already licensed technology. The university took the position that inventions should be licensed to the company best able to develop them. It noted that this stance did not preclude a company from developing more than one invention if it were best suited to bring "successor" inventions to fruition. However, other companies' bids should be fairly considered. Yet, frequently, researchers had to be involved with future as well as current technology. As a means of successfully developing licensed technology, companies often wrote in future research support for the faculty member who was named on the patent. Despite concerns about pipelining, if the company paid for the research, they were often able to negotiate a license to it.

Although uneven and sporadic attempts were made to separate business principles from research, the two were embroiled because research was central to the technologies that the UC system licensed. The dilemma the university addressed when it tried to reconcile business and research principles was that successful development of technology often depended on the continued involvement of university inventors or experts. Without them, technology development often floundered or failed. Thus, the university officially allowed inventors to work closely with licensing professionals or potential licensees to better promote commercialization. Although much UC system patent policy was focused on separating the university and faculty from engagement in the market, especially when accusations of conflict of interest were possible, a successful patent program demanded faculty and institutional market involvement.

This dilemma gave rise to a variety of conflict of interest (COI) policies, some at the state level, others at the system level, and still others at the federal level. The state COI statute (1974) held that if a principal investigator had a financial interest in equity that exceeded $2,000, then the COI policy came into play. Any project supported by the National Science Foundation (NSF) or the Public Health Service (PHS) (which included the National Institutes of Health) required disclosure of financial information; if the inventor's equity interest exceeded $10,000, federal COI policies applied. However, these policies had rather large loopholes. For the state policy, if the inventor did not directly accept an equity interest and instead the university treasurer held that interest for future conversion to cash, then the equity interest did not "constitute a positive disclosure" and the inventor was not subject to the various review committees. Although inventors did not have an immediate cash interest in the company, they had strong future stakes that might easily influence their assessments of research. The same held true with regard to federal COI policy. Further, the UC system interpreted the federal COI policy to mean that "royalty payments made in the form of cash by The Regents to the inventor also are not discloseable financial interests related to NSF or PHS-sponsored projects" (University of California 2002, Appendix D).

Involvement with the market caused greater and greater elaboration of rules and regulation. The equity policy (University of California 1996) noted that licensing had to be conducted within the framework of "the University Guidelines on University-Industry Relations (1989), the Conflict of Interest Policy (1974), the University Policy on Integrity in Research (1990) and related University policies and guidelines." Each of these policies spawned their own series of memoranda and guidelines. For example, the 1996 equity policy gave rise to Memoranda G-44 in 2002, which provided forty-five pages of guidelines for accepting and managing equity. This document included two forms inventors had to fill out and sign, a checklist, and a model agreement. The management of intellectual property contributed to contractualization and bureaucratization, creating employment for managerial professionals, such as lawyers and administrators, whose increasing presence made faculty managed professionals (Rhoades 1998a).

In many respects, these concerns were a response to the 1974 state conflict of interest laws, which set a very low threshold. To shift from a public good to an academic capitalism knowledge regime, the UC system elaborated rules and regulations surrounding academic capitalism to the point where state COI rules were substantively though not formally rewritten. The new policies permitted a greater degree of individual, institutional, and system involvement in the market than had been envisioned in the 1974 COI laws.

University of Utah

Organization and Oversight. In 1970, the Utah policy simply stated that the office of patent and product development handled all matters concerning intellectual property. A Patent Advisory Committee advised the president and the director. In 1984, a University Patent and Product Development Office replaced the previous office. This office worked with the Patent Review Committee to evaluate and recommend inventions for patenting and commercialization. The University of Utah Research Foundation was "the instrument of the university that commercialized inventions" (University of Utah 1984). The Research Foundation purchased the services of the director of the University Patent and Product Development Office to prosecute patents, explore commercialization, and negotiate agreements. In 1993, the office was renamed the Technology Transfer Office. This office, not the Patent Review Committee, evaluated disclosures for patenting and commercialization. The Patent Review Committee became an oversight rather than a decision-making committee. In 1999 its oversight function was underlined by a name change: it became the Technology Transfer Advisory Committee (University of Utah 1999a). The committee, upon request, advised the administration on disputes involving intellectual property.

Forms of Market Involvement and Degree of Faculty and Administrator Involvement in Firms. The 1999 policy referred to two other documents: "Remunerative Consultation and Other Employment Activities" (University of Utah 1999b) and "Faculty Profit-Making Corporations" (University of Utah 1999c). On the one hand, the consulting document stressed that faculty were full-time employees, and it stipulated the days per month (two) they could work elsewhere, the need to abide by COI requirements, and the need to relieve the university of any liability. On the other hand, "Faculty Profit-Making Corporations" allowed university faculty and/or administrators to participate in corporations in which they held "substantial stock interest" as "consultants, employees, members of the board of directors or as chairman [sic] of the board of directors" if the full and proper conduct of their university assignments was not impaired and COI was avoided (University of Utah 1999c). How these responsibilities were to be met with two days a month for consulting was not directly addressed. However, a clause near the end of the document suggested that faculty involved in corporate R&D for firms in which they held an interest should perform such work on "a time and material contract basis through the engineering experiment station. All work shall be on a full overhead basis and shall be subject to approval by the department head."

The document on faculty profit-making corporations opened with a general statement that endorsed energetic academic capitalism. "University faculty members are increasingly becoming involved in profit-making corporations in which they hold substantial stock interest and in which they are active participants. These corporations may have a substantial beneficial influence on the economic growth of the State; and the associations derived by the faculty member from participation in the corporations may, in most cases, have a beneficial influence on his [sic] teaching and research capabilities. Consequently, it would not be in the university's interest to preclude this type of association" (University of Utah 1999c). The document required that inventions jointly produced by the university and a corporation in which a faculty member was financially involved become the exclusive property of the university, although the corporation could have a nonexclusive license. The policy cautioned that faculty invention did not insure university licensing to a corporation in which the faculty was an active member. If a faculty member's invention were given to a "competing firm" under open bidding, the faculty member was obliged to give "full, unrestrained disclosure and assistance to the licensee firm" (1999c). Purchasing was also to be done through open bidding, with care given to not making preferential purchases from a corporation in which a faculty member held an interest. But if the faculty-owned company won the open bid, the university could do business with the firm in which the faculty member had an interest.

The Utah policy committed very strongly to a regime of academic capitalism, and the model of science was unapologetically applied. Only Utah stipulated that if faculty wanted to claim a patent, the burden of proof fell on them to prove they had not used university resources, materials, time, and research. Although the copyright policy excepted scholarly work that did not make undue uses of university resources, in principle the university treated all employee work, including that of faculty, as work for hire, an unprecedented stance in intellectual policy documents. In taking this position, Utah treated faculty as expert professionals (Brint 1994) employed in a corporation, not as autonomous professionals who were part of a universal community of scholars. In terms of royalty splits, Utah gave its faculty less than many other universities but offered more incentives designed to pull faculty toward academic capitalism. In the early years, the patent policy offered small rewards for faculty who took the initiative to patent, develop, and market their own inventions; in the later years, these rewards were large (two-thirds of royalties rather than 40% of the first $20,000 as the top end of a downwardly sliding scale).

As the documents that articulated academic capitalism suggest (particularly the document on profit-making corporations), Utah regarded its faculty as in partnership with the university to generate external revenue. Under the auspices of the university, faculty were able to run corporations built on their discoveries over a long period of time, sometimes incorporating related licenses to intellectual property that they or they colleagues had discovered. Faculty and university were not limited to licensing and collecting royalties. They were conceived of as a business partnership, committed to long-term market engagement.

Washington University in St. Louis

Organization. Washington University's intellectual property was handled by the Center of Technology Management (CTM). Its task was to "protect University intellectual property rights and to maximize the value of intellectual property to the faculty and the University" (Washington University in St. Louis 1998a). The CTM advertised technology, helped faculty find partners, negotiated and managed agreements, and provided legal support. The center provided faculty with booklets about how to establish their own start-up companies and generally promoted a variety of forms of technology transfer.

Oversight. The work of the CTM and any other technology transfer activity was overseen by the Committee for Faculty Oversight of Technology Transfer. This committee looked at the technology transfer mission, budget, resolution of disputes, and the division of intellectual property income. It made recommendations to the vice-chancellor for research, who appointed the committee. The Disclosure Review Committee advised faculty of possible conflicts of interest following disclosure.

Forms of Market Involvement. Multiple forms of intellectual property were: licensing income, "most commonly received in the form of royalties from sales or guaranteed payments"; milestone payments, which were made when "particular steps are made, ranging from obtaining a particular research result to reaching a particular stage in drug development"; equity interest, which could include "publicly tradable shares, privately held shares, or options to acquire shares"; mask work, "a series of related images embodying the original, predetermined topography of a semiconductor chip product," which was registered with the copyright office; material transfer agreements; tangible property (cell lines, software, compositions of matter); and trade secrets (1998a). Intellectual property had moved far beyond the simple licensing described in Washington University's 1971 patent policy.

Degree of Faculty and Administrator Involvement in Firms. Faculty members who patented intellectual property could also be compensated as paid consultants to the company developing the technology, or they could have positions in companies that were formed around their intellectual property. The multiple forms of market activity pursued by Washington University together with faculty's close involvement in them created many opportunities for conflict of interest. As the intellectual property policy pointed out, "the possibility of conflict of interest is inherent in the commercial development of intellectual property" (1998a). According to the conflict of interest booklet the CTM put out to guide faculty, "conflicts of interest are neither inherently wrong nor avoidable in all cases." But conflicts of interest had to be to be "disclosed and managed" (Washington University in St. Louis 1998b). The intellectual property policy rated the "risk enhancing factors" with regard to conflict of interest in market activity. They were:

a. increasing magnitude of personal compensation;
b. increasing number of financial relationships between a creator and a company;
c. increasing commitment of a creator's time to a company;
d. holding equity in a company;
e. involvement of trainees or students; and
f. involvement of patients or human subjects. (1998b)

In other words, the risk of conflict of interest increased the more closely faculty members or creators were involved with market activity. Yet the intellectual property policy continued to aggressively promote close involvement of faculty with the market. The only high-risk situation that the policy suggested might "essentially preclude" faculty (creator) involvement was "equity ownership in a company concurrent with active participation in clinical trials" (Washington University in St. Louis 1998b). But most other risk factors could be managed, including involvement of trainees or students in market activity.

Washington University is not a public university, but it is a nonprofit higher education institution chartered by the state. The development of market activity made the boundary between nonprofit and profit-taking activity less and less clear. The university, in the persons of its administrators and officers, did not make profits, but faculty did. Although administrators did not put money from intellectual property in their pockets, their salaries increased dramatically to the point where they were many times higher than that of the average professor. The university as an institution was able to capture profits on its intellectual property so long as it put those profits back into research and education. As we saw in the case of the University of California, profits could even be dedicated to making unprofitable inventions profitable. The pursuit of intellectual property was approaching institutionalization and was the hallmark of an academic capitalism knowledge regime.

Public Good. Although we analyzed the patent policies for what they said about the public good, they generally did not elaborate on a public good knowledge regime because their purpose was to give direction to technology transfer, exploitation of intellectual property, and profit-taking. In their preambles, most policies made formulaic mention of the purpose of technology transfer as serving the public good. For example, in 1985, the University of California system policy mentioned the public good only in the first four paragraphs, stating that research was conducted "primarily for the purpose of gaining new knowledge," which gave rise to applied research and "fortuitous by-products" (University of California 1985). However, the purpose of the patent policy was to find an equitable way to administer intellectual property for the public benefit, which included further support of research and education, while providing incentives for faculty and staff to use the patent system for discovery and invention. The 1990 and 1997 policies did not change. Elsewhere, at one extreme was the University of Utah, which said almost nothing about the public good, at the other was Stanford.

Stanford offered stronger support for a public good research regime, including Mertonian norms, than most institutional patent policies. Its 1993 policy proclaimed that "while the University recognizes the benefits of patent development, it is most important that the direction of University research not be established or unduly influenced by patent considerations or personal financial interests" (Stanford University 1999). In 1999, it asked for compliance with the 1996 openness in research policy with regard to grants and contracts that generated patents. Stanford's 1996 openness policy took the position that graduate student dissertation work should not be initiated if there was a strong likelihood that it would lead to a "secret thesis or dissertation" (Stanford University

1996). Nor could a faculty member involve students in projects that would cause any substantial delay to their dissertations.

Stanford valued faculty autonomy and took the position that inventors were "free to place their inventions in the public domain if they believed that would be in the best interest of technology transfer" and if doing so did not violate contract agreements (Stanford University 1999). However, the policy did not address how the best interests of technology transfer would be determined, nor did it address whether Bayh-Dole, which allowed universities to hold patents discovered during research performed under federal contract and directed profits to be shared with faculty, was a prior contract. Moreover, Stanford's comprehensive disclosure policy probably influenced faculty's willingness to place inventions in the public domain. If disclosure of all inventions was mandatory, then officials from the Office of Technology Licensing had an opportunity to counsel faculty about what were "the best interests of technology transfer" (1999). The documents referenced in the patent policy indicate that the Office of Technology Licensing was skilled at arguing that patenting was the appropriate vehicle for technology transfer.

Stanford's 1999 policy referred to the 1983 Tangible Research Policy, which captured Mertonian norms of openness and universality. Tangible research property (TRP) was a different category from intangible intellectual property. TRP referred to items produced such as biological materials (including microorganisms), engineering drawings, computer software, integrated circuit chips, computer databases, prototype devices, circuit diagrams, and equipment. Although TRP was owned by Stanford and subject to provisions similar to those in the patent policy, investigators were able to make TRP broadly available for the world research community. However, with the ambivalence that characterizes the Stanford patent policy, TRP was shared with other researchers, but its dissemination had to be "by means which do not diminish its value or inhibit its commercial development or public use" (Stanford University 1999). As with many of the policies, the strong commitment to norms characteristic of a public good knowledge regime were undercut by acceptance of exemptions, reasonable delays, and classification after research was performed.

To see if policies influenced outcomes at universities with patent programs, we drew on data from the 2000 AUTM survey to see if licensing practices and staffing patterns were associated with outcomes such as research funding, license income, patent applications, and the like (Table 3.3). We ran six separate linear regressions, with FTE (number of licensing and technology transfer employees) as the independent variable and the variables listed in the correlation table as the dependent variables. The results of the regressions indicate that in

Table 3.3 Technology Transfer Activities, Fiscal Year 2000

	FTE	Research Funding	License Income	Total Patent Applications	New Patent Applications	Legal Fees	U.S. Patents Issued
FTE	1	.326	.776	.787	.749	.850	.863
Research funding	.326	1	.187	.227	.233	.247	.268
License income	.776	.187	1	.650	.607	.799	.748
Total patent applications	.787	.227	.650	1	.954	.881	.922
New patent applications	.749	.233	.607	.954	1	.815	.844
Legal fees	.850	.247	.799	.881	.815	1	.937
U.S. patents issued	.863	.268	.748	.922	.884	.937	1

Note: Each correlation is significant at the 0.01 level.
Source: AUTM Survey, FY 2000

fiscal year 2000, an increase by one in technology transfer FTE was associated with a $135,105.98 increase in research funding related to licenses/options, a $1,959,145.70 increase in license income received, a 6.5 percent increase in total patent applications filed, a 3.9 percent increase in legal fees expended, a $121,939.03 increase in legal fees expended, and a 2.8 percent increase in U.S. patents issued. The results of these regressions suggest that technology transfer FTE is highly correlated with the number of patents filed and issued but not as highly correlated with research funding related to licenses and options. While the number of employees in a technology transfer office may contribute to the number of patents, more technology transfer officers may not necessarily contribute to the amount of research funding earned related to licenses and options. Increased capacity in technology transfer associates universities more closely with the economy and its prestige system than with the research endeavor, funded by the U.S. government, and its prestige system. It is also interesting to note that the number of U.S. patents issued is highly correlated with the amount of legal fees expended.

The system and institutional patent policies that delineated academic capitalism practices greatly expanded market managerial capacity in colleges and universities. The new functions were many: surveilling institutional employees' intellectual property activity to ensure capture by the system or institution; reviewing and evaluating faculty disclosures; technology licensing; supervision of royalty flows, including distribution of funds within institutions; reinvestment of funds in new market activities; litigation to defend intellectual property; evaluation of intellectual property for institutional equity investments; monitoring and occasionally administering corporations in which the institution held equity; overseeing initial public offerings (IPOs); and developing and monitoring market activity for conflict of interest issues. As colleges and universities become more involved in academic capitalism, they hired more managerial professional staff. The policies gave the professional staff the managerial capacity to run intellectual property activities like businesses, albeit without the same consequences, in that business failure did not necessarily terminate intellectual property programs and university-based businesses were often protected from legal suits by the Eleventh Amendment. Expanded managerial capacity institutionalized business activity in colleges and universities by allowing segments of them to directly engage the market.

The professionals hired by universities to develop patents and the many business activities that surround them had to establish working relations with faculty to be successful. They had to locate or respond to faculty willing to participate in patent activity. Together, these managerial professionals and faculty formed entrepreneurial networks within universities that linked them to external corporations. These networks constituted entrepreneurial practices and cultures, bringing the values and ethos of capitalism into academe.

Conclusion

Generally, system and institutional patent policies do not sit well with Mertonian values: communalism, the free flow of knowledge, disinterestedness, and organized skepticism. Rather than being shared, intellectual property is owned. University patent policies indicate that ownership precludes communalism (or the intellectual commons) in several ways. The object of patent policies is to contain or enclose knowledge and to detail the process of enclosure: obligatory disclosure, administrative review, advisory committee review, executive decision making. Once knowledge is enclosed or owned, it has to be managed, elaborating the enclosure process and creating policies that deal with royalties, licensing, equity, and conflict of interest, all of which more tightly fence in information. Rather than preserving an intellectual commons to which all members of the academic community have rights, intellectual property policies transform the academic community into a mine. Faculty must tunnel with the help of a small crew to unearth knowledge from veins or seams with commercial properties, which they present to technology licensing officials for evaluation.

Knowledge flows less freely when patent policies are in place. Obligatory disclosure means that administrative authorities are able to direct faculty to patent rather than publish, which keeps knowledge out of circulation for the period in which the patent is being proved, usually from three months to a year, but sometimes much longer. In an era of telecommunications, electronic journals, and prepublications, this interruption of knowledge flow can slow discovery. As the patent process details, when knowledge is owned and commodified, it becomes valuable and is no longer traded in a gift economy. Data sets are ownable, as are research tools, and faculty are charged for their use. As public-private partnerships built around exploitation of university-owned intellectual property increases, knowledge about them decreases. A number of states have passed laws that make contracts that deal with intellectual property exempt from freedom of information requests (Schmidt 2002). (As a test of the degree to which restriction occurs, request copies of your university's contracts with corporations.)

Disinterestedness stresses that scientists should not have a stake in the outcome of their research. Intellectual property policies create an interest in outcomes by attaching monetary incentives to discovery. The policies give faculty large rewards, up to 50 percent of royalty or licensing income should an invention prove profitable. It is possible to argue that these incentives do not motivate faculty because so few discoveries result in profits. However, the steep upward curve of disclosures, patents, licenses, and equity agreements from 1980 to 2002 suggests otherwise. The proliferation of conflict of interest language and rules in the policies is another indication of the death of disinterestedness.

Organized skepticism calls for scientists to question results and look for alternative approaches and answers. Intellectual property policies implicitly set up a system that rewards the opposite. If faculty and universities are rewarded through royalties derived from the licensing of products or processes, then they have no incentives to question the science on which the products or processes are built, nor any incentives to look for alternatives that, if better or more cleverly marketed, would pose a threat to their revenue stream. Concern about pipelining, the licensing of technologies related to those already patented, in the University of California system policies points to the possibility of faculty and institutional commitment to specific product and process lines, which makes unlikely faculty research in or university sponsorship of alternatives.

We have documented and described the shift from a public good knowledge regime, associated with Mertonian values and the Vannevar Bush model of science, to an academic capitalist regime, associated with basic science for use and basic technology, concepts that their framers argue allow academic and commercial values to coexist, even if uneasily. But description is not explanation. What caused the values to shift? In this chapter, we are not concerned with underlying causes, such as the shift from a defense to a knowledge economy, but with proximal causes, namely, organization.

The subtext of the Merton/Bush model was that organizational separation of universities from the state and the market was necessary for its espoused values to prevail. Academic knowledge was valuable to society precisely because it offered disinterested expertise, removed from politics and economics. The Vannevar Bush model stressed separation of university science from state and economy; basic science done in the university preceded development, which occurred in federal (state) laboratories, or application, which was accomplished by industry. Certainly these conceptions of the organization of science were self-interested in that they called for a system that gave scientists unprecedented autonomy: state subsidy with no strings. While the system was at best relatively autonomous (Evans, Rueschemeyer, and Skocpol 1985), it nonetheless reinforced a status and prestige system for science that was somewhat independent of the state and commerce. Status depended on discovery and reputation within an elaborated system of nonprofit associations—scientific associations of disciplines, umbrella associations, such as the American Association for the Advancement of Science, and universities. These organized the work of science: peer review and journal publication, which was not tightly tied to remuneration. Science depended upon the federal government for funding, but a significant portion of that funding was awarded through peer review, which distanced science from the state. Science was involved in commercial activity, but application was not at the core of the status and prestige system, mostly because scientists controlled a large portion of federal funds through peer review.

An academic capitalist knowledge regime to some degree reorganized science, changing the configuration of relations between university, state, and market, the process of which changed values. Able to hold title and profit from inventions made by faculty working on federal grants, universities became market actors. As market actors, they moved to control or enclose faculty discovery through intellectual property policy, which, as some institutions began to generate substantial revenue streams, called for more extensive management of that property and more sustained involvement in the market by universities and faculty members. The universities are the state arm that dramatically shifted federal resources from the Merton/Bush model to an entrepreneurial model. Public universities' patent programs dismantled the firewall between the state and the market, making less possible the autonomous science envisioned by the Merton/Bush model.

Although the various intellectual property policies make (uneven and sporadic attempts) to separate business from research, the two are embroiled because successful development of technology often depends on the continued involvement of university inventors or experts. Without them, technology development often flounders or fails. More and more universities officially encourage inventors to work closely with licensing professionals or potential licensees to better promote commercialization. Although conflict of interest policies attempt to separate the university and faculty from too close an engagement in the market, a successful patent program demands faculty and institutional market involvement. Indeed, the various patent policies provide powerful financial incentives for faculty to remain involved.

The status and prestige system that sustained the Merton/Bush model depended to some degree on the (relative) organizational autonomy of universities and science. From the end of World War II until roughly 1972, universities' engagement with the economy was primarily through the Department of Defense and was structured through a division of research labor, initiated in part by the Vannevar Bush model, in which universities performed basic research, the federal laboratories were involved in development, and corporations focused on applied research. As part of the Keynesian welfare-warfare state, the DOD generously funded research, offering university scientists long-term grants for projects that did not have immediate payoff and that, even though classified, were not closely supervised in day-to-day terms. Despite violating Mertonian norms of secrecy and lack of national purpose, the DOD promoted a sense of (relative) autonomy among scientists (Slaughter and Rhoades 1996). This system of organization (implicitly endorsed by the intellectual commons model, sans the DOD connection), with its degrees of separation from state and economy, sustained (some) Mertonian values. The NSF was implicitly seen as the lynchpin of this system and was portrayed as different than the mission agencies in that it sponsored basic science: open, free, disinterested research. These organizational structures—an elaborate grant and contract system that functioned through peer review and at least one federal agency not directly committed to a specific (state) mission—in a sense made Mertonian values possible.

Changes in patent policies created new circuits of knowledge between academe and the new economy. Faculty who discovered patentable products and processes in the course of their federally funded research spoke with university technology licensing officials about their discoveries before they shared them with colleagues; to protect their discoveries they had to keep them secret until the patents were awarded. If professors and technology transfer officers decided to pursue a patent, the commercial rather than the academic potential of the knowledge was foregrounded. Sometimes professors participated in the search for a corporate partner, sometimes the technology transfer officers did, and sometimes both did, often operating in separate networks. If the search was successful, complicated negotiations with the firm over the share of royalties and the conditions of licensing followed. After the agreement was concluded, faculty frequently did not simply hand over the university-held patent; they remained involved with the firm as a consultant or advisor. If a corporate partner could not be found and if the technology transfer officers were convinced of the value of the patent, universities, especially in the 1990s, sometimes decided to act as venture capitalists, taking equity shares in the corporation. If this occurred, professors usually remained closely involved, working to ensure rewards for university investment in the venture. University administrators, often technology transfer officers, were sometimes involved as well, occasionally as corporate officers. If the company was successful, there was sometimes a pipeline for new products, which often called for further faculty research involvement. The new circuits of knowledge connected faculty, administrators, and institutions of higher learning to the corporate world of the new economy.

Professors with patents did not abandon their academic pursuits. They usually continued with federally funded research programs, wrote for scholarly journals, and spoke at learned conferences. However, they had to juggle time and commitments to patent activity with traditional research activity. Even if they did not have a successful experience in the new circuits of knowledge, they undoubtedly saw the commercial potential of their work more clearly.

The state, system, and institutional patent policies powerfully demonstrated the emergence of interstitial organizations that bring the new economy into universities. As new circuits of knowledge connected academe and the new economy, technology licensing offices emerged from the interstices of other organizations—the university attorney's office, the vice-president for research's office, the foundation office—and grew rapidly. By 2002, the University of California system technology transfer office employed roughly one hundred people.

At the various institutions, technology transfer provided examples of interstitial organizational emergence. In their associated form, technology transfer officers exemplify networks that intermediate between the private and public sectors. In one of the most rapid cases of recent professionalization, they formed their own association, the AUTM. This association fosters the interests of technology transfer officers, which are to facilitate colleges and universities' success in generating external revenues from intellectual property. The network of technology transfer officers in AUTM spans the world of academe and the new economy.

Patent policies greatly expanded the managerial capacity of colleges and universities, calling for identification of patentable research and protecting and marketing that research. The policies identified more and more types of intellectual property to be managed and protected. They directly involve universities in the market through a variety of activities, including licensing, taking equity positions in start-up corporations, occasionally participating in the management of corporations, and organizing IPOs. Universities' efforts to generate external revenue from intellectual property are difficult to distinguish from businesses' commitment to extract profits from intellectual property.

Currently, the Mertonian/Vannevar Bush public good and academic capitalist knowledge regimes coexist and sometimes overlap. However, the values of both systems depend in part on the organizational structures that sustain their cultures of research. The academic status and prestige system is still concerned with discovery, fundamental (broad) scientific questions, pushing back the frontiers of knowledge, and recognition as reward. However, that system may be sustained only if there continues to be an organizational infrastructure that supports it with a degree of separation from a (relatively autonomous) state and a degree of separation from the market. The academic capitalist system is setting up an alternative system of rewards in which discovery is valued because of its commercial properties and economic rewards, broad scientific questions are couched so that they are relevant to commercial possibilities (biotechnology, telecommunications, computer science), knowledge is regarded as a commodity rather than a free good, and universities have the organization capacity (and are permitted by law) to license, invest, and profit from these commodities.

4

PATENT POLICIES PLAY OUT

Student and Faculty Life

In this chapter, we move from policy to practice, focusing on students and faculty. As we demonstrated in chapter 3, state and system policies interacted with institutional efforts to capitalize knowledge. The resulting academic capitalism knowledge regime has implications not only for faculty, researchers, and administrators involved in technology transfer but also for the educational process. Legal cases that feature students and patents let us glimpse how movement toward academic capitalism in the new economy affects students. To hear the voice of faculty involved with industry who are subject to institutional and system patent policies as well as federal conflict of interest policies and patent procedures, we draw on interviews with faculty, many from the states whose policies we analyzed, to see how they grapple with the new knowledge regime.

The student patent cases draw on the work of Althusser (1971) and Gramsci (1971), which allows us to see how power shifts relationships among market, state, and higher education as intellectual property becomes the cornerstone of a knowledge economy. The faculty interviews are framed by the norms and values theories used to examine patent policies, and they point to how values change when knowledge regimes shift. Generally, we see case law, as well as state and institutional policy, as interacting with student and faculty approaches to the market. Laws geared toward solving corporate intellectual property problems reshape students' legal status, and state and institutional policies, combined with interactions with corporate partners imbued with corporate values, renorm academic values (Slaughter and Rhoades 1990). However, these are not cases of institutions reshaping academe; the students, directed by their professors, and the faculty initiated the approach to the market, inviting the relevant institutions to reconsider boundaries.

Students, Patents, and Markets

In considering these cases, we focus on how the state, represented by the courts, refracts capital through its power, organizing production (Althusser

1971)—in this case through commodification of intellectual property—for a knowledge economy, indirectly contributing to an academic capitalist knowledge/learning regime in which students are valued as creators of intellectual property and workers rather than as learners. We also examine how the state, again through the court, contributes to the ideological hegemony (Gramsci 1971) of an academic capitalist knowledge/learning regime by legitimating the students' role as knowledge producers, affirming the importance of their contribution to the new economy. However, we are also aware that the state and markets do not simply work their will on students and faculty. Faculty, in their capacity as teachers, researchers, and entrepreneurs, direct students toward the market, and students seem willingly to approach it. Students and faculty apparently see themselves as expert professionals, part of the technoscience core of the economy (Brint 1994), and are ready to move across the traditional boundaries that have separated university and market, themselves affirming an academic capitalist knowledge/learning regime.

We analyze three cases that represent all the student cases that came before the federal appellate court since 1980 (Baez and Slaughter 2001). There are no Supreme Court cases because no student/patent litigation has yet reached that level. Although the cases are few, they are instructive. Two cases involve undergraduates; one involves a graduate student. In analyzing these cases, we look at how the power of capital and the state are deployed with regard to the state, non-profit institutions, higher education, faculty, and students.

In re Cronyn (1989)

A corporation sought to declare invalid a Reed College professor's patent application for a chemical compound used in the treatment of cancer because the information had previously been published in three undergraduate student theses. The patent holder was the students' chemistry professor and a university administrator. Legally, if the knowledge were previously published, it would be in the public domain and therefore unpatentable. The corporation argued that the student theses should be considered as published even though they were indexed in a shoebox in the chemistry department and listed in the college library by the students' last names with no reference to their contents. The Board of Patent Appeals and Interferences found for the corporation, holding that the three theses were printed publications that anticipated the patent. The federal court of appeals reversed the board's ruling, following earlier decisions that students' work was in the public domain, accessible, and thus unpatentable if it was indexed, catalogued, and shelved in a university library. The court reasoned that the Reed theses were not accessible because the cataloguing was not sufficient for anyone else to make use of the information.

In this case, the corporation was the initiating actor with regard to the courts, challenging a patent taken out by a faculty member that was based on student work. However, the faculty member, who was also the vice-provost of the college, was the initiating actor with regard to the patent, which placed the intellectual property within the commercial system, albeit under the offices of the federal patent system, which issued him the patent. Regardless of whether the professor/administrator exploited his relationship with the students in securing his patent, a point not addressed in the case, his professorial relationship with the students moved away from being based on learning to production of commercial knowledge. Once the intellectual property was in the world of commerce, via the patent, the institution was open to state sanctioned-litigation in the federal court.

Because the federal court of appeals has indicated that cataloguing student theses and shelving them in a university library put that research in the public domain, universities have supported the practice of withholding students' research results from publication or even placement in the open shelves of university libraries, so that professors or students and their corporate sponsors can patent. As universities have moved aggressively to patent, it has become standard practice, endorsed by the Government University Research Roundtable, to allow universities to withhold students' work for ninety days (Campbell 1997). Cases have been reported, however, in which students' work was withheld anywhere from ninety days to three years (Slaughter et al. 2002).

Academic capitalism thus emphasizes students' identity as producers of knowledge that can become a commodity, yet their rights to that knowledge are constrained. Universities and professors, presumably because they sponsor and supervise student knowledge production, claim title to intellectual property that students work to create. In a recursive pattern, the students learn to create knowledge that can be turned into marketable products and learn as well that they are valued as knowledge workers more than learners, extending the lived practice of academic capitalism.

National Research Development Corporation v. Varian Associates (1994)

Hoult, while a graduate student at Oxford University under the supervision of Professor Richards in the early 1970s, invented a method and apparatus for eliminating systemic noise in a Nuclear Magnetic Resonance (NMR) spectrometer. Hoult received a U.S. patent for his invention and assigned his rights to the National Research and Development Corporation (NRDC). However, while Hoult was working on his discovery, Dr. Richards attended a 1973 experimental NMR Conference in the United States. "While traveling to the conference one morning, Dr. Richards had an informal, one-on-one conversation on a bus with Dr. Stejskal, a Monsanto Corporation research scientist. During that conversation, which took place without Dr. Hoult's knowledge or explicit permission, Dr. Richards disclosed the essence of Dr. Hoult's invention to Dr. Stejskal. It is undisputed . . . that Dr. Richards at that time did not ask Dr. Stejskal to keep the information confidential and did not inform him that either he or Dr. Hoult intended to file for a patent thereon" (*National Research Development Corporation v. Varian Associates* 1994, pp. 3–4). When he got back to Monsanto Corporation, Stejskal and his colleagues incorporated Hoult's invention, as disclosed by his professor, into one of its spectrometers and has used it ever since. The NRDC filed a lawsuit against Varian Associates in 1989 for infringing its patent, and Varian claimed that the NRDC patent was invalid because Monsanto had been using the invention for years. The NRDC argued that the information was understood to be confidential, but the court disagreed, relying on Professor Richard's testimony and the 1973 conference's intended purpose of encouraging the "free disclosure of information" (p. 8).

This case underscores how the possibility of commercialization permeates relations between students and professors. Because student research has value as intellectual property, the commercial world can intrude on the professor-student, teaching-learning relationship, inhibiting the ability of professor and student to discuss freely the results of their research. Ironically, a professor's unguarded disclosure of information to an industrial scientist at a conference designed to encourage collaboration between academe and industry later penalized his student and university through the loss of patent rights. The case also illustrates the contradictory demands of the university on faculty and students who create intellectual property. Universities encourage university-industry exchanges; however, they also encourage patenting, precluding such exchanges. Professors and students have to calculate how they will best serve themselves as market actors, whether working through industry or institution.

Johns Hopkins University v. Cellpro, Inc. (1998)

When Johns Hopkins University sued Cellpro for patent infringement, the intellectual property at issue was the Civin patents, which researchers hoped would make bone marrow transplants safer. Cellpro charged that, after patenting, the university was unable to convert the patents to practice again, rendering them invalid. The university responded that the reason for this lack of progress was that its laboratory used undergraduates, who could be not considered "skilled in the art" of this research. The court agreed with the university and upheld its claims against Cellpro.

Although the court held undergraduate students to a less demanding standard than it would have professional researchers, it nonetheless affirmed the use of these students in creating intellectual property for the university. The institution's commitment to academic capitalism revalued students as workers who learned rather than as learners who worked for the university in return for instruction. Because the university construed the students as workers, it was able to claim their intellectual property. Not incidentally, students learned that even though the patented products might be crucial to saving human lives and were likely financed in part by public tax dollars used for research, the federal court of appeals gave Johns Hopkins a potentially profitable monopoly on the knowledge they helped to create. Education and ideology combined to recursively reinscribe academic capitalism on the institution and its actors.

In the three cases we have discussed in this chapter, the state, as represented by the court, did not simply affirm the power of corporations. In the Reed case and the Johns Hopkins case, corporations lost. However, in all three cases the court affirmed universities' commercial rights to knowledge and recognized faculty and students as knowledge producers and market actors. Although the state (court) did not favor capital (corporations), it aligned private nonprofit universities with the market, preferring an academic capitalist knowledge regime in which students were knowledge producers to one in which students were learners somewhat insulated from the market.

The patent infringement cases indicate the federal court of appeals' preference for institutional and private rights to profit from knowledge rather than for public rights to obtain and benefit immediately from that knowledge. In other words, the courts have generally affirmed the bipartisan legislation that made possible opening universities to academic capitalism. Universities, strengthening their units that litigate, have moved to defend their intellectual property, firmly committing themselves to academic capitalism, even when it puts them in awkward positions with regard to their treatment of students and the public trust. However, movement toward the market is not without difficulties. Academic capitalism unleashes the entrepreneurial energy not only of the institution but also of professors and students with the consequence that professors, students, and institutions frequently follow their own paths to the market, sometimes working at cross purposes, yet all legitimating universities' engagement with the market.

Professors, Patents, and the Market

In this section we analyze interviews with faculty engaged in the process of transferring technology to the market to see how their work intersects and reflects the federal, state, state university system, and institutional patent policies as well as the court cases discussed so far. We use the same theories as in chapter 3 as well as the theory of academic capitalism. Our analysis of the interviews is framed by the shift from a public good to an academic capitalist knowledge/learning regime. The professors give greater voice to values espoused by a public good research regime than do the patent policies, but they also articulate many values and practices associated with an academic capitalist knowledge/learning regime.

Our data, gathered in 1997, formed a subset of the larger National Science Foundation (NSF) study that explored faculty and administrators' relations with private-sector firms. (For methodological details, see Campbell 1997; Slaughter et al. 2002; Slaughter and Archerd, forthcoming.) We analyzed data from thirty-eight semistructured interviews with faculty who had interacted with industry in the previous five years (Campbell and Slaughter 1996). Fourteen institutions located in California, Arizona, Texas, North Carolina, and Massachusetts were selected because of their significant research interactions with industry. For the most part, the institutions were large, research-intensive universities. Our sample comprised ten department heads or center directors and twenty-eight faculty members. Nineteen were engineers, of whom five were department heads or center directors; twelve were from the sciences, four of whom were department heads or center directors; and seven were in medical schools, one of whom was a department head. While every effort was made to include professors of all ranks as well as women and members of minority groups, several members of these groups declined to participate, citing a lack of time. Only four female faculty and three assistant professors participated. The sample reflected the majority of faculty who were engaged in collaborative activity with firms: male, tenured, full professors.

The greatest points of conflict for professors were issues that pushed them to make choices between a public service and an academic capitalist knowledge regime. These issues were publishing versus patenting, access versus secrecy, and contested ownership of a wide variety of intellectual property. Publishing was tied to the free flow of knowledge and values associated with a public good knowledge regime, whereas patenting was associated with academic capitalism. Open access to knowledge characterized the Mertonian/public good knowledge regime; secrecy was more typical of academic capitalism. Communalism did not stress profit taking and was associated with the public good regime, while intellectual property was tied to broadening commitment to an academic capitalist knowledge regime. These three issues created tension between professors and firms and professors and their institutions.

Publishing versus Patenting

According to U.S. patent law, if information about a product or process is published, then it becomes part of the public domain and can no longer be patented. If a product or process is patented, first it must be "reduced to practice" or demonstrated, and an application filed with the U.S. Patent Office. The office reviews the product or process to see if it is original and then issues a patent, which ideally protects the product or process from being copied by another party for seventeen years. The average time from submission to the U.S. Patent Office to issuance of a patent is twelve to eighteen months. Among the difficulties that patents pose for academics is that patenting may hold up publication.

About 60 percent of the faculty we interviewed held patents. Almost all valued publishing research papers more highly than patenting. A few thought patents had some merit, but they were the exception. As a professor of chemical engineering explained: "A patent is hard to get, okay, but a patent doesn't need to be a scientific document . . . You can patent things that are just scientifically terrible . . . However, some people like to say, well, if you've got a patent, it shows you did something novel because you were able to get a patent. Okay. That may be true. But I think most people in academia . . . I think the thing that is valued the most is a high-quality scientific publication."

Patents were "like icing on a cake. You have to have a cake first," according to an associate professor of physics. Research was the cake. Most professors did not attend closely to how their institutions set intellectual property policy and to the share they would receive if they "got a big hit." They understood that the chance of making a great deal of money from a patent was like winning the lottery. As a center/lab director of electrical and computer engineering put it, "I remember when it [intellectual property policy] was first instituted . . . I don't think people are too concerned about the percentages because typically it's like a lottery ticket. You either get nothing or there's going to be a substantial amount. And if it's percentaged smaller . . . people don't win the big prize but win the second prize, they're still pretty happy because their chances were very much that they were going to get nothing. I think that's the way most people feel about the patent thing."

Most tenured professors with established industrial connections had figured out how to publish *and* patent. They employed a technique we call *sequencing.* Professors who had ongoing shared research agendas with corporations timed their publications so they did not interfere with patenting. As senior faculty, they did not feel pressed to publish and could afford to wait. A chemistry professor said: "Like any other collaboration, you have to be able to get along with the people . . . so there is a legitimate interest of the company in not disclosing things until patent applications are finished and so forth. Generally I have found that that doesn't have to be very restrictive. I'm slow enough in writing out my papers anyway so that another month or something isn't going to make a big difference. So, I think it is important to keep in view the academic issues of freedom to publish and so forth, certainly one doesn't want to compromise those things. In practice, I've not run into any big conflicts there." A professor of endocrinology elaborated this pattern:

> As long as publishing is fairly quick . . . as long as things are not so hidden for years, I don't think it's that big a deal now . . . if somebody was going to say "patent it or not, we're not going to tell anybody about this for five years," then, you know, I think it would [matter]. But . . . we're talking about a year or so, and I don't think [it] matters all that much . . . Even if you're writing a paper without any patent involved or anything, it's going to be a year to year and a half after you do the work before probably the work comes out, so you write the patent and you write the paper and it's going to be year, year and a half before it comes out anyway, so I'm not sure it's that much of a difference.

Because these senior professors had developed close relations with industry, they saw industry as having "a legitimate interest" in not disclosing information until patents were approved. They argued that there is little difference between publishing with a patent or without a patent, given the slow pace of publishing, a somewhat disingenuous position given the prevalence of prepublications and on-line publications in the sciences. Nonetheless, many professors had so naturalized sequencing that they saw no conflict between patenting and the free flow of information.

However, assistant professors were not so sanguine about their ability to publish and patent. A young assistant professor of biology noted that she had difficulty patenting quickly enough to get her publications out in a timely fashion. Her difficulties were with her university, not a corporation.

> If you think you have something that is commercially relevant, you are required to file a disclosure to the university before you publish it. So they are essentially sort of censoring what's being published . . . the university . . . is in business too . . . so it's annoying in one respect because being in academics, you need to have all this freedom, but if you actually read the university faculty handbook . . . anything that you think is

> commercially relevant has to be filed first and then they have up to six months to decide the fate of what you are working on . . . and that includes presentations at meetings. So, I don't know. The lines between industry and universities are sort of merging.

She understood that universities, like corporations, had become invested in profit taking, and both types of organizations now pushed for patents. As a result, the university, historically understood to be more committed to academic freedom than corporations, sought to constrain the free flow of knowledge when patents, licenses, and royalties were in the offing. Despite her insight, this professor was willing to excuse universities. "In a way, I can see the side of academics because times are getting tough and they can't just wash potential profits down the drain either."

Many of the professors we interviewed had moved from a public good conception of academe, in which industry scientists patented and professors published, toward an academic capitalist regime. Professors still believed that publications were much more important than patenting, but many were convinced they could publish and patent. This belief was most powerful among senior professors with long-term research programs who published regularly.

Secrecy versus Access

Some professors, especially those who had worked with industry, took the position that universities seeking to maximize revenue flow by patenting and obtaining licensing and royalty agreements were naive. As an associate professor of electrical and computer engineering said:

> The issue with patents is very tricky . . . you write the patent and you think that money will start flowing in the next day and then you want to move on to license it . . . writing the patent is the easy part. The hard part is what do you do once you have the patent. You need to go after certain industries to make sure that they carry it. The patent issue in big companies is more like a cold war situation. Suppose you are AT&T and I am IBM. So we both write 200 patents a year. We meet once a year, we have a coffee and we say, "Okay we just exchange and use those things. We can both use it." But once you suddenly write 200 and I have only 10 then we meet for a coffee and you say, "I'm a nice guy but I have 200 and you have only 10." So it's more like a cold war situation. Everyone has his own arsenal and they basically exchange.

Or, as a professor of organic chemistry put it, "There's no one patent you can get which will make a lot of difference to one company because if it's in an area of their major concern, they'll create a network of patents, process patents, little changes in structure and so on. So your patent can't even be independent of their patents. So I think university administrators have a very unrealistic idea about this."

These professors were making the point that industries saw patents as valuable not because they promoted discovery and free competition but because they precluded it. Indeed, these professors thought industries saw patents as a strategic means for staking out future directions for product development and thus preventing investment in these areas on the part of other firms. If universities held only one or two patents in a product area and were unable to deploy them strategically, they were unlikely to reap a rich revenue stream. If universities began to treat patents as strategic for a line of product development, as has the University of California system with regard to its biotechnology patents, then they become more like corporations, engaging in prolonged, complex, multistate litigation to protect themselves and align research endeavor with business plans, shifting higher education toward an academic capitalism knowledge regime.

If the strategic potential of patents becomes paramount for corporations, problems other than withholding publication arise. As an associate professor of biomaterials pointed out, when a product essential to the research process is patented, a whole field can be constrained.

> Patenting a product really does create some problems. Let me give you an example. There is a growth factor that we use, bone growth factor . . . you can derive it from animal bones but it takes . . . tons and tons of bones to extract it and not every place can do that. It's very expensive. They [the corporation] have a way of chemically doing it, recombinant, but that technology is licensed. It's owned by one company, and they don't give out their stuff to anybody unless . . . you sign . . . an obscene agreement. You sign your life away . . . Everything that will come out of it belongs to the company . . . Now, to me, that's a deterrent to progress because there are so many people who'd like to use that and if it was freely available, the whole field can move forward. But since one company's controlling it and wants to control everything that comes from it, I think it's negative. It . . . might make money in the long run but . . . its impeding science.

Other professors were less concerned with patents blocking whole fields of science and more concerned with industry blocking profits for universities, colleges, and faculty members. As a head of electrical engineering said: "You got to be careful because if you give the rights to industry, they can shelve it which is [what their] competition does . . . They have to have performance guarantees. So if they want to shelve it, I don't care as long as they are paying. They are paying the university. They pay the researchers. Everybody is part of this. The university gets a percentage, the researchers get a percentage . . . [The university needs an agreement with industry that says] 'Here's what we think this thing will do. You agree to this. If you don't do that, either give all the intellectual property rights back, or you pay the retainer whether you sell it or not.' "

These two professors were at opposite ends of the spectrum. The first raised questions about what happens to free inquiry when knowledge becomes alienable and patents are used as a protection strategy that keeps scientists away from data. The second insisted that industry not take university discoveries and "shelve" them so competitors were unable to use them unless industry was prepared to pay a fee for doing so. Both thought that patents were part of a larger game, perhaps even a "cold war," in which universities were peripheral players but the consequences were significant.

However, patents were not professors' major interface with industry. Professors routinely interacted with industry as consultants. As consultants, they encountered a variety of restrictions on their free use of information. They often had to sign nondisclosure agreements with industry, had to deal with industry's data management conditions, and had to submit research papers to industry for prepublication review.

Many professors were not troubled by prepublication agreements. As a chemistry professor said, "I have no problem at all with them [the sponsoring companies] wanting first glance at anything . . . the bottom line . . . is that if they can't have some way of knowing what's coming out ahead of time to do damage control if they have to, they're not going to give you a contract. It's just black and white." He was convinced the corporations he worked with would "correct errors" but not tamper with his interpretation of the data, nor hold up his publications, even if they contained material detrimental to the corporation. He interpreted the corporations he worked with as supporting his academic freedom, even though he understood they would "do damage control" prior to the release of his results, perhaps undercutting and challenging his science.

Other professors were willing to accommodate corporate requests for secrecy with regard to data analyzed as part of consulting agreements so long as they were able to publish. A professor of earth sciences explained: "With the oil companies, that's the most important thing to clarify up front . . . how much freedom do I have to publish my contributions? The scenario where the work I do remains secret is not an attractive one at all. Usually, if I'm shown the data at all, then it's available to me. Sometimes it's muted in the sense that the locality is very generalized so that I know sufficient for my purposes where the oil well was drilled. I don't know whether it was a well that produced oil or not and I don't know accurately enough which well within a large field it might be . . . So they don't necessarily give me all the data."

According to an assistant professor of mechanical engineering and materials science, he would not consult with industry if he could not publish, although he had to manipulate his data presentation to get his material past corporate reviewers and into journals. "This is a big problem with high tech industry. Proprietary rights and all this kind of stuff . . . if a company comes to you and says, 'Well, we'd like you to work on this. We have the money for it but you can't publish anything,' well, then I wouldn't do it because there's nothing in it for me because I really do need to be able to publish it. Now, frequently you can get around that by writing publications where you don't divulge all the secret recipes that they don't want to give away. Or you can wait a little bit and often for high-tech industries if you wait six months it's already old hat and they don't care about it anymore." Although this professor experienced corporate censorship, he saw it as an irritation rather than as a substantive challenge to his academic freedom. When he talked about submitting a paper for prepublication review, he related the following: "You have to go through a couple of passes, often. You write a draft proposal, a draft paper, and it goes through the company bureaucracy, and you know, it goes through various peoples' desks. And they always get paranoid about the most innocuous little words that you might have in the paper. It'll come back all red-lined and "Can you take this word out?" and yeah, of course, it doesn't make any difference. So those little things can easily be done without compromising the basic idea." In some cases, he gambled that the corporation would be so "desperate" for his work, that they would continue funding him and allow him to publish despite the company's unhappiness with the situation.

Other professors found company prepresentation and prepublication review more problematic. A professor of earth sciences recounted how a paper he and a student had planned to present at a scientific meeting was barred by the oil company whose data they were using.

> The oil companies can be a little bit paranoid about who gets to see the research when it's done. Initially, they were convinced that the work that my student wanted to do on the side was of no particular merit to the oil exploration process and that was fine. We made the mistake of talking about it as the project developed. We got permission for him to give abstracts at meetings, and others from the company decided that this is really rather interesting—we could use it. So suddenly, the project was no longer available for reading outside of the company and so, well within the first year, that project essentially folded as an option for a PhD. So we found another one and then we took the tack of not talking about it outside of the department, essentially.

Industries often required professors who consulted with them to sign nondisclosure agreements. These agreements protected any industrial data the professor might use and captured the potential profit that might accrue from intellectual property derived from faculty work. Because professors often had complex relations with a variety of companies and government agencies in order to keep their labs and graduate students funded, they sometimes agreed to keep confidential information from several companies. A professor of chemical engineering recounted that faculty had great difficulty in keeping verbal agreements straight, so his institution devised a policy whereby professors could only accept confidential (nondisclosable) information in writing. "We were sitting in a room like you and I are and we talked about something and then half a year later [the corporate representative says] 'well you can't work on that because I mentioned this to you in the room' . . . which happened before . . . it's hard, you know, especially when you're dealing with so many different companies and stuff. I can't remember who said what in that kind of detail two years down the road. So now, it's up front in the language from [his university] that if anybody . . . give[s] us any confidential information it has to be in writing that it is confidential and we both sign it so we don't get into trouble."

In contrast to the professor of chemical engineering, a professor of aeronautical engineering was confident of his ability to manage multiple nondisclosure agreements.

> Q: Many faculty have told me when they work with private data, sensitive data, they sign a nondisclosure agreement. Is that something that you've done?
>
> R: Yeah, I've signed a lot of those.
>
> Q: And do you find it hard to keep track of which ones you've signed, and, you know, do they usually have a length of time on them or is it forever and ever?
>
> R: Actually I never looked that closely. I should go look for the ones that I have. Do I—I honestly don't know that. And do I find it hard to keep track of? No. I keep them strictly separate.

Yet another professor and department head in electrical and computer engineering took pride in having signed only a single nondisclosure agreement with industry.

> My students and I have only signed one nondisclosure agreement and probably won't sign any more. Like we haven't signed one with Intel even though we have . . . extensive collaboration. It's much simpler for them. They simply don't tell us things that are very secret to them or . . . important for confidentiality. And we are working in an area where that's okay. So an example might be that we will know what materials are present in some structure they build for us, integrated circuit structure, but we may not know how exactly those materials were deposited because [knowing] the means of deposition . . . is a big competitive advantage. I don't want to be responsible for knowing what those very expensive, very important secrets are and we don't have to know that. So often when you read scientific papers, there comes a point where in the

> classic paradigm anyone with the right equipment and competence can read a scientific paper and reproduce the results. That's the ideal. That's rarely the case.

This professor disliked nondisclosure agreements because he found it difficult to keep track of what was public and what was secret. He preferred to let companies draw the line for him and keep their secrets. He realized he had violated "the classic paradigm" in which "anyone with the right equipment and competence can read a scientific paper and reproduce the results," but he did not care.

Other professors did not wait for the company to draw the line for them. *Sanitizing*, a term used by a full professor of aeronautical engineering, involved removing data from a thesis that industry wanted to protect so that the professor could publish.

> R: I mean, you know, you can, you can go in for various [types] of sanitization of a thesis, right?
> Q: Sanitization meaning . . . what do you mean by that?
> R: Well, you know, you've gotta ask . . . what's really objectionable in this thesis to the company? I mean, usually it's the specific numbers [that] might be in there . . . Usually it's not the entire thesis, right? The objection to the entire thesis is . . . a real big problem. But if it's . . . numbers, then take the numbers out.
> Q: And just don't . . . report those?
> R: Yeah.

The professors were convinced such omissions did not compromise the integrity of their research and seemed not to understand, or disregarded, that it might undermine the scientific method, which calls for the possibility of replication. Instead, they affirmed property rights that constrain the free flow of knowledge and scientific accountability.

Most professors normalized the constraints—prepresentation, prepublication, nondisclosure agreements—that corporations imposed on their consulting agreements and managed to publish regardless. Even when there seemed to be egregious violations of traditional academic norms, as in the case when a student was prevented from using data he had analyzed in a presentation and in a thesis, professors were willing to excuse it and work with the company. As they sequenced their research write-ups when they worked on patents, so they sanitized their data when they consulted. Although having multiple nondisclosure agreements with industry raised the possibility of legal difficulties should a company make the case that a professor had used its data in ways that benefited another sponsor, most professors did not seem to take this seriously.

Although university policies tried to regulate professors' behavior with regard to disclosing, patenting, and publishing, and corporations also wrote consulting contracts with professors that aimed at controlling their behavior, professors were able to some degree to manipulate their employers and sponsors. In large part that was because professors were the experts, the pioneers at the frontiers of knowledge, and their employers and sponsors often did not know enough to regulate them. Faculty in their labs were difficult to monitor because very often only they were in a position to decide whether something should be disclosed to the institution, shared with a corporation through a contract that might include a bonus for a patent, or, as we will explore below, become the basis of a start-up company. Faculty took advantage of their knowledge on the grounds that, as a professor of biochemistry put it, "extraordinary people do extraordinary things."

Start-up Stories

Approximately 40 percent of the professors in our sample were involved with start-up companies. We used the term *start-up* loosely, including companies in which professors received stock equity in return for knowledge as well as companies that professors initiated themselves. The defining characteristic of start-ups was that professors owned stock based on their discoveries, so they were simultaneously holders of human capital and shareholders with investment capital in their own knowledge.

As we noted in chapter 3 on patent policies, university acceptance of equity increased dramatically in the 1990s, creating conditions conducive to start-ups (Feldman et al. 2002a). Start-ups captured the imagination of many of our sample participants because they were emblematic of the transformations academic capitalism brought to the academy (Slaughter and Leslie 1997). Start-up stories generally emphasized the wealth available to professors able to transform discovery into public stock offerings and marketable products. Even if they had not participated in such ventures, roughly a quarter of the professors interviewed told start-up stories, suggesting the power they held over the professorial imagination. These stories sounded somewhat like fairy tales in which the hero finds an object with magical properties that convert dross into gold. In the professors' case, the object was a discovery, and the alchemical process was "taking it public" or "going public." The discovery led to a product or process, a company was formed, and its stock was sold to the public on national and international exchanges, making millions of dollars for everyone involved, often before a product was fully developed, let alone successfully marketed. Most of the elements that professors emphasized are contained in an engineering department head's story.

> You know, we had a guy . . . a faculty member in computer science where this is the easiest to do this today, he started a company . . . eighteen months ago, probably built it up to something like fifteen employees, never had a dime of profit of course, probably never sold anything, just getting going. Eighteen months old, the company was bought for $220 million. And this was in the paper. Bought by a big company, Cisco Systems. So his corporate days are over, he had 10 percent of the company. He comes back as a . . . faculty member after his eighteen-month leave of absence and he's worth $22 million. So his [university] salary becomes his pocket change . . . They always take leaves of absence . . . our new dean, our brand-new dean of engineering did this, started a company in [19]84. Two-year leave of absence, got the company going, continued to be involved after he came back from his leave of absence. The company actually was probably going to fail but the parts that it made were so important to Silicon Graphics, which is the world's foremost high-end work station, that they bought . . . [his] company because they needed the company to survive. So they captured it for themselves for $480 million. So I don't know how much our dean owned at the time as a founder, not 10 percent, but judging by his estate . . . just north of here, where the very, very wealthy people live, he got plenty. And he's forty-four.

The professors in the story are hard-working innocents ("never had a dime of profit . . . just getting by," "the company . . . was probably going to fail . . . but the parts it made were so important to Silicon Graphics") not motivated by greed. They took leaves of absence, clearly separating academy and corporation. Their work was transformed by corporate interest and investment into multimillion-dollar companies, but the professors were not captivated by the corporate world. After the corporations took over their companies, the professors returned to their origins, the university. They reaped their rewards in private lives, moving into lavish estates, perhaps living happily ever after as princes of the new economy.

The dazzling feature of the start-up story was the transformative power of corporations, conferred by their almost unimaginable wealth. What was not commented on by the tale-teller was how the professors fit back into the university, given that their salaries were "pocket change" and that the professors were now stars, although not necessarily in an academic firmament. This story, as did many of the other uncritical stories told by participants, represented an uncomplicated imaginary in which professors could profit enormously from their discoveries without changing themselves or the universities in which they worked. The start-up stories threw into sharp relief the differences in compensation packages between the academic and the corporate world.

When professors moved away from mythic start-up stories to talk about their own experiences, their accounts became more complex. The issues they struggled with were similar to those discussed previously but intensified because equity and ownership interests made the stakes even higher. Among the issues were (1) who owned what, or how to sort out faculty, institution, government, and taxpayer claims to intellectual property that was developed at least in part using (public) university facilities and federal research funds; (2) how to preserve professors' traditional use of expertise in external settings given institutional intrusion into these practices when both professors and institution shared equity in a company; and (3) how to insure that graduate students involved in start-ups were not exploited. Another issue the professors involved in start-ups sometimes faced that did not appear in other professors' relations with industry was (4) how to guarantee that the products and processes they worked on were safe and sound, given that they were not able to exercise much oversight or influence over the companies that developed their products and processes into consumable goods.

The legal line that determined whether the professor or the institution owned a discovery depended on time and use of facilities, as we saw in our discussion of state system and institutional patent policies. Universities sought a share of professors' profits, arguing that if faculty used university facilities in developing their ideas, then the ideas belonged to the university, while the professors who made the discoveries could claim only a (negotiable) percentage of the profits from university licensing and royalties. Given professors individualized use of expertise, universities sometimes encountered difficulty knowing what faculty discovered and what resources they had used.

Some professors in our sample still claimed that their intellectual work was independent of the university and they were therefore entitled to all the profits of the start-up. In making this claim, an associate professor of chemical engineering distinguished between spin-offs and start-ups. For him, a spin-off was derived from university work on federal grants while a start-up was independent. When he talked about his company, he said, "I make a real effort to keep them very distant . . . The start-up has nothing to do with my research and I have vigorously resisted having anything in my home lab . . . Now there are a variety of reasons. One of them is I'm protecting my own financial interests because if the university can claim that I used university resources to facilitate the start-up, then the university has a legitimate claim on the company . . . This would not be good. I would get crucified by my co-start-up people. But the other thing is I just don't want to create even the hint of guilt . . . I just want it to all be perfectly clear." This professor mediated multiple, conflicting claims to his knowledge: his own financial interests (personal), the interests of his co-start-up founders (private sector), and the interests of the university (public sector). He sought to evade punishment (getting "crucified" by the private corporation) by avoiding "even the hint of guilt." As if to atone for the independent start-up from which he was profiting, he said he was engaged in another one, a spin-off, from which the university too would profit.

Although this professor tried to avoid guilt, he found it difficult because crossing the boundaries between academe and industry created so many quandaries. The most obvious source of guilt was the issue of who benefits and who pays. As he noted, "We're sitting here in a building paid for by taxpayers and the stuff in my lab . . . a lot of it's federal money . . . the electricity, the lights, the ventilation and stuff are all taxpayer supplied. I draw my salary from tax bonds. And to go and say that I'm now going to start a company and it's going to be my company and it's not going to be yours . . . seems just not fair. I mean the university's intellectual property policies are reasonable . . . I can license it from them for some reasonable amount of money . . . and they can get a cut." Even though the professor seemed to be profiteering at public expense, the question of who benefited and who paid was not a black-and-white decision. As the professor noted, "The legislature probably likes [start-ups] a lot because you're creating jobs for the people of your state." There were pros and cons across the spectrum of issues. The start-up could become a "consuming interest" so that faculty "neglected their other tasks." Yet at the same time, "You can get a real sort of intellectual synergy [between the department and the corporation] because the company's poised to take what comes out of the academic fountain." Similarly, start-ups created intense competition—"there's a certain testosterone aspect," yet "it makes . . . uniformly stronger faculty." So, too, student projects could "be made too biased to the interests of the company," yet students who participated in start-ups were often "much more savvy about the job market and in the end they have jobs."

The question of ownership sometimes became far more complex than making decisions about whether the professor, the institution or the corporation owned intellectual property. In some cases, the state in effect acted as a venture capitalist, backing a professor's company. Rather than licensing the discovery to a private corporation, the state engaged in financing production and profit taking, acting, along with the professor, in an entrepreneurial capacity. In these cases there was no boundary between academe and industry.

An endocrinology professor who acted as a state-subsidized entrepreneur outlined some of the complexities of his situation. He was the head of a large bone-research group that worked on drugs for osteoporosis. In his words, "It [osteoporosis] became popular with the pharmaceutical companies because all of a sudden they realized there was an enormous market . . . they had a big-time disease out there affecting millions of people with no decent drugs . . . and the chances of enormous profits if they had a good drug . . . and so when I first starting working in research about twenty, twenty-five years ago, it was like really tiny, hardly anybody in it." His situation was transformed by corporations seeking profits in new areas. Rather than allow corporations to capture all the profits, the professor worked with his university to develop a plan from which the institution, the state, and the professor benefited.

> So, what the university has done is, we have decided on this specific area of research of direct discovery for osteoporosis . . . and they have allowed me to go out and hustle, form a separate company, and hustle companies from outside for money to support this. They get part of the equity and it's just like a sense of gift for them, and . . . I'm still a full-time faculty member . . . At this stage . . . I have a company which has gotten the right to actually license its products to any big major pharmaceutical company out there, but in addition, I'm responsible for this big operation at the school which is also dealing with other companies, but through the school. So, we have some patents which are handled through the school which involve usually pharmaceutical companies through the school, so that the school owns the patent and the school is actually doing the licensing. And, then we have this other operation where the school is like a minority shareholder. So, it's a little complicated.

This professor never touched on the many conflict of interest issues inherent in his situation. What would the professor and his institution do if the clinical trials suggested that there were health problems related to the drug? Neither university nor professor could claim to be disinterested parties to the trials, given their direct economic interest in the outcome. How did the professor decide which discoveries to channel through the basic discovery group, in which the university was a "minority shareholder," and which to route through the school, where the university owned the entire product and controlled the licensing? How did the professor avoid "disclosing" knowledge he gained in one project to participants in another, given that all the knowledge was contained in his mind, and very likely one discovery cross-fertilized others?

Start-up stories did not always avoid exploring the professional dilemmas professors encountered when they crossed boundaries between academe and industry. A chemistry professor described how he began working with a corporation as a consultant, became enmeshed in corporate decision making and the company's future, and found himself sliding toward unethical behavior. He was recruited as a consultant by a former undergraduate student because he worked on related (and federally funded) research. Because the company ran short of money, the professor took an equity position and funding for a postdoctoral fellow, who worked for the company, in lieu of consulting fees. He acknowledged the potential ethical problems in his course of action.

> That's why you have to file all sorts of financial disclosures and so forth because, of course, the university wants to make sure that you're not working your graduate students or post doctorates to death to put dollars in your pocket. And so in that case, and this was the first time I'd ever done this, it was a small company and they didn't

> have huge amounts of money and so the agreement was that they would pay me half my usual consulting fee with the other half being in stock options. And so, I mean, I didn't get a huge equity position in the company but it ended up, you know, being a smart financial move because when the company was sold, I was obliged to sell that stock but at a substantially higher price.

Although the professor understood the ethical issue of student and post doc exploitation, he nonetheless let the company fund the postdoc, perhaps because otherwise the company would have failed and he would have lost his consulting fees and stock options. He did not speak to whether the postdoc received an equity share in the company. The chemistry professor justified his corporate success by saying that there was "a new paradigm," noting that "times have changed . . . companies are . . . looking to invest money" in "university laboratories," as was the case with biotechnology.

Not all faculty were happy with their start-up experiences. An associate professor of biomaterials who held an equity position in a start-up discussed what he experienced as loss of control of his research. The loss of control came in two ways: first, he was shut out of the company with which he was working; second, he implied that he could not control the way the company presented his findings to the world, which confronted him with ethical quandaries.

He took an equity position with the company in trade for his technology. However, his equity position did not entitle him to a voice in corporate decision making, let alone a seat on the board. Within a year, he was pushed out of the company, although his technology stayed and he retained his equity position. "I've had a very bad experience [with the spin-off] . . . after we got the company up and going, we were asked to leave within a year . . . the technology [was taken] from us, it was basically my lab . . . [but] these products, or so-called products, don't really see the light of the day, especially in this area. By the time they see the light of the day they are so different and there are patents upon patents that any gain that you might get from royalties is almost nonexistent . . . And once the company starts, it's got a life of its own . . . the faculty members are not officers." He was concerned with having a voice in how his discovery was used and feared that it might be buried in the company's overall strategic deployment of patents (which would also, as he noted, diminish any royalties he might hope to receive). He also implied that corporations, perhaps even the corporation that held his technology, sometimes misrepresented what the technology could do, creating ethical dilemmas for academics.

> We see so many problems. I mean, the silicon problem, now we have polyethylene wear on the total joint. I just feel wrong in supporting something . . . that the indications [show] might be a problem. Even though it's my technology. But just because

> you have a technology doesn't mean it's working right now. It might need another five years working on it to fine tune it . . . I do believe . . . young start-up companies—not the big established ones, the big established ones don't have to worry about it too much—the young ones, in order to survive, do tread very close to that ethical line, if not cross it at times. Whereas sometimes not all the data is shown and it should be shown. You know, if you are testing one hundred animals and you put in a gray implant and three of them do well and the others don't do well. Then in the pictures you show . . . those three perfect ones as representative. Now that's kind of . . . You're not saying that all of them were like this but when you show those pictures, you imply that all your cases were like that . . . Now is that ethical? To me, it's not.

Start-ups dramatized the issues faced by professors involved with industry. Once, the boundaries between university and industry had been fairly clear. According to (mythical) custom and tradition, professors had been responsible for basic science and industry for applied, neatly separating science and commerce. Now, the professors were not only pressured and tempted by industry, but also the institution in which they worked, the university, had moved toward market values. As a full professor and head of a chemical engineering department said, "the wall [between academe and industry] was really high . . . We didn't want anybody in the world to say that . . . Joe Blow was using the state resources for gain . . . Then what happened was, about ten years ago, it shifted markedly to the sort of idea that something else could pay the toll booth . . . there was then a push and a great liberalization of what universities could do." Like industry, universities encouraged professors to capitalize their knowledge. Although universities and states had rules to guide professors' work with industry, the regulations were to some degree undercut by institutions' insistence on their rights to intellectual property and their share of profits. For the most part, professors dealt with the issues that emerged when they negotiated knowledge regimes on their own as individuals.

Generally, the professors seemed to accommodate industrial and institutional demands because they saw no other way of maintaining their core identity as teachers of graduate students and researchers. The new narratives about competitiveness, told outside universities, stressed the intrinsic value of money and the willingness of the neoliberal state to fund university-industry government ventures. These narratives made it easier for professors to elide academic and commercial values. (That professors often benefited economically from work with industry was perhaps not incidental to their accommodation.) Even when professors criticized industry and academic institutions (and they were usually more critical of academic institutions than of industry), they often recognized the utility of the new partnerships, whether these were making students more ready for the market, bringing new revenue streams to the institution or state, or building regional economies.

Our analysis of the interviews with professors engaged in technology transfer indicated they were moving away from a public good model toward an academic capitalism knowledge regime. Many still held to some values of the public good regime—for example, the importance of publishing and the corresponding value of the free flow of information—but they were willing to alter those values and sometimes delayed publication. The patent policies we discussed in chapter 3 opened up new possibilities for professors and created powerful market incentives. Professors responded by straddling both worlds, retaining a place in the university community but also assuming the role of (state-subsidized) entrepreneurs who were sometimes consultants, officials, or even presidents of their own companies.

Conclusion

The Bayh-Dole Act was passed early in the Reagan administration as part of the new federalism, which was aimed at privatizing, deregulating, and reregulating government to better serve the needs of commerce. The law was a signal to universities that academe and industry were no longer divided by a "fire wall." Some faculty, primarily in the sciences and engineering, and a cadre of administrators and professionals, like technology licensing officials, moved into the territory opened by the new regulatory climate. The biotechnology revolution, occurring at roughly the same time, spurred faculty and university interest in the market because so many discoveries had product potential. The states experiencing (periodic) fiscal crises began to support universities' technology transfer mission with their own funds, hoping to create economic miracles like Silicon Valley and Research Triangle that would increase the tax base. Corporations were very supportive because the new policies reversed three decades of federal ownership of research. Universities became conduits for cutting-edge commercial R&D, replacing industrial laboratories that in the past had focused on long-term development. Even when corporations had to pay for royalties and licenses to university intellectual property, these were less than the costs of corporate laboratories because university research was federally funded, faculty salaries were low relative to those in the corporate sector, and student labor was very inexpensive.

Theoretically, our analysis shows that values are attached to organizational forms as well as state and federal policies. These do not change the norms and values of a knowledge regime in and of themselves but rather frame opportunities for change. When groups of actors within universities form coalitions and networks in response to external opportunities, they can shift knowledge regimes. Universities are segmented, and some actors were always engaged in technology transfer, as evidenced by patent policies developed well before Bayh-Dole (1980). When the federal and state regulatory climate changed and corporations signaled interest in university intellectual property, this segment of the university—a loose coalition of faculty, administrators, and support professionals aligned with market actors—were already committed to an academic capitalist regime. After Bayh-Dole, more faculty, students, and administrators were drawn into these networks. The organizational changes that occurred in the national research apparatus over the past twenty years supported the academic capitalist regime and made sustenance of a public good regime more difficult.

Our analysis of state university system and institutional patent policies shows that rules and regulations have codified academic capitalist values and practices. Members of the university community are required to identify and disclose any inventions or discoveries with revenue-generating potential that could be patented or protected in a variety of ways. The managerial capacity of institutions to engage in academic capitalism has greatly increased. As faculty became state-subsidized entrepreneurs, administrators became venture capitalists who invested in faculty technology, participated in IPOs, and litigated to protect an increasing variety of intellectual property. Higher education institutions, arms of the state if public, and nonprofit entities, chartered by the state if private, were no longer separate from the market. They took on business functions, often run through foundations or other "arms-length" organizations that intermediated between (state) higher education institutions and the market. By the turn of the twenty-first century, increasingly broad segments of universities were involved with the market and had incorporated market functions within universities.

5

COPYRIGHT
Institutional Policies and Practices

IN THIS CHAPTER, WE explore the commodification of college and universities' core academic function—education. We pursue our analysis through the study of institutional policies and practices surrounding educational materials (e.g., lecture notes, syllabi), curricula (e.g., classes, programs), and products (e.g., course management software). These educational materials are new economy products. They are increasingly being copyrighted by colleges and universities and marketed in ways that foreground their commercial rather than educational potential. This commodification of education offers important continuities with and contrasts to the commodification of research that we tracked in chapter 3.

Institutional claims to faculty's copyrighted materials are different from institutional claims to patents. Historically, many faculty published and held copyright to scholarly and artistic materials, including instructional materials, which they created in the course of their employment at colleges and universities. In contrast, relatively few faculty patented, and by the 1950s, case law in federal courts was clear that universities, not faculty, owned discoveries professors made in the course of their employment (Chew 1992). Although recent scholarly attention to commercialization has focused primarily on patents, faculty who copyright have always engaged in commercial endeavor. They contracted with a variety of commercial publishing houses to produce and distribute their works. However, the stakes in scholarly publishing, with the exception of textbooks, were relatively small, and institutions were not interested in them. As our analysis of copyright policies demonstrates, this seems to be changing as increased use of information technology mediates instruction. Institutions are aggressively advancing claims to shares of faculty intellectual property in copyright, beginning with technology-mediated products. This is a sharp break with the past and potentially affects all faculty, regardless of field or institutional type.

Very often scholars and policy makers who address copyrighted educational materials concentrate on distance education. Although an important activity, it is located closer to the margins than to the center of higher education. Our analysis looks at distance education but also focuses on ways in which conventional, on-campus instruction is being mediated by technology. For example, a blackboard was once simply a classroom artifact on which professors wrote concepts and ideas, then erased them at the end of class. Now BlackBoard is a corporation that sells to colleges and universities platforms on which curricula are mounted and by which education is structured. It is one of several private companies with which hundreds of institutions contract to utilize a portal system for managing (and structuring) courses and integrating learning. Such a technological transformation, from slate and chalk to software, has profound implications for who owns the concepts and materials that a professor introduces in class. Usually, the greater professors' use of institutions' technological resources, the greater the claims colleges and universities are able to make on professors' copyrightable educational materials.

Generally, we argue that universities and colleges (and in some cases, students) have initiated aggressive pursuit of external revenues based on instruction and curriculum. State system and institutional copyright policies were very often introduced after patent policies but are substantively different from them, following their own legal and product trajectories. We develop the theme that knowledge in the public domain is increasingly being treated as raw material that can be transformed into products sold for (potential) private profit or generate external revenues for colleges and universities. Before examining state system and institutional copyright polices, we offer a story about faculty, universities, and students that captures key developments about copyright in the academic capitalist knowledge/learning regime.

The Story of Class Notes

Who owns the copyright to notes taken in a professor's class? Have the positions and claims of professors, universities, and private companies to the copyright of class notes changed over time? As professors have been encouraged by universities to put their syllabi, class notes, and other class materials on institutional websites, and as the on-line availability of class notes has escalated, a number of claimants to ownership of these intellectual products have emerged. Two court cases, the first in the late 1960s, the second in the mid-1990s, reveal a dramatic change in such claims and in the principles underlying them. In *Williams v. Weisser* (1969), the University of California, Los Angeles (UCLA) supported faculty members' claims to copyright of class notes in the name of academic freedom, but in *University of Florida v. KPB* (1996) the university claimed proprietary rights (Xie and Zhou 2003).

In *Williams v. Weisser*, a UCLA anthropology professor sued under California's common law of copyright, seeking an injunction against the owner of a private company (Class Notes) that had been selling his and other professors' lecture notes to UCLA students. Williams claimed the company was "infringing on the copyright of his lectures" (*Williams v. Weisser* 1969). Weisser, speaking for Class Notes, claimed the professor did not own the notes because the university "owned the copyright to his lectures under the work for hire doctrine," and, if the notes were the university's, they belonged in the public domain where they were available for use by private companies (Borow 1998, 55n). Yet the university had not claimed ownership and did not have a copyright policy until 1975 (Lape 1992). Moreover, UCLA administrators had encouraged professors to protect their copyrights: a letter from the vice-chancellor stated, "It is emphasized that the common law copyright in a lecture is the property of the lecturer rather than of the University, and therefore any legal actions for the infringement of such right must be brought in the name of the aggrieved faculty member" (*Williams v. Weisser* 1969, n. 1). In the appellate case, the counsel for the University of California filed an amicus curiae brief in support of the trial court's ruling that Professor Williams owned the copyright to his lecture notes. The university took a position consistent with that of the American Association of University Professors (AAUP), which holds that professors' lectures are their property. The California Court of Appeals upheld the lower court ruling and "found that the student's professor, and not the university the student attended, owned the common law copyright to the professor's lectures" (Simon 1982–3, 28n). The reasoning of the court was grounded partly in the university's explicit support of faculty ownership, partly in the view that the university lacked a motive for owning copyright to such materials, and partly in that such an arrangement would have unspecified "undesirable consequences" (Borow 1998, p. 154).

By contrast, in the KPB case in the 1990s, the University of Florida initiated legal action against a class notes company. As in the UCLA case, the firm (in this instance, KPB) paid students enrolled in classes to take notes, which the company repackaged and sold to other students. Professors are absent in the case, as are any professorial claims to copyright. Instead, the University of Florida claimed copyright infringement and sued KPB under the unfair competition provision of the Lanham Act, which covers interstate commerce. Florida argued that KPB was using trade practices that infringed on the university's trademark by using university course numbers in its commercial guides, and it took the position that the Lanham Act applied because the university had many out-of-state students. In other words, the university, which was in the process of developing its own note-taking company, was advancing arguments as if it were a business whose trade was being compromised. Neither the U.S. District Court nor the U.S. Court of Appeals accepted these arguments. The district court was blunt in its ruling, in a sense reprimanding the University of Florida: "Well, there is no confusion here. There is no false advertising, there is nothing. You ought to try this thing on what the main theme is, and that is, is there a copyright here and did the defendant violate the copyright? All of this other junk—and it is junk—shouldn't even be here" (*University of Florida v. KPB Inc.* 1996, n. 8).

Although Florida did not win, the case nonetheless suggests that in the 1990s institutions of higher learning took a very different stance toward copyright than they did in the late 1960s. Given the court's ruling, one might read the moral of the story to be that universities should not pursue academic capitalism as if they were businesses. However, the court essentially invited Florida to try the case under copyright law. Had Florida followed that course, the case might have had a very different outcome.

We are not suggesting that the University of Florida's stance has become the norm. For example, in response to controversy surrounding an on-line notes company, Kansas State University put a statement on its website indicating that, "Any close reproduction of a faculty member's lecture, such as is constituted by good class notes, is a use of property which, at the very least, belongs to the faculty member, who because of copyright laws may distribute, produce and prepare derivative works from lectures" (Kistner 2000). UCLA, like some other universities, has adopted a policy against unauthorized notes companies. And many universities fought against the meteoric rise of on-line notes services such as Versity.com, Study24–7.com, CollegeClub.com, StudentU.com, and AllStudents.com, which popped up in the late 1990s (and which almost as quickly as a pop-up ad, disappeared from view).

However, UCLA, University of California (UC), Berkeley, and many other institutions have identified particular companies as "authorized" note dealers that are affiliated with the institutions. Berkeley has authorized a university-run notes service, Black Lightning. The manager of that service states that, "We're not here to make money; we just want to make sure we provide the best notes and we don't lose the university any money" (Holbrook 1999). Nevertheless, the notes service and company, like other university auxiliary units, are designed to run at a profit. They are quite literally in business and in direct competition with private businesses. After the UC regents filed a lawsuit against one such note-taking service, Research & Report Corporation (R&R), that same manager of Black Lightning noted that "Black Lightning used to lose business to R&R and other firms that operated at UC-Berkeley, but the regents' lawsuit has apparently scared them all away" (Holbrook 2000). Like the two class-notes cases, this case offers an example of change in behavior with regard to copyright and educational products in some higher education institutions. In recent years, we see not-for-profit universities aggressively pursuing revenue from educational materials in ways that fundamentally alter their relations to faculty, students, and to the external marketplace.

The rise of class-notes businesses also points to a shift in the position of students in an academic capitalist knowledge/learning regime. When students sell their notes to corporations, they are both producers of educational materials and consumers of education. Some universities allow students to act as producers of marketable notes, particularly when the university runs the note-taking service, as is the case with the University of California at Berkeley's Black Lightning service. However, at the University of Nebraska (2000), the university made it a student code of conduct violation for students to sell their lecture notes to on-line services. One university regent was quoted as saying, "The basic feeling is that intellectual property belongs to the university and to professors; it does not belong to students, and students should not sell it for money" (Daehn 2000). At issue is whether students can sell what they learn from their professors as they learn it or whether the professors or their institutions should be able to sell the notes. In either case, the idea of the student as apprentice imbibing learning to which a price has not been attached seems lost.

State System and Institutional Copyright Policies

In detailing the commodification of copyrightable educational products, we draw on various data sources. The principal sources are the intellectual property policies of colleges and universities. As with the patent policies analyzed in chapter 3, we examine the copyright policies of three institutions in each of six states: California, Florida, Missouri, New York, Texas, and Utah. We also draw on secondary materials to amplify our analyses of the six states, particularly the work of Lape (1992) and Packard (2002) on copyright.

Our analysis of the data is partly framed by the literature that informed our analysis of patent policies. To what extent is there a shift from a regime that foregrounds the public good to one that foregrounds the commercial utility of knowledge, a shift from Mertonian norms to academic capitalism? Again, as in chapter 3, we are also interested in the organizational dimensions of that shift. To what extent are connections between universities, the state, and the private marketplace being redefined such that hybrid structures emerge that combine the values, activities, and missions of these formerly separate domains?

Our exploration of copyright policies and the commodification of copyrightable educational works and courses is also framed by work that speaks to the changing relationship between professionals and managers, and to the emergence of new forms of professional work in the academy (Rhoades 1998a; Rhoades and Slaughter 1997; Rhoades and Sporn 2002).[1] Whereas Jencks and Riesman (1968) spoke of an "academic revolution," with faculty power in the academy becoming ascendant in the post–World War II era, Rhoades has argued that more recently a managerial revolution (Keller 1983) has reversed the role and fortunes of faculty, making them a more managed and stratified workforce. Such a change is evidenced in reduced professional autonomy and influence, and increased managerial control over various domains of professional work, including that of intellectual property. That shift is partly a function of new approaches in difficult financial times, in which central academic managers strategically restructure universities. That shift may also be a function of higher education's move to the market, which was accompanied by a more corporate model in which university presidents became CEOs. Rhoades's work raises the possibility that the two phenomena may be linked by market activity—to some degree, the increase in academic capitalism promotes the growth of managerial professionals. Thus, we look to the copyright policies for evidence of whether and to what extent there has been a shift in the balance of power between faculty and administrators, and whether this varies by institutional type.

The new organizational structures we identified in chapter 3 involve the interstitial emergence of new professions and new forms of professional work in the academy around the activities of patenting and technology transfer. In examining copyright policies we look for the similar patterns of expanded managerial capacity to engage markets—in this case, markets for educational materials. Although most scholarship on management and restructuring in higher education focuses on faculty and central administrators, we draw on work that studies the emergence of "managerial professionals" (Rhoades 1998a, 1998b;

1. Much research on the academic profession has emerged in recent decades. Most of that work concentrates on the profession itself. For example, Bowen and Schuster (1986) wrote of an "imperiled" academic profession, and Burton Clark (1987) provided an analysis of an academic profession stratified by discipline and institutional type between "different worlds." A decade later, Finkelstein, Seal, and Schuster (1998) analyzed the changing demographics of "a new academic generation," involving a decline of full-time faculty positions and careers in the newest cohort of faculty hires. However, in these and most other studies of faculty, there was little systematic consideration of the changing relationship between faculty and administration.

Rhoades and Sporn 2002). Such personnel are managerial in terms of their work lives (eleven-month contracts, nine to five in the office), hiring and supervision, and connection to the direction(s) of (central) academic administrators. Yet they are professional in terms of having various attributes typical of professions: they receive specialized education, possess technical bodies of knowledge, belong to professional associations, attend conferences, publish in journals, and adhere to particular codes of ethics. As a category, these support professionals (as they are designated in national data bases) constitute *the* growth area of professional employees in higher education. (The proportion of administrators has increased slightly; that of full-time faculty has declined.) We are interested in whether there is evidence of such professions emerging due to the development and marketing of copyrightable educational materials and courses and the expanding managerial capacity of colleges and universities.

The research questions we ask are: Is there evidence of a shift in knowledge/learning regimes from public good to academic capitalism? Is there evidence of a shift in the balance of professional autonomy and managerial control that suggests that faculty are increasingly managed professionals, and does this pattern vary by institutional sector? Is there evidence of changing organizational structures that suggest the emergence of new managerial professionals involved in producing copyrightable materials and courses? Is there evidence that they expand the managerial capacity of institutions?

Recency of Commodification of Education

Some scholars have argued that the commodification of education in colleges and universities represents a second wave of market activity following the earlier development of the commercialization of research (Noble 2001). According to this view, colleges and universities began to claim ownership of educational materials *after* the 1980 Bayh-Dole Act, which enabled universities to own the patents generated from federally supported research and encouraged institutions to begin actively pursuing patents and technology transfer. Investigation of copyright policies suggests that this sequencing of events is not accurate. Before 1980, many universities had developed intellectual property policies that advanced some institutional claim on the ownership of copyrighted works created by faculty. As early as 1967, a number of universities had developed such policies, including Case Western Reserve, Cornell, Harvard, MIT, Michigan State, New York University, and the Universities of California, Kentucky, and Miami (Lape 1992). In a sample of the copyright policies of sixty-nine leading research universities, Lape (1992) found that fifteen established such policies by the latter 1970s.

Nevertheless, the widespread commodification of education is more a phenomenon of the late 1980s and 1990s, occurring subsequent to the commercialization of research through patents. Peterson's 1985 study, using a larger sample of universities than Lape, found that most had patent policies but did not have copyright policies. Most of the universities in Lape's sample adopted policies in the latter 1980s. As Lape notes, "none of the policies collected in this study fails to claim at least some faculty works, which suggests that the purpose of adoption was not to maintain the . . . status quo, but rather to claim ownership of certain works for the university" (1992, p. 253).[2]

Colleges and universities' efforts to claim copyrightable products created by faculty continued to expand in the 1990s. A follow-up of Lape's sample revealed that all but one of the sixty-nine universities had adopted a policy by 2001 (Packard 2002). Moreover, Packard's analysis found increased clarification of copyright ownership in ways that expanded and specified university claims to particular kinds of copyrighted materials. In 1991, twenty-five policies made explicit claims to materials produced by faculty specifically as work for hire; in 2001, thirty-seven institutions made such claims. Only six policies in 1991 made claims on works developed by faculty "within the scope of employment," language drawn from the 1976 Copyright Act, which defined any such work as a work for hire, whereas, by 2001, eighteen policies included such a statement.

The general trend is toward increased institutional claims on the copyrightable products of faculty work. The basis of many institutions' claim to ownership of faculty members' intellectual products is that their employees utilize university resources in creating the property. Over time, language about use of resources is increasingly present in the policies. In 1991, forty-two universities had policies utilizing use or substantial use language. Sixteen "narrowed the scope of works claimed under this standard by excluding . . . commonly used resources such as libraries, offices, . . . classrooms, laboratories, and secretaries," whereas twenty did so in 2001 (Packard 2002, p. 297). In 2001, fifty-seven had

2. Lape's reference to the effects of the 1976 Copyright Act is important in that this is a subject of debate among legal scholars. Some, like Lape, believe that the law did not change the so-called teacher exception to the "work for hire" doctrine, an exception that a leading legal scholar on copyright (Nimmer 1985) has argued was clearly established in the 1909 law, which first codified the work-for-hire doctrine. Others have argued that the 1976 law represented a significant change, effectively eliminating the teacher exception and strengthening the claim of employers that employees' works created "within the scope of employment" fall within the category of "work for hire" and are therefore owned by the employer (DuBoff 1985; Simon 1983). Whatever one's interpretation of the 1976 Copyright Act, university policies are an effort by universities to formally and explicitly lay claim to at least some copyrightable products created by faculty, which represents an important departure from their past practice.

policies utilizing use or substantial use language; thirty-five of those required significant or substantial use for university ownership. Although Lape and Packard's studies focused on research universities, a similar pattern can be found in other settings. Rhoades's (1998a) analysis of a national sample of collective bargaining agreements found that 75 percent of the contracts with intellectual property provisions had language related to the use of institutional resources.

Aggressive and Expansive Institutional Claims

To explore the aggressiveness and expansiveness of institutional claims on employees' copyrightable products, we turn to the copyright policies of the same eighteen institutions analyzed for patent policies in chapter 3.[3] In some cases (e.g., University of Florida), patent and copyright are dealt with in the same intellectual property policy. In other cases (e.g., University of California), copyright is dealt with in a separate policy.

Our coding categories were similar to those utilized in analyzing patent policies. We coded for expansiveness with which copyrightable works were defined, personnel covered by the policies, shares of royalties—if any—allocated to creators, expanded managerial capacity related to copyright, and mentions of the public good. In all categories we were concerned with changes over time. Changes within the categories speak to whether institutions are becoming more aggressive in their claims and whether considerations of the public good feature at all.

Two new categories were added. First, we coded for the types of property that were covered. We wanted to understand how broadly copyrightable works were being defined. Second, we searched for particular language related to exceptions in ownership. We were particularly interested in "work for hire," "within the scope of employment," and "substantial use of institutional resources." These phrases assert that institutions of higher education are able to treat faculty in the same way that corporations treat the professionals they employ: all intellectual and creative work belongs to the employer.

Type of Property

The copyright policies of the eighteen institutions reveal the broad sweep of intellectual products that were covered. Although there was considerable variation by institution and state in the timing of policy development, institutions

3. We are interested in policies related to copyrightable materials produced by institutional employees, not regulations concerning the use of copyrightable materials. The use of copyrighted materials by educational institutions is usually treated under concepts of "fair use," and while fair use has important implications for academic capitalism, considerations of length keep us from treating it.

covered quite a wide range of copyrightable products early on. For example, the 1984 policy of the University of Missouri–Columbia identified the following educational materials: video recordings, study guides, tests, syllabi, bibliographies, texts, films, film strips, charts, transparencies, other visual aids, programmed instructional materials, live video and audio broadcasts, and computer software including program, program description, and documentation-integrated circuit and data bases. In other words, the University of Missouri claimed educational materials, not creative and scholarly works. The policy did "not affect the traditionally accepted practice that faculty members have personal ownership of books, workbooks, study guides and similar materials which were not directly commissioned by the University and the preparation of which were not supported by any substantial University resources" (University of Missouri–Columbia 1984). By contrast, the University of Miami's copyright policy as early as 1976 included books, manuscripts, television or motion picture scripts or films, educational material, or other copyrightable work, claiming a share of faculty's creative and scholarly work. The City University of New York (CUNY) 1986 policy included writings, audiovisual films, slides, tapes, artistic works, instructional aids, computer programs, and all other copyrightable works.

Over time, there is no case in which the intellectual products covered in the policies become less restrictive. Instead, the most comprehensive coverage is found in the most recent policies, providing evidence of institutions' increasingly expansive claims to copyrightable works. As information technology advanced and was integrated with instruction, many institutions understood that policies regulating such technology would determine ownership of copyright. For example, the University of Florida's 1988 policy refers to instructional technology: "The State University System of Florida recognizes the increasing use of new technology, such as videotapes and computer software, to support teaching and learning and to enhance the fundamental relationship between employee and student. In order that this technology be used to the maximum mutual benefit of the university and the employee, the State University System shall develop written [copyright] policies, subject to consultation with the UFF [the United Faculty of Florida, the faculty union], that provide for such use" (State University System of Florida 1988).

Personnel Coverage

As with patent policies, the categories of coverage in copyright policies also expanded over time. At present, both sorts of policies cover not only faculty (sometimes part-time faculty and employees are specified, as in the University of Florida policy) but also a wide range of other categories of people: employees generally as well as students, graduate students, postdoctoral fellows, and nonemployees who participate in research projects. Employees can be a very broad category, as in the policy of San Diego State University, which defines employee as including "full-time and part-time faculty, classified staff, student employees, appointed personnel, graduate assistants and teaching associates, persons with 'no salary' appointments, and shall also include visiting faculty and academic professionals who develop intellectual property using University or auxiliary resources and facilities unless there is an agreement providing otherwise" (1999). There are exceptions to this pattern of expanded coverage. For example, the copyright and computer software policy of New York University (NYU) covers only faculty.

There are also cases in which policies are extraordinarily expansive in regard to students. For example, Brigham Young University's (BYU) policy extends beyond student employees.

> Students using substantial university resources or those employed by the university will be treated in the same manner as similarly situated university personnel. However, any student not employed by the university but engaging in research or development of intellectual property under the supervision and direction of a faculty member in connection with a program or activity subject to this policy shall have no ownership interest in the resulting property but may be eligible to participate in the income distribution. Faculty using such volunteer, non-employed students in their scholarly work projects should have the students sign a "Student Assignment of Ownership and Nondisclosure Agreement" form, available from the Intellectual Property Office. (2002)

In this policy students are essentially employees when faculty supervise them. Yet in the same state, the University of Utah's policy holds that "students are the Owners of the copyright of Works for which academic credit is received, including theses, dissertations, scholarly publications, texts, pedagogical materials or other materials" (2001).

As the cases of NYU and BYU suggest, we found no particular pattern by institutional type in policy coverage. Private universities were at both ends of the spectrum as were public colleges and universities. The only pattern that really stands out is that in all types of institutions copyright policies are expansive, covering not only faculty members but also many other institutional employees as well as students.

Extended Institutional Claims to Ownership

Historically, faculty have had the sole claim within their institutions to the copyrightable educational products of their labor, principally in the form of books and articles. When faculty publish they generally sign these copyrights over to publishing houses in exchange for royalties. Given this history, grounded in practice and in copyright common law in the courts, institutions generally have advanced a claim to faculty's copyrightable intellectual products only under certain conditions. Two of these conditions are embedded in language stemming from copyright legislation, such as the 1976 Copyright Act. One is the phrase "work for hire," which means the institution hired the employee specifically to produce certain copyrightable materials, as when a publisher hires a textbook writer. In using such language, universities are essentially saying that faculty are no different than corporate employees. This language reverses universities' traditional position with regard to faculty's copyrightable intellectual property and enables colleges and universities to claim the material created by faculty. Another often-used phrase is "within the scope of employment," which means that professionals are employed to produce copyrightable works along with performing other duties. Generally, this language is similar to that which corporations use to claim the copyrightable work of their full-time employees. A third phrase is "use of institutional resources" or "substantial use of institutional resources." As with patents, universities and colleges made the case that faculty use of institutional resources entitled institutional claims to intellectual property. Ironically, the institutional resources used by copyrighting faculty were often information technologies that patenting faculty may have developed and that the institution owned.

In their study of research universities, Lape (1992) and Packard (2002) noted that an increased number of policies have "work for hire" and "within the scope of employment" language, giving institutions a broader claim to property. Here we illustrate the ways in which some universities in our sample have utilized that language. Consider the University of Utah. In 1970, institutional policy held that faculty owned almost all of their copyrighted material, with one important exception. "Notwithstanding any other university policy provision, unless other arrangements are made in writing, all rights to copyrightable material (except material which is placed on video tape using university facilities, supplies and/or equipment) and all financial and other benefits accruing by reason of said copyrightable material shall be reserved to the author, even though employed by the university." The university only claimed rights to ownership when there was a specific contract between the university and a third party, or when the author was specifically hired to do the work. (In the case of videotapes, the university also claimed ownership when its facilities, supplies, and/or equipment had been used, a point we subsequently explore in discussing "substantial use" language.) In the 2001 revised policy, all faculty intellectual work is declared work for hire: "Works created by University staff and student employees within the scope of their University employment are considered to be works made for hire, and thus are Works as to which the University is the Owner and controls all legal rights in the work." The university agrees to transfer rights to faculty in some cases, such as in the case of "traditional scholarly work," but it claims ownership if materials are produced with the "substantial use" of university resources (2001).

The introduction of work for hire and within the scope of employment language is important in relation not only to faculty but also to other employees. As greater numbers of managerial professionals are employed within colleges and universities, and as they become more involved in "production" activities such as the development of copyrightable educational products, institutions expand their policies to cover more personnel and they define these personnel's intellectual products as works for hire. For example, the University of Missouri–Columbia's policy indicates that "Educational materials are University-sponsored if . . . the production of the materials is a specific responsibility of the position for which the employee is hired" (2002). The intellectual products of any managerial professional hired to develop educational materials are within the scope of their employment and become the property of the employing institution. The policy of the University of North Texas is even more explicit: "Electronically published course materials created jointly by faculty authors and others, whose contributions would be works for hire, will be jointly owned by the faculty author and the University" (2000). In short, managerial professionals have no property rights, and by virtue of their involvement in the educational production process, the university enhances its ownership claims.

In contrast, faculty work for hire is generally defined fairly narrowly. For example, at the University of Miami it refers only to "a project assigned to members of the faculty" which will be owned by the institution "only if so specified at the time of assignment by an instrument of specific detail and agreement." Similarly, in the State University of New York (SUNY) policy, "[faculty] Work for Hire shall mean work done . . . under campus consulting, extra service or technical assistance arrangements either through contract, consultancy or purchase order, but not within the Scope of Employment" (1998).

More significant by way of establishing institutional claims to ownership of copyrightable material created by faculty is language about the use of institutional resources. Most policies in the eighteen institutions we studied had such language. Generally, policies that favored faculty and other employees were found in less prestigious institutions and policies more favorable to institutional claims were found in the more prestigious public and/or private universities. Institutions in four states (Missouri, New York, Texas, and California) in our six-state sample follow such a pattern.

In Missouri, the policy most favorable to faculty ownership of copyrightable materials was that of Southeast Missouri State (1983). Its policy referred to "University support or sponsorship," but such support only required institutional cost recovery; copyright ownership remained in the hands of creators, including all employees and students. By contrast, the University of Missouri–Columbia indicates that "use of substantial University resources" necessitates a written agreement about ownership, and in the absence of such an agreement "the University may, in its discretion, claim copyright ownership and/or a share of royalties" (2002). Similarly, in the Washington University policy, "significant use of University resources" is a basis for the institution owning the copyright (1998a).

In New York, CUNY's policy is the most favorable to faculty ownership of copyrightable works. Its policy accords ownership to the author, with the university receiving a share of the revenues "where the University has made significant contributions of resources" (1985). By contrast, the SUNY policy establishes the university's claim to copyrightable works under many conditions, including when the work was "developed through the use of facilities, funds, or personnel of the University of the Research Foundation." NYU has two policies, one for copyrights (which applies to lecture notes, manuscripts, and other writings), and one for computer software copyright. Although the copyright policy awards ownership to faculty members, the computer software policy advances university claims to ownership in several conditions, including "when there has been substantial use of University resources earmarked specifically for computer software development" and "when the computer software has been developed with the substantial assistance of other University personnel, including, for example, supported graduate or undergraduate students" (1988).

The University of North Texas's policy highly favors faculty. It holds that "in all cases except work made for hire, the faculty member retains the ownership and copyright of the work as well as the ability to market the work commercially" (2000). The policy then goes on to clarify, "Faculty members thus normally hold copyright in electronically published materials they create on their own initiative." The policy provides scenarios that flesh out categories that affect ownership, including when the university provides a grant to purchase certain equipment, pays the faculty member in the summer to develop the product, and "funds production time in the Center for Media Production." The faculty member owns the property and can market it outside the institution, although the university retains a "non-exclusive commercial license to market the course outside the University." The policy of the University of Texas at Austin is also quite favorable to faculty, asserting no ownership claims to copyrightable works even when there has been substantial use of university resources, although when substantial use occurs, the institution has claims in regard to royalties and rights to nonprofit educational use. Rice's intellectual property policy also gives faculty ownership of copyrightable materials, but its computer software policy indicates that "rights to software developed by a University researcher shall vest in the University, when there was any support of the developer's efforts through the use of University funds, facilities, personnel, or other resources" (1999). Rice's policy indicates that for copyrightable educational courseware the copyright policy applies, giving ownership to faculty; however, it also states that this policy is under review for "revision and modernization," suggesting that the institution may seek to extend its ownership claims.

The policy of San Diego State University (1999) grants considerable ownership claims to faculty. In cases of "partial institutional support," faculty retain all or partial ownership. Similarly, the policy of the University of California (2002b) gives ownership to faculty; even when materials are "created with the use of Exceptional University Resources," they belong jointly to the creator and the university. However, Stanford's policy asserts institutional ownership of copyrightable materials that are created with "significant use of services of University non-faculty employees or University resources." It also states that "courses taught and software developed for teaching at Stanford belong to Stanford. Any courses which are videotaped or recorded using any other media are Stanford property" (1998).

The limited pattern of more aggressive institutional claims being found in more elite versus less prestigious institutions is consistent with Rhoades's (1998a) study of collective bargaining agreements. Among unionized institutions, Rhoades found that provisions according faculty ownership of intellectual property were more likely in two-year rather than four-year institutions. Although our sample is too small to be conclusive, pursuing the differences in copyright policies by type may repay investigation. One of the many questions to answer is whether copyright income varies by institutional type and whether less income makes institutional policies more generous to faculty, other employees, and students.[4]

However, this pattern does not hold for all the states we studied. The University of South Florida's policy (1997) makes extensive claims for the institution's ownership of copyrightable works. Although the university does "not assert

4. Currently there is no data source that tracks income from copyright for institutions.

rights to books, articles, and similar works," the policy states that, "an invention or work made in the course of University-supported effort is the property of the University." By contrast, the University of Miami asserts ownership to copyright only in those cases where the product is a work for hire. And in Utah, extensive institutional ownership claims are evident in the policies of all three institutions we studied, though most so in the case of BYU. Utah State's policy (2002) reads that if "significant university resources" are used in creating the work, then the university can negotiate an ownership claim. The University of Utah's policy (2001), which defines all works as works for hire, "preserves the practice of *allowing* faculty to own the copyrights to traditional scholarly works, and at the same time seeks to protect the interests of the university in works that are created with the substantial use of university resources" (emphasis added). The policy defines "substantial use" and "significant University funding" as follows: faculty can use the library, office equipment, computers, and support staff, but they cannot use special computing services and production facilities without ceding ownership of the material. BYU's policy (2002) even more narrowly defines substantial use of resources, including "secretarial help" and software or office supplies "purchased specifically for a creative work," and it stipulates that "use of photocopying equipment, long distance telephone costs, postage, faxes, etc., specifically for a creative work may not exceed incidental use." In other words, a few universities are defining "substantial use" to be almost anything associated with the job.

Over time, then, institutions have significantly extended claims to ownership of faculty-, employee-, and student-created copyrightable works. That is evident in the use of language such as "work for hire" and "within the scope of employment." It is also evident in wording regarding substantial use of university resources; such language is found in most policies, and its conditions apply to most situations in which copyrightable materials with commercial potential would be created.

Royalty Shares

Royalties on copyrighted materials accorded to faculty are generous. Again, however, there are considerable variations in the size of the shares and in the ways that they are calculated, with less prestigious institutions' policies offering more favorable shares in four of the six states. At CUNY shares are calculated, as in most policies, as net royalties, the monies generated over and above the costs of production: the shares are 75 percent for faculty when works are created through "university assisted individual effort" and 25 percent for works created through "university supported effort." By contrast, at SUNY faculty receive 40 percent of gross royalties if work was created "through the use of University resources." In Missouri, the shares are 55 percent of net revenue at Southeast Missouri State, 50 percent at University of Missouri–Columbia, and 45 percent of net income at Washington University. The creator's share is 50 percent at the University of North Texas and the University of Texas–Austin; Rice's policy accords only 37.5 percent to the developer. In California, the creator's share is 50 percent at San Diego State University and 33 percent at Stanford.

Some policies are quite complicated, providing shares for parties other than the faculty member and the institution, and linking different shares at different levels of net income. Royalty shares may be allocated to the university's entrepreneurial unit (27.5% to the Creative Works Office at BYU), graduate education (18.5% at Rice University), the creator's college (27.5% at BYU), department (one-third at the University of Miami), or research program. The University of Utah's policy provides differentiated shares depending on the amount of revenue in question: the creator's share is 40 percent of the first $20,000, 35 percent of the next $20,000, and 30 percent of any net revenues beyond that. BYU's policy has a clause stating that "when total income, before distribution, exceeds one million dollars from any single intellectual property in any fiscal year, an administrative review of this source of income will be activated. The academic vice-president and the administrative vice-president shall have discretion to evaluate the allocation of the funds in excess of this threshold to the college and to Intellectual Property Services" (2002). In short, the institution takes a greater share as the amounts become larger and seeks to capitalize on any major profits generated by copyrightable works.

In contrast to patents or other copyright provisions, there is no general policy pattern over time in regard to the distribution of royalties. For example, University of Florida faculty shares decreased over time, whereas the policies of Utah State increased shares to faculty. In sum, there is variation among institutions on copyright royalties, and less prestigious public universities tend to allocate more to faculty than do elite public and private ones. Still, faculty shares at all institutions are generous. However, none of the institutions give royalty shares to the growing numbers of nonfaculty employees involved in creating educational materials.

Public Good

Amid this pursuit of academic capitalism, to what extent does any mention of the public good appear, and how is that public good defined? In answering this question we should keep in mind the historic academic tradition with regard to certain categories of copyrightable materials (books, articles, and creative works) which were commercialized by faculty who received royalties from private publishing companies that produced and sold their books. What is at issue in institutional policies is whether that tradition will be continued, to what extent institutions are asserting claims to other sorts of educational materials, and the way in which these new claims intersect with some conception of the public good.

In copyright policies the public good is mentioned more than it is defined. Typical cursory statements are: "The following policy is intended to foster the traditional mission of a University to encourage the creation, preservation, and dissemination of knowledge" (University of Missouri–Columbia 2002); and "The University is entrusted with the responsibility of administering its own intellectual property in the best interests of the public" (Utah State University 2002). Of what that public interest consists, or the mechanisms through which it will be protected, are not elaborated. All that can be determined from most policies is that the public interest is served by the creation and widespread dissemination of intellectual products.

Although the policies of BYU, Stanford, and the University of Miami make no real mention of public interest, those of three other private universities do. These policies clarify a pattern evident in most—they express values of the competing knowledge regimes of public good and academic capitalism. Washington University's policy has a phrase about advancing the public good, but it also has language encouraging academic capitalism: "In other cases, to serve the common good, it will be necessary to secure protection of University intellectual property to encourage commerce and industry to invest their resources to develop and distribute products and processes for public use" (1998a). Similarly, the University of Florida's policy simultaneously invokes a public good conception—"The University of Florida believes that a university has an obligation to serve the public interest by insuring that such intellectual property is appropriately developed"—and one of academic capitalism: "Adequate recognition of and incentive to potential investors through the sharing of the financial benefits resulting from the transfer and development of patentable inventions and other marketable forms of intellectual property encourages the creation of such intellectual property. At the same time, the University's share in the financial benefits provides funds for further research at the University" (1993a). The university's interest is conflated with the public interest.

However, a few policies make clear that there are significant public interest considerations at stake. NYU's computer software policy lists several public interest considerations, from conflict of interest to the institution's own commercial interests. "From time to time there arise cases where ownership by faculty members of copyright in computer software may not be consistent with certain of the University's basic commitments, such as protecting academic freedom through promoting the publication and distribution of research and scholarship, protecting the respective interests of participants in large, long term projects, protecting against undue commercial influences on academic priorities, ensuring proper use of the University's resources, and protecting the University's legitimate commercial interests" (1988). Such phrasing points to the potential of commodification to compromise academic values. Similar concerns are evident in Rice's policy, which includes as objectives of its patent and software policy: "To create an environment that encourages and expedites the dissemination of the discoveries, creations, and new knowledge generated by the faculty and other members of the campus community for the 'greatest public benefit' . . . To encourage research and scholarship without regard to potential gains from royalties or other such income" (1999).

What we see in the recent commodification of educational materials is a shift in the stance of colleges and universities. In earlier times, the principal function of colleges and universities lay elsewhere. As Southeast Missouri State's patent and copyright policy, alone among the eighteen universities we studied, indicates, "it should be recognized that the objectives of the University do not encompass the invention or development of a product or process for commercial use. Patentable inventions, processes, etc., will instead be a by-product of the usual intellectual endeavors of the faculty and staff of the University" (1983). Commercial activity is separate from and subordinate to the institution's principal educational and research functions. Yet this is an exception that points to the rule. Generally, the public interest receives relatively cursory mention in copyright policies, and it coexists with an explicit narrative about ensuring adequate incentives for creators and reasonable returns for institutions (and, therefore, for the state in the case of public institutions) given their investment in the commodification of copyrightable educational materials.

Development of Managerial Capacity

Intellectual property policies point to organizational developments in universities that strengthen the academic capitalist knowledge/learning regime. In this section we explore the extent to which copyright policies provide evidence of an expanding managerial capacity within colleges and universities to pursue academic capitalism in the realm of copyrightable educational materials. Are such in-house facilities the same as those developed for patenting and technology transfer?

The copyright and computer software policies of universities refer to facilities that are explicitly geared to the production and marketing of copyrightable materials. These facilities are markers of institutional pursuit of academic capitalism in two regards. First, their existence justifies institutions' extended claims to ownership and revenue from copyrightable materials. Second, their existence speaks to the investment institutions are making in the development and marketing of such materials. For instance, BYU's copyright policy claims anything done "within the scope of employment" as a "work for hire" that is owned by the university. Although the university "relinquishes ownership rights to the developers of creative works when 'nominal' use of university resources is involved in the production of the intellectual property," it retains ownership when "substantial" resources are used. Substantial use is defined as "use of university resources beyond those allocated to the faculty in support of their academic work within their respective department or college." That includes use of labs, studios, equipment production, and specialized computing facilities. Any use of expertise in support units financed by the university (e.g., Center for Instructional Design) is substantial use. In fact, the policy states that high-tech course materials "will usually be developed by the Center for Instructional Design and will be owned and administered by the university even though a college or department may have originated the course concept and participated in its development" (2002). The use of institutional internal facilities justifies the university's ownership claims, even when the academic creators initiate the concept and participate in its development. Moreover, the institution's production units, which are independent of faculty control and which hire managerial professionals, may develop materials without faculty initiative or participation.

BYU's case enables us to see how far some institutions have gone in developing internal managerial and organizational capacity to commodify educational materials. BYU's policy appears to protect the public interest and discourage commodification: "The university does not generally engage in product manufacturing, company support functions, customer service, technology maintenance, or work for hire for the private sector. In general, it is not appropriate for academic units to produce, market, or sell products or to establish organizations or companies to do so." However, the policy offers an alternative path of action that points to the university's internal capacity to commodify education. "The Technology Transfer and Creative Works Offices have the responsibility to license or sell the technology or work; or they may sell university developed products to end users when sales and support do not interfere with the normal activities of campus personnel, and when the sale is consistent with the educational mission of the university." If they "deem" the action "consistent with the educational mission and academic purposes of the university," they can approve the creation of an "enterprise center" that will pursue such activity (2002).

BYU's elaboration of managerial and organizational capacity is at one end of the continuum. It has a center for instructional design for producing copyrightable works, a creative works office to oversee "the business aspects of commercializing intellectual properties and [managing] copyright issues," and the potential of enterprise centers that will further develop and market copyrightable educational materials. The policies of other institutions are not so elaborated but point to some development of managerial capacity for the pursuit of academic capitalism in the realm of educational materials. The infrastructure for copyright is not so well developed as for patenting; indeed, the administration of copyrightable works is often handled by the same office that oversees patenting, or by a research foundation (in the cases of CUNY, SUNY, and the University of South Florida). Similarly, in most copyright policies, there is no clear identification of production facilities for copyrightable works. Yet there are references from which one can infer that such production facilities and personnel exist. For instance, those policies, like Utah State's, which refer to "specifically commissioned" works suggest that there is some university investment in such projects. In some cases, as in the University of Utah's policy, there is simply a generic reference to "production facilities" as one factor determining whether "substantial use" of university resources was involved in creating the property, which suggests that such an infrastructure has been established. The University of Missouri's policy indicates that the university owns the materials if they were "created by employees . . . [as] a specific responsibility of the position for which the employee is hired" (2002). That suggests the institution is hiring such employees with such responsibilities. And San Diego State's policy refers to auxiliary shops, including print shops, photographic services, and recording studios.

Overall, it is evident that universities are developing internal, managerial capacity to create and commodify copyrightable educational materials. Such capacity and investment has not only been used to justify more aggressive institutional ownership claims to such products, but also it enables organizational production of materials independent of faculty. In contrast to patenting and technology transfer, colleges and universities can develop and produce copyrightable educational materials without the direct involvement of full-time faculty. Staff who are hired to participate in these production and commercialization activities, whether they are full-time managerial professionals or part-time faculty, generally have no claims to the proceeds of their labors, for their directed labor is regarded as a work for hire, entirely within the scope of their employment.

Under many of the copyright policies we have considered, colleges and universities could hire managerial professionals to develop curricular materials and part-time faculty to deliver them, and the institution would own the courses. Community colleges—for example, Rio Salado—are already engaged in this pattern of production of educational materials. Conceivably, four-year colleges and universities could do the same with regard to high-volume courses, for example, general education courses.

Overall, our analysis of state system and institutional policies demonstrates that there has been a shift from a knowledge/learning regime that foregrounds the public good to one that foregrounds the commercial utility of knowledge, which we call the academic capitalist knowledge/learning regime. This shift is evidenced by the growing numbers of institutions that have copyright policies, by the expansion of the institutional population covered by the policies, and by the increased claims of the institutions to property, especially when production is covered by work for hire or within the scope of employment language, or involves substantial use of college or university resources. Institutional claims to copyright seem to be clearest when intellectual property is mediated by information technology owned by colleges and universities. The use of information technology often calls for increased numbers of managerial or support professionals to operate, repair, handle, and conceptualize educational materials and curricula. With faculty, managerial professionals coproduce commercial educational products for the classroom and the new economy. Because managerial professionals report to administrators rather than to the faculty as a collectivity, whether in departments or senates, there is a subtle shift toward expanded administrative authority. We think this shift may intensify when managerial professionals organize around their interests and successfully engage the market.

College and University Partnerships with Educational Corporations

The aggressiveness of colleges and universities in pursuing potential revenues from faculty's copyrighted works is evident in more than institutional policies. It is also evident in a range of activities and initiatives that involve profit taking from the educational materials, courses, and programs developed by faculty, staff, and students. Unfortunately, there is no national database on the revenues generated from such activities; indeed, many of these activities are not categorized in ways that are captured in any data sets. Consequently, we draw on selected examples from the literature to explore emerging institutional practices.

In the context of the new information, service-based economy, various partnerships between higher education institutions and businesses have emerged. Many of these surround on-line education. One form of joint venture consists of for-profit arms of colleges and universities. Two prominent examples are Columbia University's Fathom, a for-profit distance education consortium, and the University of Maryland University College, a for-profit distance education spin-off of the University of Maryland system.

Fathom was essentially a packaging and distribution system for member institutions to distribute/sell web-based courses and seminars. The membership included the University of Chicago, the University of Michigan system, the London School of Economics and Political Science, Cambridge University Press, the American Film Institute, RAND, the New York Public Library, and the Woods Hole Oceanographic Institution. Member institutions represented an extraordinarily diverse, wide-ranging, and complex network of public and private sector organizations. Yet, after only two years of operation, Columbia University announced that it was shutting down Fathom (Carlson 2003). Columbia invested $14.9 million in the venture in 2001, and Fathom earned only $700,000 from membership fees and sales revenues. Its students numbered in the hundreds. Remarkably, in the face of this disastrous loss of revenue, the CEO of Fathom, Ann Kirschner, spoke positively of the enterprise: "I think we're going out on a high; We've outlasted nearly everybody" (Carlson 2003, p. 30). Similar ventures at NYU and Temple University have also closed. Academic capitalism can fail, though the universities that initiated these ventures live on.

The University of Maryland's University College (UMUC) offers a story with a different ending and an interesting twist in regard to the source of profits from academic capitalism. UMUC was created with private-sector investment, although in recent years it has received tens of millions of dollars in state appropriations—about $10 million per year in 1999 and 2000, $15 million in 2001, and $20 million in 2002 (Heeger 2001). Its greatest success has been in securing military funding to provide education to service men and women around the globe. Most recently, UMUC was awarded a Tri-Services Education contract from the U.S. Army, at a value of $350 million over ten years. By its own accounts, members of the military accounted for 47,000 enrollments in 2002, of a total of 87,000 for all of UMUC (UMUC 2003a, 2003b). UMUC, although designed as a for-profit venture based on private monies, has succeeded by tapping into state funds from Maryland and federal contracts with the military.

UMUC is not the only institution tapping into the military market. David Noble (2001) points out in a chapter titled "Calling the Cavalry: Defense Dollars and the Future of Higher Education" that the Army University Access On-line program, known as eArmyU (see http://earmyu.com), has various partners, including IBM, the Council on Academic Management (supported by the Sloan Foundation, and with representatives from the League for Innovation, a group of community colleges, the Western Interstate Commission of the States, and the American Distance Education Consortium), and nineteen institutions of higher education, five of which are community colleges. The program's mission is to "increase retention by allowing soldiers to earn credits, degrees and certificates at low or no cost to them while they serve on active duty . . . [and to] develop educated, technology-savvy soldiers who will succeed in the missions and on the battlefields of the 21st century" (http://earmyu.com). According to eArmyU, 250,000 students have taken more than 3,000 courses, but only 49 have graduated, mostly with associate degrees and certificates. As of March 2003, three had earned bachelor's degrees.

The networks involved in academic capitalism in the new economy are extraordinarily complex. In exploring business/higher education connections, most scholars have focused on research activities and on universities (Bowie 1994; Etzkowitz, Webster, and Healey 1998). Yet the commodification of education involves a wider range of higher education institutions. These networks extend beyond colleges and universities to include various consortia and professional and institutional associations (e.g., Educause and the League for Innovation) that intermediate among private, nonprofit, and for-profit sectors.

One other example of aggressive pursuit of profit in the information economy is the rise and rapid demise of on-line class notes companies. We opened with a story about class notes. We conclude our discussion of educational products, academic capitalism, and the new economy by noting how students figure in for-profit ventures that involve higher education. Students started some online notes companies, such as Net Notes Media. Students are also employees of these on-line companies, or independent contractors, selling their services while they are enrolled in the same classes for which they are posting their notes. In the postindustrial (and postmodern) world, students have multiple identities: they are not just customers but also producers and owners of knowledge, collectively as well as individually. For example, the Associated Students of the University of Idaho considered forming a partnership with Versity.com, a private corporation, which later folded (Henke 2000). When Versity.com was no longer available to Idaho students, the ASUI voted to allocate monies to reopen its lecture-notes operation.

The class-notes cases highlight the consumption emphasis of the new economy in higher education. In the context of a service-based economy, class notes are not simply educational supplements provided by institutions to enhance learning but Internet-based consumables valued for the convenience they afford students to asynchronously attend class. Simultaneously, they are a knowledge-based product that students themselves can sell in the academic marketplace. In an academic capitalist knowledge/learning regime, students too become academic capitalists, sometimes competing with for-profit arms of the very institutions they attend.

Conclusion

Consideration of copyright policies in colleges and universities illustrates the degree to which knowledge is now conceived of as raw material that can be legally protected and packaged as products, processes, and services to be sold on the open market. Although books, articles, and creative works are affected by the new policies, institutions are likely more interested in software, courseware, and other instructional materials because these have larger markets. The advent of digitized information technologies, which created new horizons for online education, greatly expanded these markets.

The copyright policies show colleges and universities involved in new circuits of knowledge. Rather than appealing to limited scholarly audiences for books, monographs, and journals, institutions—whether public or private, research universities or community colleges—are starting ventures like Fathom and UMUC, which involve the use of copyrighted instructional materials in broad markets for education. How such materials will be evaluated and judged, and who will make these judgments, is not yet clear.

At a few institutions—BYU, for example—interstitial organizations such as its Creative Works Office have emerged to handle copyright policies. The Creative Works Office is aligned with the Center for Instructional Design, underlining the close connection between copyright policies and broad markets for digitized courseware and instructional materials. However, at many institutions, technology transfer offices, sometimes expanded into intellectual property offices, have been responsible for copyrights. The degree to which managerial capacity to handle market negotiations involving copyrighted intellectual property has expanded is not clear. Copyright policies, as well as the products, processes, and services covered by them, are relatively new. If they follow the same trajectory as patent policies, we should expect the interstitial emergence of separate copyright offices. So too, we should expect increased managerial capacity, with a corresponding complement of intellectual property/copyright managerial professionals to handle articulation of these products, processes, and services with the new economy.

Although copyright offices are not yet widely established, other organizations that deal with copyright in educational products have emerged interstitially. These are university organizations or offices that head distance education projects or for-profit educational arms, such as Columbia's Fathom and University of Maryland's UMUC. These organizations bring business practices and procedures into universities, although they are often removed from collective faculty authority. They create precedents and models for other market-oriented ventures. Regardless of whether they succeed or fail, they very often align colleges and universities with corporations dealing with educational products in the new economy.

Frequently, the distance education projects or for-profit arms are part of networks that intermediate among the public, private, and for-profit sectors that connect the new circuits of knowledge. Many on-line, distance education ventures are run through such networks, as we described with Columbia's Fathom. Another example is Knowledge Universe, an enterprise chaired by Michael Milken that is self-described as "the parent of a diverse group of operating companies with a common theme of building human capital by helping individuals and businesses to realize their full potential" (Knowledge Universe 2003). Among the companies in the Knowledge Universe group is UNext, which has affiliations with Carnegie-Mellon University, Columbia Business School, the London School of Economics and Political Science, Stanford University, and the University of Chicago Graduate School of Business through its on-line provider Cardean University (UNext 2003). Ironically, colleges and universities often see for-profits as competing with them, yet a number of the for-profits involved in distance education and on-line universities could not operate without college and university partners, which offer highly skilled, relatively low-cost content providers (Schiller 1998). Indeed, the line between public, private, and for-profit institutions is hard to draw in the case of for-profit arms of institutions of higher learning. Perhaps the common line that connects all of them is that they are able to ask (nontraditional) segments of the public to pay more for educational materials and curricula.

Although copyright policies parallel patent policies in some regards—for example, making the use of faculty time and institutional resources the basis of claims to institutional ownership—in other regards they differ—for example, faculty who copyright rather than patent are granted much more generous royalties. Because copyright policies potentially affect all faculty, they are likely to be more contested than patent policies.

6

COPYRIGHTS PLAY OUT

Commodifying the Core Academic Function

In this chapter, we examine how intellectual property related to instructional materials and educational activities plays out in the work lives of faculty. Union contracts cover approximately 44 percent of full-time faculty in the United States, most of whom are located at two- or four-year institutions (Rhoades 1998, p. 9). The contracts provide a sense of how faculty at nonresearch colleges and universities intersect the academic capitalist knowledge/learning regime. Union contracts often have copyright as well as information technology clauses. Copyright clauses speak to ownership of intellectual property. Information technology clauses generally address distribution of profits based on courseware and other curricular materials as well as the use of these materials by full- and part-time faculty. Sometimes they even specify how use of technology-mediated products should be factored into faculty workload.

The theories we draw on are Rhoades's (1998a) work on the changing power relations within universities and our theory of academic capitalism. Rhoades's work suggests that managerial or support professionals are assuming greater control over or coproducing faculty work. The theory of academic capitalism suggests that the pursuit of external revenues creates webs of policies and procedures that call for greater use of and authority for managerial professionals. Information technology, as represented by on-line education, whether on campus or at a distance, calls for greater use of managerial or support professionals who work with faculty to coproduce educational services for new economy markets. Both faculty and administrators, whether senior or managerial, are increasingly concerned with the generation of external revenues, which push or pull them toward the academic capitalist knowledge/learning regime. Although all sincerely profess to be interested in creating "better" colleges and universities, their differing conceptions of "better" shapes how they approach copyright. Senior level administrators seek to enhance the annual operating budgets of institutions. Managerial professionals are concerned with expanding and making permanent their professional positions and services. Faculty often try to maintain their control of the curricula and expand their share of profits from external revenues derived from intellectual property. The ways in which faculty, senior administrators, and managerial or support professionals interact around the opportunities created by the academic capitalist knowledge/learning regime work to restructure higher education in ways that are both intentional and inadvertent.

The questions that arise when we ask how this plays out in collective faculty agreements and individually fall into two categories. The first are related to ownership of intellectual property: Do faculty attempt to profit from copyrighted instructional material? Do faculty try to protect values associated with the public good knowledge regime even though they may profit from intellectual property? If so, to what degree? The second have to do with on-line higher education: Do institutions attempt to expand on-line education to reach new student markets, and do they try to assert ownership over educational materials to enhance external revenues? Does expansion of on-line instruction call for greater reliance on support professionals? Do faculty try to seek a share of profits from on-line education? Do institutions or faculty try to protect values associated with the public good knowledge regime as they develop e-education?

In the following pages we explore the complex collective stance of faculty with regard to the increased commodification of educational materials. We draw on several data sources: data developed by Lape (1992) and Packard (2002) in their analyses of copyright policies in research universities, data from the state system and institutional policies we analyzed in chapters 3 and 5, and data from a national sample of collective-bargaining agreements. The sample is found in the 2003 version of the Higher Education Contract Analysis System (HECAS), a CD-ROM database owned by the National Education Association (NEA), which has 435 collective-bargaining agreements, 113 in four-year institutions and 322 in two-year institutions.[1] The contracts in the database are from local bargaining agents of the three major unions/associations, as well as some negotiated by independents. We also draw on earlier versions of this database to track patterns in the contracts over time (see Rhoades 1998a, 1999). In addition to the intellectual property policies, we draw on primary and secondary materials from the national faculty associations and unions, the American Association of University Professors (AAUP), the American Federation of Teachers (AFT), and the NEA. These enable us to consider not only the collective professorial pursuit of ownership and profit from intellectual property but

1. A far greater number of campuses are covered because many of the agreements are for state systems of universities and municipal systems of community colleges.

also the official articulation of professional concerns about the use and control of copyrightable intellectual property.

Intellectual Property Issues Identified by Faculty Collective-Bargaining Negotiators

As colleges and universities expand their provision of distance-learning courses and programs to tap into new student markets and generate new revenues, and as institutions provide professors with the opportunity to develop and deliver them, important questions arise about who owns, receives proceeds from, and controls the use of these intellectual products created by faculty members. Interviews with two faculty negotiators, one from a university and one from a community college, reflect two important themes in regard to the commodification of education. First, faculty, like institutions, pursue ownership claims and the promise of revenues from copyrighted intellectual products, and collectively have negotiated generous shares of income from intellectual property. Second, faculty sometimes negotiate peer-based quality control of their copyrighted materials.

The lead faculty negotiator in a unionized research university (Wayne State) proudly spoke of the intellectual property provision he and his team had negotiated, which preserved faculty ownership of copyrighted educational materials. A key issue in many contracts is the use of institutional facilities. The more substantial the use, the greater the institution's claim to ownership, a significant point given that educational materials are increasingly produced with advanced information/media technologies. Yet the Wayne State provision specifies "substantial use" in a way that is favorable to faculty, reducing the university's claims to ownership to include only cases in which a "work for hire" has specifically been commissioned to produce the course (Rhoades and Maitland 2000).

The lead negotiator at Mott Community College was also pleased with a similar feature of the provision he helped negotiate. "The most important language covered a deeply-held conviction; it was to retain ownership. So, the new language really protects that. It protects the intellectual property and the content of the course . . . We came to the table saying, we own it. The story we told was, a faculty member's ideas are their own . . . they are all that we have. Since the classical era, our ideas have been ours" (Rhoades and Maitland 2000, p. 30).

Beyond ownership, the negotiator at Wayne State referred to the generous shares of the proceeds from the faculty-created property that the contract provided. A sliding scale for jointly created works and works for hire accorded faculty members 90 percent of the revenue up to $50,000 and 75 percent after that (considerably more generous than the split for patents, which was 50% after $100,000). On this point, the Mott faculty negotiator articulated a sentiment that speaks to our second theme—even as they participate in commodification and negotiate their share of the proceeds, many faculty are also deeply invested in the educational dimensions of their intellectual property. "I don't think revenue is the big issue. I hope not anyway. These courses are being developed to fit the needs of our students. Not for markets, or for making profits. I guess we are competing in some sense with some big private companies. But the courses should be geared to our students. Our first priority is our students, not to compete in markets . . . That's management's view, as well, thankfully, at least at the present. But we'll keep an eye on that . . . The minute you get into making a profit, to competing in the market, then you almost change yourself into something you are not" (Rhoades and Maitland 2000, p. 31).

Concerns about educational quality are particularly evident in questions about the control and use of educational materials created by faculty members. An important consideration for both faculty negotiators was who would control the assignment and future use of materials and courses. They expressed faculty's concern regarding scenarios in which a course might either be taught by an unqualified (often part-time) instructor who would deliver an inferior course or be taught in its current form in the future, long after it should have been revised and updated. The negotiator at Mott was proud of the clause that ensured that faculty members controlled course assignment (through veto rights) as well as the decision of whether and when to revise or replace a course.

As educational materials become increasingly commodified, many faculty participate in negotiating ownership and shares of the proceeds from the products they create. As both faculty negotiators indicated, their leverage in negotiations with institutions that wanted to expand distance-education activity was that faculty needed to be given more incentive to engage in such activity. Yet even as they are complicit in the commodification of educational materials (Rhoades 2002), faculty also create some alternatives to the pursuit of profit by developing contract clauses and association positions that address quality and faculty control, which can act as professionals' protection of the public good.

Collective Professorial Pursuit of Profit, Shares, and Ownership

Shares and Ownership

Collectively, faculty claim ownership and pursue their share of the proceeds from their copyrightable educational materials. The three major faculty unions and associations have taken a clear position claiming faculty ownership of such materials. The AAUP offers the following positions:

> [I]t has been the prevailing academic practice to treat the faculty member as the copyright owner of works that are created independently and at the faculty member's own initiative for traditional academic purposes. Examples include class notes and syllabi, books and articles, works of fiction and nonfiction, poems and dramatic works, musical and choreographic works, pictorial, graphic, and sculptural works, and educational software, commonly known as "courseware." This practice has been followed for the most part, regardless of the physical medium in which these "traditional academic works" appear, that is, whether on paper or in audiovisual or electronic form . . . this practice should therefore ordinarily apply to the development of courseware for use in programs of distance education. (AAUP 1999c)

An AFT position paper advises that: "Ownership of intellectual property should be the right of all academic employees and is key to controlling the quality and duplication of their work" (Strom 2002, p. 11). The NEA statement goes further:

> NEA believes that education employees should own the copyright to materials that they create in the course of their employment. Toward this end, the Copyright Act of 1976 should be amended to expressly recognize an appropriate "teacher's exception" to the "works made for hire" doctrine, pursuant to which works created by education employees in the course of their employment are owned by the employee. This exception should . . . reflect the unique practices and traditions of academia. In the interim—unless and until legislative action is taken—all issues relating to copyright ownership of materials created by education employees should be resolved through collective bargaining or other processes of bilateral decision-making between the employer and the affiliate. In the absence of special circumstances—under which it might be appropriate for the rights of ownership to be divided between the education employee and the employer, or to make some similar arrangement—such negotiated agreements should provide that copyright ownership vests in the education employee who creates the materials and that he or she has all of the legal rights that come with such ownership. (NEA 2003)

An analysis of the collective-bargaining agreements in the HECAS data set of institutions that have copyright clauses shows that a majority of the contracts mention either use or significant use of institutional resources as a factor affecting ownership claims. Almost one-quarter of the copyright clauses in two-year institutions' policies and over one-third in four-year institutions' indicate that faculty own copyright outright, even in cases in which institutional resources have been used. The overwhelming majority, over four-fifths, have language that recognizes faculty ownership if they produce the work independently, without significant use of institutional resources.[2]

Triton College provides an example of faculty successfully negotiating ownership rights even when there is substantial use of institutional resources.

2. In several cases, this varies from the provision regarding patents and inventions, which accords ownership to the institution when significant institutional resources are utilized.

"When there is College support, the College shall have sole ownership of recorded materials; the faculty member shall have sole ownership of written materials and inventions" (2000). Cloud County Community College offers creators blanket ownership rights:

> The Board of Trustees recognizes that it has certain proprietary rights to material, including publications, instructional material and devices, prepared by staff members on college time and with the use of Cloud County Community College facilities and/or equipment . . . The Board requires that development of material by staff members for the purpose of obtaining patents, distribution rights, monetary gain or copyrights, shall not infringe upon the responsibilities that the staff member has for the position held within the College. Therefore, the College shall have no interest in such materials prepared by staff members. However, material prepared by a staff member and covered by this policy must be made available to the College without charge. (2001)

Although such clauses are not the norm, they are important for two reasons. First, they point to the aggressiveness of faculty working collectively to maintain ownership claims over copyrightable works and their right to generate revenues from them even when these works are created with the support of the institution and essentially are publicly subsidized. Second, the clauses point to the possibility of faculty in less prestigious institutions occasionally negotiating more favorable intellectual property claims than are allowed faculty in more prestigious institutions.

In other cases, faculty have not retained ownership claims, but, as in the eighteen policies we examined in the previous chapter, they have negotiated substantial revenues from or generous shares of the proceeds. Some provisions identify a specific payment for developing materials. "Each professor/instructor who voluntarily agrees to develop a new or existing course for delivery via television (two-way interactive) shall be compensated $1500" (Glen Oaks Community College 1997). Other provisions identify shares from the proceeds of intellectual property. "Twenty-five percent of all net proceeds from the sale or licensing of college supported written materials will go to the college and 75 percent will be retained by the originating bargaining unit member. Seventy-five percent of all net proceeds from the sale or licensing of college supported recording materials and inventions will go to the college and 25 percent will be retained by the originating bargaining unit member" (Johnson County Community College 2003). Again, technology matters—the college's share of proceeds from recorded materials is greater than that from written ones.

Another mechanism by which faculty have collectively bargained for revenues from distance-education courses is evident in this clause about the rebroadcasting of courses: "If the instructor who created and/or taught the course is unable or declines to administer the course, the sponsoring department may, by agreement with the Office of Telecourse Programs, recruit another instructor with appropriate expertise to administer the course, but the instructor who created and/or taught the course shall be paid a royalty of 10% of the total tuition received from all students based on the continuing education tuition rate, but not to include course fees" (Western Michigan University 2003). Essentially, there may be a bounty on distance students, for individual faculty as well as for institutions. Another type of bounty is evident in the contract of Chemeketa Community College: "Whenever the distance education class is significantly larger than common department practice, i.e., enrollment caps, the following guidelines shall be used when additional monetary compensation is given" (2003). The guidelines specify pay bonuses that accompany classes over the enrollment cap (e.g., for twice as many students the faculty member gets paid 100% more).

Unionized faculty have negotiated, with some success, to ensure that teaching courses at a distance is voluntary. They treat the teaching of such courses as an extra responsibility for which they should be paid, though almost always at a piece rate, rather than through prorating their salaries. As in the story of the two faculty negotiators, one of faculty's points of leverage is that institutions want to get more involved in distance education and faculty require an incentive to engage in this activity. That stance suggests faculty complicity in the pursuit of profits from educational activity and copyrightable educational materials.

It is very unusual for a contract to challenge the pursuit of academic capitalism in the new economy. Most of the current struggles are over who gets how much. As Rhoades (2002a, 42) notes, "The public is usually left out when the profits from academic intellectual property are divided." However, a few collective-bargaining agreements do offer alternatives to the academic capitalist knowledge/learning regime, including setting aside some monies for public good uses, discounting products that have been subsidized by public monies, and distributing all materials at cost (2002a). One exceptional piece of contract language offers the possibility of pursuing a path other than academic capitalism: "Any videotapes or audiotapes made of distance learning courses are for student use, and may not be used for any commercial purpose . . . Unless there is an extraordinary reason for preserving the tapes, all tapes of a given distance learning course will be destroyed within two weeks of the course completion" (Oakton Community College 2002). However, this is the exception that clarifies the rule of academic capitalism for faculty and institutions.

A final example of a contract provision underscores the complicity in commodification that is evident in much collective faculty behavior. Chemeketa Community College has a clause that expressly prohibits commercialization of video tapes or films. "All video tapes or films made by the College become its property with the restriction that they may not be sold or used for a commercial profit." However, reading further along, it is clear that the restriction is lifted if the creator can get a share of the proceeds. "Use for commercial profit in any form may be arranged through a negotiated agreement between the party or parties involved, or their designated agents, and the College" (2003). In other words, no profit-taking activity will be allowed unless the creator chooses to share in the revenues of that commercialization.

Professional Considerations of Quality Control

In various higher education settings faculty have articulated quality control concerns in regard to the commodification of educational products. Two sorts of policy provisions are particularly relevant to professional control and quality. One relates to *individuals'* creative control over how copyrightable works are used; the other relates to the faculty's *collective* control over disputes that arise over ownership and use of copyrightable works.

Lape states that "the most creative measures designed to protect the professor's interests are those which recognize the importance to the professor of control over dissemination of works whose copyright is claimed by the university" (1992, p. 262). In Packard's words, "some policies include provisions allowing professors to control dissemination and revision of their works and to determine whether and how long they are identified as a work's creator" (2002, p. 303). For example, the University of Washington's policy reads, "As long as the author or producer of such materials remains an employee of the University, the author may . . . request reasonable revisions of the materials prior to any instance of internal use" (Packard 2002, 141n). The University of Wisconsin's policy reads, "Copyrightable instructional materials shall not be altered or revised without consultation with the author" (Packard 2002, 141n). Yet only seven of the sixty-nine universities in Lape and Packard's studies had such policy language.

Collective faculty involvement in disputes about the ownership and use of intellectual products is also significant. A little less than half of the policies in Packard's study provide for a committee to review and make recommendations regarding any disputes over copyrightable intellectual property. All but three leave the final decision to the administration, which may be a party to the dispute. Yet collective professional quality control is particularly important in the case of educational products because this realm of activity tends to lie outside traditional academic structures—distance-education curriculum, for example, generally is developed and approved outside standard academic governance mechanisms. As institutions increasingly emphasize the use of on-campus technology-mediated educational materials, the same point holds true—their development and approval lies outside academic peer review.

Historically, the curriculum has been seen as the purview of academics. Faculty unions and associations are clear in their positions on the quality issues discussed above. For example, "in the context of distance-education courseware, the faculty member should also be given rights in connection with its future uses, not only through compensation but also through the right of "first refusal" in making new versions or at least the right to be consulted in good faith on reuse and revisions" (AAUP 1999c). AAUP recommends that "the faculty member (or an appropriate faculty body) who teaches the course (or adopts a pre-existing course) for use in distance education shall exercise control over the future use, modification, and distribution of recorded instructional material and shall determine whether the material should be revised or withdrawn from use." Similarly, in its *Guidelines for Good Practice*, the AFT identifies fourteen benchmarks for distance education. One is that "faculty should retain creative control over use and re-use of materials" (AFT 2000). Further, the AAUP recommends the establishment of intellectual property committees, composed of faculty as well as administrators, to develop policy and resolve disputes (AAUP 1999b).

Although the national faculty associations and unions specify that faculty should have final authority over technology-mediated curriculum, it is another matter to negotiate contract provisions that ensure quality and creative control. In some cases, local bargaining units have successfully negotiated some measure of creative control to faculty who develop curriculum. At the very least, faculty may have veto rights. "Tapes or other materials developed expressly for distance learning may not be reused without the instructor's written permission" (Minnesota State Colleges and Universities 1997). In other cases, provisions go beyond simple veto rights to identifying a committee that reviews disputes, thereby speaking to a more collective faculty control of educational quality matters.

> If, and when, the Office of Telecourse Programs wishes to re-use the course in its entirety, the following will apply: . . . the instructor who created and/or taught the course shall be notified and given first consideration to administer the rebroadcast of this course . . . If the instructor who created and/or taught the course deems the continued use of an electronically purveyed course to be detrimental to his/her personal or professional reputation, he/she may request that the course be reviewed by the Office of Telecourse Programs for either substantial revision or removal from circulation. If a decision is made to substantially revise a course, the instructor who created and/or taught the course shall have the first right to revise the course . . . An instructor may appeal any of the above decisions of the Office of Telecourse Programs to a

> review committee. The committee shall consist of two faculty members appointed by the Chapter and two members appointed by Western . . . The decision of the committee shall be final and cannot be grieved. (Western Michigan University 2003)

Such language is not the norm, but over one-fifth of contracts with copyright provisions afford faculty some measure of peer control over the use of the intellectual property. Most typical are provisions regarding a committee that makes decisions and adjudicates disputes, with faculty representation on the committee. In addition, individual faculty members are sometimes given veto rights over who will teach a course or whether the course will continue to be taught in the case of distance education and videotaped classes. In a few cases, the issue of use is a matter for grievance and arbitration.

In sum, our data speak to the complicit and multifaceted nature of faculty's position in relation to the commodification of copyrightable educational materials. Individually, some faculty members are aggressively pursuing profit-taking activity in copyrightable educational materials. Collectively, faculty representatives are articulating and negotiating claims to shares of the proceeds of copyrightable works. That negotiation is partly driven by the argument that if institutions want faculty to become more involved in developing copyrightable works that can be delivered in ways that may enhance institutional revenues, then there needs to be an economic incentive for the faculty-creators. Faculty are also collectively resisting institutional claims to own educational materials under an academic capitalist knowledge/learning regime. And faculty are collectively foregrounding significant considerations of educational quality and professional control as institutions become involved in academic capitalism in the new economy. Our data on professors point to the internally complex and conflicted nature of faculty's collective positions in regard to copyrightable intellectual products. In part, faculty are pursuing academic capitalism. At the same time, they are working to maintain professional autonomy and peer-defined quality control within increasingly capitalistic higher education enterprises. In short, even as faculty are complicit in academic capitalism they are also collectively working to mitigate its impact on professional autonomy and control, and on educational quality.

Technology, Property Ownership, and Access

Software nicely represents the ambiguous possibilities embedded in new technologies. It is a gray area in intellectual property policies: in some cases it is treated as patentable, in others as copyrightable, and in still other cases there is a separate policy for software. As Packard (2002, p. 312) notes, the variation may partly be a function of the different standards that apply to patents and copyright: "Software has to be 'novel' to earn a patent, but copyright applies the moment the work is produced as long as a modicum of creativity is involved."

Generally, the type of protection sought for intellectual property depends on its use. If it is used for educational purposes, it tends to be treated under copyright policy. For example, BYU's policy states that "all computer software is included in technical works except that which is clearly developed for entertainment or for instructional purposes, e.g., electronic textbooks and textbook supplements, classroom and self-study tutorials" (2002). In addition to educational purposes, many colleges and universities see technology as a basis for generating new revenues by extending claims over faculty's intellectual property, reducing instructional costs by increasing productivity, and targeting new, more affluent student markets as an additional means of generating new (and maximizing existing) revenues.

When substantial use of institutional resources is involved in the production of works copyrighted by faculty, the employing institution frequently claims ownership of the materials produced. New technologies usually belong to universities, and their use by faculty is very often framed as substantial. The rationale for institutional claims on technology-mediated works is the high cost of technology and managerial/support professionals. For example, any creation of multimedia materials is likely to draw on "substantial" or "significant" university resources, including multimedia experts. (The Universities of California, Kentucky, Michigan, and Utah have policies with substantial use language.)

In explaining the timing of institutions' copyright policy development, Lape states that "the advent of new technology and an increased interest in commercialization of faculty works are the primary reasons presented" (1992, p. 254). Similarly, Daniel and Pauken write, "As universities recognize the potential revenues inherent in the newest categories of copyrightable works—computer programs and other computer and media-created materials—more and more have begun adopting copyright policies" (1999, p. 18).

Although not all universities claim ownership of such materials (e.g., Carnegie Mellon's policy claims software but not educational courseware "because of its role in furthering the primary educational mission of the university" [Packard 2002, 111n]), about half of the universities in Lape's (1992) and Packard's (2002) samples identify software as a work that is claimed by institutions. For example, the University of Cincinnati's policy reads as follows: "Specifically excluded from this list [of faculty-owned works] are audiovisual and computer materials including audio and video tapes, slides, and photographs, films, computer programs, and computer stored information."

Faculty unions are aware of the implications of advanced technologies for ownership. In outlining the AFT's "Checklist for Collective Bargaining Negotiations," Strom states: "Bargain for ownership of as much of members' creative works as possible. However, within the realm of the evolving digital world where new questions of copyright ownership arise, recognize that faculty members will not necessarily own everything. Digital works may involve other creators and include substantial institutional support, which then complicates exclusive versus joint ownership" (2002, p. 12).

Along with ownership issues, distance-education technologies raise issues about which educational markets will be targeted. Although policy makers and institutional spokespersons often justify distance education because of its potential for providing greater accessibility to higher education, institutions pursuing the generation of external revenues may target those best able to pay. National data indicates that older students, students who are already employed, and students who have technology at home are more likely to take distance-education classes than are traditional age students (NCES 2000b).

Some unions have voiced concerns about compromising access through the increased used of distance education. The NEA's policy statement articulates this concern: "Although distance education can overcome physical and geographical barriers, its reliance on high level information technology has the potential to create new barriers based on economic and social status" (NEA 2003). One of the largest bargaining units in the country, the California Faculty Association (for the California State University System), has a contract clause speaking to technology and access, charging the Faculty Workload Committee, which focuses on issues surrounding the use of technology to deliver courses, to "evaluate and make recommendations on innovations in the delivery of education services that will increase student access to the CSU while maintaining high academic standards" (1998).

However, the faculty associations, whether national or local, that voice concerns about access and quality also have negotiated faculty ownership of copyrighted intellectual property and incentives for faculty to participate in distance education, making faculty, like institutions, academic capitalists with interests in expanding lucrative markets. Although older, employed students may be diverse, they do not necessarily enrich the campus mix of students because they are, often by choice, at a distance.

Technology and Educational Quality

Distance-education technologies have created new markets on which (some) institutions and faculty are eager to capitalize as well as new opportunities for institutions to restructure faculty work and cut costs. Faculty salaries are the greatest single expense at most institutions. If managerial professionals become responsible for the supervision of distance education, faculty work can be "unbundled," parceled out to (possibly) less costly employees or part-time professional workers. As was the case with patents and copyrights, expanded managerial capacity is the key to market engagement, in this case through technology-mediated instruction. Managerial professionals supervise part-timers who deliver distance education and work with decreasing numbers of faculty to coproduce distance education.

Distance education is increasing rapidly. From 1995–1998 the number of institutions offering distance education increased from 33 to 44 percent; the number of such classes doubled (Lewis et al. 1999). Moreover, 29 percent of students who have taken courses on-line (about 8% of undergraduates and 12% of masters students have taken distance education classes) have done so in programs that were entirely on-line (NCES 2000).

Part of the strategy for using technologies to increase efficiency is to unbundle the faculty role (Paulson 2002). Rather than having one professor do all the work involved in developing and delivering curriculum, the process is overseen by managerial professionals and broken down into various discrete tasks, ranging from designing and delivering the class, evaluation, assessment of students, technical advising, academic advising, and more. If the professor has a role, it is as a "content specialist." Rio Salado Community College embodies one end of the unbundled continuum. It has fewer than twenty full-time faculty and over 600 part-timers. Not only at Rio Salado but also throughout U.S. higher education, where the proportion of full-time faculty has declined significantly, the corollary of institutions investing in technological resources for students is that they disinvest in full-time faculty.

Faculty unions resist the use of technology when it increases class size, reduces full-time faculty, and bypasses faculty involvement in curriculum. Unions frequently juxtapose quality-of-education arguments to cost-savings justifications for distance education.

> Distance education should be used only to improve the learning opportunities for students, improve the quality of instruction, and/or improve the effectiveness of education employees. Although distance education may inevitably have an impact on the location and nature of educational employment, it should not be used—in whole or in part, directly or indirectly—for the purpose of eliminating traditional education employee positions or reducing the hours or compensation of such employees. Nor should distance education be used solely for the purpose of reducing costs, if such use has an adverse effect on the economic security of education employees. (NEA 2003)

The AFT foregrounds academic versus economic considerations in course planning. "To ensure that academic decisions are made for academic reasons, a key characteristic of quality in distance education is ensuring that faculty are in control of shaping and approving courses and integrating them into a coherent curriculum" (2001, p. 20). Through faculty unions, professors are trying to curtail the rise of managerial professionals whom senior administrators have hired to contain costs and to administer distance education.

Some local bargaining units have successfully translated quality concerns into contractual provisions. "The maximum class sizes for courses offered as distance learning shall be the same as those in the Master Course Table. The course maximum equals the total of all students enrolled at all sites" (Elgin Community College 2002). Most contracts that address this issue stipulate enrollment maximums for classes delivered with technology; many of these have additional remuneration attached to the larger class size. In other words, contract provisions are not grounded in an absolute commitment to particular class sizes simply in the interests of quality. Instead, these contracts are grounded in concerns that faculty not be overloaded with students. Faculty unions also initiate provisions that enable professors to get more pay from classes that exceed the limits. Indeed, many faculty members are committed individually to increasing their income through such "overload" work. This points again to the complexity of professors' position with regard to academic capitalism—they articulate quality concerns, but if the institution seeks revenue maximization through bigger classes, then professors ensure that they will benefit financially from the process.

Occasionally professors as a collectivity resist participation in academic capitalism. In February 2003 the Washington Federation of Teachers, representing faculty in the state's community colleges, announced a campaign to highlight the importance of class size and to build support for increased funding for public two-year colleges, which were overenrolled by several thousand students. Called the "Campaign to Protect Learning Quality" and begun at Seattle Community College, the initiative aims to convince instructors to refuse classroom overloads, thereby forcing the college to open new class sections. "When classes are chronically overloaded, we shortchange our students," says Lynne Dodson, president of the Seattle Community College Federation of Teachers. "There is less time for personal interaction with the instructor and less time that the instructor can spend on responding to individual assignments" (AFT 2000a).

A related issue surrounding instructional technology is the configuration of the faculty work force. As academic managers seek to expand part-time faculty, full-time positions are lost. Expanded managerial capacity to handle instructional technology allows more part-timers to be hired. Unbundling the faculty role, modularizing the curriculum, and delivering education through advanced technologies are all developments that make the use of part-time faculty more feasible.

Some contracts have language regarding instructional technology that protects the current workforce configuration. "Under no circumstances will audio or videotapes or computer programs be used to reduce the number of teaching positions existing at the College . . . exclusive of any one-semester only contracts" (Middlesex County College 2003). But it is uncommon to find such strong language in contracts.

Quality is not only about class size, it is about faculty control of the curriculum. In contrast to the "use" and "creative control" clauses discussed earlier, some clauses focus not on the individual creator's rights but rather on the collective faculty's responsibility for the curriculum, as a matter of ensuring quality. Two examples follow.

> No credit-bearing course taught by non-traditional methods (television, computer-aided instruction, videotape lecture, or any other electronic or other media) will be offered without the approval of the department members involved in teaching the subject area in consultation with the Department Chair. (Jackson Community College 2003)

> In approving distance education courses, the following criteria shall be applicable: (a) course approval through the traditional academic process; (b) a qualified instructor; (c) use of suitable technology as a substitute for the traditional classroom; (d) suitable opportunity for interaction between instructor and student. (Association of Pennsylvania State College and University Faculties 2002)

Although these are exceptions, they do speak to the aims of faculty unions and negotiators.

Over time, the percentage of collective-bargaining agreements with such clauses has increased. The percentage of HECAS agreements with technology clauses increased from a little over one-third in 1994 to about one-half in 2000. That speaks to the increased significance of this issue and perhaps the growing use of information technologies. However, many unionized institutions do not have clauses regarding technology.

Technology, Openness, and Academic Freedom

Instructional technologies offer the promise of enhancing freedom of expression and openness in the classroom. Some students, the argument goes, are not well served by face-to-face interaction, finding it inhibiting. By making expression anonymous, technology may increase the participation and learning of students who have not benefited from conventional classroom settings. The worldwide resources that technology makes available and brings into the classroom are also said to open students up to new possibilities.

However, there is another side to the introduction of new technologies in the classroom. The AAUP, long regarded as an association committed to protecting professorial academic freedom, puts it this way. "Institutions of higher learning in particular should interpret and apply the law of copyright so as to encourage the discovery of new knowledge and its dissemination to students, to the profession, and to the public. This mission is reflected in the 1940 *Statement of Principles on Academic Freedom and Tenure:* Institutions of higher education are conducted for the common good and not to further the interest of either the individual teacher or the institution as a whole. The common good depends upon the free search for truth and its free exposition" (AAUP 1999c). Although technology has the potential to expand freedom of inquiry, it also has the potential to inhibit free expression within the classroom and on-line. The increased use of technology to enhance and deliver instruction offers many opportunities for surveillance of individual classrooms. The old technology, such as blackboards and overhead projectors, was not easy to monitor. In a technology-enhanced classroom in which a professor's notes and overheads, as well as students' comments, are on-line and on class websites, discourse is relatively easy to track. In a distance-education course, monitoring professor/student and student/student interactions is easily accomplished. From the standpoint of accountability, perhaps that is good. From the standpoint of professors seeking to protect their academic freedom, and of professors and students seeking to engage in free expression, however, monitoring can be problematic. The more open a classroom is to surveillance, the more the participants must wonder who is watching, and they may censor (or have censored) their participation accordingly.

New technologies afford managers (and others outside the institution) the opportunity to surveil and evaluate faculty work outside faculty peer evaluation. Most collective-bargaining agreements do not contain language about surveillance; that some do is significant. "Evaluation of the unit member shall not be accomplished through electronic monitoring or taping" (Cumberland County College 2003). "Evaluation of instructors is not allowed by any electronic means such as video tape. ITV instruction shall be evaluated by the procedures set forth herein for other non-ITV courses" (Dodge City Community College 2000).

Perhaps even more central to academic freedom are recent challenges to the right of academics to pursue knowledge, given the commercialization of software and the Digital Millennium Copyright Act's (DMCA) protection of proprietary rights. One well-known case is that of a Princeton University computer science professor, Edward Felten, who, in response to a public challenge by a music industry group, successfully cracked several watermark schemes designed to protect their products. When Felten indicated that he would be presenting a paper on his work at a professional meeting, the Recording Industry

Association of America (RIAA) threatened to sue under the DMCA. Although the RIAA later dropped its suit, Felton, supported by Princeton, filed a countersuit challenging the constitutionality of the DMCA (Foster 2001a), arguing that it abridged his first amendment rights. That suit was later dismissed by a U.S. district court judge.

At least three features of the story are interesting for our purposes. First, it points to the tension between commercialization and the free pursuit of knowledge. Second, it points to the tension between faculty and external, commercial entities. Third, the situation highlights the contested relationship between property rights and academic freedom within the academy. Felten was supported by various professors, by Princeton, and by organizations that advocate the free flow of information and pursuit of knowledge, such as the Electronic Frontier Foundation and Computer Professionals for Social Responsibility.

However, others within the academy support the protection of property rights, as evidenced in a related case. In *University City Studios, Inc., v. Eric Corley,* several movie studios sued a hacker for creating a software program that circumvents a scrambling system that protects DVDs. The suit invoked the DMCA's "anti-circumvention provision." Professor Felten signed a legal brief supporting the hacker, along with sixteen other university computer scientists, including David Touretzky of Carnegie-Mellon University. Yet one of Professor Touretzky's colleagues, Michael Shamos (a computer science professor, intellectual property lawyer, and codirector of the Institute for eCommerce) took a different position. Shamos testified in court on behalf of movie studios (Foster 2001b). The story shows a professoriat not only embedded in a web of relationships and interactions between higher education and external markets but also characterized by internal divisions regarding the pursuit of academic capitalism. It also shows how technology can serve to compromise rather than enhance openness and academic freedom.

In sum, national associations of faculty—the AAUP, the AFT, and the NEA—take the position that faculty are the legitimate owners of any copyrightable intellectual property that they create. Although a number of unionized institutions have bargained intellectual property clauses that provide for faculty ownership, most have not. Increasingly, institutional policies, on which nonunionized faculty offer advice and consent, claim ownership of faculty's intellectual property, especially when substantial institutional resources, usually information technology, are used. Although institutions may own intellectual property created by faculty, most are generous in sharing royalties with faculty, as demonstrated in chapter 5. The generous royalties often act as incentives for faculty to participate in technology-mediated instruction and development of on-line educational materials and products. Organized faculty and institutions seek to capitalize on copyrighted intellectual property, faculty through holding title to and/or receiving royalty shares, institutions through generating external revenues from distance education as well as products and educational services copyrighted by faculty. The pursuit of profit and external revenues commits both faculty and institutions to the academic capitalist knowledge/learning regime.

For the most part, neither faculty nor institutions recognize the public as a partner in the creation of copyrighted intellectual property used for educational activities. Yet faculty in public institutions receive a high degree of public support because their salaries come from the state. Faculty in private institutions receive indirect subsidies through institutions' tax-exempt status, through federal and state student financial aid, which provides a part of private colleges and universities' annual operating budgets, and a variety of other public programs. As is the case with patents, the public pays for educational infrastructure, subsidizes the corporations that work with faculty and institutions to develop educational products from their intellectual property, and pays again when they or their children attend a higher education institution.

On-line education uses an array of copyrighted products developed by faculty or co-produced by faculty and institutions. According to the NCES (2000b) statistics quoted earlier, national data shows that institutions of higher education are rapidly expanding on-line education. (Some) faculty and (some) institutional administrators are eager to expand on-line education: faculty want to profit from overloads and any royalties from instructional materials, and institutional administrators hope to expand external revenues. The same data show that distance education reaches new markets. The majority of students served on-line are older, working students who have technology in their homes. Although these students are nontraditional, they are not necessarily the most needy students. By targeting working students able to afford higher education and negotiate aid and loan processes, on-line education may inadvertently divert resources for expanding access.

Although neither our data nor national statistics directly indicate an increase in managerial or support professionals in on-line endeavors, it seems likely that their numbers are growing. The AAUP, the NEA, and the AFT provide indirect evidence of the increase in managerial professionals. They have issued policy statements against unbundling, since it makes possible the restructuring of faculty work. Faculty organizations, whether national or local affiliates of nationals that bargain collectively, usually assume that they, not managerial professionals, should control the curricula because they have the specialized knowledge necessary to provide quality education. When digitized interactive information technology enabled electronic capture of that expertise, institutions argued against faculty control over curricula because it was cheaper to provide on-line education supported by managerial professionals. Neither faculty nor administrators provided a great deal of evidence for their claims. Yet both claimed their respective positions represented the public good. Faculty took the stance that as experts they should have control over on-line curricula, or institutions would use, reuse, and unsuitably alter educational materials so as to cut costs, serving students badly. Institutions claimed that faculty would use their control over curricula to ensure guildlike prerogatives that run up costs, and argued that on-line education, aided by expanded use of managerial professionals, would cut faculty costs, thereby serving students better. Both faculty and institutional administrators assumed that the students were the public, even though the number of students who were part of the taxpaying citizenry is relatively small. As is so often the case, deciding whether the public good is being protected depends on how the public is defined.

Open Source Approaches to Technology

While many institutions rushed to profit from on-line education, MIT chose another path, announcing an OpenCourseWare initiative in the spring of 2001. A brief review of this initiative enables us to see the complicated interplay of private and public interest in an academy embedded in networks of organizations and activities that connect the state, higher education, and private marketplaces.

As described by two MIT faculty members, one of whom served as chair of the initiative's management board, the original motivation was to generate revenue.

> The [planning] team, led by Dick Yue, associate dean of the School of Engineering, and assisted by a team of consultants from the firm Booz, Allen, and Hamilton, Inc., was 'to develop a recommendation to address how MIT can generate and offer [on-line educational] modules that provide the target market with a working understanding of current hot issues and emerging fields' . . . Befitting the excitement of the times, MIT's core team began with the idea of making its program generate revenue, that is, ensuring that it would be 'financially viable and sustainable'—although the question of whether it would be a for-profit endeavor was left open. (Lerman and Miyagawa 2002, p. 24)

After conducting studies, doing market research, and developing business plans, it became clear to the team, which had considered creating a for-profit arm of MIT, that it would take years before a sustainable on-line program could be developed. Indeed, the co-chair of MIT's Council on Educational Technology, which launched the planning team, said, "Our feeling about the for-profit model is that not only are you not going to make money by selling higher education on-line, many universities are going to lose money hand over fist" ("For the Record" 2002, p. 25). Only after determining that a revenue-generating program was not viable did the planning team turn to alternative ideas. It was seeking a unique strategy that would speak to MIT's sense of being a leader in technology and higher education. Several team members came up with the idea of making course materials publicly accessible on-line. Rather than posting courses or course modules on the web, MIT would make available materials such as syllabi, lecture notes, reading lists, and the like. MIT agreed that faculty would retain ownership even when support staff and professionals working in the OpenCourseWare project transformed those materials into a standard web-compatible format.

The initiative has encountered problems that have slowed its progress and that challenge its viability as a model other institutions might adopt. The planning team estimates a cost of $85 million over ten years to put materials from all 2,000 of MIT's courses on-line. Although MIT has received grants from various foundations to support the effort, it still committed $2 million of its own to the project in its first two years. At present, materials from only thirty-eight courses have been put on the web, and costs have exceeded expectations. "Collecting permissions, paying royalties, and finding other materials to substitute for copyrighted materials have turned out to be much bigger jobs than expected" (Olsen 2002, p. 3). The director of the Carnegie Foundation for the Advancement of Teaching's Knowledge Media Laboratory has referred to MIT's project as an example of "intellectual philanthropy" (2002, p. 2). That definition of the alternative path clarifies how marginal it is, and how it is available only to the very wealthy, in the larger context of academic capitalism.

Conclusion

Information technology initiated new circuits of knowledge. Rather than instructional materials being confined to the classroom or circulated through correspondence courses (Noble 2001), digital technologies made possible new and (sometimes) interactive off-site modalities for instruction. For-profit higher education institutions, such as the University of Phoenix, began to make heavy use of distance education. However, the greatest growth occurred in public and private nonprofit higher education. Very often these institutions partnered with private, for-profit corporations to establish distance-education programs, colleges, and universities (Schiller 1998). The formation of Cardean University by the for-profit company UNext is an example of such an enterprise. Cardean University, which offers an online MBA degree as well as professional development courses and corporate training, is supported by a consortium of well-known, private nonprofit business schools (Carnegie-Mellon University, Columbia Business School, the London School of Economics and Political Science, Stanford University, and the University of Chicago Graduate School of Business). These new circuits of knowledge generate external revenues for colleges and universities from the sale of educational products developed for on-line instruction and from new student markets.

In chapter 5, we discussed the interstitial emergence of copyright offices and facilities as well as the development of networks that mediate between public and private sectors with regard to distance education. In this chapter, we want to emphasize how expanded managerial capacity in the area of digital technologies is restructuring universities. These changes are not technologically determined. They would not occur without the active organization of managerial or support professionals, senior administrators, and faculty, with each group working somewhat independently. To some degree, the groups are exercising different strategies to intersect the academic capitalist knowledge/learning regime in ways that they see as best serving higher education and their own interests.

The push of resource constraint and the pull of external market opportunities turned senior administrators' attention to the possibilities the new technologies presented for containing labor costs and reaching new student markets. Consequently, senior administrators turned to hiring strategies in which the overall number of faculty—whose salaries were traditionally the largest single budget item of any college and university—were reduced and the number of managerial or support professionals increased. Information technology offered an alternative to having one faculty member per class in real time. Instead, professors' course materials could be transmitted to multiple audiences in a variety of formats and times. Interactivity, which was less possible with earlier technologies, made on-line courses comparable to live classrooms. Interactivity could be handled by less costly adjunct faculty or by managerial professionals. To senior administrators, the opportunities presented by the new technologies were legitimated by their close fit with the labor structure of services in the new economy: small numbers of highly trained and paid traditional professionals, and larger numbers of support or managerial professionals, as is the case in health care.

However, the higher educational labor structure differs from that of other service sectors and the manufacturing sector, which have cut many midlevel managers, in that it has greatly expanded its managerial or support professionals. Moreover, such professionals do not necessarily contribute to the flexibility of the higher educational labor force. Often, especially in public institutions, managerial or support professionals are permanent employees. Senior administrators may prefer them to faculty for several reasons: the managerial professionals are directly responsible to administrators; they do not have the guildlike prerogatives of faculty, for example, tenure, self-governance, and peer-evaluation; and, in the short run, they are probably less costly than faculty.[3]

The managerial or support professionals generally worked with faculty to create digital instructional technologies and were housed in a variety of organizational contexts: media centers, teaching centers, distance education centers, and computing centers. Like technology licensing officials, they quickly formed their own professional associations. These are a form of interstitial organization, in that they depend on the time and dues made possible by their members' college or university positions. Among the professional associations and consortia involved in digital instructional technologies are the National Learning Infrastructure Initiative (NLII), which is part of EDUCAUSE, the Association for the Advancement of Computing in Education (AACE), the American Distance Education Consortium (ADEC), the New Media Consortium (NMC), and the Consortium of College and University Media Centers (CCUMC). As educational technologists professionalized, they asked administrators for amenities like those faculty enjoy—funds to attend conferences for professional development, budgets for new equipment and technologies, and increased support staff.

Most importantly, managerial or support technologists made the case that they coproduced instruction with faculty. Historically, what differentiated faculty from managerial professionals was that managerial professionals did not regularly teach. Even if they held PhDs and occasionally offered courses, they had no authority over the curricula. When they coproduced instructional materials with faculty, managerial professionals moved closer to the educational function of higher education.

Over time, this expanded capacity was somewhat centralized through positions such as chief information officer (CIO), a position not widely available

3. National data systems have not yet caught up with the changes in the higher education labor force, so managerial or support professionals are an undifferentiated category, making it difficult to calculate cost savings. Both technology licensing staff and computer repair persons are included in the category. However, when a position is permanent, salaries usually increase more regularly than they do for contingent workers, raising questions about the long-term cost savings of hiring managerial or support professionals.

until a decade ago, and distance-education officer. These offices engaged the market in several ways. The extent to which campuses were "wired" was a marketing device to attract traditional students to campuses. Distance education opened up new student markets that could increase enrollment without expanding facilities, relying on "clicks not bricks" to hybridize the educational environment beyond the physical campus. These offices could be involved in selling courseware—and various other copyrighted educational materials not packaged as curricula leading to a degree—in a range of external markets.

Faculty had to position themselves in regard to the new technologies embedded in the academic capitalist knowledge/learning regime. National organizations of unionized faculty are clear that faculty should own copyrightable intellectual property, ranging from books and creative works to courseware and educational materials. Some unionized faculty in the two- and four-year colleges used their collective power to bargain the right to hold title to copyrighted courseware and educational materials and to receive overload pay when they teach larger numbers of students through distance education. Because administrators want to expand on-line education, copyright policies usually provide generous royalties to faculty, even when the college or university owns the copyright and faculty have made substantial use of institutional resources. Because faculty want to share in the profits created from their educational labors, they participate in consolidating the academic capitalist knowledge/learning regime.

Some collective-bargaining agreements point to ways in which the academic capitalist knowledge/learning regime retains aspects of the public good knowledge regime. These include setting aside some monies from royalties or external revenues from distance education for public good uses, discounting products that have been subsidized by public monies, and distributing all materials at cost (Rhoades 2002b). Although such agreements are small in number, they demonstrate that organized faculty could expand collective-bargaining provisions to accommodate both profit and the public good.

Ironically, the greater faculty's collective success in negotiating ownership of copyrightable intellectual property and increased pay for participating in distance education, the wider the range of faculty rewards and the less cohesive the collectivity. Not all faculty pursue ownership of copyrightable intellectual property. Those who do may increase their pay significantly, creating differentiation among salaries. Historically, less prestigious institutions have had relatively undifferentiated salaries, which fostered faculty solidarity and facilitated unionization. The pursuit of profits based on intellectual property may weaken that solidarity and undercut the unions that have successfully bargained for faculty ownership.

As managerial capacity increases and managerial professionals work with faculty to coproduce products based on information technology and geared to new student markets, the traditional role of faculty in colleges and universities is restructured. Faculty are not the only professionals responsible for education. Rather, they are content specialists in teams of managerial professionals that produce instruction for an academic capitalist knowledge/learning regime.

7

ACADEMIC CAPITALISM AT THE DEPARTMENT LEVEL

ACADEMIC DEPARTMENTS ARE INCREASINGLY being treated by college and university central administrators as cost centers and revenue production units (Whalen 1991). For example, science and engineering departments may be characterized, and may characterize themselves, as being "productive" of revenue and as "subsidizing" units that do not generate external monies (Gumport 1993). In this context we might expect departments to increasingly orient themselves towards activities and markets that they hope will generate revenues. The primary questions that frame this chapter are: How and to what extent are academic departments, as the basic providers and producers of education and research, collectively undertaking entrepreneurial initiatives? Has entrepreneurial culture moved from the periphery of institutions, where Clark (1998) located it, into the academic heartland? To what extent are departments engaging in academic capitalism in the new economy?

Theory and Method

In *Academic Capitalism* Slaughter and Leslie made the case that around 1980 "to maintain and expand resources faculty had to compete increasingly for external dollars that were tied to market-related research, which was referred to variously as applied, commercial, strategic, and targeted research, whether these moneys were in the form of research grants and contracts, service contracts, partnerships with industry and government, technology transfer, or the recruitment of more and higher fee-paying students" (1997, p. 8). Increased competition for external revenues directed institutional expenditures and faculty activity away from instruction.

Although faculty had long engaged in federal research grant and contract activity, Slaughter and Leslie identified the 1980s as a turning point in the pattern of universities' revenue streams. At research universities, funding from the states diminished dramatically as a share of institutions' operating budgets, from about 50 to 28 percent. Although federal grant and contract research monies increased throughout this period, from $6.063 million in 1980 to $24.241 million in 2001, as a share of institutions' operating budgets, these monies declined slightly, and the federal funding share of academic R&D also decreased from 67 percent in 1980 to 59 percent in 2001. By contrast, entrepreneurial or private research markets, though small in absolute terms, grew from 4 percent in 1980 to about 7 percent in 2001 (NSF 2003). The greatest growth in shares of institutions' operating budgets was student tuition: as these monies are more fungible than restricted monies such as grants and contracts, they were shifted away from instruction and toward the support of research and entrepreneurial activity.

The theory of academic capitalism moves beyond this initial conceptualization to explore the processes through which these behaviors manifest themselves, concentrating on how various segments of institutions of higher education intersect state and market. In this chapter, we look primarily at academic departments. The theory of academic capitalism (see chapter 1) would lead us to expect some department heads and faculty to continue to exploit federal grant and contract markets as well as to develop entrepreneurial initiatives, either pushed by resource constraints or pulled by opportunities offered by the academic capitalist knowledge/learning regime. An embedded assumption of the theory of academic capitalism is that shifting revenue streams, whether contracting or expanding, shape strategic initiatives. Given that student tuition accounts for the greatest increase in shares of operating budgets over the past twenty-five years, we would expect increased educational initiatives, regardless of field. We would expect to find departments involved in reshaping their fields to integrate with the new economy.

This chapter reports data from an NSF-supported study (Leslie, Rhoades, and Oaxaca 1999) of departments at eleven public research universities that were members of the Association of American Universities. The study was focused on five fields of science: engineering, physical sciences, life sciences, mathematics, and social sciences. Departments were the unit of analysis. In each of the fields in each of the eleven universities three departments were randomly drawn. The heads of these departments (135) were interviewed, as were three randomly selected faculty members from each of the sampled departments.

The sample consisted only of departments that generated at least some undergraduate credit hours. Analytically the focus was on whether and the extent to which there were trade-offs in departments between the pursuit of academic capitalism and the production of undergraduate education. Directors of centers or department heads of units that did not teach undergraduate students were not interviewed. That is an important omission. Much of the dynamism of universities in the past twenty years has been attributed to the emergence and proliferation of various centers and institutes (Geiger 1990, 1993). One survey of the top 150 universities found that "nearly all of the fastest growing [in research monies] research universities (82%) stressed the importance of research centers to their research growth during the 1980s" (Stahler and Tasch 1994, p. 547).

The study focused on public research universities, which are thought by many scholars and policymakers to be less responsive than private institutions to external needs, pressures, demands, and markets.[1] The study did not include less prestigious universities, liberal arts colleges, and community colleges. Although these limitations reduce generalizability, they can also be seen as strengths. The study explored activities in the academic heartland—in traditional, discipline-based departments. Such a sample represents a best-case test of the questions that underlie this chapter.

Fiscal Pressures

Across the board, department heads talked about the increased pressure from provosts and presidents to enhance productivity and generate new revenues. Throughout the institutions there was a belief that more competitive market processes for allocating state monies to academic departments were being introduced and a view that departments and faculty were being pressured to find external resources to supplement institutional funds. That sense of scarcity and increased pressure was complemented by perceptions of heightened competition for external revenues, particularly with regard to research monies.[2]

Amid the generalized sense of scarcity there was considerable variation from one institution and field to the next as to the particular levels of fiscal pressure. For example, some units had a richer array of market opportunities available to them internally and externally than did others. Moreover, departments in dif-

1. However, there is important evidence to the contrary in terms of general responsiveness (Francis and Hampton 1999). Public research universities are the sites of some of the most longstanding and aggressively pursued technology transfer activity. The Wisconsin Alumni Research Foundation (WARF) at the University of Wisconsin began in the 1930s. The University of California is one of the largest generators of patent activity and revenue. The University of Utah is renowned for its aggressive pursuit of commercialization.

2. The question of increased competition for federal grant and contract funding is complex. Federal grant and contract funding has not decreased but has grown steadily over the last twenty-five years. However, the size of the science establishment has increased, which increases competition, and the fields of science that are most richly funded have shifted. See Greenberg 2001.

ferent universities confronted different resource allocation processes, for the managerial translation of fiscal pressure by the central administration varied by campus. Some universities had set up responsibility center management budgetary systems. Others had established incentive-based budgeting systems that swept a small percentage of departmental budgets to the central administration and then required departments to justify reallocation back to their units. Still others had weak central administrative budgetary incentive systems.

The varied position of departments relative to external and internal economies and opportunities contributed to considerable variation in how departments responded to fiscal pressure. Most importantly, although many departments increased their grant and contract activity, and some were increasingly partnering with corporations in various ways, the most prominent collective entrepreneurial activities were educationally oriented. There were also many departments that showed relatively little evidence of a collective, strategic response. In these cases, department heads and faculty expressed frustration, bemoaning the changed fiscal environment, but admitted they were doing little about it. And in some cases the entrepreneurial efforts of heads were resisted by departmental faculty. Thus, the pursuit of academic capitalism was not only contingent but also debated and both actively and passively resisted.

Fiscal pressure was also linked to declining support, shifting priorities, and/or increased competition for research monies from certain federal agencies and in certain fields of work. As one astronomy head stated: "We rely on federal money. Department of Energy, NASA, they're down. And NSF has gone down the toilet. The evil empire is dead so we bite the big one." And he was not alone. A math department head noted the significance of the end of the cold war: "We are 65 percent dependent on NSF. They have cut back, not in grants, but in the amounts of money per grant. So we get the same number of grants but we get less support." The substantial majority of department heads experienced significant fiscal pressure. Nearly two-thirds of the department heads had found it necessary to substitute self-generated revenues for state monies in some category of expenditure (28% had done so for instructional funds, 45% for graduate student support, and 53% for operating funds [Leslie, Rhoades, and Oaxaca 1999]).

Research Entrepreneurism

The universities in our sample had competed successfully in federal research markets for decades, substantially augmenting annual operating budgets with external revenues from grants and contracts. Presidents and vice-presidents for research pressed faculty to maintain and expand their federal grant and contract work. From 1980 to the present, the sampled institutions substantially increased federal grants and contracts.

The research activities of scientists and engineers are profoundly influenced by external markets. Over the last fifteen years, that landscape has changed significantly. The federal government is still, by a ratio of approximately ten to one, the principal source of external support for academic research. Yet the orientation of federal funding agencies has increasingly turned toward commercially relevant research. Industry representatives now sit on many review panels for allocating grants. Federal agencies have funded a variety of organizational structures such as centers that are grounded in partnerships between the state, corporate business, and universities. The strategic planning efforts of federal agencies have focused monies on fields of work that have potential commercial and economic development payoffs (Branscomb et al. 1997a, 1997b; Etzkowitz and Gulbrandsen 1999; Feldman et al. 2002b).

It is not clear whether professors understand the degree to which the federal funding agencies have directed priorities toward economic competitiveness. Evidence from chapter 4 and from the NSF study on which this chapter is based suggests that many do not, perhaps because they prefer to believe in a system of research funding that is not tied to imperatives other than those of science. However, regardless of scientists and engineers' understanding of the changing goals of mission agencies and the funding priorities of the federal government, they see federal grant and contract funding as the key to the research prestige system and value it above all other types of external funding.

University administrators, especially presidents and vice-presidents for research, understand that such funding is the bread and butter of external revenue streams. They also understand that federal grant funding plays an important role in research prestige systems and exhort their faculty to increase competition in federal grant and contract markets. They watch the NSF R&D charts as closely as provosts watch *U.S. News and World Report* ratings.

Our 1999 study provided evidence across universities of an increased central administrative emphasis on entrepreneurial research markets. These markets involve direct work with corporations or corporate partners, although the state is sometimes a silent partner, contributing funds directly (as in the case of engineering centers) or indirectly (because relationships between corporations and departments are built around intellectual property based on federally funded research grants). This emphasis took various forms and was typically broadcast through mechanisms controlled by vice-presidents of research. The message to connect more with industry was also articulated by presidents, carried out in the creation of research parks, and promoted within institutions by managerial professionals. Yet there did not appear to be great collective enthusiasm for such activity in the basic units of the academic heartland. As one faculty member in geology stated, "I think there is a campus wide push . . . But it is not explicit at the department level . . . We get all this—encouragement to do more research, and more research that is supported by industrial monies—from the University Research Dean. It also comes from the research park, and the research institutes such as the Advanced Research Technology Institute, which is a group of units focused on technology transfer. We get a lot of that from the university. They even send people out to talk with departments."

In absolute terms, a substantial minority of the departments were involved in entrepreneurial research markets. One geology head referred to the department's strategic plan, which involved "developing closer ties with industry." Part of that strategy included targeting interdisciplinary areas important to industry. In the head's words, "We want to forge more interdisciplinary, inter-institutional, inter-college ties." This statement calls attention to an important part of entrepreneurial research initiatives: a shift to participating in the private market often means the emergence of new organizational forms in universities, layered on top of existing departmental structures.

A widening range of entrepreneurial research opportunities are available in the private sector. There are already well-established mechanisms for interaction between individual academics and these businesses, in the form of consulting relationships. The newer forms include various university-industry partnerships, patenting, and universities taking equity in faculty firms (all of which were discussed in chapters 3 and 4). Although entrepreneurial research markets have grown, relatively few faculty were involved with them. In fact, many heads and faculty spoke almost fatalistically of two reasons for such lack of entrepreneurial activity—industry is not really interested in the research we do, and we are not in a geographical location with a lot of business. Interestingly, they were referring to large, corporate enterprises, which were the focus of much central administrative attention.

The exception is biotechnology. In the 1999 NSF study, several departments in the life sciences were engaged in private, entrepreneurial biotechnology markets. This was a strategic choice, given that approximately half of biotechnology funding is private (U.S. Congress 1991). However, few departments were undertaking collective initiatives. This finding fits with earlier research that showed that in the mid-1990s about 5 percent of all U.S. life scientists were engaged in entrepreneurial research in biotechnology (Louis et al. 1989, but see also Krimsky 2003).

Despite the central administrative push for faculty and units to engage in entrepreneurial activity, there was no evidence of a systematic push across units to, for example, recruit new faculty who would connect with industry. No consistent evidence emerged of departments and department heads making hiring decisions with potential entrepreneurial activity as even one of the criteria. As a chemistry department head said, responding to a query about whether the department was recruiting in areas that would connect well with entrepreneurial funding opportunities, "We should be flexible and consider such matters. But . . . recently we got a person and sort of stumbled into a fit. But that's not why we hired him. We hired him and then we realized, hey, this guy is good in this [entrepreneurial] area. That's great. He can work on that. But that's not why we hired him." Occasionally, some faculty indicated their units were moving toward hiring to strategically intersect private research markets. As one physics professor said, "We are hiring more applied, interdisciplinary faculty who do research with application to industry." For the most part, however, we did not get a sense of such strategic hiring. When there was some movement toward applied or entrepreneurial research markets, it seemed to be change on the margins. For example, a physics head noted that his department and a few others had gotten new positions (in his case, in high energy physics) because of the contribution of these fields to the state economy. He then stated: "Yes, we are doing more applied research; but it is only 2–3 out of 31 faculty. There is an optics person with a few patents. Another person wanted to start a company."

Similarly, no consistent evidence emerged of department heads mentoring faculty, particularly junior faculty, in the direction of doing entrepreneurial work. There is a potential in this interaction for heads to suggest to new faculty fruitful avenues of research that might yield private monies and relations with industry for the department. However, we found no evidence of any such pattern of encouragement. In fact, quite the contrary was true. In those few cases when department heads mentioned entrepreneurial research markets to new hires, they cautioned young faculty against becoming too involved with industry and private sources of research support and activity. The rationale of department heads had to do partly with the unreliability of such funding and the adverse impact its loss could have on the young person's career. As one chemistry head stated: "A lot of the people we hired, the biotechs are after them. We've hired people who are being pursued by business. The faculty don't even have to ask. I tell them, 'Be careful. Make sure that you have as your base, federal monies.' With private support, one day you think you're on easy street, the next day they pull their funding and you're stuck. I've seen it happen before." The heads we interviewed focused on the individual faculty member's academic needs and interests rather than on some collective departmental market orientation or plan to generate revenue.

Generally, department heads and faculty in science, mathematics, and engineering (SME) preferred federal grant and contract markets operated by the mission agencies above all others. This was a strategic choice. Federal grant and contract funds far exceeded private, entrepreneurial research markets and were central to the research prestige system. Individually and collectively, faculty and departments' reputations depended on their ability to compete successfully in these markets. Federal grant and contract markets were also crucial to success in entrepreneurial or private markets. Most entrepreneurial ventures were built on federally funded research made alienable by Bayh-Dole (1980). As the faculty member quoted in chapter 4 said, "Patents are the icing on the cake. You've got to have the cake first." The department heads in our sample did not talk much about their strategies for success in federal grant and contract markets, probably because such behaviors are ubiquitous, given that most SME faculty worked on federal grants and contracts during their training, and peer pressure as well as merit review at the department level maintains pressure for success in these markets.

Educational Entrepreneurism

What was most unexpected about the sample was the considerable extent of collective effort to generate new revenue streams in the realm of education. The literature would lead us to believe that entrepreneurial educational efforts would be found in departments not positioned close to federal grant and contract research markets; it has not addressed any such activity in SME departments. Such a finding points to the value of the theory of academic capitalism in the new economy, which holds that departments and faculty undertake strategic initiatives partly in response to the push of resource constraints and the pull of various market opportunities beyond those in technology transfer. In the case of educational entrepreneurial activity, departments were responding to new economy pulls to develop programs for information/knowledge society employment, in which many positions are highly technical and located in large corporate enterprises, often involving the upgrading of existing personnel. Tuition dollars, the most rapidly increasing share of institutional budgets were targeted by departments as well.

Departmental competition for new students whose tuition would increase external revenue streams is closely related to competition for internal resources. Many departments were confronting increasingly competitive markets for the internal allocation of state monies. In many cases, central administrators linked student credit-hour productivity more explicitly and powerfully to internal resource allocations than they had in the past. Departments developed strategies to compete more effectively in this undergraduate marketplace, with a particular focus on lower division, general education classes that would generate significant increases in credit-hour production (Volk, Slaughter, and Thomas 2002). To some extent, departments have always competed internally to capture student credit hours. However, as universities increasingly emphasize credit-hour productivity, this competition has increased. Thus, we have concentrated on new program developments and new educational activities because they bring in external resources, which we see as a key component of academic capitalism.

Educational activity geared toward securing new streams of external resources fell into various categories. First, some units sought to increase undergraduate credit-hour production by reorganizing their curricula or developing new programs to attract more majors in their fields. Not uncommonly, such programmatic efforts were connected to conceptions of external employment markets for new economy careers, many of which had technical components that SME departments could provide. A second sort of initiative focused on expanding summer programs with an eye toward generating revenues for the department. A third type of educational entrepreneurial activity involved developing "professional" master's programs that targeted potential student populations and employment markets in corporations. Such programs were inexpensive to deliver because the labor-intensive thesis option for students was generally eliminated. They could be taught partly or largely by adjuncts and even doctoral students, and they generated more revenue because master's students generally did not require research support and sometimes paid higher tuition. In some cases the tuition bill was paid by the corporation for which the master's student worked. Fourth, some units participated in fund-raising activities that often targeted industry and that involved raising the money for educational purposes, such as supporting students and enhancing undergraduate classrooms and labs. Fifth, a few units sought to generate revenue by placing students in industry. The fourth and fifth forms of educational entrepreneurism are significant in that they are not directly "instructional" in the sense of Anderson's (2001) "instructional capitalism"; nevertheless, they were focused on educational services and activities.

Some educational entrepreneurial activity at the undergraduate level involved developing new programs designed to be more closely connected to emerging or existing employment markets. As one geology department head indicated, his unit was developing a program in environmental geology. "It's all marketing. The whole thing is marketing. The whole thing is how many bodies do you process. Administrators actually use these terms. The whole revision of the curriculum is to attract more majors. To attract the students of the [19]90s." Again, the curricular changes and new developments were being driven not so much by educational considerations as by a sense of potential opportunity structures in new economy employment markets. Another head noted the development of environmental chemistry degrees at the undergraduate level. A psychology head pointed to a new undergraduate track between psychology and biology, designed to appeal to the expanded career opportunities in biotechnology. In referring to the development of a BA (to complement the BS) in physics, the head indicated that the aim was to increase student numbers because "not all students want to go on to graduate school in physics; and physics can be a good major for getting into med school." Like biotechnology, medical substances and devices are a key growth area in the new economy and are often developed by persons with medical training. Similarly, a math head noted the development of an undergraduate program in "actuarial science as a way of recruiting students." Department heads saw the creation of new economy programs as a promising way to increase their numbers of majors.

Another entrepreneurial strategy for generating revenues from courses was increasing the offering of summer school classes and programs. The advantage of summer school as an entrepreneurial venture is that it pays immediate and direct monies to departments, independent of allocations of state monies. As one science head stated, "Summer can be quite lucrative. Chemistry 101 is like a fast dentist. It can generate lots of revenue." Of course, as in any marketplace, some units were more favorably positioned than others to succeed. Revenue-generating summer programs were more common in psychology and economics (and business schools generally), where costs are not great, and less common in departments such as geology that run expensive summer camps.

One of the most common examples of educational entrepreneurism was the development of new master's degree programs. Many departments were consciously developing graduate curricula and programs that articulated more closely with the needs of the new economy. For example, a math department head indicated that, "There is a move across the country to develop an MS in industrial mathematics. And new courses are designed to make graduates more suitable to industrial employment. It's in the works here." Public research university departments have long emphasized doctoral programs because they are central to competition in prestige markets, both nationally/internationally and within the institution. Master's degrees have not generally been treated as terminal degrees in the disciplines, except for those in which a doctorate is not available. The development of new master's degrees is a dramatic break from the past and reflects a significant reorientation at the graduate level to the external employment market and to revenue generation. Part of the strategy is to forge closer ties with business—for instance, through advisory boards that would give suggestions to departments about curricula as well as donate monies. Yet another strategy is to leverage federal money, reflecting a shift in the external market for such research funding, a shift that involved emphasizing relevance and connections to business, built, as a math head stated, into the NSF's grant competitions.

The idea underlying the new master's programs was not to prepare people for new employment but to target people already employed in business for a new kind of degree program. Called "professional master's degree" programs, these were particularly evident in engineering departments and colleges. Unlike the traditional master's degree, they did not require a thesis. The programs were market rather than educationally driven. As one engineering head said, "We have toyed with a non-thesis MA option. The professional MA in engineering might take care of that for us. It has some distance learning, some business courses, some science and engineering advanced courses. Due to the large number of mining companies in [the state] this should work. And the thesis option often kills us with people in business. There will also be more offerings in the evenings." The idea is to generate additional revenues for departments through increased graduate credit hours and tuition. A head of civil engineering noted the significance of these degrees for his department's budget. "The college has installed a professional engineering master's degree. It's a separate program. I get a check every fall for $10,000–20,000. In the next three to four years, maybe $50,000. Civil engineering is a big participant. It's continuing education. All classes are 3:30–10 PM, and most students are employed." Although he claimed that "there's nothing different about the classes" in the professional masters' degree program, his description of the department's strategy revealed a clear effort to capitalize financially on a different and lower quality student market. "We are trying to get graduate applicants who won't get a PhD accepted . . . to push them to the professional masters program. That gets them out of the statistics for our rankings in *US News & World Report.*" The new degree structure enabled the unit to tap into a new student market for continuing education without compromising its quality. As departments continue to play in the prestige market, they are developing strategies for competing in what is essentially a continuing education marketplace of institutions like the University of Phoenix.

Many of the new masters' degrees create the possibility of differential tuition, another mechanism for generating revenues from new student markets. As one economics head stated, "Business has tried to expand its MBA programs and then sought to gain a share of the increased revenues." Unlike traditional master's programs, departments get a direct economic payoff from enrollment in the new programs, gaining a share of their tuition. On the campus of the economics head quoted above, there are a few such programs—one being a new professional master's in telecommunications, bringing together engineering, computer science, business, and public policy. Very often the programs that bring external revenues to departments offer employment skills for new economy jobs.

Such programs were found not only in engineering but also, as noted above, in math and science departments. For example, one physics head indicated that his department was developing a professional master's program in industrial and applied physics because "we want to broaden our graduate student base, not just create clones of ourselves" and because such a program would strengthen connections with industry. At another institution, a physics head was more explicit about such a program's purposes. "We are trying to broaden our curriculum. The curriculum here is the traditional one. We want to go into more applied master's degrees. One is about to be approved. The idea is to have an additional fifteen students a year, who will graduate in one–two years. They will not have any support [in contrast to other students]. These students will pay their fees." These programs are cash cows, generating revenue because they cost less and the students pay more. The programs connect students and departments with the new economy and reveal the reorientation to the market embedded in educational entrepreneurial activity. However, the units noted above were not changing their doctoral programs; they were continuing to compete in the prestige market even as they developed new programmatic structures to tap into new student markets in the new economy.

Some departments also sought to connect with industry and generate revenue through courses that did not fit within graduate or undergraduate programs. For example, one head in engineering noted that there were some faculty who taught workshops and short courses to generate monies, sometimes up to $80,000 a year. Although the department had not really coordinated that activity in the past, this head stated, "We're going to do more of that as we try to do more teaming up with industry; we haven't done enough of that, and we're trying to do more."

Educational entrepreneurism extends beyond curricular change. In some cases, units went directly to the private sector, with their proverbial hats in hand, for equipment and monies. As one chemistry head said, "Occasionally we go to Dow or Lilly to get money for equipment. This is an intermittent matter, to get dollars for undergraduate classes." Similarly, an engineering head indicated that "we get significant amounts of money from mining companies in [the state] and in the U.S., and also from alumni and private citizens. But the bulk of the money comes from companies. Annually, it's about $60,000–80,000. We just send out letters and ask for direct operations support. We also get a lot of scholarship support . . . And we use it for computer facilities and running the department." This collective entrepreneurial activity was not geared primarily to research support but rather was focused on supporting students and undergraduate instruction.

Along similar lines, some units were entrepreneurial fund-raisers. Some funds raised were related to research, but in most cases they stemmed more from education (e.g., donors were alumni) and/or they involved supporting educational activities. Such fund raising was often based on relations with businesses and industries (though not always; one of the units most successful in raising monies was an anthropology department). For example, a geology department head had organized an aggressive fund-raising plan focused on alumni, many of whom worked in the oil and gas industry.

In some cases, the fund raising was grounded in an advisory board composed of well-connected individuals who helped identify and cultivate potential donors. Some particularly entrepreneurial departments had developed their own advisory boards. More typically, boards were set up by academic colleges. Departments have also hired fund-raising officers. Whereas fund raising was once primarily the province of central development officers, now the commitment to fund raising has extended into the academic heartland, academic colleges, and, in some cases, departments.

Some departments raised revenues by serving as employment agents. One example of tapping into employers' need for students in order to generate revenues is provided by a head of space sciences. "The dean, at our suggestion, started a corporate scholars program. Lots of companies are not interested in our research, because our horizon is too long term. Our research is oriented to the long term. They are oriented to two to five years at the most. But they are interested in our students. Three companies a day are calling me to interview students. They ask things like, "Do you have a good student in [a particular area]?" So we charge them now. We charge them a fee. There is also an internship program. The dean matches students and companies." This head captured a key point that helps clarify the greater extent of department-level collective entrepreneurial activity in the educational versus the research realm. In the arena of research, there are established mechanisms, such as consulting, by which companies can tap into the knowledge base of universities through individual faculty. Yet businesses are most interested in universities as a source of employees. That creates an opportunity for collective entrepreneurial initiatives in the educational arena.

The departments in our sample, most of which were SME, were active in traditional federal research markets through which they generated external revenues for their departments and universities. However, the bulk of their new entrepreneurial activities did not focus on research with corporate partners. They sought to bring in new revenue streams through education-oriented activities. Departments developed curricula related to new economy employment opportunities to attract new students. They expanded summer programs when they could capture the revenues. Professional master's programs geared to continuing education for the new economy often brought revenues directly to departments. Departments received funding for linking students up with employers, and departments raised their own funds for education by connecting with industry via solicitations, advisory boards, and fund-raising officers. Given that the new economy is a knowledge/information economy and that tuition revenues are the most rapidly expanding share of annual operating budgets, we should not be surprised that many departments are offering educational services aimed at generating external revenues.

Strategic Resistances

Given the seriousness of many departments' fiscal situations, we were surprised by what we saw as a relatively uneven level of strategic response. When departments perceive external challenges and threats, they do not always know what to do, or they are not willing to do something, or they are saved from having to strategically reposition themselves by virtue of a special commitment from central administration.

Moreover, departmental incorporation into the academic capitalist knowledge/learning regime is incomplete. There is substantial resistance to entrepreneurial activity other than competing for federal grants and contracts. Although department heads give a variety of reasons for not seeking to compete in entrepreneurial research markets or in instructional capitalism, a great deal of resistance is tied to commitment to the research prestige system associated with the public good knowledge regime (see chapter 1) in which basic science is highly valued.

Department heads often gave their geographical area as a reason for not being able to undertake entrepreneurial initiatives in relation to business. This was particularly true in regard to private research markets oriented to business entrepreneurism. In the words of one department head, "It's hard to see how astronomy can do anything about connections with industry. We are users, not builders and developers, and that's what they want." Or, as a computer science head said, "One of the reasons for the lack of a connection is that there is not an industrial environment. [The geographical region of this university] is not the Silicon Valley. There is not the same symbiotic environment as when you have industry around you." We repeatedly heard stories invoking the liability of location as a reason for not seeking out entrepreneurial research opportunities with business.

In other cases, department heads saw their fields as not competitive in private research markets. As a biology head stated, "There is a slight increase in faculty activity in this area [connections with industry], but it's only a couple of faculty. The rest of us don't work in areas that connect to business."

Pleading inability to engage in private research markets based on location or type of field legitimates resistance. The astronomy department head, accustomed to federal funding through NASA, was unable to see the opportunities presented by the commercialization of space. The computer science head, who dealt in information technology infrastructure, conveniently ignored the ways in which information technology collapses distances that limit geographical liabilities. Similarly, the biology head paid little heed to the exceptional opportunities for biotechnology in private research markets.

In many cases, department heads were openly frustrated and/or angry about pressure to find new sources of federal grants and contracts or entrepreneurial research opportunities. They wished for the good old days. One math head pointed to the end of the cold war and to changes in NSF policies as sources of increasing fiscal pressure on his faculty and department. "Grants and contracts are way down. When the evil empire died we came upon hard times. Weapons are down. The DOD and DOE are way down. The NSF has changed its policies. It used to support two summer months; now it's only one and generally it's younger people. Older people are locked out, despite their qualifications." This head was aware of a fiscal problem and of some of its sources. "The focus of the NSF, at least in math, is not hard math anymore. It is on education and on interdisciplinary studies." Later in the interview he stated bitterly, "And they turn down proposals that don't mention training and human resources. It drives me nuts. And I'm not alone in the nuthouse." His explanation as to why the NSF was changing was: "It's who's running the NSF, and I know them. Education types are running the place. It used to be basic research was really the central focus of the NSF. No more. They are going on an education bent, undergraduate education, interdisciplinary education." Yet, he had no strategic sense of the connection to the NSF's educational emphasis on workforce development, and no strategy for adapting the department to this changing opportunity structure. There was no effort, for example, to partner with math educators in education on grants. "Basic research suffers, and that's what most of us do. So where do we go? I'm not sure many of us want to go that way [to more education-focused or applied research]. The stuff that we do may not have relevance. If it does, it's twenty years down the road. Mathematicians are not willing to work in applied. They are not likely to adapt." There was little sense of willingness to shift the focus of the department's research activities, even on the margins. Instead, the response was contempt for the new direction of funding agencies, contempt based on a prestige structure of basic versus applied research, and of science versus education-focused work.

In some cases, heads did not respond to fiscal pressure because they did not feel it, perhaps because of their success in federal grant and contract markets, or because the central administration was bailing them out. Central administrators, like the heads themselves, were somewhat committed to the research prestige system rooted in the federal grant and contract system, and, even if they lacked such a commitment, they apparently felt they could not afford to dispense with the external revenues brought in through federal research markets. On several campuses it was clear that some units, generally in the sciences, were seen as central to the future of the institutions; therefore, even when they had not been particularly productive in generating student credit hours, graduates, entrepreneurial research monies, and even federal grant monies, they were still being strongly supported by the central administration as potential generators of revenue and sources of prestige. Sometimes such investments in units that had not been particularly strong or productive were driven by a commitment to success in key prestige markets of higher education. As an anthropology head indicated, "We have the biggest physics department in the country. If we don't have a first rate physics department, where is our monument? The National Science Rankings are essential; that's where the investment in this institution is. On this campus, 40 percent of the faculty are in departments which will become permanent minority status." Ironically, as he noted of his own unit, "We generate tremendous revenues for the institution [through instruction]." However, such a commitment applied overwhelmingly to science and engineering fields that were seen as able to access federal grant and contract markets.

The academic capitalist knowledge/learning regime coexists with the public good knowledge regime. Some heads and many faculty who came into the institution under an "old regime" with a different set of values attached to academic work coexist with newly arrived faculty and heads, some of whom are committed to a more entrepreneurial conception of academe. Two computer science heads exemplify this situation, illustrating different attitudes toward entrepreneurial research and educational markets. The old head was still in the department and openly questioned the entrepreneurial efforts being undertaken. He was critical of the new head's initiatives. The idea of a separate school of computer science which would expand the student market and faculty/student productivity ratios had no appeal for him. When asked about splitting up the arts and sciences college into separate colleges, which created the opportunity for a separate school, he said, "I would not like a split. I like very much the relationship with other units, and not just sciences. It encourages us to be less engineering oriented in our programs. We should consider other departments. I like being at a university. What's the point of being here? I like the fact that students take courses across different fields . . . As one college we're more attuned to the needs of students, to training the general population in computers. We would as a separate group not attend to that." The subtext of the old department head's discourse is oriented to liberal educational mission and purposes. Productivity and revenue generation do not feature at all. The old head was also openly disdainful of private, entrepreneurial research markets.

Several faculty within this computer science department were openly or passively resistant to the new head's initiatives. Their resistance undermined the new head's charge from central administration to become more entrepreneurial. Most faculty members did not pursue the private-sector-oriented entrepreneurial connections that the new head was promoting. Other heads on this campus indicated that the new computer science head was experiencing considerable difficulty in implementing his programs, and that he was beginning to fall out of favor with central administration.

A math department head offered another example of resistance to the redirection of a department's research focus. Noting a 10 percent decline in his unit's grants and contracts monies, he indicated that there was going to be an emphasis on recruiting faculty in computational math.

> We are very well placed in the balance between pure and applied math. We have quite a strong faculty in both. That helps in recruiting and in moving research agendas to take advantage of opportunities . . . We're flexible. We're actually going to move more towards computational math. The dean has pushed that. There was an external review committee of the math department that strongly recommended this . . . There has been a reasonable amount of resistance to this move in non-computational people. That new emphasis plays out in recruitment, course development, and in the

development of a new program in computational science, to be done in conjunction with other departments.

Faculty in subspecialties within departments could resist new directions. In large departments, that can make substantial change very challenging.

Sometimes the source of faculty resistance was the core clash of entrepreneurial activities and values with those of academe. For example, a psychology head in another institution pointed to an initiative he was promoting in his department to connect with industry. "We just had a retreat. One working group was outreach and entrepreneurial activity. We have made that committee permanent, to try to develop some opportunities. Faculty reaction was predictable, with research scientists and scholars. If this helps me fund my research, I'm for it. If it's to sell products, I'm against it. My angle is to bring in resources for students and postdocs." If faculty thought getting private monies would support their research, they were willing to support entrepreneurial endeavors. However they were less enthusiastic about selling products. The head hoped an educational strategy, generating support for students, would lessen opposition.

We interviewed many faculty who expressed varying levels of disdain for and hostility to research that was in their eyes more applied or that followed a logic of entrepreneurial opportunism rather than a logic of discovery. Sometimes the sentiment was expressed as a personal view about entrepreneurial activity, as in the case of the biochemistry professor who stated, "I personally think it's a disaster for faculty to ally themselves with industry and their problems. They are not basic problems. Faculty should do fundamental research, ivory tower research." In other cases, the sentiment was expressed in a simple observation about what was valued in the department. A faculty member in physics indicated that federal grant and contract research that brought prestige along with dollars should precede entrepreneurial work in private markets.

> Of all my colleagues [thirty-one] maybe one has made the transition from pretty basic to very market-oriented research. There is no example of the opposite . . . But there is no overt pressure to do that. The way we collectively view this issue, I would guess if we sampled the department you would probably get a consensus that if it happens—market direction—that's fine, but it's not our main mission. It's not something we try to do or feel bad about if we don't do it. We are a research department . . . Of course, it depends on how well you are doing. If you feel you are falling behind, then it makes sense to reconsider your direction. In our department, we don't have that feeling.

Another example speaks to a general bias against applied work. A faculty member in biology said, "I think there's a bias [in this department] against applied research. I happen not to share that bias. I think applied is fine. To me, basic and applied aren't that distinguishable." Another biology professor said, "About five to six years ago they built a research park. There was a lot of talk about how companies would come in and we would establish ties with them. It never really developed. There was sort of a revolt by faculty. We were being urged to orient our research to working with companies. As faculty explored this it seemed like it was completely unscientific. It's like we were providing a service to private companies to help them make money for their stockholders." A chemistry professor told a story of an internal departmental dispute centered on entrepreneurism. "It's up to the individual. Some individuals have chosen to do more patents. It caused a flap a few years ago. Some faculty were concerned that a faculty member wasn't publishing in open journals. He was acting like a businessman, getting the patent first. But he got tenure. He left abruptly this year. He went to industry." Each of these examples speaks to the existence of a university push and some movement on an individual level toward more entrepreneurial research activities. At the same time, they point to how and why it is problematic for departments to collectively pursue entrepreneurial initiatives in research.

In some cases, department heads were ambivalent about entrepreneurial work. One computer science department head talked about revising an "industrial board" of companies that would provide input regarding the education and training of students. Although he was pursuing this entrepreneurial initiative to enhance connections with the private sector, and hopefully to generate some revenues, he was a reluctant entrepreneur, as the following language suggests. "In a few weeks I'll have the first meeting with a steering group from the advisory board. We want to be open, but we don't want to bow to them . . . It's mostly related to education. But we know what's good in computer science education, not them. We want to address their needs, but we know what's best."

Departments in SME frequently engage in academic capitalism or the generation of external revenues. With regard to research, they prefer the federal grant and contract market above all others and do not demonstrate awareness that this research is more and more frequently aligned with the market. Their resistance is often articulated around adherence to values captured by the concepts of "basic" or "pure" research associated with the public good knowledge regime (see chapter 1). Basic or pure research gives professors the illusion of controlling research agendas and following research where it leads. Regardless of whether "curiosity-driven" research was tied into the long-term goals of mission agencies, professors were clear that they enjoyed the long time lines, generous funding, and indirect monitoring associated with (often DOD-funded) federal grants and contracts that characterized the period from 1945 to the 1980s.

Instructional Leverage amid Multiple Pressures

How can we understand the increase in collective departmental initiative and entrepreneurial effort in regard to instruction? Drawing on our interviews, we make the case that faculty develop entrepreneurial instructional ventures that intersect with recent strategic planning and budgeting processes adopted by public research university provosts and presidents in response to external political and fiscal pressures. Department heads attend to these processes but also hear contradictory, internal messages from university officials.

Provosts and deans are implementing mechanisms that make the internal allocation of state monies more competitive. Public research university central administrators now find themselves in a competitive marketplace for state monies and in a political environment that can be relatively hostile towards these institutions' research emphasis. Consequently, the target of many incentive-based budgeting mechanisms is student credit-hour production, particularly at the undergraduate level. Many department heads in our sample commented on this orientation to educational markets and productivity. At some campuses heads overwhelmingly identified the focus of provosts as being on issues related to instruction generally and undergraduate education in particular. "There is tremendous pressure from the provost to increase student credit hours. The pressure from the dean is to maintain or increase student credit hours. The main emphasis is, not to turn away students. Don't turn away students who want classes . . . The idea was that faculty numbers would stay about the same, but we would have increased numbers of students and thereby increase productivity. The formula was based on an incentive to grow" (physics head). In this case, however, enrollments at the institution did not grow, and the formula became a basis for reducing resources to departments. The head went on to say, "In internal resource allocation the deans don't look at research anymore. They look at student credit hours. We [department heads] have to keep reminding them of the purpose of a research university."

There were variations from one campus to the next in the specific mechanisms managers employed to allocate resources. There were also variations in the extent of emphasis on undergraduate education in comparison to federal grant–focused and entrepreneurial, private-sector-focused research. At most institutions, however, the issues of undergraduate education, instructional productivity, and faculty teaching loads were the focus of provosts' and presidents' budgeting processes and activities. Across institutions, nearly one-third of department heads reported an increase in the overall faculty teaching load (41% reported an increase in undergraduate teaching load). Only 7.5 percent reported decreased teaching loads. These figures suggest that provosts (and deans) had some success in the 1990s in leveraging increased faculty instructional activity, particularly at the undergraduate level.

Although in their annual budget allocation processes academic managers focused on instructional productivity, it is clear that these same managers, in addition to other administrators, were sending other messages as well. Such messages related not to student markets and educational productivity but to research and private-sector markets and the pursuit of entrepreneurial research ventures. These messages came not only from established administrative offices but from recently established offices and officials, for example, from managerial professionals such as technology transfer and research park directors. Department heads and faculty were clear that they were receiving multiple pressures and messages. As one head in space sciences related,

> There is no one in the institution that has a sense of the priorities in the university. It must be very hard to be a faculty member now, to have to do all these things. I asked the dean of the graduate school . . . which one of the tasks was most important. He can't tell me. He had no answer. I don't think there is one pressure. One of my colleagues in the math department, he gives the best description of our situation. Formerly our role was to produce top quality research and graduate education, and to do a reasonable job of teaching. Now he's told us to return undergraduates at a certain rate, to be diverse, to use technology in teaching to be innovative, to do outreach in the community, and to keep doing the research and graduate education. All with no new resources.

Similarly, a head in life sciences commented, "It's a schizophrenic situation because of higher administration. Central administration want you to be an excellent teacher. But the higher administration knows that if we stop writing grants, they'll fold up. And there's not enough merit money around to do much to reward people for teaching, or for research for that matter." In essence, these heads were saying that the university's academic managers wanted more for less. They wanted more productivity in a range of markets, with no increase or a reduction in faculty and other resources. Despite the discourse of academic managers about tough choices, many heads saw little evidence of prioritization. They were being leveraged to increase productivity in old (prestige and federal research) and new (student, educational, and entrepreneurial research) markets.

Conclusions

SME academic departments are very involved in academic capitalism. Most generate external revenues by competing for federal grant and contract funding. A relatively small number are active in private, entrepreneurial research markets. More and more departments are becoming active in educational initiatives designed to generate external revenues through new programs that articulate with the new economy.

As was the case historically, federal grant and contract work is central to SME departments. Private, entrepreneurial research markets are less so, perhaps because these markets are intersected by centers and institutes outside the departments. Entrepreneurial educational culture, however, seems to be blossoming in the academic heartland.

Departments develop various strategies to articulate with opportunities presented by the academic capitalist knowledge/learning regime. We did not locate precipitating causes but instead found general patterns. Department heads seemed to recognize two research systems, one based on grants and contracts, the other on the amount of revenues brought in. The two were not the same, although they overlapped at certain points. Federal grants and contracts were closely related to the research prestige system rooted in the public good regime. A number of heads believed that departments had to have a strong federal grant and contract base before engaging other research markets. Private, entrepreneurial research markets did not carry the same prestige with department heads as did federal grant and contract markets. According to the department head interviews, presidents and vice-presidents for research were perceived as valuing private, entrepreneurial research markets more than faculty did. However, department heads knew that these administrators had to attend to maintaining and expanding federal grant and contracts because they contributed reliably to annual operating budgets, while private research markets, although holding out the promise of very high returns, were less predictable.

Although a number of department heads tried to develop strategies for intersecting federal and private, entrepreneurial research markets, many resisted involvement with the latter. They preferred to try to maintain or expand federal grant and contract revenues rather than embark on ventures with corporations. Frequently, their preference was tied to commitment to the values of the public good knowledge regime. Even when department heads pursued a strategy that focused on both types of research markets, faculty within their departments or subspecialties resisted. The public good and academic capitalist knowledge/learning regimes coexisted.

The bulk of educational entrepreneurial activity of department heads was aimed at tuition and external monies (such as gifts) to support students and education; tuition constituted the most rapidly increasing share of annual operating budgets. The programs they crafted were aimed at linking SME fields to the new economy, capturing tuition revenues for departments. The technical components of much new economy employment made these programs relatively easy to "sell," and department heads seemed to be willing to reshape their fields to integrate with the new economy.

In short, then, academic capitalism has penetrated into basic academic departments. It has become part of the core educational activity of that academic heartland in the form of various types of educational entrepreneurism. However, the transition to an entrepreneurial culture is very much incomplete, uneven, and even contested, which is evident in some units more than others. In contrast to what the literature might lead us to believe, it is perhaps most contested in regard to an ongoing commitment to traditional conceptions of academe's role in conducting fundamental research, in the heartland of SME units that are deeply invested in federally funded research activities.

We seek to redress somewhat the limitations of the department head study by briefly considering a broader range of studies as they relate to academic capitalism in U.S. higher education. First, we note findings on centers and institutes in research universities. Second, we note studies that go beyond science and engineering and beyond public research universities, addressing the extent to which academic capitalism can be found throughout the U.S. higher education system.

The prevailing story told in the literature on higher education is that the dynamism and creativity of research universities lies more in the development of new academic units than it does in the traditional, discipline-based departments that continue to structure and produce most undergraduate education. For some time there has been a policy emphasis, at various levels, to promote the growth of centers and institutes, which link academics to external constituencies, particularly to government and business. In addition, there has been an increased policy emphasis on interdisciplinary programs. Centers, institutes, and interdisciplinary programs feature prominently in explanations for the dynamic rise of some institutions into the ranks of the nation's top research universities (Geiger 1990, 1993). Over time, the number of these units has risen significantly. Interdisciplinary structures often involve partnerships between universities and private enterprise; they are an important source of higher education's responsiveness to external corporate markets. Indeed, federal agencies have funded various types of centers (e.g., engineering research centers, and science and technology centers) that have as their explicit purposes and structures direct connections with and funding by private companies (Government-University-Industry Research Roundtable 1992; NSF 1989). As just one example, nearly 60 percent of 1,056 government-funded university-industry research centers (UIRCs), which have the explicit function of connecting universities and companies, were established in the 1980s (Cohen, Florida, and Coe 1994). The entrepreneurial significance of these centers is evident in the fact that almost 70 percent of industrial support for academic R&D is channeled through them (and a little less than one-third of UIRC budgets, on average, come from industrial sources).

In other words, much entrepreneurial initiative occurs outside basic academic departments. Organizational structures such as centers and institutes have been developed alongside discipline-based academic departments. This new mode of producing research has not replaced the old (research production continues in academic departments), but it coexists with the old, which remains the principal site for the production of undergraduate and graduate education.

A second point is that academic capitalism extends beyond science and engineering, and beyond research universities. Some years ago, we sat as participant observers on our university's technology transfer committee, which had nineteen members. All but two came from science and engineering. (The exceptions were a business school professor who studied technology transfer and a library science professor who was active in campus politics.) This committee played a key role in shaping the university's intellectual property policy, generating draft policies not only for patents but also for software and copyright. Almost without exception, committee members strongly supported the idea that material incentives were necessary to encourage professors to work toward transferring knowledge from the university to the private sector (Rhoades and Slaughter 1991a, 1991b). Committee members believed that knowledge gained value only when it reached the marketplace and that it remained worthless if it stayed in the lab and the public domain. They were involved in "renorming" science, redefining acceptable and desirable scientific practices and social relations (Slaughter and Rhoades 1990). Over two years we never heard any member suggest that a wider representation of faculty would be desirable on the committee. Indeed, the legitimacy of the current membership lay in the fact that most had engaged in patenting and technology transfer practices. There was no indication that members believed other faculty had a right to shape these early drafts, nor was there a sense that perhaps faculty outside the sciences and engineering also had engaged in technology transfer, or that faculty in other academic units created intellectual products of potential commercial value.

Such presumptions vastly underestimate the range of intellectual products developed by faculty in a variety of fields. Software is an obvious example; it is produced not only by computer scientists (and other scientists and engineers) but also by faculty in the social sciences, arts, and humanities. Similarly, in the course of their work professors in various fields produce instruments that have commercial value. For example, generally overlooked in the literature is nursing faculty's production of instruments used in clinical practice or education and psychology professors' production of measurement instruments applied to students and to populations of clients and patients. Furthermore, as shown in chapter 5, an extraordinary range of copyrighted educational materials, programs, and courses is being produced for external markets. These products and services are generated by diverse academics and units (and by managerial professionals in support units) that extend far beyond science and engineering.

Restructuring of academic units for the marketplace also occurs outside the sciences and engineering. For example, one of our graduate students has explored restructuring of the studio arts in fine arts colleges, revealing how the move to the market has led to greater investment in fields (e.g., graphic arts) perceived as close to external corporate markets, and disinvestment in units (such as the traditional studio arts of painting and sculpture) perceived as relatively distant from such markets (Lund, in progress). Similarly, one of the largest undergraduate majors nationwide has become communications, a field that did not really exist two decades ago and that is perceived by students and institutions as being connected to private-sector employment markets.

The pursuit of academic capitalism also extends beyond research universities. Even within small, private, liberal arts colleges in the United States, there is evidence of a programmatic push toward the private marketplace, particularly in less prestigious colleges. In these institutions, which advertise an emphasis on liberal arts, the national pattern in the last two decades has been of growth in degree programs connected to employment in general and business in particular (Delucchi 1997; Kraatz and Zajac 1996).

The scholarly literature on higher education tends to reflect the presumption within research universities that it is only faculty in these sorts of institutions who produce intellectual property of any value. Yet the intellectual labors of academics in less prestigious settings are sufficient to warrant entrepreneurial activity on the part of community colleges and doctoral and master's granting universities. Less prestigious universities have expanded curricular delivery through the use of high technology and, not uncommonly, through contracts with private-sector entities (Rhoades 2002b). Struggles over intellectual property are a key issue in most unionized institutions, few of which are research universities (Rhoades 1998a). Institutions have been even more aggressive in the two-year sector, where there has been an extraordinary expansion of contract education and certificates geared to employment needs and particular businesses and industries (Brint and Karabel 1989; Dougherty 1994; Levin 2001).

In sum, research universities are not the only site of the academic capitalist knowledge/learning regime. The activity we identified in the academic heartland is also evident in centers and institutes, beyond discipline-based departments. It is evident beyond science and engineering units, in unexpected fields of academic work. And it exists in institutions other than research universities. Indeed, as we expand our understanding of the phenomenon to include activities in the realm of curriculum and instruction, we come to understand the broad-ranging extent of academic capitalism in the new economy. We may also come to understand that academic capitalism is redefining the academic heartland not only in terms of what work is done in basic academic departments but also in terms of redefining whether those units are regarded as the center of the academy and the principal target of its new investments.

8

ADMINISTRATIVE ACADEMIC CAPITALISM

THE LITERATURE THAT TREATS entrepreneurial universities and intellectual property focuses almost exclusively on faculty activity. Scholars look either at faculty research that leads to intellectual property, new product development, increases in institutional revenue generation, and concomitant economic development, or at faculty participation in distance education and courseware development that brings revenue to institutions. If administrators are considered, they are usually technology licensing officials (Feldman et al. 2002a). University presidents' part in the development of an academic capitalist regime has not been extensively treated. Yet presidents are now often called university CEOs, indicating that they have management powers similar to corporate CEOs. Colleges and universities could not engage in academic capitalism without the involvement of university presidents, so we decided to explore how they contribute to market behaviors.

We analyze Internet2 as an instructive instance of administrative academic capitalism. The case has all the elements we need to explore administrative academic capitalism. The Internet2 organization includes presidents from most research universities in the United States, letting us see a large number of presidents involved in the academic capitalist knowledge/learning regime. The purpose of the organization is to span the boundary between nonprofit and for-profit sectors, creating commercial opportunity for both, allowing us to observe administrators' pursuit of market opportunities. The federal government is also a partner in that the Next Generation Internet Act (1998) works in parallel with Internet2 and provides a good deal of the funding that allows university and corporate leaders to achieve their goals. The federal government participation provides an opportunity to see how the state shapes and subsidizes nonprofit and for-profit markets, engaging in a back-door form of economic planning. Faculty perform the necessary research as well as deploy and test the infrastructure, but they are not the drivers, indeed, are usually not even formal members of Internet2. Graduate students are involved because they participate in the research and development necessary to construct Internet2. Undergraduates are central because elements of their education serve as test beds for many Internet2 products and processes.

Several theories have informed our conceptualization of administrative academic capitalism. They are: knowledge economy theory (Bell 1973; Carnoy 1993; Castells 1993, 1996, 1997, 2000; Cohen 1993; Slaughter and Rhoades 1996) aided and abetted by military/industrial/academic theories (Foreman 1987; Greenberg 1967; Melman 1982; Noble 1976;) and theories that deal with the shifting boundary between private and public sectors (Bollier 2002a, 2002b; Coombe 1998; Heller and Eisenburg 1998; McSherry 2001). Each of these treat aspects of the academic capitalism knowledge/learning regime. Knowledge economy theory considers the larger economic shifts that bring universities to the foreground. Military/industrial/academic theories point to the importance of patterns of market, state, and higher education interaction, whereas theories about shifting boundaries between the private and public sectors analyze the social and political construction of boundaries we take as fixed.

These theories deal with knowledge and research but not as they are embodied in universities and colleges as institutions. Knowledge or information economy theory deals primarily with production processes and labor force changes in the wider economy and does not dwell on universities, even though these are sites central to implementing changes. Yet university laboratories are often where production processes are developed, as in the case of biotechnology, and college and university classrooms are where the labor force is trained. Military/industrial/academic complex theories focus largely on university research that serves the military. In 2001, the federal government's research budget spent as much on civilian technology as military, which means that the military/industrial/academic complex theories leave half of all research unexplained, nor do these theories deal with education. Boundary theories often examine intellectual property patented by faculty but not the universities that own it. The theory of academic capitalism differs from these theories in that it foregrounds colleges and universities and tries to draw out and expand the implications of these theories for universities and colleges as institutions engaged in undergraduate education as well as graduate education and research.

Internet2: A Case of Administrative Academic Capitalism

Administrative academic capitalism takes a number of forms. The following types are meant to be suggestive rather than exhaustive. (1) Administrators contract with corporations that franchise (McDonald's, Burger King, Starbucks, Domino's, Barnes and Noble) in order to make student services, such as unions and bookstores, "profit centers." (2) Administrators contract with corporations to ensure universities' exclusive use of their product—such as soft drinks or athletic gear worn by sports teams. (For example, our university is a Nike/Pepsi university). (3) Administrators develop distance-education initiatives that fall outside the purview of faculty regulation for the express purpose of generating revenue. (4) Administrators engage in planning, contracting, and building infrastructure for economic development of the state, region, nation, or global economy in ways that may secure revenue for the institutions as well as for their corporate partners. Examples of these sorts of activity are the Translational Genomics Research Institute (TGEN) in Arizona, in which both the University of Arizona and Arizona State are involved, and Internet2. Faculty and students may have input into these activities, but administrators are the primary actors in creating and developing these forms of academic capitalism.

Although administrative academic capitalism is a phenomenon worth studying as a whole, if only because it is little understood and almost entirely untheorized, we concentrate on the fourth form—administrators' part in planning, contracting, and building infrastructure for economic development. We see this form as particularly important because in many respects it determines the future of the university. Resource commitments strongly influence faculty hiring, resourcing of curricula, selection of types of students for recruitment and support, state and institutional intellectual property regimes, and perhaps most importantly the boundary between public and private sectors. Although this form of administrative academic capitalism has far-reaching consequences for institutions, usually faculty senate, student government, and alumni leaders are not involved in deliberations about institutional commitment to these endeavors, largely because they are perceived as ancillary by administrators and the university community as a whole.

The case we have selected to illustrate this form of administrative academic capitalism is Internet2. As its website says,

> Internet2® is a not-for-profit consortium, led by over 200 US universities, developing and deploying advanced network applications and technology, accelerating the creation of tomorrow's Internet. With participation by over 60 leading companies, Internet2 recreates the partnership of academia, industry and government that helped foster today's Internet in its infancy . . . Close collaboration with Internet2 corporate members will ensure that applications and technologies are rapidly deployed throughout the Internet. Just as email and the World Wide Web are legacies of earlier

> investments in academic and federal research networks, the legacy of Internet2 will be to expand the possibilities of the broader Internet . . . A key goal of this effort is to accelerate the diffusion of advanced Internet technology, in particular into the commercial sector. (www.internet2.edu/html/faqs.html)

The "principals" are presidents of universities, many of which are research universities, and the corporate leaders, who are most often CEOs of telecommunications corporations. The explicit purpose of the consortium is to repeat the success of the earlier partnership among government (Defense Advanced Research Projects Agency, or DARPA), universities, and industry that led to the development of a dispersed computer network that made possible e-mail and the World Wide Web, which then became an opportunity structure for a wide variety of forms of e-commerce, not least of which were real-time networks that allowed the development of global financial markets.

Theory and Method

Knowledge economy or new economy theory addresses the shift from an industrial economy in which workers in factories characterized by assembly line production (Fordism) made goods for national consumption to an economy where educated workers in flexible organizations produce goods and services for global consumption. Colleges and universities play a major part in this shift because they serve as milieus of innovation (Castells 1996), creating the research and discovery for the telecommunications infrastructure that undergirds the global knowledge economy and for the products and services that are traded in the global economy. They also serve as milieus of use where people are educated to use technoscience products and processes. Technoscience is at once science and product (Aronowitz and DiFazio 1994; Lyotard 1984; Touraine 1974). Universities, whether through R&D or education and training, are the font of technoscience for postindustrial economies. and play a major role in the construction, dissemination, and use of products and processes such as artificial intelligence, telecommunications, and biotechnology (Sassen 1991; Kevles and Hood 1992). In terms of our case, Internet2, knowledge economy theory points to the importance of universities as milieus of innovation and use for new technologies, specifically, telecommunications infrastructure.

Knowledge economy theorists usually see knowledge and related technology as the driving force in change. We see them as an important force but argue that the state and corporate sectors of society play an important role, particularly in the organization, dissemination, and distribution of new knowledge and technologies. The state, particularly the Defense Advanced Projects Agency (DARPA) played a major role in creating the telecommunications infrastructure on which the global knowledge economy rests. Indeed, a number of theorists argue that without government, particularly military, investment in telecommunications and artificial intelligence, development of the knowledge economy would not have occurred or would have been much slower (Greenberg 1967; Melman 1982). However, military technology was not necessarily fitted for global civilian markets, and in the 1980s, a split developed among corporate elites over how to subsidize research. A number of business leaders argued that using the military to subsidize research was inefficient, made U.S. products unfit for competitive civilian markets, and was too costly (Slaughter 1990). Business pressure on government created a bipartisan competitiveness coalition in Congress that supported research funding for civilian technology and research (Slaughter and Rhoades 1996). The end of the cold war accelerated this move toward federal support for civilian technology policy. In 2000, for the first time in thirty years, research funding for civilian technology matched that for defense (Slaughter and Rhoades 2003). At the same time, the several states began funding civilian technology, sometimes quite heavily, in an effort to spur economic development (Isserman 1994). In terms of Internet2, military/industrial/academic theory indicates that the state, often leveraged by corporations and universities, is a major player when it comes to changing economic/knowledge regimes. The centrality of the state to economic development and innovations suggests that it is important to attend to the role the state plays with regard to civilian technology.

Elite theory allows us to deal with actors external to the state. At its most rudimentary level, elite theory suggests that persons who head institutions of great wealth and power (corporations, armed services, universities) in society are able to exercise disproportionate influence on politics and policy (Domhoff 1990, 1996; Domhoff and Dye 1987; Useem 1984). However, our understanding of how such power is exercised is contested, sometimes focusing on class as the vehicle through which elites exercise control, other times looking at power elites or an institutional class, and often at positional/managerial authority. Rather than enter those debates, we focus empirically on the network of positional elites who constitute the membership of Internet2, who form an intermediating network, and we try to understand how that network draws together representatives from universities, the corporate sector, and government to build Internet2. We are particularly interested in the dynamic role played by university presidents, who have historically participated in elite policy formation but usually not as the central actors.

Finally, we are interested in theories that deal with the shifting boundaries between the public and private sector: theories about civil society, a (perhaps mythical) space in which the citizenry were free to debate issues of public concern free from the pressures of state or economy; theories about the "commons" that draw on historical accounts of common law claims to community land/space that were essential for sustaining and replenishing society and that are currently applied to the idea of an "intellectual" or knowledge commons (Bollier 2002; Heller and Eisenberg 1998; Slaughter and Rhoades 1996); theories about privatization, deregulation, and commercialization of the public sector. All of these theories recognize that the boundaries between the private (commercial), public (state), and nonprofit sectors are flexible and are currently in a state of flux. These theories turn our attention to how the Internet2 community, which has interests in both free circulation of knowledge and the commercialization of knowledge, draws these boundaries.

The specific questions provoked by the theories we consider in relation to our case are:

1. Who are the leaders of Internet2, how do they work together, and how do they leverage the state for supportive policy and funds?
2. What role do the several branches of the state (including those public universities that are "arms of the state") play in funding and shaping Internet2, and what consequences does this have for universities?
3. How does Internet2 draw the boundary between public and private sector, given that it has an express intent to commercialize? Specifically, how is public knowledge or "the academic commons" defined, and how is commercial knowledge defined?
4. How does Internet2 shape universities as milieus of knowledge innovation and use?

Our method is qualitative and primarily relies on document analysis. The major source of data is the extensive Internet2 website and the many hyperlinks Internet2 provides to related websites (www.internet2.edu). The Internet2 site itself contains several hundred pages of text; the related hyperlinks provide over a thousand. We answer our first question by looking at membership, minutes, money, and organizational processes. To answer the second question, we look at Internet2 funding and at the mechanisms by which various state agencies and corporations participate. Our third question is answered by analyzing all materials that deal with the *intellectual commons,* a term used by the Internet2 community, and following all the links that lead from this material. We contrast that with the Internet2 "intellectual property framework," which establishes rules for commercialization, and follow all the links that lead from that, including examples of ownership and commercialization of specific technoscience products and process developed as a result of Internet2 funding and/or participation. To answer our fourth question, we look for specific research projects and technologies supported by Internet2 to understand the technoscience innovations at issue; we also look at test-bed projects in which the university community is treated as a milieu of use.

Internet2 Leadership

The presidents of thirty-four universities started Internet2 in 1996. They joined together to deal with the problem of congestion on the Internet, which had developed when NSFNET was commercialized in 1995. Commercialization had so clogged the Internet that scientists and engineers had difficulty doing research. The university presidents who came together were by and large the same group that had been involved in the early construction of the Internet (1960–1985) in collaboration with the DOD (ARPANET and the Advanced Projects Research Agency) and a small number of defense contractors. In the first phase of Internet construction (1960–1985), neither privatization, deregulation, nor commercialization had figured in the designers' plans. The purpose of the early Internet was defense, education, and research (Frischmann 2001). In the second iteration of the Internet, the planners were very clear that one of their purposes was to rapidly diffuse to the commercial world the new technologies developed through Internet2, creating an economic boom like that associated with the dot.coms in the late 1990s. A year later, Internet2 needed a more formal structure and organization. A brief analysis of the initial thirty-four member group of university presidents reveals that they were roughly the same group that was initially involved with the construction of the early internet. In October 1997, the University Corporation for Advanced Internet Development (UCAID) was established as a nonprofit corporate base for Internet2, with a membership of eighty-six universities (Van Houweling 2000).

An analysis of the 2002 UCAID board of trustees and council members reveals a slightly different picture. In 2002, UCAID was comprised of fourteen members who serve staggered three-year terms. The board is self-perpetuating, and three new members are selected each year. In 2002, most UCAID members were white male presidents of research I universities. (Two women were added in 2001.) Six are presidents of public universities (North Carolina, Indiana, Texas at El Paso, Illinois at Chicago, Texas at Austin, Wisconsin); four are presidents of private research universities (Northwestern, MIT, University of Southern California, and Princeton). Two UCAID members are not research university presidents. One is head of the Washington Advisory Group, a nonprofit policy organization, and was formerly head of the Council on Competitiveness. The other is president of the Andrew W. Mellon Foundation and was formerly a university president.

UCAID works with a series of self-perpetuating councils whose new members are chosen through election. They are the Applications Strategy Council, the Network Policy and Planning Advisory Council, the Network Research Liaison Council, and the Industry Strategy Council. Other than the Industry Strategy Council, which will be discussed below, the majority of the membership on these councils is from universities. In 2002, of the thirty-eight council members, sixteen are professors, almost all in science and engineering, very often in computer-related areas. The one woman on this council is a professor of art and design. Fourteen of the council members are directors of university information technology. Eleven of the directors are in the Network Policy and Planning Advisory Council, which includes three women. Many use the new title CIO (chief information officer) or special designations such as vice-president for scholarly technology, the name of the office at USC. The majority of the professors are on the Network Research Liaison Council, on which there are no women. There are eight nonuniversity members across these three councils, most of whom represent nonprofit organizations concerned with information technology as well as hybrids such as Educause, which, like Internet2 crosses the boundary between private and public sectors. Three members represent private firms, one of which is Cisco Systems. The several councils' membership represents twenty-four public and five private universities.

The Industry Strategy Council is the group through which UCAID relates to its corporate partners. There are twelve members, three of whom are from public universities: a professor from the University of Michigan, a vice-provost for information at Penn State, and a vice-chancellor for information technology at the University of North Carolina at Chapel Hill. The corporate members are from Qwest, NASDAQ, WorldCom, Packet Design, Evans Telecommunications, Sun Microsystems, Diamondhead Ventures, Nortel, Palm, IBM, Lucent Technologies, and Microsoft Research. Among the corporate members are a director, a vice-chairman, and three vice-presidents, all in areas related to information technology; three presidents and CEOs; a managing director; two division presidents, both related to research; and a program director. Three members are women, two from the corporate world, one from the university. The top leadership in Internet2, as represented by UCAID and the Industry Strategy Council, clearly represent elite institutions.

There were eighty-six charter university members, fifty-nine public, twenty-seven private. In the initial years of Internet2, these universities had to put up about $500,000 each, in part to pay for the construction of Abilene, the GSI (Government Services, Inc.) very high-speed network overseen by UCAID. Almost all of these members were NSF High Performance Computing and Communications (HPCC) awardees as of September 1998. Their HPCC awards paid part of the costs, particularly for construction of and connection to Abilene. After the initial contributions, the universities pay about $110,000 annually, in part for access to Abilene. Corporate members, partners, sponsors, and affiliates also contributed but not as much. Corporate members have promised about $20 million over three years, while UCAID universities have paid about $50 million per year. These same corporations are often involved in constructing the infrastructure for Internet2/GSI. For example, Qwest, Cisco Systems, and Nortel (Internet2 corporate partners, each of whom committed to contribute $1 million dollars or more) secured contracts to develop and build the network (Dugan and Trump 1999).

In Internet2/UCAID, we see university presidents from both public and nonprofit sectors act as planners of an Internet that has both nonprofit and for-profit dimensions. The case is interesting in several regards. A number of university presidents can be considered state actors, in that they are heads of primarily state-funded organizations, if we consider their federal research funds, student aid monies, and state block grants. The other university presidents are not heads of state organizations, although they too have federal research funds and student aid monies, often from both state and federal government; they are considered heads of nonprofit organizations. In our current neoliberal political climate, the obvious explanation is that Internet2 is a case of market failure, in which government intervention is justified. "When an investment involves sufficiently high fixed costs, government intervention (subsidization) may be necessary because market actors will under-invest due to capital constraints, free-riding, and attenuated time horizons for investment recovery" (Frischmann 2001, p. 11). However, this is not an instance of government intervention into a market, but, as Frischmann points out, of "*market intervention into government.*" Her point is that the Internet was originally construed as serving public good functions (defense and education) of government, not as a commercial endeavor that needed government support due to underinvestment by business. For the market failure argument to work, the Internet would have had to have been initiated by commercial entities, like power companies, and then subsidized by government when the commercial endeavor failed and there were public good issues (e.g., energy, transportation) at stake. The case of Internet2 is not a case of market failure but of privatization.

Neo-Marxians offer alternative explanations. It is possible to see the university presidents in Internet2/UCAID as state or quasi-state actors, in an Althussarian sense, organizing the economy for the corporate sector. However, the presidents are not the usual suspects (politicians and state bureaucrats). Instead, the presidents are actors from a segment of the state not usually involved in forward economic planning. Perhaps universities have become so central to a knowledge economy that their presidents believe they must act as forward planners.

It is also possible to think of the presidents and universities in a Gramscian sense, as being part of a segmented state. Gramsci (1971) did not see the state as monolithic but as composed of different segments, often having separate in terests. The separate state interests could align with other segments of the state and various outside actors to shape policy. However, only the public university presidents can be thought of as heads of organizations that are "arms of the state;" the private universities are nonprofits and do not fit neatly into Gramscian theory.

Perhaps Internet2/UCAID is best conceptualized as an intermediating organization, linking together segments of state agencies, universities, and corporations to construct a network that spans the three types of organizations and performs functions that each would have difficulty doing by itself. Intermediating organizations such as Internet2/UCAID may be particularly important to the academic capitalist knowledge/learning regime because they provide ways to cross public/private, nonprofit/for-profit boundaries. Internet2/UCAID is different from many other intermediating organizations in that the presidents of universities are the leaders, rather than state officials or corporate executives.

UCAID uses a railroad metaphor to describe Abilene, the high-performance network it developed and paid for in partnership with Cisco Systems, Juniper Networks, Nortel Networks, Qwest Communications, and Indiana University: "The Abilene Project is named after a railhead established in Abilene, Kansas during the 1860's. In its time the ambitious railhead of the 1800's staked a claim on what was then the frontier of the United States; the Abilene Project establishes a foothold from which to explore and develop pioneering network technology. The links of last century's railway changed the way people worked and lived. The Abilene Project is transforming the work of research and educators today" (www.internet2.edu/abilene/html/faq-general.html).

In this metaphor, UCAID does not mention the federal government, which supplied the railroad with public lands that subsidized the costs of building a national transportation infrastructure, in much the same way that the DOD granted universities funds to do research which subsidized a Keynesian welfare/warfare state. Instead, UCAID likens itself to a private agent, the railroads, equating itself with the commercial rather than the government aspect of the venture. In other words, UCAID claims properties associated with private, for-profit activity in networking the nation. The railroad metaphor is an interesting choice. Railroads were made possible by generous grants of federal lands to railroad companies for develop of transportation in the West. Once railroads were established, cut-throat, free market-competition was so intense and counterproductive that many railroads failed, and the federal government had to intervene in the form of the Interstate Commerce Commission to regulate rates and administer profit (Kolko 1963). The UCAID identification of Abilene with pioneering capitalist activity stresses the movement of university presidents from selected engagement in the economy, usually in roles that focused on their research and technology knowledge, to a broad engagement as members of an intermediating network, who play a part in organizing and producing the information economy.

As members of the knowledge barons' network, university presidents use their institutional funds (which are no longer "purely" public in that many universities now have commercial streams of income from royalties and licenses, equity holdings, and other profit-making activities in which administrators and faculty engage) to invest in Internet2. For example, Abilene is paid for by the universities and corporate partners, not by the federal government. (Of course, the universities would not be able to make such investments were they not able to use "discretionary" federal and state funds, as well as their tax-free status, to "accumulate" "surplus" monies for such investments, again pointing to the difficulty with categories like private and public.) As noted above, UCAID pays roughly two-thirds of the costs, corporations one-third. Yet UCAID is also able to "leverage" federal funds, primarily through the NSF and the Next Generation Internet.

Role of the State

Our general argument with regard to the state is that the National Science Foundation and the National Institutes of Health (NIH) are to the knowledge economy what the Department of Defense was to the defense economy. The DOD was integral to creating and managing the Keynesian welfare-warfare state initiated after World War II (Melman 1982). We see the NSF and the NIH as creating and managing the privatized/commercialized state that is developing in the twenty-first century. The NSF is central to the telecommunications and information technology industries and the NIH to biotechnology and pharmaceuticals. In this chapter, we concentrate on the NSF and telecommunications and information technology.

The DOD initiated the Internet when the Advanced Research Projects Agency (ARPA) created ARPANET, which connected four sites: the Stanford Research Institute, two University of California campuses (UCLA and UCSB), and the University of Utah (www.wpi.edu/Admin/IT/Internet2/history.html). But the DOD "recognized a potential conflict between its primary mission of military defense and the network externalities of a broader network base" (Frischmann 2001). The DOD split ARPANET in two. One network, known as MILNET, was used to link military sites in the United States, and the other, named ARPANET, continued to be used for research (Kahn 1995).

The NSF gradually took over from ARPA, began to manage and coordinate among academic and government networks, "and became the central funding and decision-making agency for interconnecting networks" (Frischmann 2001). The turning point came in the early 1990s, when the NSF moved toward two new and related policies concerning "commercialization and privatization. Under commercialization, the mission of the Internet was broadened from its initial focus on supporting research, education, and defense to include commercial . . . activity. At the same time, privatization shifted responsibility for the design, implantation, operation, and funding of the Internet from the Federal government to the private sector" (Chinoy and Salo 2002).

Because the Internet was congested with traffic in the early 1990s, the NSF built NSFNET in a cooperative agreement with a nonprofit organization, Merit. Merit became the interconnection backbone for the early Internet, which was still primarily focused on promoting collaboration among researchers. The cooperative agreement with Merit opened a window to new arrangements. The NSF had previously worked under government procurement; under cooperative agreements, it had the ability to enter flexible, contractual relationships with corporations and maintain an active role in organizing the rapidly evolving Internet. When the cooperative partners became private corporations, the NSF was also able to leverage (some) private funds, which perhaps seemed enough, compared to no private funds. MCI built the next backbone as a cooperative partner with NSF, and many of the technologies that were part of the Internet came from industrial partners, "such as IBM mainframes and workstations and MCI's digital cross-connect system" (Frischmann 2001). Because the Internet was still governed by an acceptable use policy that allowed information flows only for education and research, the NSF organized a joint venture between commercial backbone operators through Commercial Internet Exchange (CIX) that was financed by corporate partners and became a commercial version of the Internet. Pursuing privatization, the NSF then managed the transfer of its backbone, including finance and management, to industry. The transfer was completed in 1995.

However, the commercial network quickly became so congested that academic researchers, accustomed to a network that served only education and research purposes, found it inadequate. Enter Internet2 and UCAID, which deliberately leveraged the federal government through various NSF computing programs and the Next Generation Internet (NGI). These initiatives overlapped and fed on each other.

After privatizing its backbone, the National Science Foundation continued to play an organizational and management role in Internet2 and the NGI. The NSF's vBNS (very high speed backbone network) served as Internet2's national interconnect. The NSF also has a variety of programs through its Advanced Networking Program that allows Internet2 member organizations to connect to the vBNS (www.educause.edu/pub/er/review/reviewArticles/33316.html). Although the NSF is one of many agencies involved in the National Coordination Office for Information Technology Research and Development, it has taken the lead with regard to civilian technology and, particularly, commercialization. For example, the NSF Supercomputer Centers have "extensive industry involvement" in "partnership and affiliate relationships, cooperative efforts in technology development" (National Coordination Office for Information Technology Research and Development 2002).

The NSF is deeply involved with the Next Generation Internet (NGI). The NGI Research Act of 1998 authorized "the National Science Foundation, the Department of Energy, the National Institutes of Health, the National Aeronautics and Space Administration, and the National Institute of Standards and Technology (the supporting agencies) to support the Next Generation Internet (Program)." Included among the program objectives were "(1) increasing Internet capabilities and improving Internet performance; (2) developing an advanced test bed network connecting research sites; and (3) developing advanced Internet applications that meet national goals and agency mission needs" (Next Generation Internet Initiative 1998). The NSF had the position of lead agency among the non-defense research mission agencies.

The Next Generation Internet Research Act of 1998 does the following:

> (1) authorize(s) research programs related to high-end computing and computation, human-centered systems, high confidence systems, and education, training, and human resources; and (2) provide(s) for the development and coordination of a comprehensive and integrated U.S. research program which will focus on a computer network infrastructure that promotes interoperability among advanced Federal com-

> puter networks, high-speed data access that is economical and that does not impose a geographic penalty, and flexible and extensible networking technology. Amends the High-Performance Computing Act of 1991 to include among its purposes: (1) promoting the more rapid development and wider distribution of networking management and development tools; and (2) promoting the rapid adoption of open network standards. (Next Generation Internet Initiative 1998)

In other words, the NGI does for the federal government what UCAID proposes to do for colleges, universities, and the commercial Internet.

In UCAID's words, "the university-led Internet2 and the federally-led NGI are parallel and complementary initiatives based in the United States." UCAID points out that Internet2 and NGI work together in many areas. For example, "through participation in a NSF NGI program, over 150 Internet2 universities have received competitively awarded grants to support connections to advanced backbone networks." The aim of joint work is to "ensure a cohesive and interoperable advanced networking infrastructure for research and education, and the continued interoperability of the global Internet" (Internet2.2002).

Internet2/UCAID is able to leverage the NSF and NGI programs because its aims coincide with theirs. Like the NSF, Internet2/UCAID is concerned with privatization and commercialization. In most cases, Internet2/UCAID university presidents have long-established ties with the NSF, which facilitates cooperation. So too, NGI, whether under Clinton or the elder or younger Bush, has pursued many of the same goals as the NSF and Internet2/UCAID. All three groups are intent on building the information infrastructure, management tools, and quality of service standards that will promote global markets, which they present as having both commercial and educational dimensions.

The NSF has shifted from procurement to cooperative arrangements with telecommunications corporations in an effort to defray the costs of building Internet infrastructure. Although exact figures on what corporations contribute are difficult to find, none of the figures we have located thus far suggest that corporations pay more than about one-quarter of the costs. These figures raise a number of interesting accounting problems. Is a cooperative one-quarter (or less) of costs better than a procurement relationship? Is some contribution from corporations better than none? How much leverage do corporations buy through their cooperative arrangement? As we have seen, the hardware, software, and design interests of cooperative partners were incorporated in the design of the vBNS and Super Computers.

Internet2 has adapted many of the same practices as the NSF, leveraging the state and the private sector. Internet2 depends on the NSF for connectivity, backbone, and research grants and treats the NGI as a "parallel and complementary" initiative that provides funds, personnel, research opportunities, and some design leadership. Internet2, the NSF, and the NGI share a constant flow of leaders and especially researchers, who weave together the several organizations' efforts to build a global information superhighway, dominated by the United States. Internet2's niche in this initiative seems to be in research and design for the short term (three to six years out) and milieus of use, particularly as test beds. There is some irony in Interntt2 holding this niche, in that this was the niche university presidents in the late 1980s described as appropriate for corporations (Office of the Vice President for Research 1996).

Although UCAID has been able to leverage state and corporate monies, Internet2 nonetheless represents a large commitment of institutional funds to building telecommunications infrastructure. Internet2 built Abilene as its own backbone. Even though corporations and the NSF contributed, the institutions spent considerable sums. Regardless of the exact figures and the complicated ratios of state/corporation/institutional contributions, universities committed these funds as an investment in the future, which means other investments cannot be made. UCAID committed universities to building and testing the global information superhighway in partnerships with corporations and a variety of state agencies that direct universities toward a high-tech, privatized, commercialized future appropriate for an academic capitalist knowledge/learning regime.

The Intellectual Property Framework

"Internet2's goal is to maximize the no or low cost availability of deliverables to the Internet2 membership while permitting project participants to retain ownership and control of the intellectual property they develop in the course of an Internet2 project" (Internet2 2002a).

As noted above, an explicit purpose of Internet2 is commercialization. Internet2's founders seek to repeat the success of the earlier alliance between the DOD, universities, and corporations, particularly the dot.coms that flourished in the mid- to late-1990s after the NSF privatized its backbone. However, the founders, and later UCAID, want to reach this goal more rapidly than did the earlier DOD-sponsored Internet, and to more deliberately steer the project toward commercial outcomes, as their cooperative arrangements with corporate partners suggests.

The three major initiatives undertaken by Internet2 were middleware, quality of service, and bandwidth. These were essential to commercial users. The middleware initiative focused heavily on security, without which e-commerce and financial markets could not operate. Improving quality of service focused on upgrading the quality and interoperability of video conferencing, tele-immersion, digital sound, the Internet, the World Wide Web, and personal computers (PCs), all of which were necessary for expanding cyberspace commercial products and processes, patented and copyrighted. Increasing bandwidth meant increasing the amount and kinds of data that can be handled on the Internet, which is very important for commercial ventures that make software programs with ever-expanding capacity. These three initiatives were planned to result in "deliverables" that ranged from academic papers to intellectual property.

While these initiatives—middleware, quality of service, increased bandwidth—also benefited universities, they were not necessarily crucial to education and research, the telecommunications aspects of which could have been conducted as extra-net activities confined to universities and colleges on a much smaller scale than Internet2. As it stands, the majority of the Internet2 university community does not have access to Abilene or Internet2 projects; these are still reserved for a very small number of researchers. The products and processes resulting from Internet2 may well be commercially available to most students before they are available on campuses, unless a particular campus serves as a test bed.

Internet2 has an elaborate intellectual property framework that deals with ownership of the fruits of collaboration among the cooperative partners. It runs for fourteen pages and presents principles, processes, sample agreements, answers to frequently asked questions, methods, and examples. The principles cover intellectual property developed by Internet2 projects and initiatives. The principles are as follows:

1. Maintain and contribute to the accessible, standards-based character of the Internet, and promote appropriate, flexible, and easily administered open source arrangements.
2. Where open source or royalty-free arrangements are unworkable, encourage members to make intellectual property developed as part of an Internet2 effort available to UCAID and members of the Internet2 community. Terms and conditions should promote further innovation and reflect the contributions of the community and its members to the development of that intellectual property.
3. Encourage the broadest possible distribution of the technology.
4. Encourage rapid deployment of the technology. (Internet2 2002e)

Nowhere do the principles suggest that there should be an intellectual commons rather than intellectual property. An "accessible, standards-based" Internet is ownable and more valuable because it is accessible. Open source arrangements mean that members are able to modify and innovate with software, not that the software cannot be owned. In the principles and elsewhere, Internet2 says open source and royalty-free arrangements (which do not mean that intellectual property is not owned, only that Internet2 members are not charged for it) are preferred. However, like the rest of the document, the principles mostly address what members should do when open source or royalty-free arrangements are "unworkable," rather than suggesting ways in which such arrangements can be expanded. Instead, they suggest that ownership should promote innovation (ironically, something that ownership often impedes) and reflect the contributions of the community, which means that member universities as well as their corporate partners should derive revenue from intellectual property. Rapid distribution and rapid deployment mean rapid returns to monetary and human capital investments.

The process section of the intellectual property framework stresses the importance of up-front agreement on intellectual property and of disclosure. Internet2 suggests that "project participants should agree on the intellectual property approach to be taken before commencing work" (Internet2 2002e). Internet2 asks participants, often universities partnering with corporations, to disclose in writing any knowledge of intellectual property claims that may be infringed by the groups' work, and stresses that the obligation to disclose is ongoing. This request seems aimed at faculty to ensure that universities capture intellectual property. In these partnerships, faculty are usually the experts and innovators, developing new technoscience and software. Should they chose to withhold potentially alienable discoveries, either to put them in the public domain or to later patent and form their own companies, neither institution nor corporation would benefit, impairing cooperative arrangements and causing the loss of revenues and/or profits. (Chapters 3 and 5 explain the importance of disclosure to institutional intellectual property holding. Several universities have vigorously prosecuted students and faculty who did not disclose and instead attempted to exploit their discoveries on their own.)

Internet2's methods of handling intellectual property are: open source, freeware/shareware, discounted commercial licenses, and public domain. In open source, the property remains that of the creator, but is "licensed to anyone who wants to use it for free, and the source code is included." In freeware/shareware, "one or more of the participating organizations retains ownership of the deliverable, and distributes it for free (freeware) or for a fee after use (shareware) to all, with or without the source code." A discounted commercial license lets the participating "organizations retain rights to the deliverable, and makes it available to Internet2 Regular Members under very favorable terms, but without source code" or "the rights to modify and use it" (Internet2. Intellectual Property Framework 2002). In each of these instances, faculty cede intellectual property to universities and/or corporations through Internet2. Inclusion of source code allows continued innovation within the Internet2 community, building on the synergy derived from collaborative research. Discounted commercial licenses allow the Internet2 community to use at a low cost products and processes that are very likely ready for the commercial market. However, given that universities probably contributed to the development of the property, it is not clear how much "business" sense this makes.

As Internet2 notes: "Outside the Internet2 Regular Membership, the owner is free to market the deliverable without restriction" (Internet2. Intellectual Property Framework 2002). This includes university and corporate owners, who partner in developing products and processes, and is the heart of the Internet2 intellectual property framework. Within the Internet2 community, partners, whether universities and/or corporations, receive shares in intellectual property according to their contributions. (Unfortunately, the details of these arrangements are not clarified by the examples offered on the website). Presumably universities and corporations will sign up-front agreements defining what percentage of the property is owned by whom. The property is shared within the community to facilitate innovation, but it is also sold to those outside Internet2, presumably generating profits and revenue streams for the corporate and university partners.

Internet2 recommends that creators of the "deliverable" do not place it in the public domain so that they do not lose control over who uses it and how it is used. This is a curious recommendation, in that were the creators to place a discovery in the public domain, they would *expect* it to be freely used in a variety of ways. LINUX provides an example of public domain Internet deliverables. Perhaps what Internet2 means is that public domain precludes ownership, the position from which control and use is exercised.

Generally, the intellectual property framework seems to close the space in which knowledge can move freely, as exemplified by rejecting public domain as a concept for handling intellectual property. The framework then fences off an area—the Internet2 community—in which knowledge can move freely among paying members, some of which are corporations. Within this administratively created space, university and corporate leaders seek to capture the innovative energy, intellectual ability, and managerial panache of the faculty. If faculty are allowed to operate freely in this space, then perhaps they will create (ownable) things such as LINUX, the alternative operating system to Microsoft, that continues to be modified, managed, and updated by faculty and other computer devotees, and is still distributed free of charge. Unlike LINUX and the many programs created by the free and open software movement in which many computer scientists participated in the early days of the ARPA-defense industry-university partnership, knowledge circulates freely only within the Internet2 community. Although this community may be a deliberate attempt by CIOs and CEOs to recreate the milieus of innovation that stimulated the rapid development of the Internet and the World Wide Web, Internet2 closely bounds the free space, and intends to privatize and commercialize when a deliverable emerges.

The corporate partners who participate in the intellectual property framework gain a great deal. They share in the innovative space created by university administrators. They are able to make better calculations about the future of technoscience and software; to build their equipment and standards into projects, ensuring future markets; to use universities as test beds for jointly developed projects; and to own and commercialize intellectual property that emerges from specified projects. Informally, they are also able to recruit highly talented employees from faculty and graduate students with whom they work on projects. They are also able to develop projects with faculty independently of Internet2, as long as they do not use Abilene or other Internet2 resources. Although the partners in the intellectual property framework are supposed to receive rewards in relation to their contributions, it is not clear how contributions are measured. If corporations are able to leverage their hold on intellectual property in the same way that they have leveraged their monetary contributions to Internet2, they receive a good deal.

Universities too gain a great deal from the intellectual property framework. They are able to build on the synergy created by the Internet2 community to build the university of the future, each reducing their costs through partnerships with others. By sharing the community with paying corporate partners, they are able to access funds that would otherwise not be available to them. Corporations often donate and share equipment, again contributing to the community. (Whether these funds "reduce costs" is a debatable point when the investments and maintenance costs for hardware and software are considered.) At this point, we cannot be sure about who benefits most from the intellectual property agreements, universities or corporations, because it is too early to know. University leaders are seeking to recoup the costs of building the information infrastructure of the future through Internet2. However, as the intellectual property framework makes clear, they seek to go beyond recovering costs—through ownership of innovative deliverables, universities privatize and commercialize research and educational work and become market actors.

The Intellectual Commons as Test-bed

When we planned the methods for this chapter, we thought we would contrast the intellectual property framework with the Internet2 Commons project. The language of the "commons" (Heller and Eisenberg 1998; Bollier 2002a) suggested a contrast to the marketplace. According to Bollier, the idea of the intellectual commons captures "the social 'gift economy' that has been such a productive engine of academic knowledge. The gift economy is a system by which members of a distinct community, joined through shared values and commitments create valuable artifacts and services for each other without using money, legal contracts, or other market mechanisms" (2002a). Although the academic gift economy that characterized nonmilitary U.S. research culture is being eroded by the academic capitalist knowledge/learning regime, we thought that the Internet2 Commons would be an effort to preserve a free space within the more broadly privatized and commercialized Internet2 community. Instead, we discovered that the Internet2 Commons was a test bed, in which many universities tested telecommunications companies' infrastructure technologies.

We did not understand immediately that the Internet2 Commons was a test bed because the "commons" language connotes nonmarket activity. The Internet2 Commons was presented in such a way that its commercial component was not immediately obvious. It was portrayed as "a large-Scale, Distributed Collaborative Environment for the Research and Education Community." Videoconferencing technologies were foregrounded—H.323, VRVS, AG, MPEG2, and others—along with other collaborative technologies such as data sharing, instant messaging, voice/IP, electronic notebooks, peer to peer, and collaboratories (Internet2 2002f). ViDe, Accord, and RADvision were named, but their status as corporations traded on public stock exchanges was not mentioned, nor were the immediately recognizable Cisco and Microsoft named, although they were also partners. Initially, the website told us that Internet2 and ViDe had formed a partnership to provide the "best effort of service." Pages later, when we discovered the goal was to begin at a "best effort" level of service and move to a "production" level of service, we began to realize that the Internet2 Commons was a test bed.

The corporate partners were first introduced through the Internet Commons Network Infrastructure hyperlink. A graphic appeared that showed Abilene, the Internet2 backbone, in the form of a cloud, floating above the Commons infrastructure. The infrastructure was provided by Cisco (router and switch), RADvision (MCUs, gateways), Accord (MGC), Starbek (Torrent CES), and APC (master switch and power switch). The infrastructure providers were not labeled as private, although all but Starbek (including ViDe, aka Video Display Corporation) were publicly traded corporations, almost all in the telecommunications industry. The financial arrangements between the infrastructure and the Internet2 Commons project were never clearly described. We did not find the word *test bed* used until we pressed the ViDe hyperlink, at which point we were given the background to the project. "ViDeNet was formed by ViDe, the Video Development Initiative, to be a test bed and model network, in which to develop and promote ViDe's goals for multi-organizational, multi-location highly scalable and robust networked video technologies." ViDe was short for Video Display Corporation, which manufactures and distributes cathode-ray tubes and related parts for the replacement market. Its components go into televisions, computer monitors, data display screens, medical equipment, and military displays, and it is a very acquisitive corporation (Hoover 2002).

The Internet2 Commons White Paper most clearly outlined the scope of the project.

> The Internet2 Digital Video group (I2DV) recognizes the importance of video conferencing over Internet2 and is undertaking the task of promoting discourse and information-sharing targeted towards the realization of an international scale IP-based digital video conferencing capability. . . As an Internet 2 working group, the I2DV shares a goal of "bringing together member technical issues to enable advanced applications for higher education's research and education missions." Implicit in this goal is the need to consider how to develop and improve new IP-based technologies (developing the capability) but also the need to foster and support new applications for these technologies (delivering a service). *The former requires research, innovation, test-beds, and vendor/developer partnerships. The latter requires delivering new functionality in such a way that it is reliable enough for the intended end-users to envision themselves using it, and to be successful in that use.* For the national and international environment that is being discussed here, several key technical issues will need to be addressed at both the R&D and service levels. These include:
>
> - a global dialing plan
> - a global directory service
> - a scheduling mechanism for the use of shared resources
> - improvements and coordination in "back room" equipment functionality and con trol, and
> - interoperability with other significant communication services (gateways). (Internet2 2002b, italics ours)

The Internet2 Commons project was not about a gift economy; it was about a market economy. The universities that participated were serving as a test bed for the telecommunications infrastructure of their corporate partners: Video Display Corporation, RADvision, Microsoft, Cisco, Starbek, and others.

Universities as test beds serve as milieus of innovation and of use. As milieus of innovation, they provide research, contributing to hardware and software innovation. They directly and indirectly leverage federal funds for the project through the NSF and other mission agencies by using expertise and knowledge faculty have developed on other federally funded research projects. The university researchers are also expected to provide peer support for the technology, which means that they use their expertise to work out the glitches without turning to their corporate sponsors for support. When universities serve as milieus of use, researchers and site coordinators (who can also be researchers) deploy the telecommunications on their campus to ensure that "intended end-users" will be instructed and supported until they are able to work happily with the telecommunications technology. The universities' faculty and students, not necessarily involved in or aware of the Internet2 Commons, are guinea pigs for the technology. The campus environment provides a test bed unlike any other in that scientist and engineers contribute their innovative expertise to deploy and support these technologies; faculty and students serve as intelligent users and are also the ideal future consumers for such products, processes, and services.

The global and interoperable scope of the project is breathtaking. Currently, it includes fifty-two universities (most of them in the United States and all necessarily members of Internet2, unless sponsored by an Internet2 university), eight organizations the status of which is unclear (i.e., MOREnet, Advanced Network & Services), and Ford Motor Company. The financial arrangements are not detailed, so at this point we are not sure whether the universities are paying all or part of the costs of deploying the infrastructure or whether the infrastructure is donated by corporations in return for using the universities as test beds. Although Internet2 urges that intellectual property rights be settled at the beginning of all projects, the way the framework works for the Internet2 Commons project is not included on the website.

Regardless of how the funds go, the Internet2 commons is a prime example of administrative academic capitalism. The UCAID leadership has designed a global project that seeks to make use of all the creative properties of the academic commons, drawing on the innovative skills of academic researchers; their willingness to exchange information freely and improve the products, processes, and services they work on without expecting recompense; and their commitment to peer support. However, the intermediating network has "enclosed" this commons because the infrastructure is private. The corporations that participate will greatly improve their technologies by deploying them in universities, which serve as milieus of innovation and use, and they will not have to pay for these improvements or tests. The technologies and related services will be sold commercially, and the corporations will reap profits, while it is not clear what universities receive in return—perhaps royalties. Although the Internet2 Commons site speaks to the architecture of the technology involved, it does not address how this is simultaneously an architecture of control, committing universities to particular types of technology, enlisting faculty to participate in them, training graduate students to work with them, and undergraduate students to use them.

Conclusion

Given the way knowledge production is structured in the United States, universities were poised to play a major role in the knowledge economy because of their generation of (federally funded) research. Indeed, the knowledge economy was in large part the product of the historic relation among the DOD, universities, and defense contractors. In an effort to protect DOD command central from attack and destruction by invaders, the DOD hit upon the notion of dispersing information to numerous sites, thereby laying the foundation for the Internet, the World Wide Web, and the knowledge economy.

Faculty and administrators exuberantly created computers and telecommunications, far exceeding the bounds of DOD requirements. As the possibilities of the Internet appeared, universities not hooked to ARPANET were able to connect themselves, expanding the potential of telecommunications much more rapidly than bureaucracies or policies intended. Hackers and geeks experimented wildly and freely shared their products and software with anyone who wanted them.

However, as noted in chapter 2, federal policy powerfully structured the U.S. knowledge economy. In the 1980s and 1990s, a bipartisan congressional coalition legislated the privatization and commercialization of federal research. Although the coalition was bipartisan, it was political. The coalition drew together Democrats and Republicans who worked with the business class (Useem 1984) to develop neoliberal policies that fostered privatization, deregulation, and commercialization under state auspices and with state support. The business class in the United States had decided that civilian technology was as important as defense and acted to establish funding and opportunity for corporate activity in a global economy. This necessitated (but perhaps unintentionally) a knowledge economy because a global economy could not operate without a telecommunications infrastructure that made possible real-time trading and vastly increased numbers of traders. As technological discoveries, often university based, interacted with the creation of a global economy, the knowledge economy emerged, sharpening corporate leaders' interest in restructuring intellectual property so that increasing amounts and types of knowledge were alienable, privatizable, and commercializable. Universities' interest in privatization and commercialization was cemented with the Bayh-Dole Act (1980). By the time the DMCA was legislated, universities were committed to a neoliberal intellectual property regime that featured privatization and commercialization.

As has historically been the case in the United States, the bureaucratic arms of the federal and several states (quasi) independently played an important role in creating the knowledge economy. The NIH began to expand rapidly in the 1970s, contributing to the growth of the biotechnology and pharmaceutical industries. The NSF greatly expanded its role when the cold war ended, providing that agency with unprecedented opportunity. During the cold war, the NSF was often spoken about as the balance wheel among the federal research agencies, ensuring that national needs were met. In practice, the NSF received much less funding and had much less research scope than the constellation of defense-related mission agencies (DOD/DOE/NASA). When the Berlin Wall was precipitously torn down, the NSF had room to expand. It had already begun developing initiatives that involved privatization, commercialization, and deregulation, particularly in engineering.

The NSF and NIH became to the knowledge economy what the DOD was to the cold war economy. The NSF was not forced to move away from a "basic" science mission to an entrepreneurial mission. Rather, its leaders helped to create neoliberal ideas that emphasized the importance of civilian technology and saw privatization and commercialization as vehicles for rapid dispersion of these ideas. For example, Frich Bloch, former head of the NSF, became head of the Council on Competitiveness, a private policy group that advocated neoliberal competitiveness policies, and is now head of another think tank, the Washington Advisory Group, which is an Internet2 member. As we have recounted, the NSF created the backbone for the commercial Internet, privatized it, and is now in the process of organizing its next iteration, which is explicitly geared to commercialization. The NSF uses its resources for building the infrastructure for the knowledge economy, grants resources to universities, and mobilizes other agencies, currently through the NGI, to put their resources into telecommunications infrastructure. Privatization and commercialization are made possible by continued state subsidy.

The emergence of the knowledge economy made university presidents, who headed institutions that created knowledge, more important actors than they previously had been. Historically, some presidents, particularly physicists after the cold war, connected universities, the defense state, and defense contractors to the economy. However, the defense economy was directed primarily toward military security. Economic development was a by-product, not an end. Research related to defense was often classified and performed in special laboratories. With notable exceptions, such as the first successful experiment with the atomic bomb at the University of Chicago, the technology was not used on campuses and not used by the majority of faculty and students. In contrast, the knowledge economy eventually involved most members of the university community.

The rapid development of technology, combined with neoliberal policies of privatization and commercialization, heavily subsidized by the state and federal governments, created an opportunity for presidents of research universities to become administrative academic capitalists. The niche they occupied was forward planning in research, innovation, deployment, and testing of infrastructure, products, processes, and services for the knowledge economy. However, they chose not to do this as a public service, as universities historically had, as illustrated by land-grant universities and agricultural experiment stations. Instead, the presidents in Internet2 shared neoliberal ideology with their counterparts in government and business, and chose to develop the knowledge economy as a privatized and commercialized enterprise in which they participated and in whose revenue streams their institutions shared. There is scant evidence that they considered alternatives, although alternatives were available, given LINUX and the free software movement. Although all of the groups discussed—corporate leaders, political leaders, state agency leaders—contributed to the development of the knowledge economy, university presidents occupied a quasi-independent niche as administrative academic capitalists who created, managed, tested, and deployed the new technologies.

Administrative academic capitalists are part of different networks than are the faculty academic capitalists and the offices that directly support them. (However, support offices such as technology transfer and intellectual property also have lives of their own, independent from the faculty they support, and they contribute heavily to the development of academic capitalism through their national networks.) Administrative academic capitalists often operate through intermediating networks—for example, Educause, Internet2, and the League for Innovation. State and regional examples abound, as manifested in networks of economic development officers. These networks are separate from but related to faculty entrepreneurial networks. The distinction between the two types of networks is more than academic. Administrative academic capitalists speak for the institution as a whole and are able, partly by virtue of their external functions and invocation of connections to the economy, to make policies that affect everyone in the university communities.

Generally, we think our Internet2 case—and particularly the account of the intellectual property framework and the Internet2 Commons—suggests that the boundary between the public and the private sectors is no longer well defined. The categories of public and private no longer work well in a number of cases, particularly those that involve public/private partnerships (a phrase that in and of itself suggests erosion of the categories). Yet most theories of the state, whether pluralist or Marxian, depend upon a clear boundary between public and private. Nor do market theories replace state theories because the markets we have discussed depend on continued and substantial state subsidy.

We suggest a somewhat different interpretation. The labels public and private (which were always socially constructed categories) no longer serve to distinguish between the commercial (private) economy and the public (noncommercial) sector. Historically, the private sector has always benefited heavily from state subsidy. Indeed, many high technology oligopolistic corporations (nuclear power, pharmaceuticals, aerospace, electronics) achieved their economic positions through various forms of federal subsidy. However, putatively public institutions taking on commercial functions is new. If important segments of the private sector were historically subsidized by the state, and if segments of the state that have important connections to the economy now engage in commercial activity, then the categories lose their edge, and we need to think of new theories and categories to address these developments.

9

NETWORKS OF POWER
Boards of Trustees and Presidents

THE CASE OF INTERNET2 points strongly to the dynamic role that networks of presidents play in forward planning that contributes to the academic capitalism knowledge/learning regime. That case led us to ask if trustees have networks and what part they play with regard to academic capitalism. Because trustees are usually not involved in the day-to-day running of universities but have formal legal and fiduciary responsibility for them, we thought their networks might be somewhat different from those of presidents. We analyzed the networks of a small sample of private and public research universities, which formed a pattern of tightly interlocked boards. After analyzing network densities and patterns and contrasting them with presidential networks, we came to the conclusion that the boards of trustees comprise one of several networks crucial to the management of universities. Boards have to approve universities' adoption of policies and activities that contribute to an academic capitalist knowledge/learning regime, whether they are new policies, legal strategies, or activities such as Internet2. When boards are cognizant of the possibilities of an academic capitalist knowledge/learning regime, they participate more fully and knowledgeably in decision making. However, private and public boards seem to serve somewhat different functions, and presidents of public universities may use their knowledge about private university trustee networks' practices to leverage their boards of trustees.

Theory and Method

There is not a great deal of theoretical literature on boards of trustees. Generally, scholars assume that university presidents (now CEOs) are the key decision makers and institutional leaders. The bulk of the literature on boards of trustees is descriptive, surveys of trustee characteristics, or proscriptive, aimed at educating trustees so they understand their duties (Chait, Holland, and Taylor 1991; Kerr and Gade 1989; Hill, Green, and Eckel 2001; Madsen 1997). The proscriptive literature makes the case that the function of public-sector trustees is to serve as a buffer between universities and nonacademic groups, primarily government, while the function of private-sector trustees is to protect academic autonomy from donors, alumni, and government. Networks of trustees are neither studied nor theorized.

We turned to scholars of business organizations to see if they could shed light on the role of trustees. Much of the literature on corporate boards from the 1930s to the 1980s made the case that CEOs, not boards of directors, were the decision makers for corporations (Berle and Means 1932; Toffler 1970). However, research beginning in the 1950s began to study interlocks among boards of corporate directors. Interlocks occur when a member of one corporate board sits on the board of directors of another corporation. From the 1950s to the 1970s, these studies were relatively few in number and viewed interlocks as "elements of capitalist class integration" (Mizruchi 1996, p. 279; see also Domhoff 1967; Mills 1956; Useem 1979, 1984; Zeitlin 1974). As the study of organizations moved from examining single organizations to considering organizational fields and interorganizational relations in the 1980s, boards of business corporations began to receive much more attention. Tightly interlocked boards were seen as important business networks rather than simply as vehicles for class domination. The interlocks were retheorized as avenues for interorganization information transmission, ranging from specific practices, such as total quality management (TQM), to business strategies that gave firms competitive advantages. As network methodology and analysis became more sophisticated, the study of interlocking corporate directorates burgeoned.

What compelled researchers was the density and flexibility of the network formed by corporate boards (and its amenability to quantitative analysis). "Directors of the median Fortune 500 firm . . . collectively sat on the boards of seven other Fortune firm boards, and some firms . . . shared directors ['interlocked'] with 40 or more large firms. The aggregate result is the creation of an interlocking directorate linking virtually all large American firms into a single network based on shared board members" (Davis 1996, p. 154). In 1999, "any two of the 4760 directors of the 546 largest US firms . . . could be connected by 4.3 links, and any two of the boards are 3.5 degrees distant" (Davis, Yoo, and Baker 2003). From 1982 to 1999, there was substantial turnover in the identities of the firms and directors that created the network among the Fortune 500 firms, but the network nonetheless remained tightly linked. As Davis, Yoo, and Baker put it, "The interlock network created by overlapping board memberships has proven to be a potent medium for the spread of corporate practices and structures . . . [which] . . . spread through shared directors like a virus, cumulating into substantial changes in the character of the largest corporations." As they note, boards meet quite often—several times a year, sometimes as often as ten. The directors, who sit on multiple boards, bring information learned on one to problems faced by others. If the distance between directors is shorter, the information flows faster. The Fortune 500 corporations are so closely linked that Davis, Yoo, and Baker use a metaphor of contagion rather than of communication to capture the rapidity of knowledge flow among boards.

Higher education researchers have not studied college and university boards of trustees as networks (for an important exception, see Thomas, Pusser, and Slaughter, forthcoming). A few historical works studied corporate boards on which trustees sat, and, after noting the numbers of large corporations represented, made the case that these trustees and regents were the means through which business leaders' exercised conservative control over higher education (Veblen 1918; Sinclair 1923; Beck 1947; Smith 1974). However, these studies did not focus on the interlocks among the various boards.

Our sample was defined by the membership of governance boards of twenty of the nation's leading research universities in the academic year 2000. Using the National Science Foundation's report of federal obligations for fiscal year 1999, we chose the ten leading public and ten leading private universities in terms of the federal dollars devoted to science and engineering obligations.

Members of the governing boards of these twenty universities were identified directly from institutional records. Each board's membership list was then compared to listings of boards of directors from publicly held U.S. corporations that ranked within the top thirty best capitalized firms and those appearing in the top 500 of the NSF's ranking of firms' expenditures on research and development (National Science Foundation and the United States Department of Commerce 1999). The source for the corporate board memberships was EDGAR Online, Inc. This comparison of board memberships allowed us to identify individuals who sat both on university governing boards and the publicly held corporations identified for our sample. Because our sample is quite selective, it likely underrepresents the density of interlocks.

Aggregating the total linkages observed for any university allowed us to develop a matrix representing the number of ties between each university and each corporation in the sample. If, for example, university X trustee Jane Smith was a director at Xerox and at IBM; and university X trustee John Stevens was also a director of Xerox, university X would have a total of two ties to Xerox and one to IBM.

The data contained in this matrix can be subjected to descriptive analyses yielding a number of measures useful to social network analysts. The typical focus of such analyses includes measures of network density, width, degree of connectivity, and centrality. While we use GAUSS and SNAP for our preliminary descriptive analysis there are a number of other software packages that have been designed specifically for this purpose. These descriptive measures can provide a wealth of information about the characteristics of the linkages between boards such as those of interest to us.

Corporate and University Interlocks

In 2000, the top ten private research universities, as defined by annual R&D funding, had as trustees one hundred people who sat on the top thirty capitalized corporations in the United States or on the boards of the NSF's top 500 research performing corporations, representing a total of sixty-one firms. Thirty-nine (39%) of the corporations shared board members with more than one university board of trustees. None of the private research universities were more than two steps away from each other. Most were multiply linked through the corporate board members who sat on their boards of trustees. For example, trustees of MIT served as members of the board of directors of twenty-four corporations in our sample. MIT was interlocked through six corporations to Johns Hopkins University (see Figure 9.1). Johns Hopkins had thirteen trustees who were members of corporate boards in our sample, as did Cornell; they were interlocked to other top ten universities, Cornell to all ten, Johns Hopkins to six. Washington University had twelve members from corporations in our sample, only four of which did not link directly to other universities. Harvard had eight of our sample's corporations, five of which were connected directly to other universities. Duke, Columbia, and Stanford each had six, most of which linked to the other universities, as was the case with Yale, with five. The density of the network is extraordinary.

After discovering the density of the network of members of corporate boards of directors who sit on boards of private research universities in 2000, we wanted to check to see if the network had changed over time. However, we had difficulty compiling historical data, given the lack of any easily accessible public archive. We were able to locate 1981 data on only four of the twenty universities we studied in 2000. Two were public and two private. We realize that such a small data set does not constitute baseline data and were tempted to discard it as a comparison point. In the end, we decided to retain it but acknowledge that it is at best suggestive.

The 1981 data (see Figure 9.2) show as many chairs of corporate boards holding seats on private universities as in 2000, although they are not as tightly interlocked. The lack of linkage may be due to having information from only

Top 10 Private Research Universities, 2000

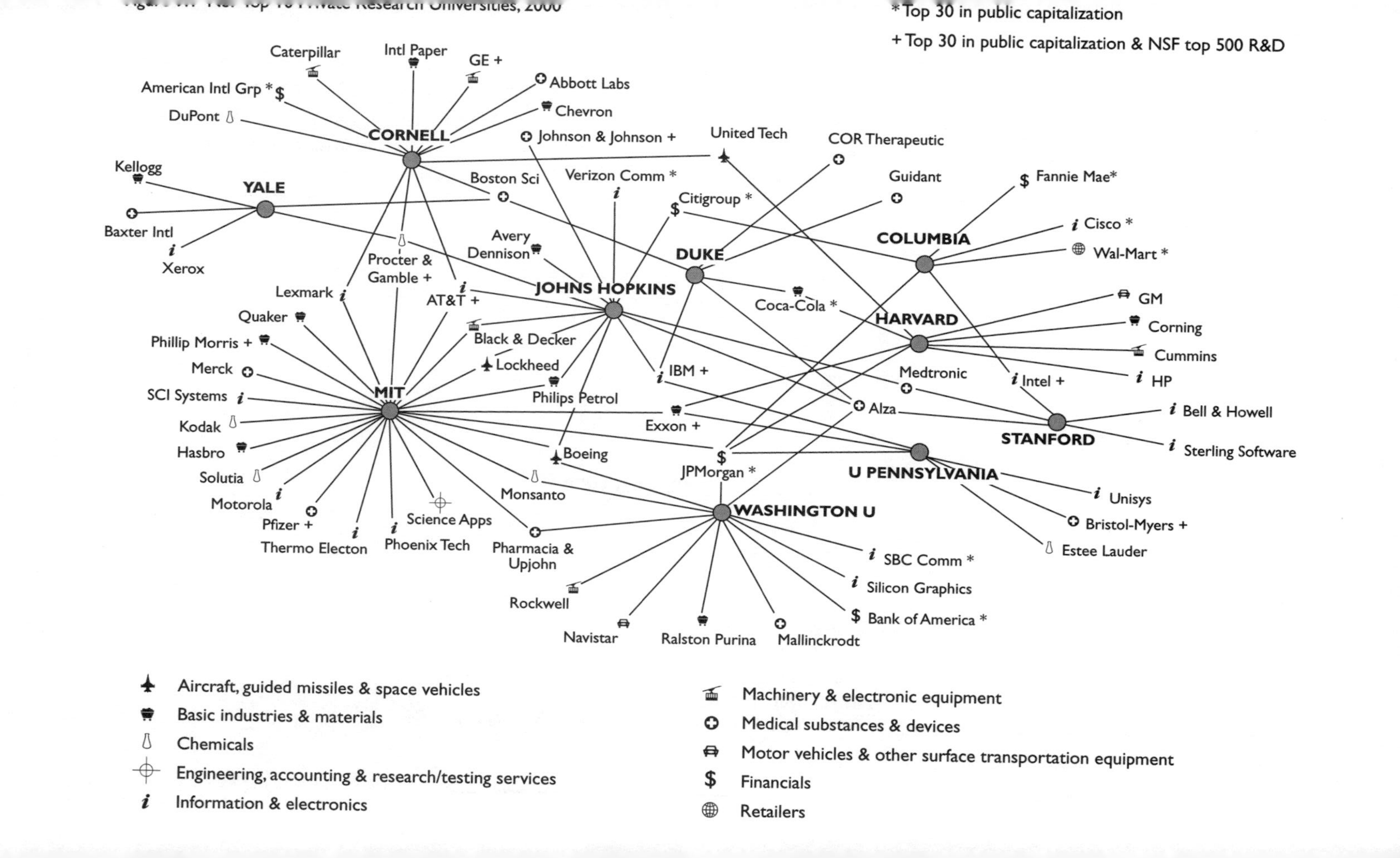

Figure 9.2 NSF Top 10 Public Research Universities, 2000

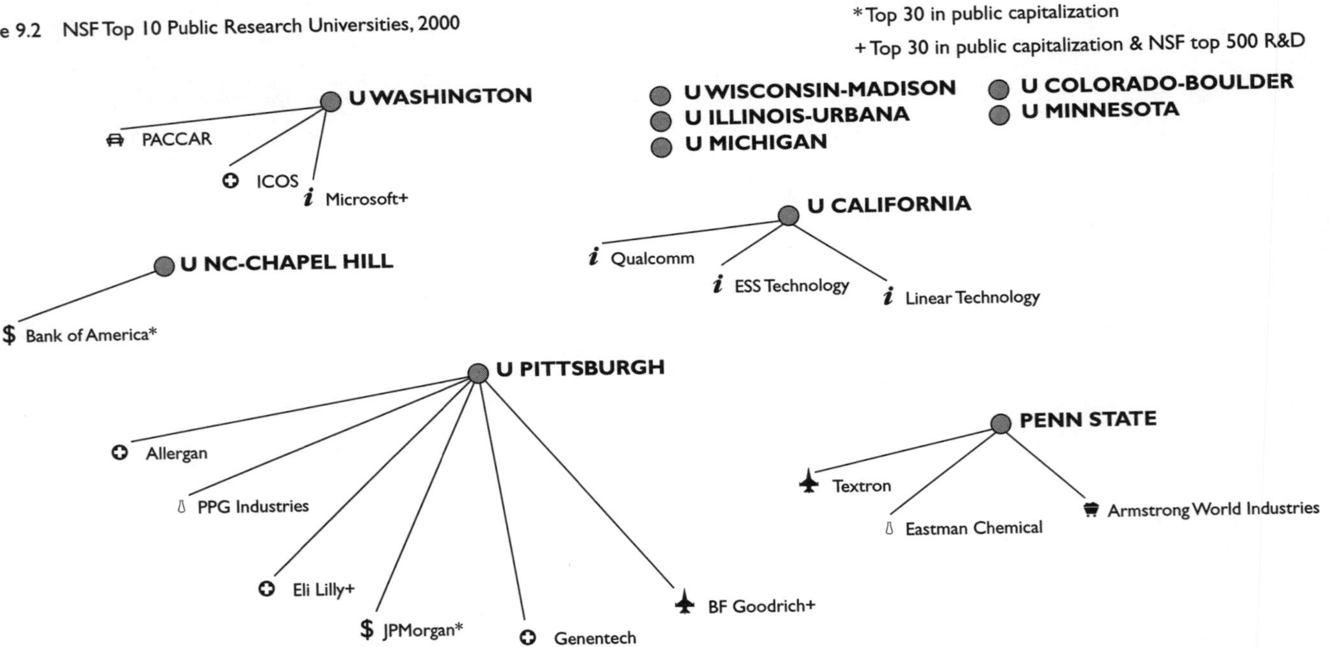

Figures 9.1 and 9.2 cont. Standard and Poor's Major & Detailed Industry Categories*

- **Aircraft, guided missiles & space vehicles**
- **Basic industries & materials**
  - Food & kindred products; tobacco products
  - Misc. products (leather, toys, jewelry, musical inst.)
  - Oil & gas extraction; petrol. refining & related ind.
  - Paper & allied products
  - Stone, clay, glass & concrete products
- **Chemicals**
  - Industrial chem.; plastic & other synthetic materials
  - Other chem. (soaps, ink, paints, fertilizers, explosives, etc.)
- **Engineering, accounting & research/testing services**
- **Information & electronics**
  - Calculating/accounting mach. & office machines
  - Communications services (phone, satellite, radio/TV, cable, etc.)
  - Computer networking communications equip.
  - Computer peripheral equip. (printers, scanners, etc.)
  - Computer storage devices
  - Electronic components (semiconductors, coils, etc.)
  - Electronic computers & computer terminals
  - Multiple & miscellaneous data processing services
  - Prepackaged software
  - Radio, TV, cell phone & satellite communication equip.
  - Ophthalmic goods, photogrph. equip. & clocks
  - Laboratory controlling and measuring instruments
- **Machinery & electronic equipment**
  - Electrical equipment (industrial & household)
  - Machinery (indus., farm, services, mining & construction)
- **Medical substances & devices**
  - Drugs: in vitro, in vivo diagnostic substances
  - Drugs: pharmaceutical preparations
  - Medical instruments
- **Motor vehicles & other surface transportation equipment**
- **$ Financials**
- **Retailers**

*Categories only for those corporations appearing in this analysis

Figures 9.1 and 9.2 cont. Corporation Index, by Major Sector & Detailed Sector

Corporation	Major sector	Detailed sector
Abbott Labs	Medical substances & devices	Drugs: pharmaceutical preparations
Allergan	Medical substances & devices	Drugs: pharmaceutical preparations
Alza	Medical substances & devices	Drugs: pharmaceutical preparations
American Intl Grp	Financials	Financials
Armstrong World Industries	Basic industries & materials	Rubber & misc. plastic prod. (tires, plastic footwear, etc.)
AT&T	Information & electronics	Communications services (phone, satellite, radio/TV, cable, etc.)
Avery Dennison	Basic industries & materials	Paper & allied products
Bank of America	Financials	Financials
Baxter Intl	Medical substances & devices	Medical instruments
Bell & Howell	Information & electronics	Calculating/accounting mach. & office machines
BF Goodrich	Aircraft, guided missiles & space vehicles	Aircraft, guided missiles & space vehicles
Black & Decker	Machinery & electronic equipment	Machinery (indus., farm, services, mining & construction)
Boeing	Aircraft, guided missiles & space vehicles	Aircraft, guided missiles & space vehicles
Boston Sci	Medical substances & devices	Medical instruments
Bristol-Myers	Medical substances & devices	Drugs: pharmaceutical preparations
Caterpillar	Machinery & electronic equipment	Machinery (indus., farm, services, mining & construction)
Chevron	Basic industries & materials	Oil & gas extraction; petrol. refining & related ind.
Cisco	Information	Computer networking communications equip.
Citigroup	Financials & electronics	Financials
Coca-Cola	Basic industries & materials	Food & kindred products; tobacco products
COR Therapeutic	Medical substances & devices	Drugs: pharmaceutical preparations
Corning	Basic industries & materials	Misc. products (leather, toys, jewelry, musical inst.)
Cummins	Machinery & electronic equipment	Machinery (indus., farm, services, mining & construction)
DuPont	Chemicals	Industrial chem.; plastic & other synthetic material
Eastman Chemical	Chemicals	Industrial chem.; plastic & other synthetic material
Eli Lilly	Medical substances & devices	Drugs: pharmaceutical preparations
ESS Technology	Information & electronics	Electronic components (semiconductors, coils, etc.)
Estee Lauder	Chemicals	Other chem. (soaps, ink, paints, fertilizers, explosives, etc.)
Exxon	Basic industries & materials	Oil & gas extraction; petrol. refining & related ind.
Fannie Mae	Financials	Financials
GE	Machinery & electronic equipment	Electrical equipment (industrial & household)
Genentech	Medical substances & devices	Drugs: pharmaceutical preparations
GM	Motor veh. & other surface transport equipment	Motor vehicles & motor vehicle equipment
Guidant	Medical substances & devices	Medical instruments
Hasbro	Basic industries & materials	Misc. products (leather, toys, jewelry, musical inst.)
HP	Information & electronics	Electronic computers & computer terminals
IBM	Information & electronics	Electronic computers & computer terminals
ICOS	Medical substances & devices	Drugs: pharmaceutical preparations

Intel	Information & electronics	Electronic components (semiconductors, coils, etc.)
Intl Paper	Basic industries & materials	Paper & allied products
Johnson & Johnson	Medical substances & devices	Drugs: pharmaceutical preparations
JPMorgan	Financials	Financials
Kellogg	Basic industries & materials	Food & kindred products; tobacco products
Kodak	Chemicals	Industrial chem.; plastic & other synthetic materials
Lexmark	Information & electronics	Computer peripheral equip. (printers, scanners, etc.)
Linear Technology	Information & electronics	Electronic components (semiconductors, coils, etc.)
Lockheed	Aircraft, guided missiles & space vehicles	Aircraft, guided missiles & space vehicles
Mallinckrodt	Medical substances & devices	Drugs: in vitro, in vivo diagnostic substances
Medtronic	Medical substances & devices	Medical instruments
Merck	Medical substances & devices	Drugs: pharmaceutical preparations
Microsoft	Information & electronics	Prepackaged software
Monsanto	Chemicals	Industrial chem.; plastic & other synthetic materials
Motorola	Information & electronics	Radio, TV, cell phone & satellite communication equip.
Navistar	Motor veh. & other surface transport equipment	Motor vehicles & motor vehicle equipment
PACCAR	Motor veh. & other surface transport equipment	Motor vehicles & motor vehicle equipment
Pfizer	Medical substances & devices	Drugs: pharmaceutical preparations
Pharmacia & Upjohn	Medical substances & devices	Drugs: pharmaceutical preparations
Philips Petrol	Basic industries & materials	Oil & gas extraction; petrol. refining & related ind.
Phillip Morris	Basic industries & materials	Food & kindred products; tobacco products
Phoenix Tech	Information & electronics	Prepackaged software
PPG Industries	Chemicals	Other chem. (soaps, ink, paints, fertilizers, explosives, etc.)
Procter & Gamble	Chemicals	Other chem. (soaps, ink, paints, fertilizers, explosives, etc.)
Quaker	Basic industries & materials	Food & kindred products; tobacco products
Qualcomm	Information & electronics	Radio, TV, cell phone & satellite communication equip.
Ralston Purina	Basic industries & materials	Food & kindred products; tobacco products
Rockwell	Machinery & electronic equipment	Electrical equipment (industrial & household)
SBC Comm	Information & electronics	Communication services (phone, satellite, radio/TV, cable, etc.)
SCI Systems	Information & electronics	Electronic components (semiconductors, coils, etc.)
Science Apps	Engineering, accounting & research/testing	Engineering, accounting & research/testing services
Silicon Graphics	Information & electronics	Electronic computers & computer terminals
Solutia	Chemicals	Other chem. (soaps, ink, paints, fertilizers, explosives, etc.)
Sterling Software	Information & electronics	Prepackaged software
Textron	Aircraft, guided missiles & space vehicles	Aircraft, guided missiles & space vehicles
Thermo Electon	Information & electronics	Laboratory controlling and measuring instruments
Unisys	Information & electronics	Electronic computers & computer terminals
United Tech	Aircraft, guided missiles & space vehicles	Aircraft, guided missiles & space vehicles
Verizon Comm	Information & electronics	Communication services (phone, satellite, radio/TV, cable, etc.)
Wal-Mart	Retailer	Retailer
Xerox	Information & electronics	Ophthalmic goods, photogrph. equip. & clocks

two private universities from this period. However, private research universities may have been less tightly interlocked with each other then.

Although the network created by interlocks among university boards has not been studied, corporate interlocks, as we noted earlier, are receiving more and more attention. Studies indicate that the overall network established by corporate interlocks creates a general communication system through which information important to corporations quickly travels (Davis, Yoo, and Baker 2003). Sitting on external boards allows corporate leaders to run a "business scan" to understand what other corporations are doing (Useem 1984). Interlocking boards created social cohesion within the business class which unifies them as political actors. Interlocked firms have similar Political Action Committee (PAC) contribution patterns and give voice to similar political positions at congressional hearings (Mizruchi 1989, 1990). Patterns of interlocks predict a range of corporate strategies: provision of "golden parachutes" (Wade, O'Reilly, and Chandratat 1990), adoption of the multidivisional form (Palmer, Jennings, and Zhou 1993), engagement in acquisitions (Haunschild 1993), and TQM (Westphal, Gulati, and Shortell 1997).

Corporate board members have long sat on university boards of trustees, where they have been the dominant occupational group since the 1890s (Veblen 1918). There are several interpretations of this behavior, which fall into three broad categories: altruistic service, social cohesion among elites, and self-interested exercise of power over universities. Because many trustees are successful alumni, their board service is often seen as dedication to the institution at which they were educated. Business persons may also see a university board seat as conferring status and prestige. Private, non-profit boards are self-perpetuating and selective, and service is a mark of social cachet (Domhoff 1967). The corporate board members in our sample, especially the 40 percent who sit on more than one board, meet with each other specifically about university concerns several times a year. The interorganizational literature on corporate boards suggests that perhaps interlocked university trustees, like corporate trustees, do something other than support the president/CEO. For example, they may form a communication and learning network in which information about practices and strategies flows rapidly among the boards. If this is the case, then boards of trustees very likely influence institutional management, especially with regard to decisions relevant to their university's interorganizational field.

Only sixteen (16%) of the corporate board members were from the thirty most highly capitalized corporations that were not also part of the NSF top R&D 500, and they represented only ten (16%) firms, five (50%) of which were financials. Although financial firms do not invest heavily in research, they are among the heaviest users of information and electronics research (NSF 1999). Nine firms were in the top thirty most highly capitalized and in the NSF top R&D 500: four produced medical substances and devices, largely pharmaceuticals, and three were information and electronics companies. The corporate board members who were trustees at the top ten private research universities were more likely to be from research intensive firms than highly capitalized firms.

Our concentration on firms from the NSF top research 500 at first glance suggests that we deliberately selected new economy firms. However, the economy has so reshaped itself over the past twenty years that most firms—other than financials—in the Fortune 500 also appear in the NSF top research 500. In part, this is because *Fortune* changed its definition in 1995 to include all industries, not just manufacturing, a change which deals with the shifting boundaries among manufacturing firms and service industries (Davis, Yoo, and Baker 2003). Moreover, about one-third of all 1980 Fortune 500 firms had been acquired and merged by 1990, and even more were merged during the 1990s. Many new firms entered the Fortune 500, often from the information and electronics or medical sectors. By 2000, the Fortune 500 exemplified many of the characteristics of the new economy.

The one hundred seats held by corporate board chairs at the top ten private research universities represented the following sectors: information and electronics (26); medical substances and devices (19); basic industry (15); chemical (12); financials (9); aircraft and guided missiles (8); machinery and electronics (6); motor vehicles (5); engineering and accounting (1). When contrasted with the firms represented on private university boards in 1981, the marked change is the decrease in seats held by corporate board members in machinery and electronic equipment and the increase in seats of companies representing information and electronics, and medical substances and devices. In 1981, seventeen, or 73 percent, of the trustees represented basic industrial and materials firms, chemical firms, or machinery and electronics firms. In contrast, only 34 percent of the 2000 trustees represented such firms. In 1981, there were only three firms (15%) in information and electronics or in medical substances and devices. In 2000, these same sectors accounted for forty-five (45%), or almost half, of the one hundred interlocks.

Information and electronics and medical substances and devices are at the cutting edge of research in the new economy. A number of university and corporate leaders have identified universities as the appropriate sites for research six to ten years away from development (Council on Competitiveness 1996; Office of the Vice President for Research University of Michigan 1996; Stokes

1997). Some scholars go even further and argue that research universities already serve the functions that industrial labs formerly did (Worthington and Varma 1995). The top research universities are repositories of knowledge valuable to the members of boards of directors of new economy firms.

Trustee positions very likely provide corporate board members with a "research scan" (Useem 1984) that allows them to get the big picture of the direction of university research in fields with which they are concerned: information and electronics, biotechnology, and medical substances and devices. Although trustee/corporate board directors have other means of accessing information about research—for example, through partnership programs such as MIT offers, or through their Vice-Presidents for Research, who meet as an Association of American Universities subgroup, or through technology licensing officials, who also meet as a group—they may attend more closely to information shared by other corporate directors/trustees because it is immediate, direct, and presented by their fellow directors (Haunschild and Beckman 1998). The "big picture" may also involve discussions about the commercial potential of research from the perspective of corporate leaders who have research investment portfolios that are different in scope and magnitude than those held by any single university or covered by any organization of university actors.

In contrast to the private research universities, and contrary to our expectations, the top ten public research universities, defined by the amount of research funding they received in 2000, had only sixteen corporate board members from our sample (see Figure 9.3). Again in sharp contrast with the top ten private universities, none of the corporate boards linked any one university to another. Indeed, half (5) of the top ten public research universities are not linked to *any* of the corporations in our sample. Only one corporate board, JP Morgan, links a public university to the private research universities. Because JP Morgan interlocks with four private research universities, the University of Pittsburgh is connected to the dense private research university network, the institutions of which are at most two steps away from each other.

Like the private universities, public universities have the heaviest representation from information and electronics and medical substances and devices (8, or 50%). However, the number of firms is not great when compared to the number connected with the private research universities. The only other strong pattern among the public universities is that all three of the University of California's corporate board members come from the information and electronics sector.

There are several explanations for the differences between private and public boards of trustees. First, the private research universities had a much larger

Figure 9.3 NSF Top Research Universities, 1981

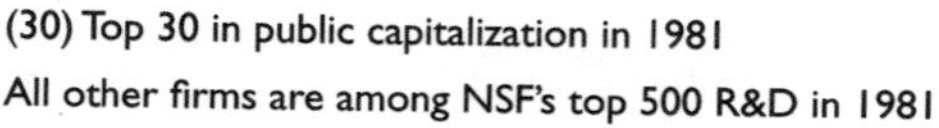

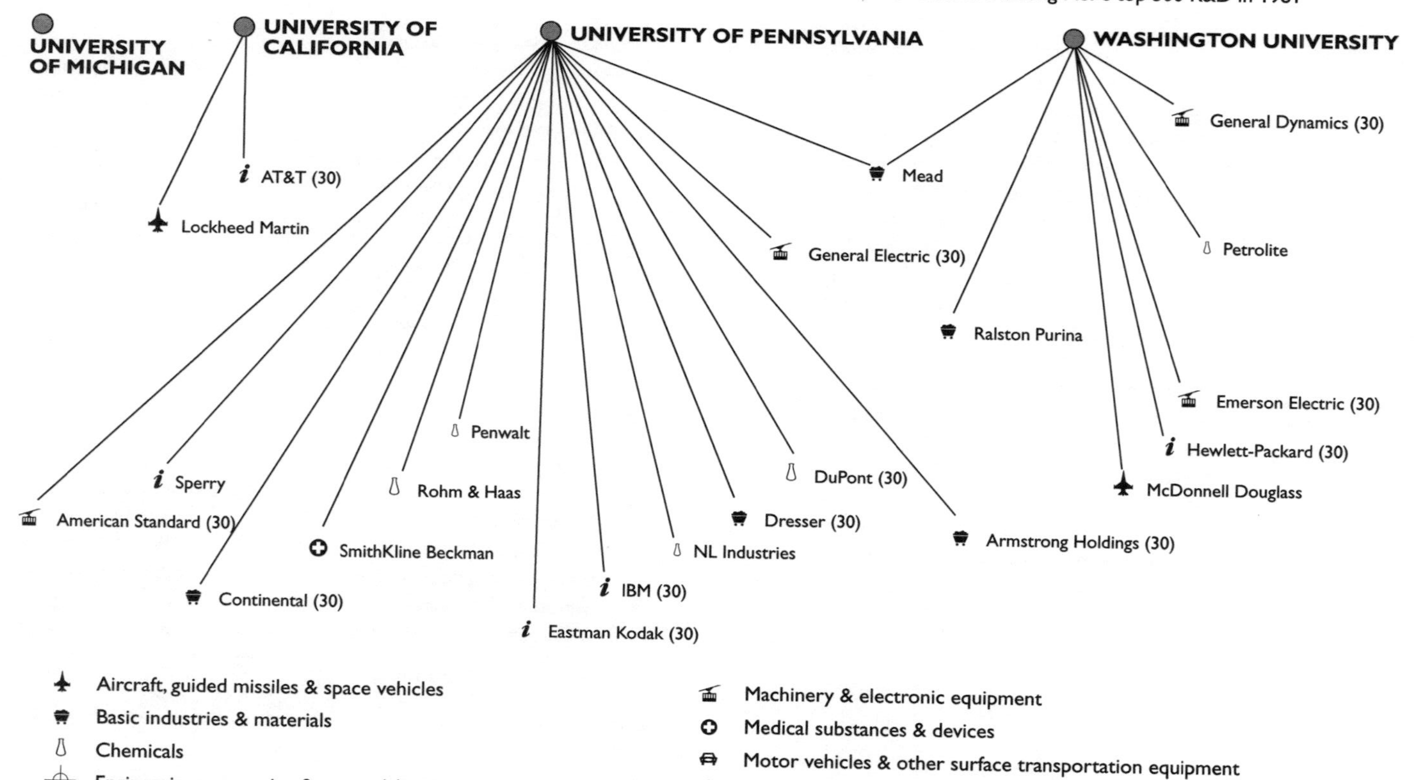

Figure 9.3, cont. Corporation Index, by Major Sector & Detailed Sector

Corporation	Major sector	Detailed sector
American Standard Companies	Machinery & electronic equipment	Electrical equipment (industrial & household)
AT&T	Information & electronics	Communication services (phone, satellite, radio/TV, cable, etc.)
Armstrong Holdings	Basic industries & materials	Misc. products (leather, toys, jewelry, musical instruments)
Continental Group	Basic industries & materials	Misc. products (leather, toys, jewelry, musical instruments)
Dresser Industries	Basic industries & materials	Oil & gas extraction; petroleum refining & related industries
DuPont de Nemours & Co.	Chemicals	Industrial chemicals; plastic & other synthetic materials
Eastman Kodak Co.	Information & electronics	Ophthalmic goods, photography equipment & clocks
Emerson Electric	Machinery & electronic equipment	Electrical equipment (industrial & household)
General Dynamics	Machinery & electronic equipment	Machinery (industrial, farm, services, mining & construction)
General Electric	Machinery & electronic equipment	Electrical equipment (industrial & household)
Hewlett-Packard	Information & electronics	Electronic computers & computer terminals
IBM	Information & electronics	Electronic computers & computer terminals
Lockheed Martin	Aircraft, guided missiles & space vehicles	Aircraft, guided missiles & space vehicles
McDonnell Douglass	Aircraft, guided missiles & space vehicles	Aircraft, guided missiles & space vehicles
Mead	Basic industries & materials	Paper & allied products
NL Industries	Chemicals	Industrial chemicals; plastic & other synthetic materials
Penwalt	Chemicals	Industrial chemicals; plastic & other synthetic materials
Petrolite	Chemicals	Industrial chemicals; plastic & other synthetic materials
Ralston Purina	Basic industries & materials	Food & kindred products; tobacco products
Rohm & Haas	Chemicals	Industrial chemicals; plastic & other synthetic materials
SmithKline Beckman	Medical substances & devices	Drugs; pharmaceutical preparations
Sperry	Information & electronics	Computer peripheral equipment

number of trustees: 467. The number of trustees ranged from seven to seventy-nine, with the average being forty-three trustees per board. In contrast, the public universities had 165 trustees, with each board having from eight to twenty-seven, with an average of sixteen. The private research universities have many more opportunities than publics to appoint trustees from new economy, research-intensive corporations. Second, there may be different rationales for the appointment of private and public board members. Private boards are self-perpetuating and may select corporate CEOs that they see as at the cutting edge of the new economy, reasoning that they have the greatest value as future donors. State governors usually appoint trustees to public boards and often repay campaign activists or contributors by naming them (Pusser 2004). Third, private universities may define themselves as national in scope through their trustee appointments, while governors may have to represent large state voting blocks through their appointments.

Do interlocks matter? Recent work on private enterprise suggests that board interlocks encourage adoption of underlying decision processes that can inform many policy issues: examples are R&D spending, advertising, acquisition activity, and executive compensation (Westphal, Seidel, and Stewart 2001). Not all practices and strategies diffuse throughout the network. Characteristics of boards (active versus passive) and alternative sources of information (membership in organizations such as the Business Roundtable or the Business Council) as well as other factors influence patterns and their outcomes. However, interlocks do seem to shape corporate communication, learning, social cohesion, and political activism.

Although the university boards have not been the subject of interorganizational interlock literature, activity similar to that of corporate boards may occur in research university boards of trustees or regents. Like corporate boards, university boards (and their corporate members) meet several times a year, and the information that flows through the network is "personal, vivid, and concrete" (Haunschild and Beckman 1998), very likely making it persuasive to board members. The network created by the interlocks among private research university boards may give them advantages that public universities lack.

If the private research university network conveys advantage, we should be able to distinguish among behaviors and strategies of public and private research universities, especially with regard to activity related to academic capitalism, because corporate CEOs should have information and opinions on what "works." Yet the two sets of research institutions seem to follow similar practices, strategies, and scripts with regard to policy changes that call for trustee endorsement, as our chapters on patents and copyright have shown, even though the two sets of institutions are quite different with regard to resources, legal constraints, and the size of their student bodies.

Similarities between public and private boards may occur for a number of reasons. Although our sample corresponds to the Fortune 500, it is not congruent with it: the top ten public research universities may have members of Fortune 500 corporations as trustees who are not in our sample. These corporate board members, who are privy to the same information as are those in our sample, may behave in similar ways. Similarities may also occur because presidents of public universities have alternate sources of information that allow them to access information flowing through the private research network. Research on what influences corporate decisions show that decision-shaping information flows not only through interlocks but also through CEOs' membership groups and the business press (Haunschild and Beckman 1998). Presidents of public research universities regularly meet with corporate board directors who sit on private university boards: in organizations like the Business-Higher Education Forum, the Business Roundtable, the Committee on Economic Development, and the Council on Foreign Relations (Slaughter 1990); on the boards of university foundations; and on advisory boards that serve specific colleges and schools in their universities. University presidents also sit on a number of corporate boards. In a 1983 sample of thirty-eight university presidents who were members of the Business Higher Education Forum, half of whom were heads of public institutions, 55 percent sat on at least one corporate board, and half of the public presidents sat on two (Slaughter 1990). In two separate studies of a larger sample of Research I and II universities, one in 1998, the other in 2000, researchers found that about one-third of the presidents in both studies served on from one to five corporate boards and that more than half of the presidents who so served were public university presidents (Goldschmidt and Finkelstein 2001). Many of these were the same boards from which the corporate members on the top ten private research universities boards were drawn. Overall, public university presidents have alternate sources that are likely to provide them much of the same information available to private university presidents and corporate board members who are university trustees.

Presidents may use this information to educate boards that are passive with regard to market practices and political issues (see Zajac and Westphal 1996, on the differences between active and passive corporate boards). More likely, non-Fortune 500 university trustees may be eager to emulate the practices of their corporate counterparts and actively develop similar scripts (see Westphal, Seidel, and Stewart 2001 for board members' scripts and organizational learning in the corporate sector). They almost certainly regard the top ten private research universities as their peer group and would be ready to adopt practices and strategies that make them more similar (see DiMaggio and Powell 1983, for neoinstitutional explanations of why organizations are similar).

Innovation Management in Public and Private Universities

If interlocking boards provide private research universities advantages over publics, then we should be able to see differences in adoption of strategies, practices, and behaviors between the two sets of institutions. Market activities should be most likely to differentiate the two. Private research universities, which have heavy representation of corporate board members from firms that overlap with the Fortune 500, should rapidly communicate information about business practices and market activity relevant to higher education. Public research universities, which are only indirectly connected to this knowledgeable network in a single instance, should have more difficulty gaining access to information about the same business practices and market activity, or at least lag substantially behind private research universities.

Three recent practices in terms of which to compare the two sets of research universities are: increased compensation for professors; presidential compensation; and taking equity interests in companies, often based on faculty discoveries, in exchange for giving the companies the right to use university intellectual property. The corporate board directors of the top ten private research universities likely have information about and interest in all of these practices. Approval from the boards of trustees at private and public research universities is necessary for adoption of any of them.

Private university trustee networks may play an important part in setting faculty salary ranges. Beginning in the 1980s, salaries for professors increased much more rapidly at private-sector universities than public (Alexander 2001). By 2000, there was a noticeable gap between private and public salaries. On average, professors at private universities made $15,000 more than professors at publics. University trustees at private research universities, many of whom are also CEOs at competitive new economy firms, may have seen the competitive edge private universities could gain through attracting the "best and the brightest" with higher salaries. The network of private university trustees undoubtedly exchanged professorial salary setting practices as part of their learning process and may have acted to consolidate gains.

Public-sector research university trustees and presidents have also increased professorial salaries but, lacking the same resources, have done so much more unevenly than private universities. As publics compete with privates with regard to salaries, they likely increase salary differentiation within their institutions. In effect, public research universities may have internal segments composed of centers and departments, perhaps even colleges, which are similar to private research universities, while the university as a whole behaves more like other public institutions. The concentration of resources on some units likely heightens internal stratification within public research universities.

Presidential selection is one of boards of trustees' most important functions. Often the corporate board members who are trustees of universities are themselves CEOs. The salaries of CEOs have risen dramatically in the past decade. If the networks of corporate directors and trustees are dense and overlapping, then as CEO compensation in the corporate sector increases, we likely will expect to see CEO compensation in private universities increase.

Before the mid-1990s, very few private research university presidents had annual compensation packages that topped $500,000 per year. In 1994, two made more than $500,000, but by 2001, twenty-seven did (*Chronicle of Higher Education* 2002a). Rather than speaking of salaries, pay for top leaders began to be referred to as "presidential compensation packages." Pay became more than salary, including bonuses for meeting performance objectives as well as various forms of deferred compensation. Among the targeted performance goals for presidents are admissions and finance performance, upkeep and construction of campus facilities, faculty and staff firing and retention, and overall reputation of the university. By 2000–2001, seven of the top ten private research university presidents had presidential pay and benefits over $500,000, and all had compensation packages above $400,000, while the median pay for the president of a doctoral university in 2001–2002 was $243,360 (*Chronicle of Higher Education* 2002a).

Presidential salaries for public research university presidents fell far behind those of privates in the 1990s. By 1999, the gap between private and public university presidents' salaries had widened to as much as 30 percent. Presidents and search firms began to tell public boards of trustees that they would have to increase salaries to compete. When state legislatures were unwilling to raise presidential salaries, private sources began to make up the difference. A 2002 *Chronicle of Higher Education* survey found that about a third of the 131 public university presidents received base-salary supplements from private sources that "equaled and sometimes far exceeded their state salaries." Most of the presidents led state systems or flagship or large land-grant institutions with large foundations. In some cases, "new presidents have signed two contracts. One is with the university, and one covers compensation from its affiliated private foundations" (2002a). Increasingly, public university presidents are also joining what the *Chronicle* calls the "$500,000 Club." For example, Mark Yudoff, president of the University of Texas system, has a total compensation package of $787,319, of which only $70,231 and a house comes from the state. John Shumaker, president of the University of Tennessee system, receives total annual compensation of $733,550. The state contribution includes $365,000 base salary, $20,000 expense allowance, a house and car, and $98,000 performance bonuses. His private contract has $250,000 in benefits that include executive stock options purchased by the University of Tennessee Foundation and performance bonuses from the foundation. Mark Emmert of Louisiana State University receives $590,000. The state pays $259,160 and provides a house and a car. The private contribution is $230,840 base salary with a $100,000 a year bonus if he completes his five-year contract.

While only a few of the presidents among the top ten public research institutions are members of the "$500,000 Club," many may join in the near future. The public sector institutions lag behind the private, but presidents use information about the private sector from various sources, ranging from search firms to the *Chronicle of Higher Education*, to push their trustees to develop similar practices. The market in presidents spans private and public sectors and, as long as supplemental private resources are available, allows the public to use private-sector practices to leverage their boards for similar compensation packages.

Private research universities' densely interlocked boards may not provide long-term strategic advantages over elite publics, at least with regard to presidential compensation packages, even though their network seems to give privates a short-term edge. Although the two sets of institutions may end up with similar practices and strategies, we think they do so through a different set of dynamics. We see information about practices and strategies traveling rapidly—like "contagion"—through the dense private research university network and boards of trustees as quickly adopting new practices such as complex, high-reward presidential pay packages (Ehrenberg, Cheslock, and Epifantseva 2001). The top public-sector boards, drawing on alternate sources of information from networks that overlap the private-sector board of trustees network, implement similar packages but rely on nonstate sources. In taking this course, the public boards make public institutions more like private. As Derek Bok, the former president of Harvard notes, some research university presidents now make twice as much as the president of the United States, four times that of the Secretary of State (Bok 2002). In other words, the compensation structure of public institutions approximates that of private institutions, both of which are closer to the general structure of pay for CEOs in the corporate world than to the structure of pay in most public organizations. When public and nonprofit universities adopt compensation packages that are structured like those of the private sector, they become more committed to an academic capitalist knowledge/learning regime.

Equity deals did not occur frequently among research universities until the 1980s, when we see an academic capitalist knowledge/learning regime gaining ascendancy. The number of equity deals spread among research universities, slowly at first, and starting in the 1990s, quite rapidly. Taking equity positions rather than licensing intellectual property and receiving royalties became a market strategy for research universities. According to Feldman et al. (2002a), equity provides three advantages over licensing. First, equity gives universities options or financial claims on companies' future income; second, equity deals align interests of university and firm with regard to rapid commercialization of technology; third, equity signals interested investors about the worth of the technology. These scholars attribute the rapid growth of universities taking equity positions to organizational learning through technology transfer offices and do not consider the role of boards of trustees. However, this is precisely the sort of organizational learning that interlock researchers see as spreading rapidly through linked boards. The second and third advantages are relevant to corporate board members in their roles as corporate leaders and as university trustees. As university trustees and corporate board directors, they would have an interest in using equity to align the interests of the start-up and the university, the better to foster rapid and efficient development of the technology. So too, they can easily send and read the signal that universities send about their belief in the promise of the technology when they take equity in a faculty company.

In 2002, Feldman, Feller, Bercovitz, and Burton surveyed sixty-seven Carnegie I and II research universities that had active technology transfer operations. Of these institutions, 76 percent had taken equity in a company and altogether had participated in 679 equity deals. Public universities appeared to make *greater* use of equity when compared to their private research university counterparts. Public universities took more equity in companies than did private universities, even though thirteen of the public universities (19% of the total sample) were prohibited by state laws from holding equity in companies. Ten of these public universities were able to circumvent state statutes by forming independent entities (501(c)3s), usually research foundations or other intermediary institutions, that were able to take equity in corporations based on faculty intellectual property. Although the study does not address whether public or private universities initiated the first equity deals, this market strategy spread rapidly through both, even more rapidly among the public than the private, despite the barriers to public institutions taking equity. This suggests that public institutions unconnected to the interlocked network in which private research universities participate did not suffer. Indeed, both sets of institutions adopted the same strategies geared to increasing external revenue streams.

Ironically, public research universities' adoption of practices and strategies similar to privates' may steer public institutions' trustees toward more aggressive market activity. Public research universities do not have the same resources as privates. Even the highest endowments of the top ten publics do not compare to the endowment of the average top ten private. To pay presidents, public trustees have to support other revenue-generating practices, such as increasing revenue from intellectual property. As noted above, public institutions are more likely than private to take equity positions in faculty intellectual property, even if that means circumventing state law or, as we saw in chapter 3, working to change state law to allow such practices. Public institutions may become more entrepreneurial than privates so that they can keep up. Public trustees may find it easier to build up the foundation than to get funding from the state legislature to compete with privates. However, private subcontracts with presidents and private revenue streams diminish the boundary between public and private, privatizing parts of public universities. Such practices also valorize market activity and undermine the public (nonmarket) mission of public universities.

Our small sample of corporate directors who are trustees at the top public and private research universities suggests that the composition of boards has changed over time. In the past, boards represented basic industry; currently they represent the information economy. As board composition changed, the commercial potential of university research may have become more salient to board members. They may have played a part in developing the federal and state policy changes detailed in chapters 2, 3, 4, and 5 that created the conditions for academic capitalism to flourish. In addition to general concerns with the commercialization of intellectual property, corporate board members who sit on university boards of trustees may have specific interests in university-industry partnerships of various sorts that touch on information and electronics (computers and telecommunications) and medical substances and devices (biotechnology). Practices that shape the climate for the academic capitalist knowledge/learning regime, such as pay packages that make university presidents more like corporate presidents than leaders of nonprofit enterprises, seem to flow through the network created by interlocked private boards. In turn, these seem to influence public universities. Market or academic capitalistic practices also seem to flow through the network and diffuse through the public sector: taking equity positions based on university intellectual property moves universities more directly into the market than licensing did. Trustee networks very likely participate in the interorganizational communication that makes this strategy for generating external revenue possible.

We need to know much more about the part that networks of trustees play in an academic capitalist knowledge/learning regime. The differences in density between private and public networks may have underlying causes that we are not able to explore given the limitations of our data. The extraordinary density of private university trustee networks may stem from their need for a partitioned resource space in which they can consider issues unique to themselves, for example, management issues involving their large endowments. Alternatively, private universities may be engaged in increasingly direct competition with each other and may use the network to reduce uncertainty.[1]

Networks of trustees overlap with networks of presidents. The presidential networks may constitute the creative force for university involvement in the new economy, but many university trustees are heads of corporations that are committed to a knowledge economy. The trustee network likely has a deep interest in fostering an academic capitalist knowledge/learning regime because such a regime creates a milieu for their products and services. For example, if Internet2 uses universities as test beds for advanced computing and Internet electronic products, they create a milieu of use in which students learn to use sophisticated products with which they might otherwise never come in contact. Universities as milieus of use advertise, induct, and instruct students about products and career possibilities in the knowledge economy. Trustee networks may endorse policies that enable an academic capitalist knowledge/learning regime and support presidents in their ventures in boundary-spanning intermediating organizations.

Conclusion

Like the presidents who organized to develop Internet2, trustees form another type of intermediating network between private and public sectors. Networked trustees may have intermediated between private and public sectors since the last quarter of the nineteenth century (see Veblen 1918; Sinclair 1923). However, in each epoch, the network of trustees integrated colleges and universities with different economies—at the turn of the twentieth century, with the industrial economy, at the turn of the twenty-first, with the knowledge economy.

Trustees are more likely to sit on the boards of the NSF research 500 corpo-

1. Thanks to Ken Koput for these suggestions and for his reading of this chapter.

rations than the thirty most highly capitalized corporations, illustrating the trustees' close connection to the new economy. Trustees undoubtedly played a role in shaping many of the practices we have discussed in earlier chapters: championing legislation at national and state levels that created a policy milieu that supported the academic capitalist knowledge regime, and contributing to patent, copyright, and information technology policies, including Internet2. At the least, trustees had to endorse these policies. At most, they actively campaigned for them. All of these policies shape how knowledge is valued in the new economy, converting knowledge into products that provide public and nonprofit support for new economy corporations.

At a more specific level, trustees may in some cases initiate and in other cases endorse specific practices, such as compensation packages for presidents, universities taking equity positions in corporations built on faculty patents or copyright, and professorial salaries (and compensation packages). Information about such packages likely travels instantaneously through trustee networks.

While in this chapter we limit our consideration to a basic description of these ties, our ongoing work considerably extends this presentation. Much of our work in progress employs more sophisticated measures of the frequency and strength of these ties. Perhaps more importantly, however, we can specify models that allow us to estimate the net impact of these linkages on outcomes such as faculty salaries, extramural grant productivity, patent revenues, and a number of other outcomes of capturing institutional behaviors central to academic capitalism (Thomas, Pusser, and Slaughter, forthcoming).

The differences between networks of private and public trustees need further study. As indicated at the beginning of this chapter, the size of our sample makes us less than confident about our data. If our sample were expanded in either direction—to include more corporations and/or more research universities—the results might be very different. As well as expanding our sample, we should explore alternative connections that public universities may have to the new economy. For example, public universities might be tied to regional or niche economies through a variety of intermediating advisory boards at the level of colleges and or/centers.

Public university trustees should be studied to see if they form networks that are grounded in public good purposes. Such a study would involve identifying public university trustees' shared organizational connections to see if they constitute networks embedded in the public good or other knowledge/learning regimes. Perhaps these networks support, initiate, or preserve public good practices. For example, the role of trustee networks in developing or defending affirmative action practices might repay investigation.

10

SPORTS 'R' US
Contracts, Trademarks, and Logos

Samantha King and Sheila Slaughter

Intercollegiate athletic departments usually claim that they generate external revenue. The most profitable sports are football and basketball. At the small number of universities with winning sports programs, they draw large audiences that generate revenues from box office receipts, television contracts, boosters, and corporate sponsorship. If we define academic capitalism as generating external revenues, intercollegiate athletics departments have been in the business for a long time.

However, if we see academic capitalism as a knowledge/learning regime created by the interstitial emergence of complex new networks of actors within colleges and universities who enter into alliances with groups outside the university to create new organizations, reshape old ones, and redefine the purposes of the university so they articulate more closely with the new/knowledge/information economy, this gives us another perspective on the networks of actors engaged in new market strategies for intercollegiate athletics. We use two cases to make our point. The first is the case of all-school contracts, which increased noticeably in the 1990s. In an effort to have sponsors become central to the identity of universities, companies such as Nike and Adidas endorsed entire schools rather than individual coaches or teams. At the same time that corporations were "branding" universities with their trademarks—the Nike swoosh, for example—universities began trademarking their own logos—wildcats, gophers, badgers, and bears, as well as images of Native Americans. Our second case deals with university development of trademarks as "branded" intellectual property aimed at generating external revenues. In the 1990s, a number of universities established trademark offices that began licensing logos to a variety of external corporations and aggressively policing the use of names, logos, and mascots. We conclude our examination of university trademark licensing with the story of Chief Illiniwek, the University of Illinois mascot, a particularly egregious illustration of university involvement in profit taking based on intellectual property.

Branding strategies are a new economy phenomenon. Neither athletic shoe companies nor universities manufacture the products on which they imprint their names, logos, and mascots. In most cases, the branded products are not even produced in the United States; rather, they are made overseas as part of a globalized production system. Branding sells images and identities, not particular products.

All School-Contracts

The case of all-school contracts is based on critical studies of contemporary consumer culture (Goldman and Papson 1996; Klein 2002). This literature sees brand image as more important than product and emphasizes establishing the brand as a university identity. At stake are university student consumers, who constitute a large part of the market for "athleisure" wear.[1] While corporations seek out universities for all-sport contracts, "corporatizing" the university, universities compete to offer corporations the most lucrative contracts. Universities see themselves as equal partners in fair contracts and are willing to sell their identities to generate external revenues. At the same time, universities are emulating corporate strategies, using their logos to brand all manner of products. Like corporations, universities police their logos, intent on maximizing external revenues. Corporations attempt to overlay their identities on universities to capture student markets just as universities are intent on selling institutionally branded products to students who are captive markets.

The commercialization of college sports has received considerable scholarly attention in recent years. Research by Duderstadt (2000), Shulman and Bowen (2001), Sperber (1990, 2001), Thelin (1994), Thelin and Wiseman (1989), and Zimbalist (2001) has highlighted the increasingly large sums of money the top athletic departments derive from boosters, television rights, licensing, and corporate sponsorship. These scholars have also questioned the effects of commercial relationships on the academic performance of athletes, gender equity, the pay and working conditions of athletes and coaches, the disparities between rich and poor programs, and on the values of higher education more broadly. In most cases, these issues have been explored in the context of growing concerns about the number of programs—a majority—whose expenditures outstrip their revenues.

We build on the work of these scholars by examining the recent emergence of "full-program" or "all-sport" apparel and equipment contracts between Di-

1. *Athleisure* wear is a term used in the contracts to describe apparel such as golf shirts and knitted vests.

vision 1A universities and corporations. These contracts have been mentioned in passing by some (Shulman and Bowen 2001) and analyzed in more detail by others—Zimbalist (2001) discusses the controversies that have surrounded the signing of such contracts. However, the history of the emergence of these agreements, the relations between corporations and universities inscribed therein, and their importance for understanding the broader terrain in which universities now operate have not been subject to in-depth analysis.

In exploring these questions, we are particularly concerned with moving beyond an approach that focuses either narrowly on the effects of commercialization on structures, relations, and values *within* college athletics or generally—and often vaguely—on the "educational mission" of the university. Instead, we build on critical studies of contemporary consumer culture to explore how the marketing strategies enshrined in full-program contracts are helping to reconfigure in concrete ways the culture of the university, as part of a broader shift toward the branded society characteristic of the new economy (Ewen 1988, 2001; Frank 1997; Goldman and Papson 1996; Klein 2002; Savan 1994; Schiller 1989; Twitchell 1996).

In her best-selling book, *No Logo* (2002), Naomi Klein argues that the effect of contemporary branding strategies is to push the "host," or sponsored, culture into the background so that the brand emerges as the "star." The idea, she writes, "is not to sponsor the culture, but to *be* the culture" (p. 30). Drawing on this insight, we argue that corporations such as Nike and Adidas are aiming not simply to sponsor the university but to *be* the university. This is evidenced in, among other things, the hyperpolicing of corporate logos, the guarantee of office and retail space on campus to corporate partners, agreements to give corporations first refusal on signage for any new spaces that become available, the growing corporate control of recruitment of athletes and the general student body, and the addition to contracts of nondisparagement clauses that ban criticism of corporate partners by members of the university community. In addition to evaluating these stipulations, we suggest that a situation is emerging in which universities are competing to offer corporations the most lucrative contracts, often with the least accountability to students and faculty, and with the potential to further exacerbate disparities between rich and poor institutions.

Methods

Even very basic information about full-program contracts, such as which schools have contracts, when they were signed, and their monetary value, has proved difficult to gather. Attributing their secrecy to concerns about competitive advantage, the major sponsors of college athletics—Nike, Adidas, and

Reebok—were not even willing to reveal to us the names of the schools with which they had contracts.[2] Written requests for data in the form of a simple survey sent to the 110 schools in the top level of Division 1A yielded twenty-three responses. Telephone calls to those schools that did not reply to the survey, in addition to media coverage of contract signings, generated information about a further fourteen schools. Media coverage was particularly important for obtaining information about private universities, which, without exception, said that they were not obligated under law to participate in the study.

Zimbalist (2001) claims that Nike sponsors between fifty and sixty universities (figures include full-program contracts, partial contracts, and contracts that include no cash compensation). Based on the information we accumulated, we were able to establish that at least twenty-three universities in the top level of Division 1A have full-program contracts (fifteen with Nike, seven with Adidas, and one with Reebok). We then filed Freedom of Information Act requests for copies of the contracts of the nineteen public universities in the sample. The analysis presented here focuses on eight contracts: Adidas's agreements with Arizona State University, the University of Louisville, and the University of Wisconsin–Madison and Nike's agreements with the University of Arizona, the University of Kentucky, the University of Michigan, Texas A&M University, and the United States Air Force Academy.

Historical Context: Branded Culture

It goes without saying that corporations pursue all-school contracts because their brand-building potential increases profits. Placing logos on the uniforms and "athleisure" wear of athletes and coaching staff guarantees exposure to students. Students are a prime market segment who spent an estimated $80 billion on goods and services in 1998. Live audiences also provide a great deal of exposure. In 1997, 37 million people attended college football games, 28 million men's basketball games, and 7.4 million women's basketball games. Millions of people also tune in to watch college sports on television. In the 2001–2002 season, an average of 12,174,000 households watched each college football game, 4,370,000 watched each men's college basketball game, and 368,000 each women's basketball game (Zimbalist 2001).[3] College sports fans also represent an appealing demographic. They are dominated by men in the coveted eighteen-to-thirty-five-year-old market segment, who have an average income of $55,000

2. Reebok appears to be withdrawing from college athletics sponsorship. They had an agreement with Wisconsin from 1996 to 2001, but we cannot find evidence of any other full- or partial-program contracts.

3. These figures exclude tournament and bowl games.

(Zimbalist 2001). This form of advertising, moreover, provides a more cost-effective form of promotion than the purchase of a thirty-second commercial slot. When Penn State and Michigan play football on ABC, the prominently placed logos on the uniforms of the athletes transform the game into a four-hour commercial for Nike. Zimbalist cites a study by Joyce Julius and Associates, a sport-marketing firm, that estimated that the exposure Nike gained from having the swoosh displayed on the Florida State uniforms in the 1996 Orange Bowl was worth $2.6 million (2001).

While the claim that corporations engage in sponsorship of college athletics in order to build brand awareness and increase sales among a lucrative market segment is not new, research on the history—particularly the recent history—of marketing in the United States provides key insights that extend and complicate this claim. This scholarship (Ewen 2001; Goldman and Papson 1996; Klein 2002) tells us that the first branded products appeared in the United States in the second half of the nineteenth century in order to distinguish among the uniform mass-produced goods that were beginning to flood the market. Until the post–World War II era and the emergence of the notion that a company *as a whole* could have a brand identity, brands were viewed as little more than a catchphrase used in advertising campaigns or a picture printed on the label of a product (Klein 2002). It was not until the 1960s and 1970s that the idea of brand as corporate identity, as embodying the "consciousness" of a corporation, became part of marketers' search for the "true meaning" of the brand.

The understanding that although corporations manufacture products, what consumers actually buy are brands did not elicit an immediate shift in corporate attitudes toward production. The corporate world continued to maintain the philosophy that its core business was production and that branding was an important add-on. This changed in the 1980s with what Naomi Klein calls the emergence of "brand equity mania." This period in marketing history was exemplified by Philip Morris's 1988 purchase of Kraft for $12.6 billion—six times what the company was worth on paper. The price difference, executives explained, lay in the cost of the word *Kraft*. While marketing executives were aware that marketing added value to a company over and above its assets and annual sales, the Kraft purchase demonstrated that a large dollar value could be placed on something that had previously been abstract and unquantifiable. A new philosophy emerged that rested on the idea that the more you spend on marketing and the more creative your marketing strategies, the more your company will be worth.

"New" corporations such as Nike, Reebok, Starbucks, Tommy Hilfiger, Calvin Klein, Intel, Microsoft, and the Gap led the way in this new approach to branding. These corporations claimed that producing things was only an incidental component of their operations. Taking advantage of recent moves toward trade liberalization, they were able to have the majority of their products made by subcontractors, most of whom were located overseas in places where labor is cheap and workers have few protections (Ballinger 1998; Enloe 1995; Korzeniewicz and Gereffi 1994; Ross 1997). The primary undertaking of the new, "lighter" corporation was to make not products but images of its brand. Nike, which from the *beginning* had its products made overseas (it started as a sneaker-import business), is the archetype of this model, only having ever owned two small factories for brief periods of time in the 1980s. As founder and CEO Phil Knight describes it, "Nike's mission is not to sell shoes but to 'enhance people's lives through sports and fitness' " and to keep "the magic of sports alive" (Klein 2002, p. 23). Rather than compete on the basis of price, companies such as Nike and Reebok have actually driven up their prices as they pour money into their marketing budgets in order to sign star athletes to huge endorsement contracts and universities to sponsorship arrangements. In 1987, Nike spent approximately $25 million on marketing, and by 1997 this figure had reached $500 million (Klein 2002). Nike's spending on product development in the late-1990s—about $73 million annually—appears meager alongside its marketing budget. By the mid-1990s, the Nike "swoosh" was so familiar that its products and advertisements no longer needed to carry the company name.

While major athletic shoe companies have depended on athlete endorsers for at least twenty years, sponsorship of entire university athletic departments is a newer phenomenon. The roots of this strategy go back to 1977, when the Converse Corporation signed a deal with Jerry Tarkanian, men's basketball coach at the University of Nevada, Las Vegas, giving Tarkanian two free pairs of shoes for every pair he bought for his team. Nike soon caught on to the idea and in 1978 offered Tarkanian free shoes and warm-up suits for the entire team and $2,500 for himself (Zimbalist 2001). The terms of these sponsorships have increased substantially since that time—especially since Nike hired Sonny Vaccaro to recruit coaches as endorsers of its products. John Thompson of Georgetown University was one of the first signees, reportedly earning several thousand dollars in the early 1980s in exchange for having his team wear Nike shoes (Slater 1999). By the late 1990s, Nike was paying top coaches (money that went to the coach, not the athletic department), such as Mike Krzyzewski of Duke University, over $1 million a year, plus stock options, a range of perquisites, and assistance in their recruiting efforts (Zimbalist 2001).

Because new corporations such as Nike depend so heavily on marketing for their success, they must continually build their brands through the appropriation of new images and spaces. This need, which emerged against a backdrop of dramatic decreases in government spending on education, leisure, health, and the arts, saw corporate sponsorship of public events, spaces, and institutions shift from being a "rare occurrence [in the 1970s] to an exploding growth industry" (Klein 2002). Indeed, according to a 1998 *International Events Group Sponsorship Report,* corporate sponsorship spending in the United States increased 700 percent between 1985 and 1998 (quoted in Klein 2002). The move from endorsing individual coaches to endorsing entire universities, which took place in the mid-to late-1990s, can be explained in this context. That universities with full-program contracts are popularly known by the name of their sponsors—as "Nike schools," for example—gives some indication of the strength of the association between the brand and the university. This linguistic connection is concretized in the ubiquitous presence of the Nike swoosh on the uniforms of athletes, coaches, trainers, and other athletic department employees; on nonathlete students' everyday wear; on signage; in print and electronic media; and on a range of merchandise for sale at locations across the sponsored campuses.

Full-Program Contracts

The Nike contracts in our sample are remarkably similar to one another. They all involve a form of base compensation, ranging from $82,500 over five years for the United States Air Force Academy (USAFA), to $8.4 million over the course of seven years for the University of Michigan, to $13.5 million over the course of ten years for the University of Kentucky.[4] In addition to base compensation, Nike agreements include the provision of clothing and equipment for teams (the Michigan contract specifies the retail value of products at $14 million over seven years, but other Nike contracts specify only the number of items—jackets, shoes, etc.—allotted to each team); university-sponsored camps; and, in some contracts, a one-time cash payment to the "university" (Kentucky) or the university president's office (Texas A&M).

Although the Adidas contracts share many similarities with those of its rival, there are some important differences. The yearly base compensation paid by the corporation to the universities appears to be lower: Arizona State University receives $275,000 per annum and the University of Wisconsin–Madison gets $200,000 for the first year and $250,000 for the next three. Adidas pays no base compensation to the University of Louisville. In addition, the Arizona State

4. The USAFA is different from other "Nike schools" because as a government agency it is not permitted to promote one corporation over another.

University contract (signed in January 2000 and amended in 2001) requires that the university must purchase a minimum number of products to be sold on campus in exchange for the free products supplied to the athletic department and team coaches. If the university does not meet the minimum requirement, it must pay Adidas 35 percent of the total shortfall. Similarly, the Wisconsin contract requires that the university order a minimum of $40,000 worth of Adidas products per year for its camps and clinics in addition to paying a one-time "transition and start-up cost" of $525,000. Wisconsin's agreement with Adidas also ensures payment of bonuses (at varying rates depending on the team) to coaches and teams for reaching the Final Four (in men's and women's basketball and men's hockey) or for winning national championships, bowl games, conference championships, or coach-of-the-year awards. In addition to support in the form of cash and products, both corporations pay the universities for the license to manufacture and sell their products bearing university trademarks. The amount of royalties paid ranges from 7.5 percent (Arizona, Arizona State, Kentucky, Texas A&M) to 10 percent (Michigan).[5]

In addition to the conditions discussed below, corporations receive in return for their sponsorship a range of perquisites including free tickets to home games,[6] VIP parking passes, space for hospitality events, use of the university golf course for tournaments, and use of university facilities for "community programming" events.

Policing of Logos

The contracts provide a great deal of detail about where, when, and how corporate logos must appear. All contracts stipulate that athletic department coaches, athletes, and staff must wear official Nike or Adidas wear in program activities (e.g., practices, games, exhibitions, clinics, sports camps, photo sessions, and interviews) and may not wear products bearing brand identification other than that of their corporate partners. In addition, the contracts allow no change to the size, placement, design, or number of logos on any particular product; products must not be altered to resemble a nonpartner product, and personnel may not wear nonpartner products that have been altered to resemble partner products.

The exceptional circumstances described in the contracts illustrate the extent to which the appearance of logos is micromanaged. For instance, several con-

5. Royalties are not mentioned in the Louisville contract, and Wisconsin's agreement sets the rate in accordance with the university standard in effect during each year of the contract.

6. In most cases, the contracts stipulate how many tickets the corporation shall receive and where the seats will be located.

tracts allow coaches to wear dress shoes rather than official sneakers when a particular public appearance requires more formal dress. In addition, athletes who must wear other products due to a "bona fide" medical condition require physicians' notes and must cover up competing logos "so as to completely obscure such manufacturer's identification" (University of Kentucky 2001, p. 9).[7] Injured athletes are also prohibited from wearing tape or bandages that hide a logo. These stipulations, of course, prevent small acts of resistance among athletes who do not want to act as walking billboards for corporations, but they also reshape athletic training practices. For instance, in most cases, athletes are required to obtain medical certification before they can tape over ("spat") a logo (Arizona, Arizona State, Michigan, Wisconsin), and some contracts prohibit spatting, without any mention of medical exceptions (Kentucky, Texas, USAF). The Kentucky agreement, for instance, reads: "University acknowledges that "spatting" or otherwise taping, so as to cover any portion of the Nike logo, the Nike athletic shoes worn by members of the Teams . . . is inconsistent with the purpose of this Agreement and the benefits to be derived by it by Nike and is a material breach of this Agreement" (University of Kentucky 2001, p. 9). If a university with an all-school contract needs products that the corporation does not make, the university has to ask permission to use an alternative supplier and that supplier's logo must be removed. According to employees of the University of Arizona athletic department, Nike representatives visit on a regular basis to ensure that universities are complying with the terms of the contract.

The Creeping Commercialization of Campus Space

A reading of full-program agreements also reveals how they enable the creeping commercialization of public space. Standard features of these agreements oblige the university to supply radio and program advertisements, electronic message board endorsements, and public address system announcements on behalf of corporate sponsors, as well as camera-visible signage in the form of billboards, website banners, goalpost pads, basketball bench chair backs, hockey dasher boards, and back-lit concourse signs. In three cases, universities must help corporations secure retail outlets on campus if the corporation so desires. In four cases they must help their partners place products in their bookstores and in one case (Arizona State University) must provide office space and near-campus housing if asked to do so. In Wisconsin's first full-program contract, with Reebok, the corporation was allowed access to university mailing lists. This is also the case with Arizona State University's current contract with Adidas. In

7. All schools except Louisville and USAFA.

the University of Kentucky agreement, there is a clause to ensure that when future spaces for signage become available, Nike will have first refusal to occupy the space. This is also the case if a branch campus of the University of Kentucky decides to seek corporate sponsorship of its athletic program.

The colonization of space is accompanied by the infiltration of employees' workloads by obligations to the corporate partner. In seven of eight contracts (the University of Arizona is the exception), head coaches are required to make a minimum number of appearances for the corporation each year. The number of appearances usually ranges from two to four, but for Wisconsin coaches the obligation is set at eight eight-hour days per year. Arizona State University's contract with Adidas also gives the corporation access to "players and player locker rooms" (Arizona Board of Regents 1999, p. 5).

We might argue then that the function of university athletic departments and their employees and athletes has become blurred. Not only do they help market the school (a role they've been playing for over 100 years), they are also now increasingly enlisted as marketing representatives and strategists for the sponsoring corporations. In addition to undertaking appearances for Nike and Adidas, at three schools in our sample (Kentucky, Michigan, and Texas A&M), university staff are required to act as design and marketing consultants. The University of Michigan contract outlines these obligations as follows:

> NIKE shall continue its efforts to produce high quality Products through consultation with coaches and staff of successful athletic programs such as UNIVERSITY and whose full cooperation is important to NIKE, as such individuals have knowledge than can be useful in the research, development, and production of NIKE products, and is of the essence of this Agreement. Upon request by NIKE, UNIVERSITY shall request designated Coaches and Staff to provide Nike with written or oral reports concerning the NIKE Products supplied to each through NIKE's product development and testing program. (Regents of the University of Michigan 2001, p. 13).

The blurring of boundaries between corporate sponsors and the recipients of their sponsorship is also illustrated by the increasing role played by Nike and Adidas in the recruitment of college athletes, particularly men's basketball players. Wertel and Yaeger's (2000) describe how corporations such as Nike now sponsor middle and high school boys' basketball teams and camps, in addition to university, professional, and national teams. By Zimbalist's account (2001), the strategy behind Nike's decision to sponsor high school camps is two-pronged: First, by running these camps, Nike is able to build links to the top high school players in the country, and by providing shoes to the players on summer teams and to the schools in which they were enrolled, Nike develops a direct connection to youth in neighborhoods across the country. Second, by building relationships with top prospects, their coaches, and schools, Nike is able to develop lasting bonds with future Michael Jordans.

For college coaches, these relationships also aid in their recruitment efforts. As Texas Tech coach, Bobby Knight, has said, "I see lots of high school sophomores and juniors who don't have money—taking visits to college campuses. They're given a choice, a list of four or five schools they can visit, all expenses paid, and what a coincidence: They're all schools that wear the same brand of shoe" (Zimbalist 2001, p. 140). Along similar lines, a recent article in the *Arizona Daily Star* revealed that a top basketball recruit picked the University of Arizona over Arizona State University because he prefers Nike to Adidas. We are reaching a situation, it seems reasonable to suggest, in which athletes on Nike high school teams attend Nike camps and eventually Nike schools. We might argue than that these corporations are recruiting athletes on behalf of universities, recruiting their athletes to what are becoming their schools.

Disparagement Clauses

Three of eight contracts (Adidas's agreement with Arizona State and Nike's agreements with Kentucky and Texas A&M) include a disparagement clause that bans criticism of corporate partners by members of the university community. The Arizona State clause reads: "University shall not, during the Contract Term and for a period of two (2) years following the termination or expiration of this Agreement, disparage the Adidas brand name, Adidas Products, or Adidas" (Sponsorship Agreement 1999, p. 9). In his discussion of disparagement clauses, Zimbalist (2001) describes how the University of Wisconsin's 1996 agreement with Reebok met opposition when members of the campus community discovered the inclusion of a clause that read: "University will take all reasonable steps necessary to address any remarks by any University employee, agent or representative, including a coach, that disparages Reebok" (p. 144). Campus members found the clause particularly troubling in light of the international controversy about athletic apparel companies' overseas labor practices. Would the clause mean that someone at the University of Wisconsin who was opposed to the use of sweatshop labor be prevented from expressing their views? In the Wisconsin case, Reebok agreed to remove the clause, but our research shows that disparagement continues to be addressed in certain agreements.

The inclusion of clauses requiring corporations to meet university antisweatshop/human rights policy codes is testament to the success of antisweatshop campaigners at campuses across North America, although how these clauses might be enforced varies considerably. In our sample, four of eight contracts (Arizona, Arizona State, Michigan, and Wisconsin) included such as clause. The Michigan and Arizona contracts require the use of an independent monitor to determine if Nike is in breach of the universities' respective labor standards policies. In the case of the University of Arizona, however, the "independent monitor" is selected by the university and the corporation and no budget is outlined for funding the monitor's work. The time limit for Nike to rectify a breach is set at thirty days, but this can be extended if the situation is impossible to fix within thirty days. The main limit of this clause, however, is that the university is under no obligation to terminate the contract should the corporation be found in violation. The lack of the university's response to violations brought to its attention by the campus Students Against Sweatshops group shows that the inclusion of antisweatshop clauses are not always effective.

Semiotic theory tells us that the relationship between the signifier (the Nike swoosh) and the signified (the corporation/sweatshop) is arbitrary and open to multiple interpretations. This insight helps explain why those who hold the intellectual property rights over signifiers attempt to control the signs' circulation and their meanings. As critical legal theorist Rosemary Coombe (1999) argues, by creating monopolies in fields of representation (as Nike does through full-program contracts), the law inserts signifiers into systems of political economy that, according to Baudrillard, "reduce symbolic ambivalence in order to ground the rational circulation of values and their play of exchange" (Baudrillard 1981; Coombe 1999, pp. 146–47). As the preceding reading of full-program contracts reveals, corporations such as Nike and Adidas attempt to deny the multiple meanings of visual symbols through legal contracts that protect exchange value by micromanaging when, where, and how their trademarks appear.

University Trademarks: Names, Logos, Mascots

Independent of corporate branding strategies, networks of actors in colleges and universities took advantage of the strengthened protection offered to their putatively public names, logos, and mascots, registering them as trademarks, intellectual property from which to generate external revenues. For a university, name and logo are the equivalent of the corporate brand, able to signify the consciousness and identity of the university. In the 1980s and 1990s, trademarking became a standard university practice. Even Harvard University trademarked its name in 1991 (Lattinville 1996). In 1984, there were about seventy schools with licensing programs. By 1998, approximately 300 U.S. colleges and universities licensed "the commercial use of their name, mascot and other graphics" (Revoyr 1998). By 1995, university trademarks were generating billions in external revenues.

The university logo or name encapsulated the symbolic value associated with the status and prestige system in which the particular institution was located and simultaneously represented economic value when attached to a wide range of products. Through marketing products branded with their logos and names, universities derived an increasing amount of cash value from sales, trading not only in products but also on student processes of identity formation, family and fan loyalty, and alumni allegiance.

The Lanham Act defines a trademark as "any word, name, symbol or device or any combination thereof" adopted and used by manufacturers or merchants to identify their goods or distinguish them from those manufactured or sold by others (Coombe 1998, p. 42). The justification for trademark protection is commercial. Companies like Coca Cola, Kleenex, and Xerox fought successfully to own their names when they became synonyms for all similar products, which gave them a tremendous market advantage. As Coombe notes, trademarking at the federal level developed in the late nineteenth century because "the legal protection of imagery as private property provided a means for marrying mass production of goods, mass reproduction of cultural forms, and the mass interpellation necessary to transform a mass of immigrants into similar consumers" (1998, p. 173). University trademark licensing programs became possible when federal legislation enhanced trademarks to strengthen the new economy, thus creating opportunities for universities to extend protection of their symbols, covering icons and images previously understood as having a public dimension, as in the case of university names, logos and mascots.

Organization and Growth of University Trademarking

University trademarking seems to have followed a pattern similar to that of technology licensing. As with patents, for many years trademarked products did not account for a significant portion of university revenue. So too, branded product sales were relatively unorganized at the periphery of universities. Again paralleling patents, when the revenue-generating potential of trademarks began to draw the attention of universities, commercial activity was handled by external, nonprofit organizations. From the 1930s through the 1970s, two nonprofit patent firms, University Patents and Research Corporation, handled patents for most universities. Currently, approximately 10 percent of U.S. colleges and universities operate programs that license their own logos, but the majority use licensing agents. Two account for most postsecondary business: the Collegiate Licensing Group and Licensing Resource Group. Their work is augmented by Royalty Management Associates, an organization led by a former Disney auditor, which provides compliance review services to licensors, including colleges and the Collegiate Licensing Group. As technology transfer officers organized the Association for Technology Managers, the collegiate licensing representatives formed the Association of Collegiate Licensing Administrators (ACLA) in 1986. Like the Association of University Technology Managers (AUTM, see chapter 3), which emerged around patenting, the ACLA is an example of interstitial organizational emergence, in which actors located in universities network with the corporate world, bringing businesses into the academy.

Most collegiate licensing administrators were housed in athletic departments or associations, auxiliary services, or university bookstores. Although the ACLA does not have a journal, it offers educational seminars, publishes reference materials on licensing, and shares information via an electronic bulletin board. If the ACLA follows a course similar to the AUTM, it will develop a journal and establish data sets that allow tracking (and legitimating) of licensing activity.

Just as universities moved away from relying on external agencies to handle patenting, developing their own internal capacity through offices of technology transfer, some universities are beginning to develop internal capacity for licensing logos. Notre Dame, for example, operates a self-contained, full-time licensing department. Ohio State, Stanford, the University of Texas, UCLA, and the University of Southern California also have their own licensing programs. The "independents," as they are referred to, tend to be institutions with winning sports teams, a key factor in successful licensing programs. As was the case with offices of technology transfer, licensing programs create managerial capacity for colleges and universities to engage in market activity.

In 1995, revenues generated by the sales of officially licensed collegiate products reached $2.5 billion (Lattinville 1996). Royalty rates are variable, ranging from 4 to 10 percent, with the majority of products generating between 7 and 8 percent. Many large institutions do not report their royalty income, perhaps because they do not want to attract the attention of the Internal Revenue Service. "Several years ago the IRS began looking at royalty income as Unrelated Business Income and wanted to make it taxable" (Revoyr 1998). Although that did not happen, the IRS interest indicates that trademarking and licensing programs are very close to the boundary that divides nonprofit activity from commercial activity.

College and university branding is not confined to the United States; it has global reach. The National Collegiate Athletic Association (NCAA), the governing body for intercollegiate athletics in the United States, serves as the licensing agent for overseas companies interested in using their members' logos and signs. By 1979, overseas royalties brought in $30 million, with UCLA, which had become very popular in Japan, accounting for the majority of sales (Revoyr 1998). The NCAA did not start a domestic program until recently, and its current work is focused largely on the Final Four.

Apparel forms the basis of licensing activity, but collateral products that have been licensed by schools include toilet paper, fishing lures, and coffins. There was even an attempt to license condoms (Latinville 1996). Universities also engage in cross-licensing marks, which most often involves licensing one school's mark with a corporate mark so that both logos appear together on merchandise.

Policing of Logos

The law of trademark compels holders of this form of intellectual property to protect their marks from unauthorized use. If colleges and universities do not actively police their marks, illegal vendors of the marks can claim "abandonment" and escape any consequences for their acts. Colleges and universities can use civil and criminal litigation against illegal sales.

There are a variety of legal strategies available to colleges and universities (Bearby and Siegal 2002). These strategies have multiplied as the knowledge economy has grown. Often college and universities begin their policing efforts with pregame education programs, notifying potential infringers that trademark laws will be strictly enforced. Initially, they often seek voluntary compliance and surrender of unlicensed products. Sometimes colleges and universities are able to obtain "site orders," which provide an anticounterfeit zone around the school before and after an event. Using this legal strategy, colleges assert not intellectual property rights but a property right in the football or other sports stadium, and clear out trademark infringers. Should this not work, colleges and universities are able to use the Anticounterfeiting Consumer Protection Act of 1996, which allows them to obtain court orders authorizing the seizure of goods bearing the counterfeit trademark. Sometimes colleges and universities also draw on state and local statutes that provide for seizure of counterfeit products and for strong criminal penalties.

Scott Bearby, Associate General Counsel for the NCAA, and Bruce Siegal, Senior Vice President and General Counsel for the Collegiate Licensing Company, writing in the *Journal of College and University Law* describe the work of a typical enforcement "team" on a game day:

> Relationships with law enforcement have proven to be the key to successful on-going enforcement. An effective criminal enforcement action requires the coordination of efforts of several players. The enforcement team typically includes a representative of the trademark owner, local police and possibly private investigators. On a typical collegiate game-day operation, representatives of the trademark owner will team up with local law enforcement officers to scour the area surrounding the venue for infringing products. Each team will include someone trained regarding the trademark licensing requirements, who will inspect the products being sold to determine whether they are licensed or infringing. The law enforcement officers will seize any unauthorized prod-

> ucts . . . and arrest or cite the violator. Infringing products are maintained under the control of law enforcement as evidence. At some events, particularly when multiple teams are working, a central command location is established where violators are processed, and the products are counted and placed in inventory. . . If developed correctly, the team approach helps ensure that enforcement actions will be conducted properly and safely. (2002)

University representatives and the police work together to protect what are essentially university "brands." The power of the university is asserted against aspiring small business persons who do not share in the monopoly the university has been granted in its intellectual property. The argument against infringers is that they create confusion for buyers over the source or sponsorship of the goods or services. While that may matter with regard to professional services, special ingredients, or misrepresentation of what a school stands for, the purchaser of athletic apparel likely cares more about price than brand "source."

The effort to police logos brings together university representatives and their corporate partners. When universities send "logo cops" out on the streets to seize counterfeit goods, they are working in conjunction with their "all-school" corporate partners because the goods are often cross-licensed. Policing is not an abstract exercise. At the University of Arizona, for example, game-day enforcement teams go out "on the hunt" with representatives from the Collegiate Licensing Company and Nike (Low 2002).

Policing efforts are not limited to individual institutions. College and university licensing organizations have been very active in protecting their commercial rights. In 1992, the Collegiate Licensing Company, which licenses logos for a number of universities, joined with professional sports leagues (MLB Properties, NBA Properties, NFL Properties, and NHL Properties) to form the Coalition to Advance the Protection of Sports Logos (CAPS) (Bearby and Siegel 2002). Since its establishment CAPS has developed a network of private investigators and law enforcement officials that brings civil or criminal action against trademark violators. They have confiscated over $171 million in infringing products and equipment across a number of states, and their actions have led to the detainment or arrest of 2,300 persons. In so doing, universities have aligned themselves with commercial sports, aggressively policing trademarks as a form of intellectual property.

Sweeping Commercialization

The Internet provides a new venue for protecting and profiting from trademarked university names, logos, and mascots. The impetus for increased vigilance in cyberspace was the 1999 Anticybersquatting Consumer Protection Act.

Cybersquatting refers to bad-faith, abusive registration of Internet domain names. The anticybersquatting law protects against "prominent companies being coerced into buying their names or trademarks from other parties who have registered those trademarks as domain names for a variety of purposes, including for future sale to the trademark owner" (Peret 2003). However, as critics have noted, the law might also be used to stifle parody, social criticism, and free speech (Clark 2003; Lessig 1999).

Arbitration under the anticybersquatting law occurs under the Uniform Domain Name Dispute Resolution Policy, which is governed by the Internet Corporation for Assigned Names and Numbers. Both nonprofit organizations are loosely affiliated with Educause, which intermediates between private and public sectors on Internet matters when .edu suffixes are involved. Four arbitrating organizations have been identified, including the World Intellectual Property Organization, which hears the majority of the cases. The domain names of the Internet, the infrastructure of which is public, are administered by private nonprofit organizations that are not formally responsible to the public. Penalties for violating the anticybersquatting law are decided by arbitrators from global management entities connected to many nations. Wildcats, bruins, bears, and beavers, as well as Chief Illiniwek, are connected by networks of university actors—trademark licensing officials, logo enforcement teams, athletic department officials, faculty oversight committees—to the new economy by a dense web of emerging interstitial organizations.

The results of arbitration for protecting college and university interests in cyberspace are inconsistent. To win a case, the entity bringing the arbitration must prove the other party was acting in "bad faith" and attempting to confuse or mislead potential consumers. In some cases, arbitrators have refused to support colleges and universities or the umbrella organizations on which they depend for their sports activity. For example, arbitrators refused to transfer the domain name finalfourseats.com from a ticket broker to the NCAA, even though the NCAA claimed "finalfour" as a trademarked property. Similarly, the NCAA did not want its name used in connection with gambling and went to arbitration to have revoked such names as ncaabasketballodds.com. The arbitrators found gambling to be a legitimate business and ruled against the NCAA. However, in many instances when domain names incorporate NCAA trademarks, the arbitrators have found for the NCAA, giving them control of what they see as their domain names (Bearby and Seigel 2002). Perhaps less important than the results of any one case is the increasing commodification of cyber properties and universities' and college athletic associations' growing vigilance in protecting them.

Should arbitration fail, universities and colleges can turn to litigation at the nation-state or state level to protect their marks. Again, bad faith is the issue. The defendant must prove that domain names are identical or confusing and that the plaintiff is using the name in bad faith to profit unjustly from the trademark or logo.

College and universities are also beginning to take action against the use of their names *within* websites. At issue are metatags, or search engine responses to a user's entry of a college or university name. If search engines bring up nonowners' sites in response to the command or metatag, which depends on the number of times the name is used in the site, sites with the high incidence of nonowner use can be charged with trademark infringement (Bearby and Seigel 2002).

As important as any specific case or decision is the growth of legal capacity for commodification of intellectual property and the development of organizational apparatuses for policing and enforcing it up to and through the international level. Signs and symbols, integral to the work performed by members of colleges and universities, are no longer valued only for their meanings but for their commercial potential. Institutions are actively participating in the transformation of signs and symbols into commodities under trademark law.

Trademarks as Contested Educational Terrain

Trademarks, logos, and mascots are potent symbols and images that contain many layers of meaning. That is why they are valuable and protected by law. Sometimes trademarks appropriate the image of the extinguished or vanquished. For example, many teams are named after animals that people see more often in zoos than in the wild: golden bears, lobos (wolves), wildcats, badgers, and wolverines. These animals were hunted, often to the point of extinction, to open the wilderness to farmers and tradespersons, and were exhibited as trophies that symbolized "man's" conquest of nature. Athletic teams were named after these fierce and often predatory animals (the golden gophers aside) only after they were tamed. Similarly, teams appropriated names associated with Native Americans, who occupied the land before Northern European settlement. After prolonged warfare, when Native Americans were "safely" on reservations, college and university athletic teams adopted names such as Redskins, Warriors, Braves, and Savages in an assertion of the power of the colonizer. While these names—and more tribe-specific ones, such as the Fighting Sioux—recognized the ferocity of former enemies, they also trivialized, appropriated, and distorted their images, and celebrated the authority of the colonizer. Perhaps most importantly, they taught students lessons about the power associated with whiteness.

When the social movements of the 1960s began, Native Americans began to protest the use of these trademarks. The general tenor of their arguments against the use of such mascots and logos was perhaps best captured by *McBride v. Motor Vehicle Division of Utah State Tax Commission* (1999). The Utah Supreme Court disallowed the use of *Redskins* on vanity license plates. Although the decision was complex, issued at the state level, and may not apply directly to colleges and universities, the case dramatized what Native Americans saw as the offending properties of mascots/logos. The Native American petitioners argued that the term *redskin* was descriptive of an early practice in the colonial United States whereby the British Crown offered "a bounty for the scalps of Native American men, women and children." In order to collect the bounty, the colonials were required to "skin the body of the Native American and bring in the 'red skin' as proof of the kill" (Cummings 1999). The Native American plaintiffs argued that the redskin trademark affirmed genocide.

At least fifty-eight colleges and universities still have Native American logos, mostly smaller colleges, which use names like Warriors, Braves, and Indians. Although no college or university uses Redskins, several have Red Raiders, and one has the Redmen as their emblem. The McBride case underlines the brutality layered in the naming of teams after conquered peoples. The names used are always the names given by the colonizer, which has displaced the native peoples' own names for themselves, reminding the conquered persons of the appropriation of their own history and of the trivialization of the pain, suffering, and bloodshed entailed in the process. (The dynamics of appropriation, trivialization, and affirmation of whiteness are complex and theorized by many authors working from the cultural studies perspective. See, for example, Coombe 1998; King 1998; McCarthy 1993; Root 1996; King and Springwood 2001.)

As Native American students increasingly protested the use of "Indian" logos and mascots, many colleges and universities that had taken them as mascots in the middle years of the twentieth century began to reconsider. One of the first to change its team name was Stanford. Some schools, for example, Dartmouth, only changed after considerable struggle.

However, some colleges and universities have retained their trademarked mascots and logos. Perhaps the most well known are Florida State University (Seminoles) and the University of Illinois (Chief Illiniwek). These schools have kept their logos and mascots at least in part because they are "brands" that school authorities and alumni feel capture the consciousness of the universities, both in terms of the status and prestige system central to the identity of students and alumni, and as a commercial property, bringing in external revenue. The two systems—the knowledge and prestige system and the academic capitalist knowledge/learning regime—have become so entwined as to be almost inseparable. The trademark is valuable because it represents a particular place in the knowledge and prestige system; the trademark becomes more commercially valuable with the increased attachment of students, alumni, and fans, and the increased product sales.

In terms of revenue generation from trademark licensing programs, the Florida State Seminoles were the number-two recipients of fees in 1994–1995. Florida State is committed to its trademark at least in part because it generates substantial funds through sales of branded athletic paraphernalia. Florida State's website illustrates the way logo and commerce are joined in the new economy; the Seminole logo presides over links to e-purchasing of branded sports paraphernalia.

There has been substantial protest over the Seminole logo, and Florida State may be attempting to retire it. On the main page of the website there is only an arrowhead, a more dignified representation of Native Americans than the wide-mouthed, screaming "Indian" profile that is the Seminole logo. However, the Seminole Indian profile vividly remains on the athletics and alumni pages, and, as we noted above, on links to the e-commerce webpages.

The University of Illinois has been engaged in conflict over the use of Chief Illiniwek for over a decade but has not given him up. Native American students, recruited through student services programs aimed at promoting diversity, found Chief Illiniwek an affront to institutional claims to support that diversity (Johns 2000). Native American students began to protest the chief as reinforcing racist Indian stereotypes, misappropriating sacred ideas and objects, presenting a narrow and inappropriate image of Native Americans to American youth, and misrepresenting the Illini tribe (King and Springwood 2001).

The chief is not used on the Illinois webpage. Instead, a stylized *I*, reminiscent of a Greek column, represents the university. The chief no longer figures on any of the products available through e-commerce via the bookstore. Indeed, surfing the website for the University of Illinois–Urbana-Champaign (UIUC) offers no glimpse of the chief.

However, the chief is still alive and well. He appears for his half-time ceremony at games, and his image is plastered across many local businesses. The pro-chief lobby at UIUC argues that the chief is a unifying symbol for "the community" and portrays any attack on the chief as an attack on the heritage of UIUC. However, the "community" at UIUC, a land-grant institution, is multifaceted and diverse, and claims made against the chief are made by a wide variety of groups that assert they speak for the good of the community.

In spring 1994, members of Native American Students, Staff and Faculty for

Progress filed a federal complaint against the university, claiming that use of the chief was a breach of civil rights at a federally funded and state-funded university. In 1995, after heavy lobbying from U.S congressmen from Illinois who claimed the case was a state issue, the Office of Civil Rights decided that there was not enough evidence to support the claims made by the group. That same year, the Illinois state legislature passed a law requiring Chief Illiniwek to be the University of Illinois symbol in perpetuity. The governor vetoed the law (King and Springwood 2001).

Native Americans are not the only group who would like to recall the chief. Faculty members and students agitated against the chief by informing prospective athletes, whose games would be marked by the chief's performance, about sentiment against the chief, including the widespread perception that the chief is a racist stereotype. The university responded by attempting to prohibit faculty members and students "who do not represent the athletic interests of the university and who do not intend and will not recruit prospective athletes" from talking to the recruits about the chief (*University of Illinois News* 2001). In spring 2001, the faculty and students were successful in having a temporary restraining order against the University of Illinois issued. Another tactic professors have used to retire the chief is pressuring Illinois's accrediting association, the North Central Association of Colleges and Schools, to withhold accreditation (Rybarczyk 2002). Numerous departments at UIUC have issued statements calling for the chief's retirement, pointing to the difficulty of teaching about Native American history and politics when the chief is employed as a central symbol of university identity.

The chief has symbolic value and emotional resonance as a token of a past when the white majority were able to dictate the terms in which "diversity" appeared on college campuses—often as the exotic "other," romanticized by the dominant culture only after any threat to that culture was extinguished. However, the chief also has value as a trademark, an alienable symbol possessed by the university as a corporate body. The chief bridges a not-so-innocent past and the new economy in which brands are more important than products, and are sold and made in global markets. The chief organizes alumni sentiment, which, even though his image is not visible in the bookstore, still mobilizes certain alumni's purchases at the physical site and over the internet. Although the logo cops do not police the chief—a tarnished symbol—alumni, the legislature, and congresspersons have mobilized to defend him. Above all, the chief shows us the power of image or brand to organize networks of actors, both in support and resistance.

Conclusion

All-school contracts and the marketing of university logos, mascots, and names are exercises in branding. Corporations and universities attempt to sell the image of the product or school to student consumers as well as other audiences. All-school contracts and university programs to market trademarked materials coexist uneasily. The entry of shoe companies into all-school contracts in the mid-1990s seems to have cut into profits from logo licensing, which stagnated after steady growth throughout the 1980s and early 1990s. Commenting on this development, Jack Revoyr, head of the UCLA licensing program for many years, says, "The best hope for collegiate licensing may be to forge more strategic alliances with these licensors [e.g., Nike, Adidas, Reebok] ... If nothing else, collegiate licensors should follow their example ... A critical part of this effort should be the development of a brand strategy" (1998).

In this comment, we see the boundary between corporate and university marketing dissolve. Neither product nor education matter as much as image. Students are not so much consumers able to discipline universities by exercising market choice, as captive audiences available to marketers. The marketers are not only external corporations but also the universities themselves, seeking to profit from the spending power of their student bodies.

Through the legal power signified in contracts that dictate how signs, symbols, and images must be displayed, corporations and universities, often working together through cross-licensing goods, seek access to students' psyches in a market-based form of student development. When students make the transition from high school to college, their integration into the institution is marked by the purchase of athleisure wear and trademarked paraphernalia that symbolizes their new identities (Tinto 1993). As they develop an attachment to the institution, their expanding moral development is theorized as moving from being rooted in local mores and norms associated with their home towns to accepting universalistic, rationalist, justice-based norms (Kohlberg 1981). This change is paralleled by commercial development, through which students move away from the emblems and tokens of their high schools and home communities to identification with the names, logos, and mascots of their universities, demonstrating their changing allegiance through purchases, until they become alumni, who show their loyalty to the institution through gifts. The students have dual institutional identities as educated persons and as loyal consumers of an increasing variety of intellectual property.

This branded intellectual property is brought to students by actors forming networks in the interstices of the new economy. On the one hand, corporations have staff that promote all-school contracts, police logos, recruit students through a variety of activities surrounding their logos, and set up offices on university campuses. On the other hand, networks of actors within universities reach out to these corporations, seeking high prices for all-school contracts, which are often administered through trademark licensing programs. The trademark licensing programs are staffed by administrators, marketers, attorneys, and enforcement teams. Exercising strategies at odds with freedom of expression, academic freedom, and the free flow of ideas, these networks of actors often seek to deny the multiple meanings of visual symbols. They do so through creating legal contracts that protect exchange value by micromanaging when, where, and how their trademarks appear so as to control disparagement of the symbol and to restrain parody and satire.

Although, to a certain extent, contracts and logo police enable such denial and the restriction of brands as both public culture and private property, the intensified meaning, "value," and emotion invested in logos also prompt struggles over meaning. As Coombe writes, "to the extent that specific legal infrastructures create particular forms of signifying power, they also enable, provoke, or invite particular forms of resistance or alternative appropriations" (1999, p. 262). The policing of logos, in other words, is never complete. For example, the Nike swoosh has been successfully appropriated by antisweatshop activists and incorporated into campaigns aimed at drawing attention to the conditions of workers who produce Nike products. In one example, students reinvented the Nike symbol: an image of a smiley face accompanied by the caption "happy worker" sits alongside a frowning face in which the swoosh is substituted for the mouth and is accompanied by the caption "Nike worker." As production moves offshore and the corporate presence in the public sphere is reduced to brand image, public relations, and the presence of logos, Coombe argues, the focus of commodity fetishism shifts from products to sign values that can be made to imbue products with significance. Distinct logos may thus be the most valuable assets corporations and universities own as well as the most valuable assets available to activists who seek to undo the exploitative and culture-cannibalizing practices on which corporations rely.

11

UNDERGRADUATE STUDENTS AND EDUCATIONAL MARKETS

In tracing the emergence of academic capitalism, Slaughter and Leslie (1997, p. 44) pointed to the public policy commitment in the 1970s to "making students consumers in the tertiary education marketplace." Yet they argued that students had not been well served in the competitive higher education marketplace. In the 1970s and 1980s, at the very time student tuition monies expanded as a proportion of total college and university revenues, the proportion of institutional expenditures devoted to instruction declined. Although the government had chosen to strengthen market forces in higher education, channeling financial aid to students as consumers rather than giving direct institutional grants to colleges and universities as producers, that did not result in increased institutional commitment to education or more satisfied customers.

We build on yet modify Slaughter and Leslie's thesis. Academic capitalism involved turning away from students, ignoring them despite their tuition monies, which are undesignated and can be shifted for use in noninstructional areas, and turning toward entrepreneurial science, as evidenced by the increased institutional expenditure for research in the 1970s and 1980s. By contrast, academic capitalism in the new economy involves institutions turning toward students as targets for the extraction of revenue, including but extending beyond tuition. Colleges and universities are initiating marketlike and market practices, and forming partnerships with business to exploit the commercial potential of students. As institutions adopt more of an economic, proprietary orientation to students, the consumption versus the educational dimensions of a college education become increasingly emphasized.

This chapter is organized around three basic themes related to institutions, their students, and their educational focus. The first theme is marketing to students in ways that serve colleges and universities' economic interests. We offer examples of institutions' marketing activities and explore the student markets that are targeted. The second theme explores how institutions are moving to serve more privileged student markets. We examine how institutions "craft a class" (Duffy 1998) and how increasingly they do so in ways that enhance the opportunities for more economically privileged student populations rather than for historically underserved populations. The third theme is marketing consumer capitalism to captive student markets. We consider how colleges and universities increasingly emphasize consumption. In analyzing these themes, we utilize some primary data (largely national statistics), but for the most part we rely on secondary sources.

Generally, we see a combination of market and prestige orientations to students that undermines a broad commitment to access. Therefore, we consider patterns of access to higher education before elaborating on our three themes. We frame the discussion of access with higher education marketplace research grounded in economics and sociology. The marketplace is also treated in terms of the new economy and its implications for higher education, drawing on literature about patterns of employment and of increased focus on consumption in the knowledge-based economy. The changing structure of employment in the information-based economy leads to increased demand for higher education, particularly in cycles of retraining over a lifetime of multiple careers. The increased emphasis on consumption and convenience in a service-based economy affects the behaviors of higher education institutions and the attitudes of consumers toward them. We see students not as empowered customers but more as targets for consumer markets and as captive markets being socialized into consumption-focused capitalism. (We also see them as exploited employees; see Rhoades and Rhoads 2003 on graduate student employees.)

Patterns of Access in the Higher Education Marketplace

Nearly thirty years ago, when federal policymakers were moving to emphasize a market model in supporting higher education, Leslie and Johnson noted, "The percentage of individuals attending college from higher socioeconomic backgrounds is two or three times greater than the percentage of those from lower socioeconomic backgrounds" (1974, p. 5). That pattern was also identified by the Carnegie Commission on Higher Education (1971). Moreover, two leading higher education scholars, Jencks and Riesman (1968) detailed patterns of unequal access in U.S. higher education. Devoting a chapter to "social stratification and mass higher education," they analyzed patterns of access over time and between social classes. They found evidence of enormous expansion of educational opportunity, as the system of higher education became more of a "mass" than an "elite" system (Trow 1973). Just before World War II, only one in six (Anglo) *men* was entering college; by the mid-1960s it was two in five. Yet the gap between the college-going rates of Anglo men from different social classes was increasing. "When we first looked at these trends we assumed, like most other observers, that rapid growth in enrollment was largely a consequence of increased lower-middle and working-class access to and interest in college. In point of fact, however, this does not appear to be the case. The increase in enrollment among upper-middle class children seems to have been even greater than among lower-middle and working-class children" (Jencks and Riesman 1968, p. 95).

In a table (Table V), they mapped out the percentages of high school graduates going to college the next year, based on five categories of academic aptitude and five of socioeconomic status (SES). The percentage of high-SES males with low-middle academic ability going to college (57%) was higher than that of low-SES males with upper-middle academic ability (44%). The differences in percentages were similar for females, although a significantly lower percentage in every income category except high SES went to college. The percentage of high-SES males with low academic ability going to college (40%) was four times that of low-SES males with low academic ability (10%). However, Jencks and Riesman suggested that, as there was little room left for future increases for high-SES children (81% of males and 75% of females from high-SES families went to college), "it follows that further increases in the proportion of people entering college will now have to come mainly from the lower cultural strata" (1968, p. 96).

Despite Jencks and Riesman's prediction, and despite policy efforts (particularly in the 1970s) to redress inequities in access to higher education, similar inequities prevail. Overall, access has increased for students of all social backgrounds and ethnicities. From 1973 to 1992, the number of students making the direct transition from high school to college increased from 47 percent to 62 percent (Baker and Velez 1996, p. 83). At the same time, estimated chances for students getting a baccalaureate degree by the age of twenty-four by family income quartile saw an expanded separation between the top income quartile (40% in 1970 to 80% in 1994) and the rest (e.g., the second quartile increased from 15% in 1970 to 29% in 1994; the bottom two quartiles increased from 10% and 6%, respectively, in 1970 to 14% and 9% in 1994 [Mortenson 1995, p. 1]). Although women have made great gains in college enrollment (from 38% of women entering college in 1960 to 62% by 1989 [Baker and Velez 1996]), ethnicity-based inequities persisted. From the 1970s through the 1990s, the numbers and proportion of African Americans, Hispanics, and Native Americans achieving baccalaureate degrees increased (though some of the gains of the 1970s were lost in the 1980s; see Baker and Velez 1996). Yet the wide gap between their college achievement and that of Anglo Americans has continued. In 1974, 20 percent of the Anglo population between twenty-five and twenty-nine, as compared to 8 and 6 percent, respectively, of African Americans and Latinos, had completed four years or more of college; by 1995 those percentages were 26, 15, and 9, respectively) (Mortenson 1997, p. 5). (Asian Americans are an important exception in educational attainment, although their gains in education have not translated into a corresponding level of occupational attainment [Barringer, Takeuchi, and Xenos 1990].)

In recent years scholars have focused not only on access to college but also on particular college destinations. Hearn found that choosing selective versus nonselective institutions (and those that spent more or less per student) was shaped primarily by measures of academic merit, but that "nonacademic factors, particularly socioeconomic background, [also] affected graduates' postsecondary destinations" (Hearn 1991, p. 158). He concluded that "all else being equal [for students of equal ability and achievement] offspring of higher income parents tended in 1980–81 to enroll in more selective institutions, compared to other students" (p. 168). Similarly, a later study that in part replicated Hearn's, concluded, "The results of this comparison can be summarized by pointing to the continued and increasing relative effects of background—especially of father's education and parental income—on the selectivity of institutions between 1980 and 1992, even after academic variables have been taken into account" (Karen 2002, p. 200).

Students' ethnicity is also very much related to segmented markets in U.S. higher education. In 1995, about 17 percent of all African Americans enrolled in college were at historically black colleges and universities (HBCUs), which account for only 2 percent of all higher education institutions and account for about 28 percent of the baccalaureate degrees granted to African Americans (Allen and Jewell 2002). Another ethnicity-related segmentation is that Latinos, as a group, are most likely to attend a community college: in the eighteen-to-twenty-four-year-old college population, about 40 percent of Latinos, as compared to only about 25 percent of Anglo Americans and African Americans, are in community colleges (Fry 2002). (That percentage varies significantly by national origin subgroup—for example, Cuban-Americans are less likely than Mexican-Americans to go to community colleges.) Market segmentation impacts the baccalaureate attainment of different ethnic groups because starting at a community college substantially reduces a student's chances of getting a bachelor's degree, despite equal academic ability and family background (Dougherty 1992).

Economics, Sociology, and the Changing Higher Education Marketplace and Economy

Over time, states have shifted the burden of financing higher education from state appropriations to tuition revenues in a conscious commitment to high-tuition, high-aid policies (Griswold and Marine 1996; Leslie and Johnson 1974; Slaughter and Leslie 1997). The idea has been to give an increasing share of monies to students through financial aid and to decrease the share given directly to higher education institutions. One of the rationales underlying the policy is the growing idea that higher education is largely a private good, with the benefits going primarily to individual students (who are increasing their human capital), so students and their families should be expected to bear a larger share of the costs. The externalities of higher education, the social benefits beyond the student, are overlooked and undervalued in the high-tuition policy. Over time the benefits of any expanded public investment in broader access to higher education has come into question. At the federal level that has led to a reversal of the balance between grants and loans—loans are now the main form of student aid. At the state level, that has generally led to high-tuition, and often low-aid, policies.

For higher education finance scholars, grounded in economics, the key questions about access and the higher education marketplace have to do with the conception of the perfectly competitive market, and with the proper balance between the operation of market and government forces. For sociologists of higher education, the key questions have to do with the existence of privileged players and segmented markets (linked to social stratification) in the higher education marketplace that is tied to the economy.

As early as the 1970s finance scholars were questioning the premises that underlay the new federal and state public policies in regard to student aid. Higher education does not meet the conditions of a perfect market (Leslie and Johnson 1974). One of these conditions is related to the first theme of our chapter—that the marketing activities of colleges and universities serve the interests of the institutions more than the interests of the students. A key condition of the perfectly competitive market is that "producers, consumers, and resource owners must possess perfect knowledge" (Leslie and Johnson 1974, p. 6). Yet in the context of the academic capitalism knowledge/learning regime, colleges and universities have substantially increased their marketing activities, seeking to shape the perceptions and choices of consumers in the student marketplace. Such activities do not necessarily maximize, and certainly do not prioritize, student needs. Institutions are not likely to advertise their weaknesses and shortcomings; they are likely to publicize their strengths or to portray themselves in ways that suggest they are more desirable educational commodities than they actually are. In short, imperfect consumer knowledge may derive from college and university marketing efforts that are aimed at influencing consumer choices.

Another condition of the perfectly competitive market, the mobility of economic players, or the free flow of buyers and sellers, is related to the second theme of our chapter—institutions move to serve the privileged segments of the market. Although the student market for elite institutions in higher education has been transformed in the past fifty years into a nationally integrated market (Hoxby 1997), most students continue to be largely restricted by place and price. Yet institutions are increasingly moving to national and international student markets because public colleges and universities can charge these students more. The increased significance of revenue considerations that comes with academic capitalism leads to a greater concentration of institutional energies and monies on students already privileged and served by higher education, with a lesser focus on those student populations that historically have been underserved.

A third condition of the perfectly competitive market, the homogeneity of products, is related to the third theme of our chapter, marketing consumer capitalism to students. Clearly, all college educations are not the same, in rate of return or in consumption value. Moreover, in the context of academic capitalism in the new economy, higher education becomes more of a commodity to be marketed and consumed; more monies are thus likely to be devoted to noninstructional services, buildings, and personnel to make the institution a more attractive consumption item.

An ongoing concern of finance scholars in higher education is how to counterbalance the operation of the market in order to mitigate its adverse effects on low-income students and equity. In a competitive market the low-income students lose. For example, Hoxby (1997) demonstrates that the rise of a nationally integrated market increases competition and contributes to the rise of tuition. Similarly, McPherson and Schapiro (1998) detail the pressures and processes that push institutions (and states) to compete for high-quality, high-SES students, reducing commitment to lower-SES students. They track the increase in net tuition for low-income students and the increase in institutional commitment to merit- versus need-based aid. From 1983–1984 to 1991–1992, merit-aid expenditures grew annually by 13 percent, compared to 10 percent for need-based aid. By 1991–1992, well over half (56%) of student aid monies in public institutions were merit based. McPherson and Shapiro call for a renewed commitment by the federal government to need-based student aid. A competitive higher education market for students, unleashed by government policies, leads to socially undesirable results.

Sociologists such as McDonough (1997) and Bowles and Gintis (2002) identify two other mechanisms by which privilege is perpetuated. First, the already advantaged population of high-SES students is further privileged by virtue of their parents' willingness to purchase additional advantage in negotiating access to an institution of their choice. McDonough (1997) wrote of an emergent profession of private counselors or agents hired by upper-middle-class parents to enhance their children's chances of gaining entry to selective colleges and universities. These counselors provide students with advice about where to apply, they assist with the preparation of college applications and essays, and they also interact (lobby) and work directly with the admissions offices of the institutions to which their clients have applied. McDonough finds that parents who hire such counselors tend to do so for students who are not high ability. They seek to purchase market expertise and advantage so they will not endanger their class position.

A second mechanism that perpetuates privilege is the connection between the worlds of education and of work, and patterns of stratification within them. Although Bowles and Gintis (1976) proposed their "correspondence principle" nearly thirty years ago, it is relevant today. In revisiting their classic work, they show how evidence of intergenerational mobility and student socialization patterns over the past three decades supports their initial thesis (2002). What they say about schools inculcating in students the personal characteristics and behavior patterns appropriate to their particular socioeconomic position in the workplace can be applied as well to postsecondary education. At the time of their 1976 book, the workplace was the hierarchical corporation. Although large corporations persist, the nature of employment in the new economy has transformed. The new economy couples education and employment closely. The knowledge economy calls for white-collar, service workers to repeatedly upgrade their skills to keep pace with changes in the technology-intensive workplace. Increasingly, these workers turn to continuing education and distance education. We believe this process expands existing socioeconomic inequalities. The white-collar workers that colleges and universities have targeted as markets are part of an already employed class of professional and managerial workers. Colleges and universities pay less attention to expanding initial access for growing numbers of historically underserved student populations.

Alongside the structural changes in employment are cultural changes. Thus, scholars write of "consumer capitalism" (Schiller 1992) and a "regime of accumulation" and consumption (Webster 2002, p. 75) in a post-Fordist era in which consumption is emphasized more than production. The character of the consumption is evident in the work of George Ritzer, including *The McDonaldization Thesis* (1998) and *Explorations in the Sociology of Consumption: Fast Food, Credit Cards, and Casinos* (2001). In Schiller's words, "all spheres of human existence are subject to the intrusion of commercial values . . . the most important of which, clearly, is: CONSUME" (1992, p. 3). The implications of such developments for higher education are profound. A college education becomes another consumption item, increasingly marketed by institutions to students, especially on-campus ones who are captive markets for private enterprise and for colleges and universities that partner with business to access this market.

Theme One: Marketing in College and Universities' Economic Interests

Marketing Practices

In marketing, the needs and interests of the enterprise take precedence over the needs of the customer. The aim of marketing activities is to persuade the consumer to buy (to increase revenues) rather than to inform the consumer in some neutral sense so that they can make the best choice. In the case of higher education institutions, a marketing campaign may have multiple aims having to do with the characteristics an institution wants in its freshman class. In the context of colleges and universities pursuing academic capitalism, the criteria of the students' ability to pay, generating revenue for institutions, becomes increasingly emphasized. Institutions have to market to and attract more applicants and/or applicants who will pay more for the education being offered. Given this calculus, the marketing process often gives less attention to educational matters such as the appropriate "fit" between student and institution.

These considerations underlay the warning and critique offered by the late Ernest Boyer (1987), then president of the Carnegie Foundation for the Advancement of Teaching. One of the nation's most prominent spokespersons for students' quality experience, Boyer (1987, p. 22) recommended that "the path from school to college be better marked," not more marketed. "What is involved is not new marketing procedures. Rather, the goal must be to provide more helpful information and make it possible for students to begin with confidence an educational journey that will lead them to the right college and extend far beyond the college years" (1987, p. 40). In referring to "the right college," Boyer was not suggesting that for any one student there is only one best college; rather, he was suggesting that with intensified marketing and competition, institutional economic interests took precedence over the educational interests of the students, and there was an increased likelihood of bad matches that would not serve the students well.

Based on visits to twenty-nine institutions, Boyer found cause for concern. "The publicity material is, we found, attractive and well written. Still, promotional booklets and brochures are more visually appealing than informative and, if we judged from the pictures, it would be very easy to conclude that about half of all college classes in America are held outside, on a sunny day, by a tree, often close to water. One admissions officer told us: 'Market strategists have figured out that students want to be near water. So brochures appear with oceans, lakes, and rivers. I know one college that shows an oceanfront even though they are miles from the shore'" (1987, p. 14). Although he attested to the largely ethical nature of institutions' recruitment practices, Boyer expressed concern that as competition for students intensified, "increased marketing may become the means that drives the end," "abuses are likely to increase," and there will be more cases of institutions that are "more interested in filling slots than in serving students" (p. 22).

Boyer was not alone. Five years after the publication of his book, Professor Richard Chait, another significant voice in higher education, wrote an article for the *Chronicle of Higher Education* entitled, "The Growing Hucksterism of College Admissions." Chait's lead paragraph was: "Over the past twenty years, college admissions have shifted from essentially a selection function to a marketing function. For those who believe that the battle for student bodies has become as commercialized and as intense as it can get, remember the words of P. T. Barnum's circus barker: 'Mister, you ain't seen nothin' yet.' In the next several years, I predict that market conditions will radically alter the landscape and ground rules of college admissions" (1992, p. B1). Chait's observations suggest that some of Boyer's concerns were not only justified but had already materialized. However, Chait, unlike Boyer, was not critical of these developments. Rather, Chait argued for the benefits of a "market-driven academy." He predicted that this was just the beginning, that far more dramatic changes would soon come. Some of his projections have come to pass. One scenario he offered was the possibility of "admissions consolidators" who would "purchase a block of open seats at an under enrolled college for resale to students in search of a low-cost higher education. Unthinkable? Several small companies already provide a similar service by recruiting foreign nationals as undergraduates for American colleges with empty seats" (p. B1). In contrast to Chait, who suggests that such arrangements benefit the enterprise and the consumer, it seems to us the situation is ripe for institutional abuse through exploiting students who have imperfect knowledge of the U.S. higher education marketplace and of the value of different colleges, and that it likely will increase inequities in patterns of access.

The principal focus of much policy commentary, reporting, and scholarship on higher education recruitment and admissions processes is on four-year institutions. Yet community colleges have also been aggressive in marketing their services to various student populations. This trend may seem counterintuitive, given that such colleges are explicitly focused on serving their local communities. However, community colleges are increasingly reaching further. They go beyond the bounds of their communities when they engage in distance education and international education. In both cases, the aim is to increase institutional revenues. Tuition for distance-education courses is often higher than it is for on-campus courses. Distance education points to the significance of the changing structure of employment and careers in an information-based economy. Employment runs in cycles that call for retraining, which can be accomplished through continuing distance education. Just as information now flows more easily across state and national borders, so too do academic programs and students.

The international student market has become attractive to community colleges for its revenue-generating potential. Historically, community colleges have been known for their low tuition. Even over the past twenty years as tuition has dramatically increased for public and private four-year institutions, community colleges have remained a low-cost option. Nevertheless, from 2001 to 2003, public two-year institutions' tuition and fees increased between 11 and 26 percent in ten states, and from 6 to 10 percent in another twenty-one states (NCPPHE 2003). International students afford the opportunity of even more dramatic increases; in some cases colleges charge such students more than ten times the tuition of in-state students (Golden 2002). For community colleges, charging international students more is similar to public and private research universities setting differential/increased tuition for students in some fields, an increasingly popular strategy. By entering international student markets, community colleges are serving more privileged students than they have in the past. Since 1993, the number of international students studying in the United States has increased by 30 percent; enrollment growth has been greatest at community colleges, where the numbers of such students have increased by 61 percent since 1993, and 7 percent in both 2000 and 2001. As of 2002, community colleges enrolled 98,813 international students, which represents about 17 percent of all international students in the United States (IIE 2002).

A recent article in the *Wall Street Journal* focuses on the misleading marketing practices of some community colleges (Golden 2002). Golden identifies several colleges that make inflated claims in their promotional materials about the transfer destinations of graduates. In brochures and websites targeting international students, colleges advertise that selective universities, such as Cornell, Harvard, MIT, Stanford, and other elite institutions, are typical transfer destinations. Upon further investigation, Golden found that the claims generally fell far short of the truth. In some cases, there was no record of such transfers, and institutional representatives indicated that the promotional materials were referring to the institutions students aspired to attend or were "encouraging our students to set their sights high." Golden sums up the situation with the following quote, "'Community colleges are often more interested in income than enrolling students who are a good match,' says Linda Heaney, President of Linden Educational Services, in Washington, D.C., which organizes college-recruiting tours overseas" (2002, p. 8).

The international recruiting practices of some community colleges extend beyond brochures and websites that target prospective international students. In some cases, institutions pay recruiters a commission that is a percentage of the first year's tuition. Such a practice is "explicitly forbidden" by the guidelines of the National Association of College Admission Counselors (NACAC) (1998, p. 2). Indeed, in response to scandals a decade ago, such commission-based recruitment of students who qualify for aid was banned by the U.S. government. Because international students are not eligible for federal financial aid, the ban does not apply to them. The official of one college that employed such a practice claimed that the use of agents abroad is widely accepted. Colleges and universities have become like some private-sector businesses that market and sell goods abroad that are banned in the United States.

Admissions Practices

In recent years, some admissions policies developed by four-year institutions, in both elite and nonelite sectors, have taken on elements of marketing initiatives. In seeking to attract top students in a competitive environment, institutions are turning to admissions practices that more effectively market the particular college or university. As with marketing practices generally, several of these programs have generated commentary from scholars and professional practitioners about the extent to which they serve the educational interests of students or of society at large versus the economic interests and market position of the institution.

A recent study of the effects of *U.S. News & World Report* rankings on institutional behavior provides an example of scholarly criticism of market-oriented activities by colleges and universities that many consumers and society may see as problematic. In describing how the rankings are calculated, Ronald Ehrenberg (2003), former vice-president at Cornell, addresses some institutional behaviors that stem from college and university managers seeking to enhance their ratings. Ehrenberg's first example is of institutions that manipulate their acceptance and yield rates (the proportion of applicants accepted and the proportion of accepted applicants who enroll) in order to raise their selectivity score. Ironically, some schools that are not in the most selective group reject highly qualified applicants whom admissions officers believe really plan to go elsewhere but are using a less selective school as a "safety school." Citing a recent analysis of such practices, Ehrenberg notes, "According to Golden [2001a, see also Golden 2001b], Franklin and Marshall is only one of a number of private institutions that include, as part of their admissions criteria, their estimates of the probability that a student will actually enroll if admitted" (2003, p. 152n).

A second example of institutions manipulating their selectivity scores in ways that do not serve consumer interests is the recent practice of several selective colleges to make SAT scores optional for applicants. The strategy's effectiveness has been documented by Yablon in "Test flight: The scam behind SAT bashing" (2001). The aim is to enhance a school's acceptance rate and average SAT score by making the scores optional. Less qualified students are encouraged apply, but only high-scoring students are likely to submit their test scores.

A third example of an institutional practice aimed at enhancing the school's selectivity score is the early decision admissions process. Employed by highly selective private colleges and universities, students commit to enrolling in an institution if they are accepted (they are notified earlier than those who apply to the regular process). Such a practice increases the institution's yield rate, ensuring an almost one-to-one ratio of admitted students to those who will enroll. That assurance enables the institution to lower its acceptance rate and thereby enhance its market position. Yet, early decision programs may not serve the interests of prospective students or of society. In forcing earlier and earlier decisions that may not be freely informed by a range of options, they represent a case of inherent market inefficiency, of what Roth and Xiaolin (1994) have referred to as "unraveling." Such a system may tend to disadvantage students who have less access to good counseling and less knowledge of the admissions process, characteristics that disproportionately describe students from lower socioeconomic backgrounds. Indeed, these programs tend to undermine efforts to enhance the demographic diversity of entering classes, a fact that led the University of North Carolina, Chapel Hill to eliminate its program, and Richard Levin, president of Yale, to call in 2001 for the collective abandonment of such programs among selective institutions. This call has yet gone unheeded, including at Yale (Flores 2002).

The controversy about early decision programs is such that the relevant professional association, the NACAC, has revised its "Admissions Decision Options" policy in several places, with the explicit rationale that the changes clarify and protect student rights. In the case of one change the rationale was to "place a strong emphasis on the rights of students and the protection of their interests" (2001, 2). The addition stated: "The primary goal of NACAC is to assist students in their transition from secondary school to postsecondary education. Therefore, our members believe that admission plans must be implemented in a fair and unbiased manner that does not propel students into making premature commitments, restrict them from considering their full range of educational options, or otherwise disadvantage students in the admission or financial aid processes" (2001, p. 2). Early decision programs (which are distinct from early action programs that are not binding), are found in about 19 percent of higher education institutions. Fifty-three percent of these institutions report an increase in early decision applicants (NACAC 2002, p. 5). Equally important, the report states that "counselors reported that students were being urged to apply early decision" (p. 4).

A new book on the topic (Avery, Fairbanks, and Zeckhauser 2003) enables us to speak more concretely to the effects of such programs. Based on a study of admissions records at fourteen elite institutions, and interviews with 400 college freshmen, the authors found that early admissions enhances an applicant's chances of being accepted by up to 50 percent, despite that early admission students are often less qualified academically than students applying through the regular process. Noting the different levels of knowledge students from different schools and social backgrounds had, one of the authors said in an interview, "As it stands, the strategic nature of early applications has got to be enhancing the advantage of the wealthiest" (Young 2003).[1]

On-site admissions, which is being implemented at a growing number of institutions, may help institutions attract high-achieving students. On-site admissions are in-person, instant admissions decision programs. In contrast to the early-decision process, the decisions are not binding; the student may decide not to attend the institution. Moreover, the decisions of the instant admissions process are made in person, during the prospective students' campus visit. The process can be seen simultaneously as "a service to students and a savvy marketing tool" (Hoover 2002). Instant admissions benefits students, reducing the paperwork, time, and anxiety of the admissions process, and humanizing it.

1. Not all admissions marketing practices work more clearly in the interests of higher education institutions than in those of prospective students. There may be cases in which (and select bodies of students for whom) the practices work to the benefit of both "sellers" (colleges and universities) and "buyers" (prospective students and their parents) of educational services.

As Barmak Nassirian, associate executive director of the American Association of Collegiate Registrars and Admissions Officers, says, "This is a way for colleges to take a customer-oriented approach" (Hoover 2002). At the same time, colleges that utilize this process also benefit in a variety of ways, ranging from good publicity (cited by the program director at Virginia Tech, which has had such a program since 1997) to increased efficiency by virtue of a significantly higher yield rate. It is noteworthy that this type of admissions program is more typically found at less selective institutions (e.g., at California State Universities versus Universities of California, at Virginia Tech and Radford University versus the University of Virginia, and at many community colleges). By employing this process they are more likely to gain access to higher achieving students, who are more likely to apply for instant admissions. In short, the institutions are able to leverage advantage in the marketplace, recruiting students who might otherwise go to more prestigious institutions.

Therein lies part of the problem, say skeptics of "snap apps." Institutions accelerate admissions, leading students to make decisions on the spur of the moment. Making the choice easier and more immediate for prospective students in some sense restricts their choice (though not in a legal sense). It reduces the likelihood of prospective students shopping for colleges and exploring options that might prove to be better fits. On-site admissions can be seen as a "hard sell" approach to recruiting students, leading students to make their decisions during their campus visits, rather than encouraging them to reflect on and deliberate about their options over time.

The debate surrounding on-site admissions points to the multifaceted dimensions of marketing in higher education. Colleges and universities are not simply subject to the power of consumer choice; they engage in aggressive marketing to strategically shape those consumer choices. More than that, in order to enhance their market positions, institutions are targeting certain student markets that sometimes take them away from the student populations and educational functions that they have served, and that turn them away from historically underserved populations. The bottom line is that under an academic capitalist knowledge/learning regime, institutions are employing market(ing) practices focused on the bottom line.

Theme Two: Moving to Serve More Privileged Segments of the Student Market

As recent scholarship demonstrates, there are many considerations that underlie how colleges and universities "craft a class" (Duffy 1998). Selective colleges and universities look for the academically bright, "well-rounded" students who create an incoming class that represents a broad spectrum of academic and extracurricular strengths and interests. Many institutions consider athletic prowess as well as legacies of attendance and giving (Shulman and Bowen 2001). Not all institutions are of a size and selectivity to afford admissions officers the same options in crafting a class that those at highly selective institutions have. However, the pattern throughout higher education in recent years has been for institutions to recruit and craft classes that pay immediate and long-term dividends to the prestige and revenue interests of the institution. There is a push to attract higher performing students who can pay more for their higher education.

The first part of attracting more academically able students resonates with a longstanding commitment in the academy to meritocracy. There is greater competition for and movement of monies toward meritorious students, defined in traditional terms. As Richard Chait has pointed out, "the total dollars going into merit scholarships—that is, aid not based on need—have increased 1,438 per cent over the past 20 years at private colleges. In other words, some colleges are purchasing academically gifted students" (1992, p. B2). A decade later, a NACAC survey indicated that "counselors noted that financial aid, particularly merit-based aid, figured more prominently in colleges' marketing efforts" (2002, p. 5). Indeed, the pattern of competing for so-called "super students" extends to elite public as well as private universities (Geiger 2002). At the same time, second-tier institutions are increasingly seeking to enhance their standing nationally by attracting such students. As we described earlier in this chapter, there has been a shift at the state and institutional levels towards increased investment in merit-based aid. For some very able students (by traditional standards of merit), it is a buyer's market, though such a market may not always serve their educational interests or the interests of society. One of McPherson and Schapiro's findings about the increased use of merit aid is that "less selective institutions in both the public and private sectors are far more involved in merit aid than their more prestigious counterparts" (1998, p. 130). In short, less prestigious institutions are buying "better" students who could go to "better" institutions, and are using more of their monies to do so, reducing their expenditures on instruction (and underserved students) in the process.

However, a market orientation is increasingly entering the equation. In the context of an emphasis on revenue generation, it is not just highly able students that colleges and universities are targeting, it is also moneyed students who can afford to pay full tuition with no financial aid. The two considerations are related: an institution's improvement in its *U.S. News & World Report* ranking translates into increased yield rates and reduced grant aid to attract its entering class the following year (see Monks and Ehrenberg 1999). Academic capitalism in the new economy has contributed to a shift in institutions' admissions and financial aid practices and orientations. "The simplest way to describe the change over the past decade in the way private colleges and universities approach student aid is to say that business officers, with few exceptions, don't think that way anymore. Rather than viewing student aid as a kind of charitable operation the college runs on the side, most private colleges and universities—and increasing numbers of public institutions—now regard student aid as a vital revenue management and enrollment management tool" (McPherson and Schapiro 1998, pp. 15–16). An even more graphic description of the shift is offered by one of the authors in an interview.

> Twenty-five years ago, colleges really saw student aid as a charitable operation run within the college. If the finance office took an interest, it was essentially to make sure they kept their budget under control," said Michael McPherson, [then] president of Macalester College in St. Paul, Minnesota, who has studied college finances. "Over the last 15 years you could see the light bulb go on with a lot of financial vice presidents who came to see that rather than a charitable operation, financial aid was, at least in part, a strategic tool that could be used to manage both the quality of the class and the net revenue of the class," McPherson said. (Crenshaw 2002, p. 1)

As one commentator has suggested, "In some ways, American colleges and universities have become like airlines and hotels, practicing 'yield management' to try to maximize the revenue generated by every seat or bed. But in most cases, unlike hotels and airlines, colleges also care about who is in those seats and beds" (Crenshaw 2002, 1).

The changing orientation of colleges and universities to financial aid is shaped by the larger economic context of reduced government support (Slaughter and Leslie 1997). In that context, support units and academic units in universities are increasingly being perceived as cost centers that must maximize and generate revenues. That may affect the mindsets of office personnel, leading them to take on a market orientation. More than that, in student aid there has been a reorganization of the decision-making structures that shape these policies.

> As colleges have come to appreciate better the strategic significance of financial aid, they have also changed the institutional structures through which aid is managed. When aid was seen as a charitable sideline, most institutions were content to leave the details to the professionals in the student aid office, with the main high-level concern being that of keeping the aid operation within budget. Student aid officers, who had collaborated on developing the elaborate needs analysis apparatus that governed the allocation of need-based student aid, formed strong professional and ethical bonds . . .

> and something of a tradition of holding their operation aloof from institutional goals. These days, financial aid policy and practice at private and public institutions alike is frequently the province of high-level consultants and close presidential attention. Following on the heels of their colleagues in the admissions office, financial aid officers have come to find their duty hazardous, with a high level of accountability for results in terms of meeting institutional goals and limited patience for qualms based on professional ethics. (McPherson and Schapiro 1998, p. 18).

The storyline about professionals in admissions and financial aid underscores how the economic interests of institutions are prioritized over the interests (and codes of ethics) of professionals and their clients (the students). Managerial professionals are experiencing the same pressure and internal shift of orientation that academics are experiencing in terms of the commodification of research and education. Their relations with students are being commodified in the sense that students are framed in terms of commercial rather than educational/professional considerations.

In noting the increasing share of institutional revenues coming from tuition and the decreasing share of institutional expenditures going to instruction, Slaughter and Leslie (1997) argued that this paradox was a function of two factors: the fungibility of tuition revenues (they are undesignated and can be used in various expenditure categories, in contrast to revenues from research grants, which must be expended in designated categories) and the prioritizing of entrepreneurial research activities. However, academic capitalism in the new economy creates another layer of complexity and causality. Precisely because tuition revenues are an increasingly significant share of institutional revenues, colleges and universities move to attract consumers who have more money and seek to extract as much revenue as possible from them. In contrast to a marketplace defined by the metaphor of students as empowered consumers, the situation suggests a marketplace in which there are preferred, exploited, undervalued, and overlooked customers.

Various admissions and financial aid practices characterize the academic capitalist knowledge/learning regime. Many institutions employ "need conscious" admissions, which means that some applicants who can pay full price will be admitted although they are less academically qualified than some who cannot afford to pay the full sticker price. Or institutions will seek to allocate aid in ways that will most likely leverage a decision to enroll. The price students pay will partly be a function of the institution's sense of whether they are more or less desirable, qualified, and likely to attend. Such practices have led to "strategic enrollment management" (SEM), which focuses on maximizing yield rates and quality, and minimizing tuition discounts and financial aid. This approach has become the focus of annual meetings and several publications sponsored by the American Association of Collegiate Registrars and Admissions Officers (AACRAO). It has also become a cottage consulting industry. (Our aim here is not to exhaustively review admissions and financial aid policies; for such a review, see McPherson and Schapiro 1998).

The trade-offs embedded in targeting already privileged students is encapsulated at the City University of New York (CUNY), which in 1999 adopted tougher admissions standards, eliminated remedial classes at its senior colleges, and hired a new president to give the institution a new image and take it in a new direction. The new academic management wants to enhance the pursuit of excellence within CUNY, through a public relations effort as well as the introduction of an honors college. To recruit students into the honors college, the university offers various enticements, including "free tuition, a laptop computer, free admission to many New York attractions, and a $7,500 expense account they can use over four years for 'academically enriching' items, such as a digital camera or study-abroad expenses" (Hebel 2002, p. A20). Critics of this shift in direction, including many faculty, charge that the change reduces access for the less advantaged and immigrant populations that the institution has been renowned for serving. The new direction is a dramatic shift for an institution that experimented with open access admissions in the 1970s. Whatever one's judgment of past policy in terms of academic merit, scholarship has demonstrated that it contributed to the expansion of a middle class of color in New York City (Lavin 1996).

Moving to the high end of the market, and to enhanced marketing of higher education, involves maximizing and benefiting not simply the meritorious but also the moneyed. We can see this pattern in the recruiting of undergraduates at four-year colleges and universities as well as in the case of other student populations. In community colleges, and in university masters' and professional programs, there is an increased investment of institutions' time, resources, and personnel in serving students who can pay (and often who have already benefited from higher education). Increasingly, that involves educational programs that are oriented more to training for (re)employment in the new information-based economy than to educational growth.

In community colleges, enrollments and programs are growing in contract, continuing-education, and distance-education programs. Almost all community colleges (94%) teach at least one class by contract; at half of the colleges, one-fifth of the students are enrolled in contract courses (Kane and Rouse 1999; Lynch, Palmer, and Grubb 1991). Each of these growth areas is defined by its ability to serve employees in companies and organizations that often pay for part or all of the tuition. It is also defined as much by ongoing training as by in-depth education. Similarly, the number of associate's degree recipients grew by 24 percent in the past ten years, as compared to only 18 percent for baccalaureate degrees (NCES 2001). And those numbers do not begin to match the dramatic growth in certificate programs in community colleges, which again are very much linked to employment.

Similarly, in graduate education, professional, thesis-free master's programs in the sciences and engineering are emerging across the country, targeting business employees who can pay full tuition. (Doctoral students in these fields are generally supported with assistantships and other forms of financial aid [Rhoades 2000].) The explicit aim of such programs is training rather than education. At the beginning of the 1990s, master's programs were labeled the "silent success" of U.S. higher education in terms of recent growth and responsiveness to the market (Conrad, Haworth, and Millar 1993). (However, there is silence about whether or not such programs expand access for historically underserved populations.) Throughout the 1990s, the number of master's degrees continued to grow, by 41 percent, faster than for any other degree level (NCES 2001).

The growth of such employee- and employment-oriented programs in community colleges and at the master's level represents an important shifting of institutional focus. In emphasizing programs that target students more likely to be able to pay more (older, employed students), institutions are reducing their commitment to serving traditionally aged (potential) student populations that have been historically underserved and that are growing disproportionately.

Coming full circle, then, from the concept of "crafting a class," we argue that colleges and universities are increasingly contributing to the sharpening of class divisions in society. Focusing on certificates, programs, and degrees for students who will pay for training and continuing education in hopes of landing new economy jobs moves institutions away from important admissions aims and functions. Higher education moves away from serving a broad spectrum of students and from serving societal needs by broadening access to higher education for historically underserved populations and toward serving narrow institutional aspirations and economic interests, and the interests of already relatively privileged students.

Theme Three: Marketing Consumer Capitalism to Captive Student Markets

A central feature of academic capitalist knowledge/learning regime is the commodification of higher education. Institutions increasingly foreground the consumption character and attractiveness of higher education. The emphasis is not on education but on services that all of us consume in daily life, from communication and dining services to shopping and residential facilities to services surrounding leisure activities and entertainment.

The particular types of "consumer capitalism" (Ritzer 2001) being marketed vary by institutional type and by segment of the student market. Institutions such as community colleges that cater to mass markets may emphasize values such as speed of service and convenience of access. Commuter institutions may look to enhance the convenience of their service delivery by setting up "one-stop" centers where students can receive all sorts of services, following a pattern found in the private sector (Ousley 2003). In the process, they may also market higher education as an item to be consumed quickly, and on the run, while students are working.

We concentrate on more elite or moneyed segments of the student market because of the pattern we identified earlier of institutions moving to serve privileged student markets. In this case, the institutions' marketing may feature more luxury services or high-culture consumption. What is often emphasized is the quality and exclusive character of the brand name—Stanford, Chicago, Duke. (See chapter 10 for a discussion of "branding.") In our discussion of the theme of institutional marketing of consumer capitalism, we first focus on what institutions feature in their college tours. How do they try to sell themselves to prospective students? Second, we discuss the implications of institutional marketing of consumer capitalism in terms of institutional expenditures.

In order to recruit prospective students, higher education institutions feature, and increasingly invest in, services and facilities that are aimed as much or more at attracting applicants than at educating them. Colleges and universities are coming to be marketed more as attractive places in which to live, consume services, and play than as challenging places in which to learn and become educated. Ironically, public policy increasingly emphasizes the workforce and economic development roles of higher education, yet in their recruitment efforts institutions are increasingly addressing prospective students' desires as consumers of various consumption item services, as if colleges were a combination of private-sector enterprises and services such as hotels/resorts, restaurants, boutiques, and exercise/fitness facilities.

Consider what is featured in college tours (and college guides). In a national survey of students, Boyer found that over half of prospective students visit a college campus as part of their information-gathering and decision-making processes. What was most important to students during those visits was the physical environment and appearance of the campus: "The appearance of the campus is, by far, the most influential characteristic during campus visits, and we gained the distinct impression that when it comes to recruiting students, the director of buildings and grounds may be more important than the academic dean" (1987, p. 17). In describing the typical campus tour, Boyer notes the focus on sprawling student unions, with their mini-mall character, the review of various nonacademic services (from entertainment to financial), the tour of athletic, exercise, and residential facilities, and the fact that the guide takes the group "*past* the library and classroom buildings" (p. 16). The last note is ironic, given the pattern in recent years among all institutional types of a dramatic decline in libraries' share of institutional expenditures. Along these lines, it is also interesting that library holdings are not a criteria utilized in the calculation of the *U.S. News & World Report* rankings (Ehrenberg 2003).

Consistent with the emphasis on physical appearance, attractiveness, and public image, a recent NACAC survey "revealed that 70 percent of postsecondary institutions reported undertaking a public image overhaul to attract more students" (2002, p. 5). That means colleges and universities are investing in the provision of more and more nonacademic services, for which they can then charge students more tuition and additional fees. On most four-year campuses that investment generally involves construction of enhanced residence halls, student unions, and recreation facilities. For example, a dean of admissions at Emory University explained expenditures of over 30 million dollars on a student center and an athletic center by saying that, "if you look at the schools we compete with, we could not compare favorably with them if we had not built the recreation center or the student center or the residence halls" (Collison 1989). Often, the enhanced amenities are financed by increases in student fees (Rhoades 1995). In an expression of academic capitalism in support services, some of these services are organized as auxiliary enterprises, which operate as revenue-generating operations. The clearest example of this is residence halls. A large share of the student affairs budget comes not from the state but from a variety of revenue-generating auxiliaries and from fees.

Information technology is a new-economy service that is used to attract students. Campuses are now being rated in terms of how "wired" they are. In order to attract prospective students, campuses have built in Internet (and cable TV) access in residence halls as well as in student unions; they have then increased housing fees. Such practices illustrate two mechanisms of academic capitalism in the new economy: institutions contract with private-sector services to generate revenue, and institutions pass along increased fees to students to pay for such services, generating another stream of revenue. These practices also speak to the fact that students are a captive market in the negotiation between institutions and various vendors, in this case cable and telecommunications companies, but in other cases vendors in the areas of food and beverage, financial, and other services.

One particularly striking example of the extent to which colleges and universities are partnering with private companies is Yeshiva University's arrangement with American Express to pay for a mailing from the Office of Student Finances. In a warning letter that was sent to students who were behind in their payments, there was a suggestion that one of the options for families was a loan from American Express. Yeshiva was not alone in the practice. Indeed, the *Chronicle* article on Yeshiva reported that "Keith Jepson, director of the Office of Financial Aid at New York University, said it was not uncommon for a lending institution to finance a mailing for an institution. When NYU began a loan program for international students last fall, Citibank paid for the mailing" (Gose 1998, p. A44).

As early as the late 1980s, criticism was emerging about expenditures on nonacademic services that take money away from academic activities even as tuition continues to rise (Collison 1989). The criticism partly was about choices of where to invest and spend scarce monies. Nonacademic expenditures also speak to academic values. In the words of Robert Iosue, (then) president of York College of Pennsylvania, "We should be marketing educational quality, not trying to market materialism" (Collison 1989).

Here lies an important difference between academic capitalism and academic capitalism in the new economy. Slaughter and Leslie (1997) identified a pattern, across public and private four-year institutions, of decreased shares of expenditures on instruction. Their explanation and focus, like that of other scholars and policymakers, was the increased expenditure shares on research. The pursuit of entrepreneurial science was taking attention and monies away from undergraduate instruction. By contrast, we see one of the important factors in institutions' declining investment in education as being the investment of monies in nonacademic personnel and activities. Such investment is a national pattern; the growth in administrative and nonacademic support professionals and expenditures has outpaced that of academic personnel and instruction for more than twenty-five years, through good and bad fiscal times in U.S. higher education (Gumport and Pusser 1995; Leslie and Rhoades 1995). In the 1980s, there were increases in the expenditure shares of student services, particular in private universities and in public two-year colleges. There have also been substantial increases in institutional support, particularly in private universities, and in public four and two-year colleges. Those patterns of increases in expenditures on administrative categories continued to hold in the 1990s. Referring back to

Figure 1.1 in chapter 1, instruction's share of institutional expenditures continued to decline (slightly) between 1990–1991 and 1995–1996, from 31.1 to 30.4 percent. The share of research remained the same throughout this time at 9.2 percent. One of the significant growth areas was student affairs, which increased from 4.8 to 5.1 percent.[2]

Not all the investments in providing new services are divorced from academic benefit. One of the dimensions of renovated residence hall facilities has been to provide study lounges, seminar rooms, and computer facilities that make the dorms not just living but learning environments. Such facilities may enhance students' academic performance. Or, they may simply make studying more convenient for students to do in the residence halls, thereby keeping them out of the libraries and other campus learning facilities that the residence halls are seeking to replicate, with no overall benefit to academic performance. Notably, academic services such as advising and tutoring have not received greater investment. Academic support has had only a slight increase in its share of institutional expenditures (from 6.9 to 7%).

The uncertain educational benefit of some services is particularly evident in the case of Internet connectedness and the introduction of high-tech equipment into renovated classrooms. Across the country, colleges and universities are investing enormous amounts to ensure that students have Internet access and computer support in various sites: residence hall rooms, libraries, computer labs, classrooms. To a considerable extent, these services are intended to be directly connected to educational activities. Yet there is often a gap between intentions and outcomes. Emerging evidence about students' use of the Internet calls into question just how educationally and developmentally beneficial connectedness is to students. They use e-mail more for social contact with parents and friends back home than for dialogue with faculty and support professionals on campus, and they also use the Internet for a variety of nonacademic, and occasionally illegal, activities (Gatz and Hirt 2000).

Similarly, there are significant opportunity costs to investing in high-tech classrooms that may call into question the wisdom of the extent of current investments. Most institutions plan to increase their investment in training and support personnel surrounding instructional technology (NEA 2000). But what are the educational benefits and opportunity costs of investing in this tech-

2. Interestingly, much of the student affairs budget is outside state monies, derived from entrepreneurial auxiliaries and student fees. Institutional support and public service have also increased as a share of overall expenditures. Unfortunately, the data are so aggregated that we cannot separate out expenditures for marketing or for particular areas of noninstructional expenditures. Nevertheless, the general pattern is striking.

nology? What if even half the monies invested in technology had been invested in new faculty and other direct educational expenditures, reducing student/faculty ratios and increasing the academic resources available to students; would the educational benefit have been greater? Institutions are not asking these questions, in part because market competition ensures that campuses are characterized by high-tech, state-of-the-art facilities to attract students (and faculty).

Technology has become a marketing tool and a consumption item, above and beyond, and perhaps divorced, from its educational value. The prevailing view of students as potentially empowered consumers assumes that they are in pursuit of quality education and that their choices can leverage educational improvement in colleges and universities. However, students may be more interested in consumer services and consumption benefits that may only minimally include some measure of educational quality or of knowledge consumption. That seems to make sense in an information-based economy in which speed of *processing* information is prioritized over the quality and contemplation of information, knowledge, and wisdom.

Our point in this section has been to underscore the extent to which increased marketing is transforming higher education from a site of educational activity and processes to a site of consumption of various, largely nonacademic services. Such a transformation has implications for how colleges and universities approach and recruit students, and, alternatively, for how students themselves approach colleges and universities and conceptualize the college experience. Such marketing of higher education as a consumption item also involves a shift in patterns of institutional expenditure, with trade-offs in terms of opportunity costs and commitment to educating the general population of students that higher education institutions claim to serve. Finally, such a shift encourages colleges and universities to partner with private enterprise to capitalize on the captive market potential of their students.

Conclusion

The academic capitalist knowledge/learning regime is not the only regime in higher education and is not unchallenged with regard to the framing and treatment of students. In student recruitment, admissions, and financial aid, there is clearly more going on than the pursuit of enhanced institutional prestige and the maximization of institutional revenues. A comprehensive overview of activities and issues in these realms, for example, would be woefully inadequate if it did not address diversity issues in general and affirmative action programs in particular. Our objective in this chapter has been neither to undertake such a review nor to call into question or assess the commitment of professionals and other personnel toward students in the realms of marketing, recruitment, admissions, and financial aid. Not only are individual practitioners sometimes uncomfortable with the practices of institutions, national professional associations in these realms have often produced guidelines that caution against approaches that do not prioritize the best interests of students.

Colleges and universities have highly segmented markets. Elite colleges and universities work their "brand," which is associated with prestige related to the research and scholarship of the faculty, and associated with perceptions of high returns to students' investments in their human capital. A relatively large number of upper-middle-class students compete for a relatively small number of places in the elite market segment. However, niche markets, which attract students unable to place at the top, are increasingly opening up. Schools of modest reputation recast themselves as private "bargains," or as "public Ivies," and are marketed to the affluent for escalating tuition dollars.

However, the majority of four-year colleges and universities as well as community colleges interact with the new economy in a more mundane fashion. Corporations in the new economy require well-educated workers in business-related areas—science, engineering, medicine, law—to create and protect knowledge-based products, processes, and services. Corporations also need employees able to deal with the high-technology products and services characteristic of the new economy. At the undergraduate level, business has become the core curricula. The majority of all courses taken in four-year schools are in business fields (Adelman 1999).

Many institutions—ranging from elite to community colleges—interact with the new economy by providing distance-education programs. Again, markets are segmented. Elite universities offer expensive MBAs or executive seminars to managers at Fortune 500 corporations, while other programs—such as the University of Maryland University College and Rio Salado Community College—target the employed adult. These programs are targeting the high and low ends of new-economy employment markets. The elite programs provide continuing education and confirm upward mobility, while the other programs provide training that modestly increases opportunity. Very often employees at nonelite institutions recycle through different programs as the new economy shifts to new technologies.

Whether at elite colleges and universities or community colleges, marketing activity has created new circuits of knowledge. Institutions are as attuned to *U.S. News and World Report* ratings as they are to evaluations of fields by associations of learned disciplines. These new circuits of knowledge can create an arc between an institution and a market that is able to bring in many new applicants. Marketing activity requires many new managerial professionals. As noted earlier, student personnel services grew during the past decade, although funds for instruction did not. Enrollment management became a profession, emerging interstitially as did patenting and copyright professionals.

12

THE ACADEMIC CAPITALIST KNOWLEDGE/LEARNING REGIME

IN THE EARLY YEARS of the twenty-first century, the academic capitalist knowledge/learning regime is ascendant. It is displacing, but not replacing, others, such as the public good knowledge regime or the liberal learning regime. Although other knowledge regimes persist, the trend line in emphasis and investment is the academic capitalist knowledge/learning regime, as evidenced in public policy, in relations among market, state, and higher education organizations, and in the employment structure and work practices of the academy.

Many scholars acknowledge the changes to which we point, whether they refer to them as the commercialization of higher education (Bok 2003, Noble 2001); as entrepreneurial universities (Clark 1998); as a triple helix that weaves together higher education, state, and market (Etzkowitz, Healey, and Webster 1998); or as corporatization of higher education (Soley 1995). The contribution of our work has been to develop a theory of academic capitalism in the new economy. We track and explain how the change from one regime to another occurs; in contrast to much work in the field, we point to the active, sometimes leading role that the academy plays in marketizing higher education, rather than portraying it as the victim of external, encroaching commercial interests. In addition, we demonstrate the degree to which market behaviors have come to permeate almost *all* aspects of colleges and universities, from research to instruction, including administration; by contrast, most other work concentrates on the commercialization of research. Furthermore, we point to how academic capitalism in the new economy restructures work in colleges and universities in ways that mirror and diverge from patterns of professional employment in private enterprise. Finally, we conceptualize how higher education as an institution embodies the changing social understanding of what is "public." The idea of an academic capitalism knowledge/learning regime captures the many ways and means through which market and marketlike behaviors as well as a market ethos and ideology have been incorporated in postsecondary education.

In this chapter, we offer a theoretical reprise that concentrates on how the theory of academic capitalism explains the shift from earlier knowledge regimes to an academic capitalist knowledge/learning regime. Rather than focusing on the macro level—the growth of global markets, the rise of neoliberal states in the world—we concentrate on borders between colleges and universities and external agencies, whether located in states or markets. Attention to the borders among market, state, and institutions of higher education lets us comprehend the complex networks and mechanisms that promote the academic capitalist knowledge/learning regime.

The theory of academic capitalism in the new economy sees groups of actors within colleges and universities—faculty, students, administrators, and managerial professionals—as using a variety of state resources to intersect the new economy. These groups of actors are drawn from different institutional segments and do not always act together. However, their organized activity is directed toward the opportunity structures created by the new economy, which channels their efforts in similar directions. They create new circuits of knowledge that link the university to and bring it into the new economy. They form interstitial organizations that bring the corporate sector inside the university. They join organizations that intermediate among public, nonprofit, and for-profit public sectors. They build expanded managerial capacity to supervise new flows of external resources, to invest in research infrastructure for the new economy, and to expand programs to market institutions, products, and services to students and other customers in the private marketplace. Their individual decisions to engage in organized activities that promote market and marketlike activities consolidate the academic capitalist knowledge/learning regime.

Although market language dominates discourse about entrepreneurial universities and academic capitalism, the state continues to provide the largest share of resources for the shift in knowledge/learning regimes. Colleges and universities are not seeking to become private enterprises; rather they wish to maintain the privileges of not-for-profit status while at the same time entering the private-sector marketplace. Academic capitalism does not involve "privatization"; rather it entails a redefinition of public space and of appropriate activity in that space. The configuration of state resources has changed, providing colleges and universities with fewer unrestricted public revenues and encouraging them to seek out and generate alternative sources of revenue. These new configurations and boundaries change our conception of what "public" means.

The new configurations and boundaries also represent new circuits of knowledge, which are the harbinger of knowledge regime change. Following the new circuits of knowledge points out the segments of the economy and the state to which college and universities are connecting and with which they are integrated, and gives us a diagram of the components of the academic capitalist knowledge/learning regime and how it is wired.

Interstitial organizations are the leaven for change in established organizations, the means through which actors with mutual interests related to yet not at the core of their institution join together to express new goals and purposes for the institution. When interstitial organizations are successful, they often intersect new opportunity structures that the institution comes to see as within its purview—for example, opportunities created by the rise of the new economy. The set of interstitial organizations that figure in the academic capitalist knowledge/learning regime were organized by the faculty as research centers and institutes and also by professionals who are neither faculty nor administrators, but are interstitial personnel who possess higher degrees and whose purpose very often is to manage the market dimensions of faculty work.

Like interstitial organizations, intermediating organizations (Metcalfe 2004) intersect new environmental opportunities, in this case, opportunities created by the new economy. Unlike interstitial organizations, intermediating organizations do not originate within colleges and universities and connect similar professionals at various colleges and universities. Instead, intermediating organizations are often composed of high level administrators and span the boundaries between public, non-profit and for-profit institutions, reshaping the boundaries that divide them, redirecting and revaluing organizational purposes. In working in such intermediating organizations, academic managers enhance the academic capitalist knowledge/learning regime by developing and facilitating market and marketlike activities across public, nonprofit and for-profit institutional and sectoral boundaries.

Expanded managerial capacity is a response to the increased market and marketlike activity generated by new circuits of knowledge, and interstitial and intermediating organizations. The exploitation of intellectual property, the expansion of endowments, and the marketing of educational services require staff able to compete with other institutions and organizations to capture market shares. The more the market activity, the greater the managerial staff; the more the managerial staff, the greater the institutional effort to expand markets, as these professionals become an interest group seeking to expand its domains and career opportunities.

All of these processes—creation of new circuits of knowledge, interstitial organizational emergence, intermediating organizational activity among public, nonprofit, and for-profit organizations, and expanded managerial capacity—contribute to restratification among and within colleges and universities and often to the restructuring of faculty work. Stratification among institutions is enhanced by their differential capacities to access segmented student markets and external revenue streams related to educational products, processes, and services. Stratification within institutions is increased by colleges' and departments' differential capacities in the same arenas, their perceived potential to intersect and capitalize on new economy student, employment, research, and service markets. Restructuring of faculty work is often undertaken to maximize educational efficiencies and to enable some faculty to attend more to research and technology transfer in fields believed to have revenue-generating potential in the new economy. Such restratification of institutions and restructuring of faculty work reshapes access for students. More institutional and faculty attention is directed to those student markets that can afford to pay more, and fewer opportunities are available to low-income and historically underserved students of color, who are less able to pay and less likely to be flowing into new economy fields of employment. As colleges and universities shift toward revenue generation through academic capitalism, they invest less in historic, democratic missions of providing increased access and upward mobility for less advantaged populations of students.

In the current context of apparent reduced public commitment to subsidizing higher education, the need for new revenues and the language of the market makes the ascendance and expansion of an academic capitalist knowledge/learning regime seem inexorable. Yet the market logic embedded in academic capitalism is problematic. For example, notwithstanding the connotations of academic capitalism, all of the markets we consider—ranging from markets in students to patents and start-up companies—depend heavily on state subsidies, whether in the form of federal and state student financial aid or federal and state subsidies for research from which college and university intellectual property is derived. Academic capitalism in the new economy involves a shift, not a reduction, in public subsidy. Moreover, despite the implications of applying market logic to colleges and universities, many, even most, are not particularly successful capitalists. Academic capitalism involves institutions picking, investing in, and betting on certain winners in the marketplace, in developing interstitial organizations, expanding managerial professions and managerial capacity, and in restratifying academic fields. Two particular patterns and problems define academic capitalist institutions: they move toward similar opportunities rather than to any niche competitive advantage; and they are not particularly effective as venture capitalists, investment bankers, or investors in the (stock) market. However, their market failures tend to be underwritten by consumers (in the form of higher tuition) or by state subsidy. Further, academic managers and policy makers are selling the appropriateness of market and marketlike competition in higher education to the public on the grounds that academic capitalism in the new economy will make colleges and universities more self-sufficient and will decrease costs to the public. Yet state allocations to public higher education continue to increase, and tuition continues to escalate dramatically in public and private higher education. Finally, making the students consumers was supposed to empower them, but institutional funds are increasingly concentrated less on teaching and more on research, public relations, and revenue-generating activity.

In the first part of this chapter, we review the realms of federal policy, patenting, copyrighting, departmental entrepreneurial activity, administrator and trustee capitalism, and marketing in brands and to students. In the second part, we move from theoretical reprise and review to a consideration of fault lines in the structure of the new knowledge/learning regime, and of alternatives within and beyond academic capitalism in the new economy. We identify some of these fault lines in the academic capitalist knowledge/learning regime, and we close by exploring alternatives within and beyond academic capitalism in the new economy.

Policy

In chapter 2, we considered two major federal initiatives that provided a policy framework for what we call an academic capitalist knowledge/learning regime. The initiatives were federal student financial aid policy that gives money to students rather than institutions (student as consumer), and competitiveness policy—which includes patent law and policies, copyright law and policies, and information technology laws and policies—all of which created incentives for commercialization within colleges and universities.

The policies were the product of a bipartisan congressional coalition that promoted U.S. competitiveness in global markets. The coalition enacted policies in keeping with a neoliberal state that undercut welfare functions and supported programs and segments of the state that supported large, private-sector corporations. The neoliberal state concentrated funding in state agencies oriented to the production of economic growth, revenue generation, and private wealth—for example, research funding for corporations and academe. The neoliberal state worked to build the "new" knowledge or information economy and attempted to articulate national economies with global economies. To provide funds to reshape the economy, the neoliberal state instituted processes of deregulation, commercialization, and privatization, reregulating to create a state that no longer provided "entitlements" such as welfare, or that restructured and reduced general services such as health care and social security. The benefits of the neoliberal state tended to accrue less to the broad citizenry and more to large corporations, the wealthy, and the upper middle class closely associated with the growth of the new economy.

Although we begin with the federal government, we do not see the federal government as the sole policy driver for the academic capitalist knowledge/learning regime. Federal and state laws as well as institutional policies interact in complex ways to produce knowledge/learning regimes. They do not so much dictate a new academic capitalist regime as create opportunities for academic capitalism, on which new networks of academic managers, faculty, staff, and students act. States have an array of initiatives that promote economic development. Many of these initiatives, ranging from workforce preparation of students to fostering industries that contribute to the states' economic base, feature participation of colleges and universities. Indeed, the states frequently devised innovative solutions to pressing national problems prior to the federal government's involvement. So, too, colleges and universities are not simply acted upon, or "corporatized." There are actors within them who participate in creating new knowledge/learning regimes by networking and partnering with external actors. Segments of the administration and faculty work to shape the politico-legal climate that fosters an academic capitalist knowledge/learning regime, and they actively and ardently engage in commercialization. Their activities are reinforced by judicial decisions, administrative law, executive orders, bureaucratic procedures, and institutional policies at the state and federal levels.

Patenting

Chapters 3 and 4 deal with patenting. The changes in patenting policies and behaviors in colleges and universities dramatically illustrate the theory of academic capitalism. Although such changes occurred largely at research universities and in science and engineering, their influence extends beyond these realms. Moreover, changes in patenting were the precursor of changes in other forms of intellectual property—copyright and trademarks—that were adapted within all sectors of higher education and across a wide variety of academic fields.

The patent policies we analyzed provided strong incentives to faculty to patent. Over the years, policies elaborated their coverage to include other professional staff (revealing investment in managerial capacity to develop, market, and sell intellectual property) and students. Universities reduced exceptions to institutional claims to ownership, and policies increasingly specified use of institutional resources as a crucial factor in determining ownership.

The aggressive institutional pursuit of revenue generation through patents, as evidenced in institutional policies, was matched by faculty and students' aggressive pursuit of academic capitalism. Appellate court cases and interviews with faculty and students involved in technology transfer revealed a move away from a public good model toward an academic capitalist knowledge/learning regime. Many faculty still held to some values of the public good regime—for example, the importance of publishing and the corresponding value of the free flow of information—but they were willing to alter those values, sometimes delaying publication, sometimes "sanitizing" data to preserve opportunities to patent. Professors straddled two different worlds, retaining a place in the public space of the university but also assuming the role of state-subsidized entrepreneurs in the private marketplace, working as consultants, officials, or even presidents of their own companies. They were constructing new circuits of knowledge.

New Circuits of Knowledge

Patents precipitated new circuits of knowledge by connecting university actors to external actors and organizations intent on building the new/information economy. Historically, circuits of knowledge connected the Department of Defense to universities through federally sponsored research projects, the knowledge from which moved to federal laboratories, then to corporations that made defense and defense-related products, and sometimes serendipitously spun off civilian technology that reached nondefense markets. New circuits of knowledge, characteristic of the academic capitalist knowledge/learning regime, connect the National Institutes of Health, the National Science Foundation, and the Department of Commerce to universities through sponsored research, frequently in partnership with corporations. Not only are different agencies involved, but in recent years they have more directly involved representatives from business in defining research agendas and reviewing grant proposals. Companies themselves have expanded their support of academic research. Like the federal agencies, the corporations in the new circuits of knowledge are different. Rather than defense and aerospace corporations, the corporations in the new circuits of knowledge produce civilian technology: pharmaceuticals, medical substances and devices, biotechnology (NIH); information technology and telecommunications (NSF); and high-technology products for global markets (DOC). Faculty and university administrators also create new circuits of knowledge when they start up corporations in which universities hold equity and faculty hold administrative positions. These circuits are usually connected to the broader civilian technology grid that integrates colleges and universities with the new economy.

The new circuits of knowledge affect and are reflected in faculty work. The traditional tripartite faculty role of teaching, research, and service altered during the period from 1980 to 2004. In response to surveys, faculty indicated that they preferred teaching to research until the mid-1980s, after which an increased preference for research began to emerge (Finkelstein, Seal, and Schuster 1998). Concentrating on research allows faculty to give more time and attention to work that may result in discoveries that can be patented. In fact, the rate of faculty/university patenting has increased dramatically. Prior to 1980, about 250 patents per year were granted to universities; in 1998, the number was 3,151. "As a result, academic patents now approach 5.0 percent of all new U.S.-owned patents, up from less than 0.5 percent two decades ago" (NSB 2002). In addition, faculty publication patterns are more closely aligned with industry. In 1988, faculty coauthored 20.3 percent of their publications with industry. In 1998, approximately 25 percent were coauthored with industry. As the National Science Board (2002) notes, "The Federal Government has long sought to stimulate . . . collaboration across sectors (e.g., industry-university . . . activities)" (p. 544). As we have pointed out, universities also sought to stimulate such collaboration. Academic institutions were at the heart of cross-sector relationships, linking private nonprofits, private for-profits, the federal government, FFRDC's, and institutions of higher learning (2002).

At the same time that faculty patenting has increased and faculty are publishing more often with industry coauthors, the number of scientific and technical articles by U.S. authors has declined. The national output across all research-producing organizations in 1999 was down by 10 percent from 1992. This trend diverged from growth in most other OECD countries during this period and is a reversal of three prior decades of consistent U.S. publication growth. The decrease in articles produced within academia was slightly less pronounced (9%), but, because of the sector's high share of total output, it accounted for 64 percent of the overall decline. In academia, almost half of the decrease was in the life sciences, perhaps because they have undergone the most rapid commercialization and are the academic fields in which withholding of research results is most common (NSB 2002).

As scientific publications declined, the number of patents referencing scientific articles increased dramatically. In the mid-1980s, patents referenced about 22,000 scientific articles, but in 1998 they referenced 310,000 (NSB 2002). Many explanations can be offered for the rise in patent citations, from the growth of biomedical patents to changes in international patent law. However, patent citation of scientific articles points to creation of new circuits for academic knowledge. This knowledge no longer flows primarily among scientific communities but frequently through circuits that connect it to knowledge application and the corporate world.

As new circuits of knowledge emphasized entrepreneurial research and university-industry partnerships, universities shifted their research expenditure patterns. In the period 1977–1996, all institutions increased their research expenditures from 19 to 21 percent. At public colleges and universities, the share rose from 17 to 21 percent; the increase was greatest at public doctoral granting I (6–13%) and II (16–25%) universities, suggesting that they were eager to intersect the academic capitalist knowledge/learning regime, perhaps to capture increased streams of external revenues to emulate research I and research II public universities. Alternatively, they may have received lower shares of state resources and charged lower tuition rates, which pushed them toward research activity as a means of leveraging external resources. As all public institutions increased expenditures devoted to research by roughly four percentage points, they decreased expenditures for instruction by approximately six percentage points.

Private institutions behaved somewhat differently. During the same period, research declined from 24 to 21 percent of their expenditures. The most dramatic declines were in private research I and doctoral granting II. Private research I university expenditures declined from 42 to 36 percent, and the private doctoral II expenditures from 18 to 14 percent. However, private colleges and universities did not expend increased funds on instruction, which remained relatively constant. Rather, as a group private institutions increased their expenditures on public service, a category "established primarily to provide noninstructional services beneficial to individuals and groups external to the university" (NSB 2002).

Thus, as they engage in the academic capitalist knowledge/learning regime, colleges and universities are either decreasing instructional expenditures or holding them constant, even as they are significantly increasing tuition.

Interstitial Organizations

As universities became more involved in patenting, and as federal legislation encouraged the development of organizational structures within universities to manage patenting, professionals with law and science degrees were hired in new or expanded technology transfer and/or intellectual property offices. These new professionals joined the Association of University Technology Managers (AUTM), an intermediating organization that operates outside of universities but that intersects technology transfer managers from various public and private sectors. Formed by "seven visionaries" as the Society of University Patent Administrators in 1975, AUTM has dramatically grown in membership and has broadened its focus beyond patents (AUTM 2003a). In 1986 its membership was only 381, but it had grown to 771 members by 1990 and 3,200 by 2003

(AUTM 2003b). These numbers reflect the expansion of patenting and other technology transfer activity among a wider range of universities and the increase in size of technology transfer offices within those institutions.

The national association collects data on university patenting and has a journal that provides information on patenting, licensing, royalties and start-ups. The association and the journal created a normative discourse that emphasized the degree to which intellectual property contributed to university generation of external revenues as well as the contributions university intellectual property made to the new economy and the welfare of the citizenry. Because the success of their offices depends on increased streams of revenue, technology transfer officers make every effort to expand the numbers of faculty disclosures and to patent the promising ones, linking faculty and administrators directly to corporations in the new economy. In short, AUTM illustrates how professionals other than faculty within colleges and universities respond to opportunities created by the new economy.

Yet faculty and academic units have also created interstitial organizations. Various sorts of centers and institutes in the sciences and engineering have been designed to facilitate the interaction and intersection of higher education, state, and market organizations. Such centers are in considerable part a response to a push by federal funding agencies to promote closer cooperation and partnerships between universities and business.

Intermediating Organizations

In spanning public, nonprofit, and for-profit entities, mediating among the sectors and often reshaping their boundaries, intermediating organizations play a significant role in the postsecondary community during regime shifts. In the case of patents, another important intermediating organization (in addition to AUTM) was the Business-Higher Education Forum (Slaughter 1990). It was made up of CEOs primarily from large corporations and research universities, who met on a "principals only" basis. The explicit purpose of the forum was to increase U.S. productivity and ability to compete in global markets for civilian technology. The forum circulated its policy documents widely, and spokespersons met regularly with members of the executive and legislative branch of the federal government to advance their positions.

Research university presidents committed to these goals at least in part because corporate leaders affirmed research universities' right to hold patents to discoveries faculty made when working on federally sponsored projects. The first widely distributed forum report was written about the same time (1983) that President Reagan signed an executive order that altered Bayh-Dole (1980), allowing large corporations as well as small business and universities to patent discoveries their scientists made when working on federally sponsored research. Although the change benefited research universities, it also benefited large corporations, which engaged in far more federally sponsored research than universities.

The Business-Higher Education Forum spanned the boundaries between public, nonprofit, and for-profit entities and engaged in reshaping them, working to allow corporations and universities to take out patents on research that was previously publicly held. The Business-Higher Education Forum was committed to creating a new economy rooted in civilian technology that was based on intellectual property. Corporations were able to use federal funding of research to make profits from patents; universities were able to use federal funding to generate external revenues from patents. The presidents of institutions of higher learning worked with the Business-Higher Education Forum to create a policy climate in which federal funds for civilian technology would be plentiful for corporations and universities. They reshaped public/private boundaries so that universities could easily participate in economic activity with corporations or on their own.

Enhanced Managerial Capacity

In order to more aggressively pursue the promise of patents, colleges and universities greatly expanded their internal managerial capacity to participate in external markets. The new functions were generally handled by technology transfer offices and included reviewing and evaluating faculty disclosures; technology licensing; supervision of royalty flows; reinvestment of funds in new market opportunities; litigation to defend intellectual property; evaluation of intellectual property for institutional equity investments; monitoring and occasionally administering corporations in which the institution held equity; overseeing initial public offerings (IPOs); and handling bids for downstream research related to patented technology already in the market. As institutions become more involved in academic capitalism, they hired more managerial professional staff. College, university, and state system patent policies gave professional staff the managerial capacity to run intellectual property activities like businesses. The growth of such managerial capacity is evident in the growth of technology transfer offices, economic development offices, trademark offices, and corporate relations offices.

Copyrighting

Chapters 5 and 6 deal with copyrighting. Like patenting, changes in copyrighting dramatically illustrate the growth of the academic capitalist knowledge/learning regime. Unlike patenting, which deals primarily with intellectual property discovered by faculty during the research process, copyrighting covers the instructional aspect of faculty work. After the advent of digital technologies, the possibilities of generating external revenues from instructional materials transformed the academic capitalist knowledge regime into an academic capitalist knowledge/learning regime.

New Circuits of Knowledge

Traditionally, faculty owned copyrights to their scholarly and creative works, or traded royalties for copyrights from third-party organizations, in the form of publishing companies. Other than textbooks, these works had relatively small audiences, made little money, and did not figure in revenue generation strategies of colleges and universities. As digital telecommunications technologies grew more sophisticated, colleges and universities began to see instructional materials offered via distance education as a source of external revenue from off-site student tuition. Many institutions developed copyright policies from the mid-1980s through the 1990s. These policies often let faculty retain ownership of scholarly and creative work but made institutional claims to instructional materials, particularly when these were produced with the use of university facilities or resources. These instructional materials were often used in distance education.

Prior to the 1990s, most colleges did not have distance-education programs other than correspondence, audio tapes, or closed circuit television. The Internet technology and telecommunications revolution of the 1990s stimulated enhanced distance education. By 2001, 48 percent of all college and universities offered distance-education courses, and 22 percent offered graduate-level courses (NCES 2003). In 2000–2001, 2,876,000 college-level credit-granting distance-education courses were offered, 82 percent at the undergraduate level. Forty-eight percent of public two-year, 31 percent of public four-year, and 19 percent of private four-year colleges' enrollments were via distance education. Public four-year institutions (48%) are most likely to offer virtual degrees, taken entirely through distance education, followed by private four-year (33%) and public-two year (20%) (NCES 2003).

Participation in distance education often inducts administrators and faculty into the academic capitalist knowledge/learning regime. Administrators have to purchase or lease and maintain the physical infrastructure that makes distance education possible, construct teams of producers and content providers, and market the product to student consumers. They often work in partnership and consortia with private-sector partners. Sixty percent indicated they worked in consortia, most often statewide (NCES 2003). Unfortunately, national data on how many consortia members are corporations was not available. However, we know from Schiller (1998) that many colleges and universities have corporate partners, as discussed in chapter 6.

Faculty who develop instructional materials for distance-education courses often receive generous royalties for use. However, the nature of their work changes. Rather than being in charge of a classroom where they interact face-to-face with students, they become content providers on teams of distance-education producers. In this process, nonfaculty academic professionals who participate in the teams do not receive royalties even if they contribute to course design because their work is considered work for hire.

Distance-education courses offer the promise of new student markets, increased tuition revenues, revenues from educational products, and enhanced efficiencies in the delivery of educational services. As in the dot.com debacle in the private-sector economy, so too, many of the for-profit ventures undertaken by colleges and universities often fail to fulfill the promises of the new economy. However, other strategies and ventures have been more successful. The efforts of community colleges to market courses and programs to international students and of science and engineering departments to market "professional masters degrees" to employed businesspersons have often succeeded. These efforts mark a substantial change in orientation to education, shifting the focus to the efficient delivery of educational services. For a price, circuits of instruction now encompass campus, state, region, or world, encouraging even "community" colleges to direct attention away from local students and employers in an effort to intersect with the global, new economy.

Interstitial Organizational Emergence

A number of organizations have emerged to manage, promote, and regulate distance education. As with patenting, AUTM stresses strategies for institutions to capture and exploit faculty copyrights. Among the many associations that deal with distance education are the United States Distance Learning Association and the International Association of Distance Educators. There is also an accrediting agency for distance education, the Distance Education and Training Council, which works with the U.S. Department of Education. Web resources for distance education are too numerous to list.

Many established organizations in higher education have also developed copyright and distance-education policies, and undertaken conventional interest-group activity around these issues. For example, the American Association of University Professors, the American Federation of Teachers, and the National Educational Association have issued statements about copyright and distance education. These organizations generally seek to retain faculty copyright ownership of new, digital forms of intellectual property, including instructional materials used in distance education. Although they articulate some traditional stances concerning professional control of work and standards of quality, by endorsing faculty claims to new forms of intellectual property these organizations also promote faculty complicity with and commitment to the academic capitalist knowledge/learning regime.

Important new players in distance education are for-profit, postsecondary institutions. The lobbying by these entities of state boards of education and regional accrediting associations has served to legitimate and advance an academic capitalist knowledge/learning regime. Their lobbying efforts have relaxed restrictions and created exceptions to professional quality standards regarding the percentage of classes that are taught on campus, the percentage of staff who are part-time, and the involvement of faculty in curricular matters. For-profit distance education treats education as an information service like any other service.

Intermediating Organizations

Many organizations intermediate among public, nonprofit, and private entities concerned with copyrighted intellectual property. Members from the educational and corporate sectors in these intermediating organizations are committed to improving education through information technology. Their education goals operate in tandem with commercial objectives. EDUCAUSE and the League for Innovation in the Community College are among the most well-known organizations that link colleges and universities to corporations that market information technology hardware and software, often in packages that can be sold to campuses as discounted systems.

As its mission statement says, "EDUCAUSE is a nonprofit association whose mission is to advance higher education by promoting the intelligent use of information technology." EDUCAUSE membership is composed of colleges and universities, professional associations, and corporate members, largely from the information technology sector. For corporations, the EDUCAUSE meetings are a venue for marketing their information technology products. For educators, who are generally managerial professionals rather than faculty, EDUCAUSE meetings are a place to learn about and purchase products to incorporate information technologies into campuses and the delivery of educational services. Both parties work through EDUCAUSE to develop strategies for increasing the use of information technology on campuses. These strategies are legislative, to commit more state and federal resources to information technology; interinstitutional, to build consortia promoting information technology use; and institutional, to enhance the capacity of individual institutions with regard to information technology.

The League for Innovation in the Community College serves many of the same purposes. Organized in 1968, it works to integrate community colleges with corporate labor markets. In the 1990s, it turned increasingly to information technology. Like EDUCAUSE, the league has corporate partners and offers programs at which these partners have vending rights, depending on their partnership status. Among recent partners are 3dimensional Holographic, Avenet, eFolio, Citrix Systems, College Collaborative Network, CompTIA, Condensed Curriculum International, Cyberlearning Labs, Elsevier-Evolve, Endeavor Information Systems, Hawkes Learning Systems, Learner's Library by Knowledge Ventures, School Web Services, Silicon Chalk, Soft Chalk, and Sun Academic Initiative. The league's corporate partners are purveyors of products that are used within the information systems developed by colleges and universities.

These intermediating organizations span the boundaries of public, nonprofit, and private entities, and expand higher education institutions' commitment to information technology. They pursue legislative strategies that increase public monies for information technology, subsidizing tighter connections between colleges and universities and corporations. They support distance and on-campus education delivered through more advanced information technologies, which encourages new economy corporate production and sales. It also encourages colleges and universities to market distance-education and educational materials to new student markets, as a new information and educational service intended to generate new revenue streams. Intermediating organizations, then, support the commitment of colleges and universities to an academic capitalist knowledge/learning regime.

Enhanced Managerial Capacity

Like patents, copyrighted instructional materials must be managed to enhance revenues. Although technology transfer offices often manage copyrighted intellectual property along with patents, college and university commitment to distance education and to copyrighting of instructional materials has also resulted in the creation of new offices to manage these initiatives. For example, many institutions have distance or continuing education offices that manage virtual education, including its many physical manifestations—networking infrastructure, computer labs, one- and two-way video equipment—and marketing. In addition, most institutions now have offices that encourage the use of technology in on-campus education, from teaching centers to professional development centers that develop or help faculty develop and incorporate information and multimedia technologies into their instruction.

Enhanced managerial capacity also means expanded managerial capacity. The use of information technology generally calls for more support professionals to operate, repair, handle, and conceptualize educational materials and curricula. Part of what is driving the increase in support professionals is the establishment of a new production process for the delivery of information and educational services, which involves a matrix of professionals rather than a single professor in constructing and delivering a course. Faculty are being decentered not only in absolute numbers, and by the increased numbers and percentages of part-time faculty, but also in the educational process itself. Because managerial professionals report to administrators rather than to the faculty as a collectivity, whether in departments or senates, there is a shift toward expanded administrative authority.

In a related development, many colleges and universities have established the position of CIO (chief information officer) in the past decade. The CIO manages infrastructure for information technology, ranging from technology-infused classrooms to high-speed computer wiring systems for dormitories. These officials also develop forward planning for the institutional information technology system. Furthermore, they represent a new force promoting the increased use of and investment in information technology.

Enhanced and expanded managerial capacity links colleges and universities to the new economy and commits them to academic capitalism. Very often CIOs are involved in partnerships rather than simple procurement relations with corporations. They join in strategic alliances with information technology firms in which they act as test beds for new products, perfecting products for the corporations in return for discounted technology. Distance-education offices, teaching centers, and professional development offices market new instructional technologies to faculty and students in ways that increasingly directly intersect education with new economy corporations that redefine educational materials and processes. They are shifting the academy from an era of chalk and blackboards to one in which Blackboard is a new economy corporation marketing its information technology platform to colleges and universities, which themselves are developing their own products and platforms to market in the private sector. In the process, colleges and universities are becoming further integrated into an academic capitalist knowledge/learning regime in the new economy.

Departments

Chapter 7 deals with departmental involvement in the academic capitalist knowledge/learning regime. We found departments very involved in academic capitalism, but in unanticipated ways that speak to the complex and sometimes conflicted nature of academic commitment to entrepreneurial activity. Although most departments we studied generated external revenues by competing for grant and contract funding, we were somewhat surprised at the relatively limited collective initiatives to pursue entrepreneurial research markets. More common were educational initiatives designed to generate external and internal revenues through new programs that articulate with the new economy.

New Circuits of Knowledge

Several examples of new circuits of knowledge were evident in the activities of academic departments. New masters programs targeting prospective students in business were established. These "professional masters' degrees" were terminal and did not require a thesis. The idea was to make them more attractive to employed persons who would not have time to do thesis work and who would be neither interested in nor able to pursue a doctorate in the field. Such programs were cheaper to run because there was no provision for tuition waivers or assistantships for students, and little was needed to hire additional faculty since the courses could be taught by doctoral students. The new programs represent a substantial shift from past practices, which treated masters' degrees as a step on the way to a doctorate, which was largely a step on the way to academic employment. Traditional academic departments that are reconfiguring their professional masters' degrees can be seen as providing a form of continuing education that trains and upgrades employees for the new economy.

Intermediating and Interstitial Organizations

In the mid-1980s most public universities began large capital campaigns. Some years later, colleges within these universities began to hire their own development officers and to appoint advisory boards. Such initiatives were initially most common in business and engineering colleges but have since expanded. Now, we are finding evidence of academic departments within the colleges developing these sorts of links to the private-sector market. Essentially all of the academic colleges in our sample had development officers, and some departments had undertaken fund-raising activities. One of the organizational mechanisms for pursuing such efforts was advisory boards, which included members who represented or were connected to large corporations and potential donors. These boards mediated between the worlds of academe and industry. Although they were largely focused on fund-raising, their existence also made possible a more direct flow of feedback from the external world to the department in regards to employment needs.

A more longstanding organizational form in universities is centers and institutes. In the past two decades, new types have emerged, with more direct partnerships and connections with private enterprises. At the initiative of federal funding agencies such as the National Science Foundation, many such centers and institutes require and promote university/industry partnerships. These entities facilitate the movement of faculty and students between academic and business worlds. Like advisory boards and development offices, they normalize and expand universities' managerial capacity, to some degree displacing long established but uncoordinated faculty networks with corporations.

Despite the ascendance of the academic capitalist knowledge/learning regime, elements of and some commitment to old (public good) regimes and prestige systems persist. Even those department heads who sought aggressively to intersect their units collectively with the business world were clear that they had to maintain and expand federal grant and contract revenues. Such peer-reviewed grants were considered by almost all heads and faculty as more prestigious than private-sector support and as key to the tenure and promotion process of individuals, as well as to the collective prestige of the department. Some resistance to the academic capitalist knowledge/learning regime was grounded in a continued commitment to alternative conceptions of the functions of a university.

In this sense there is clearly a coexistence of academic capitalist and other knowledge regimes. At the same time, it would appear that the prestige system is increasingly being defined in academic capitalist terms. That is, grant-revenue rankings are increasingly important relative to National Research Council prestige rankings, and the prestige of the institution as well as the academic unit is increasingly being defined by how much money it can command from external markets. Such developments, in our view, speak to the ascendance of the academic capitalist knowledge/learning regime.

Administrators and Trustees

Chapters 8 and 9 study how administrators and trustees intersect the academic capitalist knowledge/learning regime. Their networks are distinct from faculty's. Senior academic administrators, such as presidents, and trustees of colleges and universities advance the academic capitalist knowledge/learning regime and intersect the new economy directly through intermediating and interstitial organizations that foster the development of new circuits of knowledge and involve expanded managerial capacity.

Intermediating Organizations

We analyzed Internet2 as an intermediating organization that networks public organizations and private corporations. Internet2 was initiated by presidents of research universities but now encompasses postsecondary institutions from across the spectrum. The purpose of Internet2 was to create new Internet infrastructure that was not overly burdened by commercial traffic and that tested and deployed hardware and software for new economy telecommunications corporations.

The network unites its participants around the electronic infrastructure and commercial purpose that play a part in building the new economy. Internet2 enables corporations and public and nonprofit entities to adopt the others' practices, enhancing potential profit/revenue streams and expanding markets. Corporations benefit from the network in that new infrastructure is constructed which may be privatized, allowing corporations to benefit from public- and nonprofit-sector resources. Colleges and universities benefit in that they build infrastructure that expands their telecommunications capacity, furthering research and educational service delivery goals that depend on that capacity. Colleges and universities are able to reduce the costs of Internet2 through corporate contributions. Corporations are able to deduct their contributions as either research tax credits or charitable donations, yet are often given contracts to construct components of Internet2. As colleges, universities, and corporations build Internet2, they create intellectual property in which they hold shares according to their agreements, and they profit from the marketing of knowledge economy products that are by-products of Internet2 construction. Colleges and universities serve as test beds for corporate information technology products, often receiving deep discounts. Corporations benefit from the knowledge generated by student use and faculty expertise.

The networks created by intermediating organizations such as Internet2 normalize corporate-university relations around commercial activity. They create new organizational fields across very different sectors (DiMaggio and Powell 1983), operating through fluid networks rather than stable fields. These new networks create common ground for actors to develop shared values and norms, and the organizations within the networks become more similar.

Interstitial and Intermediating Organizational Emergence

Many of the organizations affiliated with Internet2 have emerged from the interstices of public entities to connect them to for-profit entities, often through intermediating boundary-spanning organizations such as Internet2. For example, Media Center North Carolina (MCNC) was founded by the North Carolina General Assembly in 1980 to drive technology-based economic development by partnering with universities, business, and government (MCNC 2003). The public entity promotes economic development in North Carolina through three lines of business—research and development, venture funding, and grid computing and networking services. Many Internet2 affiliates are other boundary-spanning organizations located at state higher education systems level and devoted "to enhance[ing] the educational, social, and economic development of . . . citizens through effective and collaborative use of telecommunications and information technology," as the Indiana Higher Education Telecommunication System (IHETS) puts it (2003). Other affiliates with a similar mission are LaNet (Louisiana), NYSERnet (New York State), and the University of Florida System. In other words, Internet2 replicates itself through its affiliates, expanding the networks that experience commercialization as normative in higher education.

Intermediating and Interstitial Organizational Emergence: Trustees and Fund Raising

As faculty academic capitalist networks are distinct from but related to presidential networks, so presidential networks are related to but distinct from trustee networks. The trustee networks are another form of intermediating organization. Historically, trustees may not have been tightly networked. Currently, private-sector trustees at elite research universities directly connect those institutions to the new economy. Many of the corporations represented on private university boards of trustees are new economy corporations. Such boards are likely to make policies that enhance the directions in which they are expanding—for example, building biotechnology research facilities, approving partnerships with corporations in a variety of businesses generally related to the new economy, expanding Internet and telecommunications facilities, and approving litigation strategies that strengthen intellectual property. Their work may frame the forward planning in which presidents participate in their own intermediating organizations, such as Internet2.

Public university trustees, aware of private trustees' network and resource advantages, may engage more aggressively in commercial endeavor in an effort to compete successfully. Despite not participating directly in the private trustee network, public university trustees may embrace academic capitalism more closely in hopes of generating external revenues to keep the resource gap between private and public from further widening. Although we found that elite public research universities are not directly linked to new economy corporations through their boards, they are indirectly connected through other networks they share with private universities. Moreover, direct connections very likely can be found in interstitial fund-raising entities that have emerged and expanded within public universities since the mid-1980s. Public universities aggressively have taken on development activities, which are coordinated not only by central offices and foundations, separate on paper from the university but directly connected, but also through advisory boards of the academic colleges. These boards link colleges directly with the external world, particularly with large companies and potential donors. Although the records of the central offices and the college boards are difficult to access, there is good reason to believe that they have numerous connections with new economy corporations, particularly in the boards of professional schools such as agriculture, architecture, business, engineering, and medicine.

New Circuits of Knowledge

Presidents networked in intermediating organizations such as Internet2 create new circuits of knowledge, different from but aligned with those created by faculty, technology transfer officers, and corporate licensees or partners, or faculty, distance-education officers, and corporate licensees or partners. The presidents, in organizations like the Business-Higher Education Forum, EDUCAUSE, Internet2, and biotech consortia, create new circuits of knowledge when they engage in forward planning for research, deployment and testing of infrastructure, and developing products, processes, and services for the knowledge economy. In effect, these new circuits of knowledge lay the groundwork for orienting faculty research and teaching in commercial directions. They augment, expand, and enhance opportunities for faculty and staff to become academic capitalists.

New circuits are evident as well in the activities of trustees and development officers in their interstitial and intermediating organizations. At the central level, as well as at the level of colleges and departments, boards and donors open up new economy opportunities that encourage and channel faculty research and educational activity in directions seen as potentially generating new revenues. These new and expanding organizations create opportunity structures, realized through closer interaction with and direct engagement in the market.

Enhanced Managerial Capacity

The forward planning that takes place in intermediating organizations like Internet2 makes university presidents central actors in planning the economic future of the nation. Internet2 named its backbone Abilene and frequently compares the construction of the net to the building of the railroads. However, nineteenth- and early twentieth-century university presidents and their institutions were not involved in planning and financing the railroads. Rather, they were beneficiaries of railroad wealth, as was the case with Johns Hopkins and Stanford. In the late twentieth and early twenty-first centuries, university presidents have been involved in the design, financing, and deployment of new information superhighways, and have contributed to corporate profits by developing shared commercial products and financing infrastructure that corporations are likely to use in the future. The managerial capacity of twenty-first-century university presidents (and of their CIOs) has been greatly enhanced, in large part through the many opportunities for commercialization presented by the new economy.

In the case of fund-raising and development, we see an expanded managerial capacity that is comparable to the growth of personnel managing patents and copyrights. In the past twenty years, development offices have increased substantially in size and activity, and have emerged at the level of academic colleges, expanding the number of personnel there as well. Increasingly, these managerial professionals, focused on generating entrepreneurial revenues from closer connections to the private sector, have a role in and impact on the strategic direction and initiatives of private and public universities.

Markets in Students and Marketing to Students

Chapters 10 and 11 deal with college and university marketing to students and alumni as well as institutional competition for student markets. The theory of academic capitalism explores new levels of marketing and consumption within the institution by focusing on school logos as brands. It also moves beyond students as consumers to institutions as ever more sophisticated marketers, increasingly able to capture the student markets they target. Student markets are heavily state subsidized, whether through state block grants or state and federal student financial aid funds. Nonetheless, the greater the degree to which tuition dollars constitute a share of colleges and universities' annual operating budgets, the more aggressive institutions' marketing behaviors. Moreover, as the academic capitalist knowledge/learning regime intensifies, students, once recruited, are transformed into captive markets to which institutions market branded products as well as an array of other revenue-generating products and services.

New Circuits of Knowledge

Branding is a new economy marketing strategy that colleges and universities use to sell goods and services to matriculated students, who are captive audiences. Colleges and universities brand products and services with trademarked college and university logos, which they sell to students and alumni to increase external revenues. Like for-profit and nonprofit marketing activities, the stores and websites that sell logo-ed paraphernalia are virtually indistinguishable from their commercial counterparts.

When college and universities are constructed as new economy consumption goods rather than educational institutions, their circuits of knowledge increasingly intersect external, but connected, for-profit entities. For example, entities such as the Princeton Review sell books, live and on-line courses to prepare students for college, and tools for guidance counselors. They also sell on-line tools for "prospect management," a euphemism for students interested in specific colleges and universities. Other for-profit corporations, such as GDA Integrated Services, provide additional services, including admissions operations assessment and consulting, branding/positioning, financial and program assessments, and packing packaging/leveraging consulting, market research, and fund-raising communications (GDA Integrated Services 2003). Commercial college guides, such as *Peterson's,* and college-rating systems, such as *U.S. News and World Report,* are important in establishing institutions' consumption value. These new circuits of knowledge, based around marketing colleges and universities to students, bring postsecondary institutions closer to commercial entities marketing similar educational goods and services. Of course, colleges market themselves as consumption items, offering a range of consumption and leisure items to prospective students. Some of these services and amenities are provided through contracts with businesses, others are run by the colleges themselves.

However, college and universities have gone beyond marketing to students; they also market their students. Many regard their study bodies as negotiable, to be traded with corporations for external resources through all-sports, test-bed, single-product, and information market (names, addresses, telephone number) contracts. When students graduate, colleges and universities present them to employers as output/product, a contribution to the new economy, and simultaneously define students as alumni and potential donors. Student identities are flexible, defined and redefined by institutional market behaviors.

Interstitial and Intermediating Organizations

Trademarking groups have their own interstitial organizations that emerged in the 1980s, including the Association of Collegiate Licensing Administrators, which is more comprehensive than the older, less commercially oriented licensing groups. Their work is augmented by Royalty Management Associates, an organization led by a former Disney auditor, which provides compliance review services to licensors, including colleges and the Collegiate Licensing Group. Sometimes interstitial organizations and intermediating organizations overlap. In 1992, the Collegiate Licensing Company, which licenses logos for a number of universities, joined with professional sports leagues (MLB Properties, NBA Properties, NFL Properties, and NHL Properties) to form the Coalition to Advance the Protection of Sports Logos (CAPS). Since its establishment, CAPS has developed a network of private investigators and law enforcement officials that brings civil or criminal actions against trademark violators, protecting college and university commercial assets.

For-profit, nonprofit, and public organizations have emerged around postsecondary marketing opportunities. For example, the Independent Educational Consultants Association (IECA) is a national, private, fee-for-service organization of counselors who aid high school students applying to colleges and universities. In 1994, the National Academic Advising Association, the nonprofit counterpart of the IECA, emerged to share information about how to help prospective students choose colleges and universities. The University Marketing Professionals Association was established in 1999 and performs functions similar to associations organized by for-profit marketers. Xap, a for-profit corporation, provides on-line application services, intermediating among educational associations, colleges and universities, other companies, and the U.S. Department of Education. Xap enhances college and university marketing by making it easier for students to apply. Xap's functions do not differ greatly from those of the College Board, a nonprofit that also helps (for a fee) students apply to college and write on-line essays. The line that distinguishes among for-profit, nonprofit, and public entities shifts depending on the tax status and profit-distribution requirements of organizations rather than their functions.

Enhanced Managerial Capacity

The new circuits of knowledge, interstitial organizations, and intermediating organizations call for enhanced managerial capacity in colleges and universities. If institutions increase their enrollment management capacity, they hire staff, just as they do if they develop stores to sell products branded with trademarked logos. When colleges and universities develop facilities and services to recruit students to campus and sell products to them after they arrive, they hire new support professionals. Recreation centers and mini-malls require personnel. Even when business opportunities are outsourced—to Starbucks, McDonald's, or Barnes and Nobles—colleges and universities have to manage the licenses and external revenues. Enhanced managerial capacity creates a stratum of on-campus professionals who are committed to expanded commercial opportunities.

Fault Lines in the New Knowledge/Learning Regime

Several fault lines are evident in the academic capitalist knowledge/learning regime. These undercut its market logic and claims of increased efficiency. First, academic capitalism blurs the boundaries between public and private sectors, but it sustains a substantial level of public subsidy of higher education. Second, there is simultaneously a redefinition of public space in the academy, and a shifting of public monies to subsidize different activities, fields of work, and professionals. Third, in many cases, academic capitalism is not very successful in generating net revenues, and it leads to unanticipated, undesirable practices and outcomes. Fourth, in the context of a conception of institutional purpose that is reduced to revenue enhancement, the academic knowledge/learning regime leads to an expanded range of educational services geared toward a reduced range of traditional-aged students. Finally, as colleges and universities seek to enhance revenue by intersecting global information systems and markets, they reduce distinctive involvement in local communities.

The federal policy changes we reviewed in chapter 2 created new opportunities for public and nonprofit entities to engage in commercial activities. In redefining public space in ways that foreground and feature market activity and logic, these federal policies continue a pattern of substantial public subsidy in various forms. When the neoliberal state withdraws broad support for social services and promotes entrepreneurial activity, ironically, nonprofits proliferate. U.S. nonprofits tripled in the past three decades, growing from about 300,000 in 1970 to approximately one million in 1998. In 1975, their total revenues were less than 6 percent of the GNP, while in 1990 they exceeded 10 percent. Between 1980 and 1990, paid employment in nonprofits increased by 41 percent, more than double the growth of employment in other sectors.

Perhaps even more ironically, nonprofits are turning to commercial activity to expand their operations. The legislation enacted by the competitiveness coalition created commercial opportunities not just for colleges and universities but also for the majority of nonprofit organizations (Weisbrod 1998b). Commercial activity increased across nonprofits, from gift shops in museums to health clubs in hospitals. Many nonprofits are forming for-profit subsidiaries. Public and private colleges and universities have led the nonprofits that have engaged creatively in commercial activity.

As commercial activity expands in the not-for-profit sector, it may become an end in its own right. James (1998) suggests that there may come a point when nonprofits become "false nonprofits" or, as Weisbrod (1988) calls them, "for-profits in disguise." That certainly is a possibility in private, not-for-profit higher education as well as in some sectors of public higher education. Public colleges and universities have no interest in becoming for-profits, but many public research universities make the case that they should become "private" entities because appropriations from the states in some cases provide as little as 15 to 30 percent of institutional revenues. However, they do not want to pay taxes, whether on property, the proceeds for their intellectual property, or their commercial revenue from an array of marketing activities, all of which are currently not taxed so long as they are used for institutional rather than individual purposes. Nor do not-for-profit colleges and universities want to forego public subvention in the form of state and federal student financial aid and loan programs. In short, they want the best of both worlds—the protections and continued subsidies of the public sector, and the flexibility, opportunities, and potential revenue streams of the private sector.

Although colleges and universities usually present their commercial activity as win-win, building the economy, generating external revenues, and expanding educational capacity, the commercial activities of institutions can be problematic in several ways. First, higher education institutions are often not very successful capitalists, and students and the public have to pick up the tab for their failures. For example, while technology transfer brings external revenue to colleges and universities, it also takes funds from them. Colleges and universities or state systems have to pay for legal fees and for technology transfer offices. Nationally, legal fees are in the hundreds of millions of dollars. The magnitude of nonreimbursed legal fees has increased about 250 percent over the eleven years that AUTM has surveyed technology transfer activities. (These costs could be substantially higher, since AUTM modified its definition of legal fees in 1999, omitting major litigation to better focus on benchmarking patent prosecution costs.) A relatively small number of universities are responsible for the lion's share of patenting activity and run their technology transfer efforts in the black. In the 1990s, the one hundred largest universities received more than 90 percent of all patents awarded. Income from patents was also concentrated in the top one hundred institutions; the most recent survey indicates that two-thirds of the monies were generated by thirteen institutions. However, most doctoral granting institutions (RI, II, doctoral granting institutions I, II) maintained technology transfer offices, as did a few comprehensive universities. In other words, a number of universities bore the expense of technology transfer offices but reaped relatively few rewards. Similarly, many for-profit ventures in the realm of on-line and distance education have gone bankrupt.

Other undesirable outcomes can attach to the entrepreneurial activities of colleges and universities. For example, those who support patenting argue that it will contribute to economic growth beneficial to the citizenry as a whole. However, the overall pattern of the new economy, at least as configured in the United States, has resulted in greater income and wealth stratification within and outside the academy than was the case under the public good knowledge regime. Actors in patent networks often present commercialization as an activity that benefits taxpayers through new discoveries made through university-industry partnerships, which obscures the continued contributions made by federal tax revenues to pay for R&D. Similarly, the discourse in patent networks is about making up for lost state revenues, and glosses over the fact that patent income is often not used to offset education costs. Instead, most institutions dedicate patent income to generating more intellectual property. Despite an elaborated market discourse, the public sector continues to bear the lion's share of the costs of technology transfer.

As more students and professors engage in entrepreneurial research markets, more knowledge becomes "propertized," or owned. When information and knowledge are owned, they circulate less freely. Sometimes information is strategically incorporated into companies' growth strategies and removed from markets. In a perverse inversion of purpose, patents are used to keep information from the market. Granstrand (2000) makes the case that "if the rate of knowledge growth is consistently larger in the private domain than in the public domain, then at some point in time privately held knowledge will start to dominate" (p. 24). If private knowledge control dominates, then public science and technology as well as education become more difficult to maintain. The academic capitalist knowledge/learning regime may contribute to this process.

We are not making the case that universities should not patent. However, the academic community needs to debate the question of where to draw the line between public, non-profit, and for-profit activities, as well as who should draw the line. Also of concern is what sorts of products are promoted. Currently, colleges and universities do not have policies about how they select discoveries to patent or exploit commercially. Some are more likely to patent when a corporation will pay the cost. Others are likely to patent when the market for the product looks promising. Because social utility is not a criteria, colleges and universities are as likely to patent cosmetic properties, for example, Retin-A, as they are discoveries that might contribute broadly to the social welfare of the citizenry, for example, AIDS vaccines. Currently, college and universities follow a market rather than a social welfare logic. However, as nonprofit and public institutions, they might well increase their public support and legitimacy by commercializing in areas of great public utility and seeking less than the maximum profit the market will bear when selling products.

Commercializing copyrightable materials increases educational costs in terms of tuition and of educational materials. Institutions meet the cost of technology in part by raising tuition. Courseware packets, CDs, or other technology-enhanced educational materials are an added expense for students. Indeed, institutions sometimes generate revenues from selling students educational materials on which they hold the copyright.

Academic capitalism also restructures work in the academy, with some undesirable and unintended consequences. As in industry, colleges and universities have downsized and essentially outsourced their instructional production workers, replacing full-time with part-time and contingent faculty. The percentage of faculty who are part-time has doubled in the last twenty years despite research pointing to the significance of contact with faculty for student learning, satisfaction, and success. Part-time faculty are by definition and by working conditions (e.g., no office space) less available to their students than are full-timers.

In contrast to the pattern in industry, where the numbers of middle managers have declined, colleges and universities have greatly expanded middle management, whether to supervise commercial endeavor and engagement with various external communities or to support students and information technology. The managerial, nonfaculty professionals who manage infrastructure, economic development, endowment, and entrepreneurial activity are less directly focused than are faculty on teaching and research, and more closely linked to intermediating networks of senior administrators involved in promoting university-business cooperation and partnership, and new economy academic capitalism. Institutional expenditures for administration go up, while expenditures for instruction go down (see Figure 1.1).

In addition to restructuring professional work, the academic capitalist knowledge/learning regime brings restratification of and competition among academic fields. This can be a very healthy development, but it can also be problematic. Among the problems that stem from stratification and competition are a narrow conception of college or university education, a heightened and counterproductive sense of struggle between and within academic units, an orientation to short-term educational markets that prioritizes market share and revenue enhancement over educational quality, and internal resistance to some of the directions embedded in academic capitalism.

As institutions move more aggressively to intersect with new economy corporate and employment markets, conceptions of a college and university education are constrained by market opportunities. The idea of a college or university as a space for public discussion, debate, commentary, and critique is pushed to the background. Instead, colleges and universities focus increasingly on preparing students for new economy employment. Professional master's degrees are one example of this trend, as are the contract education and certification programs offered by community colleges.

From the standpoint of academic departments seeking to survive and thrive in an environment that promotes academic capitalism, there is an increasingly short-term perspective that focuses on productivity measures in research, grants, and student credit hour production. Academic units are conceptualized as cost centers seeking to maximize their productivity. That can lead them to compete with each other for students in some counterproductive ways (Rhoades 2000b). It can mean reducing standards for general education students or majors, or expanding student numbers beyond those that make sense for local labor markets. It also can inhibit patterns of collaboration and interdisciplinary activity, pitting departments within the same institution against each other in a cutthroat and cannibalistic competition for internal university resources.

Academic capitalism is sometimes met with confusion or resistance at the department level, as was evident in our analysis of department heads and faculty in science and engineering. Heads responded unevenly to the possibilities of entrepreneurial activity. In some cases, they seemed unsure what to do strategically or how their department could possibly fit within the current agenda of their institution. In some other cases, heads were resistant to the push from central academic managers for more entrepreneurial activity and engagement with business in the area of research. One of the fault lines within academic capitalism is that there are often disjunctures between where presidents, provosts, and other senior academic administrators want to take an institution, and the commitments and interests of significant numbers of faculty within the institution.

Nevertheless, presidents and senior administrators operating in intermediating institutions have greatly enhanced managerial capacity. They direct the forward planning of their institutions by committing resources to projects such as Internet2, shaping future directions for decades to come. However, members of the intermediating organizations often do not consult extensively with their internal institutional constituencies, which may undercut local support and willingness to participate in the projects. Members of intermediating organizations often redraw the boundaries of public, nonprofit, and for-profit entities. In cases such as Internet infrastructure (Internet2), distance education (Educause, the League for Innovation), and start-up corporations (boards of trustees), the functions of public, nonprofit, and for-profit entities are indistinguishable. Nonprofit institutions, whether public or private, seek to maximize profits on market activity, ranging from taking their start-up companies public through IPOs to marketing computers to students in bookstores. For-profit corporations become deeply involved in the business of education, using colleges and universities as test beds and developing and marketing educational products. Only their designation, and the costs and benefits that stem from it, are different. When public, nonprofit, and for-profit entities combine in intermediating networks, each seeks to attain as many of the benefits and as few of the costs attached to the others' status as possible. The greatest problem stemming from such intermediation is that public resources are transferred to private networks that underwrite the new economy. This transfer, which is not subject to broad public debate nor voted on, may undermine public trust in colleges and universities, manifesting itself in less public support for state and federal resource allocations to postsecondary education.

Densely networked boards of trustees who share information but whose institutions compete with each other may move colleges and universities from nonprofit to "disguised forprofits" (Weisbrod 1988). When we were writing the first draft of this book, the *Chronicle of Higher Education* featured an article on "the $500,000 club" for presidential salaries. More recently, the *Chronicle* documented million-dollar presidential compensation packages. Four presidents of private universities earned more than $800,000 in the 2002 fiscal year, and, if pay for serving on corporate boards is included, the compensation for three went over the million dollar mark (Basinger 2003a). James (1998) sees this as an indication of nonprofits becoming disguised for-profits: "nonprofits maximize profits and distribute them in disguised form (as higher wages and perks), or they may maximize revenues that lead to power and prestige for their managers" (p. 273). The trustees, who intermediate between universities and the corporate sector, normalize presidential salaries that far outstrip the salaries of most other U.S. professionals, making some university presidents salaries more like salaries in the for-profit sector than the nonprofit. Unlike heads of charitable nonprofits, no university presidents have gone to prison for violation of the charter of their organizations. However, Peter Diamondopoulos was removed as president of Adelphi University in the early 1990s for earning more than $500,000 (Weisbrod 1998b).

The compensation packages that put presidents in the $500,000 or $1 million club in the twenty-first century are justified by trustees on the basis of intense competition for leaders. However, these compensation packages raise the "disguised for-profit" issue and may be beginning to undermine public support for postsecondary education. In 2003, Florida legislators capped public university presidents' state salaries after a number received large pay raises. In Ohio, a bill is before the legislature that prohibits state university presidential salaries from exceeding that of the governor, whose salary is considerably lower than $500,000. At Louisiana State University faculty and students have protested what they see as excessive presidential compensation packages (Basinger and Henderson 2003). In July 2003, the Internal Revenue Service ruled that stock-option plans for presidents "violated a federal tax law that prohibited such types of deferred compensation for executives of tax-exempt institutions. Presidents will now need to restructure those accounts or face paying interest, penalties, and back taxes" (Basinger 2003b).

Marketization of student recruitment raises questions of access. When elite public and nonprofit colleges and universities compete for students who score well on standardized tests and are able to pay high tuition, low-income and minority students are less likely to attend. The heavy attendance of low-income and minority students at community colleges is in part a reflection of the marketing strategies of elite colleges and universities. Marketing of distance education to nontraditional students, even when such projects are arms of elite schools, contributes to bifurcated access patterns, in which increasing numbers of students are educated off-site. Competition for student markets does not reduce tuition; on the contrary, it may have increased tuition as institutions vie to offer students more noninstructional activities.

Alternatives within and beyond Academic Capitalism in the New Economy

The academic capitalist knowledge/learning regime is ascendant and, as we have argued, is embedded in a complex array and network of policies, intermediating and emergent interstitial organizations, and actors and practices. It is not inevitable, in its current configuration, and it does not stand alone. In this book we have mapped the general pattern that is in place. However, what academic capitalism in the new economy means concretely for the future direction and work of individual colleges and universities in the United States is yet to be fully defined.

Just as there are many forms of capitalism, so can there be many forms of academic capitalism. Academic capitalism does not have to take laissez-faire form. Rather than simply seeking to maximize external revenue generation, academic capitalism could seek to enhance the social benefits of intellectual property and educational services. Colleges and universities' commitment to revenue generation could also encompass commitments to increased access for underserved populations and expansion of opportunity for women and minorities.

For many universities, a current principal target of investment is biotechnology. However, all universities are unlikely to succeed in the biotech arena; competition is too intense. Instead, colleges and universities could try to discover distinctive niches that build on their research strengths or their geographic locations. These niches might well be targeted because they provide opportunities for social benefits. For example, there is enormous potential in the realm of environmental engineering, sustainable environment, and clean energy alternatives, which are all significant sectors of the new economy. In the case of our own university, there would be great promise in an initiative that focused on environmental issues and enhancing the quality of life in the borderlands. Such an initiative would involve investing not only in the sciences but also in various social sciences, humanities, and fields of education, integrating in interdisciplinary ways that creatively cut across the divide between science fields and the rest of the university. The promise of such an initiative would be to intersect successfully with growth areas in the new economy and to impact positively the region within which the university exists. Such a strategy would play not only to the geographic location of our university in the southern Arizona borderlands but also to our academic strengths in environmental sciences, arid land studies, borderland studies, anthropology, sociology, American Indian Studies, bilingual education, linguistics, and higher education, among others.

In addition to biotechnology, many higher education institutions are seeking to intersect with the information technology sector of the new economy. Community colleges and comprehensive and urban universities see this general realm as a target for substantial investment. In pursuing such a strategy, colleges and universities are intersecting with a global economy in ways that do not always pay dividends for local economies and regions. They prepare relatively privileged students for computer-related careers or generate revenues through distance education that serves audiences far from their geographic locations.

We see an alternative for such institutions. They could focus on local needs, attending to issues of immigration and integrating immigrant and low-income populations into the middle layers of the new economy. What does that mean concretely? It could mean a community college combining a computer-tech program with an ESL program targeting immigrant populations. It could mean a comprehensive university combining an information technology program with a teacher preparation program, training educators who would contribute to enhancing urban populations' ability to intersect with and work within the new economy. The point is to leaven the new economy focus on technology with the ongoing and emergent human challenges and opportunities that we confront in a globalizing world. We believe such an approach would yield substantial dividends for the higher education institutions as well as for the communities in which they are located.

Of course, these are not either/or choices. The issue in most colleges and universities is how to balance various alternatives. We are simply suggesting the foregrounding of possibilities that currently are very much in the background and that involve human sciences and services fields that are currently the target of disinvestment in many higher education institutions.

The educational mission of higher education could be reinvested in by judicious use of the proceeds from intellectual property. Alternatives to current patterns of faculty and institutional ownership of and claims to royalties from intellectual property could be explored. A share of revenues generated by intellectual property could be placed in a public trust that could have as its purpose directly aiding students and communities in a variety of ways, whether through scholarships, research internships, or direct grants toward community development.

Rather than focusing only on the revenue potential of intellectual property, colleges and universities could provide some discount for the sale of products developed by faculty, which, after all were publicly subsidized in their production. Faculty and university involvement in the production of goods and services could ensure that these goods be treated as generics, with less focus on maximizing revenues than on the wide distribution and availability of the products. The implications in the field of biomedical products would be enormous.

Each of the above alternatives requires a network of policies, organizations, and actors to become viable, as was the case with the academic capitalist knowledge/learning regime. We must imagine a new university with organizational structures, incentives, and rewards for the kind of society we want, and then create the new circuits of knowledge, interstitial organizations, and intermediating networks to achieve it. This is a task that will take time, patience, and commitment and will have to be linked to appropriate organizations and social movements outside the university. Perhaps we could begin by developing networks of citizens, faculty, academic managers, and students to formulate policies that frame the terms of engagement of colleges and universities with corporate partners, that create incentives for developing products that have socially productive purposes, and that work out ways for shares of revenues from intellectual property to be directed to undergraduate instruction.

REFERENCES

Abbate, J. 1999. *Inventing the Internet.* Cambridge: MIT Press.

Abbott, A. 1988. *The system of professions: An essay on the division of expert labor.* Chicago: University of Chicago Press.

Adelman, C. 1999. *The new college course map and transcript files: Changes in course-taking and achievement, 1972–1993.* 2d ed. National Institute on Postsecondary Education, Libraries, and Lifelong Learning, Office of Educational Research and Improvement. Washington, DC: U.S. Department of Education.

Alexander, F. K. 2001. The silent crisis: The relative fiscal capacity of public universities to compete for faculty. *Review of Higher Education* 242:113–29.

Allen, W. R., and J. O. Jewell. 2002. A backward glance forward: Past, present, and future perspectives on historically black colleges and universities. *Review of Higher Education* 253:241–61.

Althusser, L. 1971. Ideology and ideological state apparatuses: Notes towards an investigation. In *Lenin and philosophy,* trans. by B. Brewster. New York: Monthly Review Press.

American Association of University Professors (AAUP). 1999a. Special committee on distance education and intellectual property issues. www.aaup.org/Issues/DistanceEd/Archives/speccmt/deguide.htm (accessed December 5, 2003).

———. 1999b. Suggestions and guidelines for ownership of intellectual property. www.aaup.org/Issues/DistanceEd/Archives/speccmt/ipguide.htm (accessed December 5, 2003).

———. 1999c. Statement on copyright. www.aaup.org/statements/Redbook/Spccopyr.htm (accessed December 2003).

———. 2001. *Policy documents and reports.* 9th ed. Washington, DC: American Association of University Professors.

———. 2002. The annual report on the economic status of the profession 2001–02. www.aaup.org/surveys/02z/z02rep.htm (accessed February 27, 2003).

American Federation of Teachers (AFT). 2000a. AFT news from the national archives. http://aft.org/higher_ed/news_events/news.html (accessed February 25, 2003).

——— . 2000b. *Distance education: Guidelines for good practice.* Washington, DC: American Federation of Teachers.

———. 2001. *A virtual revolution: Trends in the expansion of distance education.* Washington, DC: American Federation of Teachers.

Anderson, M. 2001. The complex relations between the academy and industry: Views from the literature. *Journal of Higher Education* 722:226–46.

Apollo Group. 2002. *Annual Report.* Phoenix, AZ: Apollo Group.

Arizona Board of Regents on behalf of the Arizona State University and Adidas Promotional Retail Operations, Inc. 1999. Sponsorship agreement. Available from Arizona State University, Tempe.

Aronowitz, S., and W. DiFazio. 1994. *The jobless future: Sci-tech and the dogma of work.* Minneapolis: University of Minnesota Press.

Association of Pennsylvania State College and University Faculties. 2002. Collective bargaining agreement. Available through Higher Education Contract Analysis System, 2003. Washington, DC: National Education Association.

Association of University Technology Managers (AUTM). 1999. FY 2000 Annual AUTM Licensing Survey. www.autm.net/surveys/99/survey99A.pdf (accessed February 27, 2003).

———. 2003a. President's message by Patricia Harsche Weeks. www.autm.net (accessed November 20, 2003).

———. 2003b. Membership information brochure. www.autm.net (accessed November 20, 2003).

Avery, C., N. Fairbanks, and R. Zeckhauser. 2003. *The early admissions game: Joining the elite.* Cambridge: Harvard University Press.

Baez, B., and S. Slaughter. 2001. Academic freedom and federal courts in the 1990s: The legitimation of the conservative entrepreneurial state. In *Handbook of theory and research in higher education,* ed. J. Smart and W. Tierney. Bronx, NY: Agathon.

Bailey, S. 1975. *Educational interest groups in the nation's capital.* Washington, DC: American Council on Education.

Baker, L. 2003. Deer cloning aims to bring in bigger bucks. *Battalion,* February 18. www.thebatt.com/news/514727.html (accessed December 2, 2003).

Baker, T. L., and W. Velez. 1996. Access to and opportunity in postsecondary education in the United States: A review. *Sociology of Education* (extra issue): 82–101.

Ballinger, J. 1998. Nike in Indonesia. *Dissent* (Fall): 18–21.

Barley, S. 1986. Technology as an occasion for structuring: Evidence from observations of CT scanners and the social order of radiology departments. *Administrative Science Quarterly* 31:78–108.

———. 1996. Technicians in the workplace: Ethnographic evidence for bringing work into organization studies. *Administrative Science Quarterly* 413:404–41.

Barnet, R. J., and J. Cavanagh. 1994. *Global dreams: Imperial corporations and the new world order.* New York: Simon and Schuster.

Barringer, H. R., D. T. Takeuchi, and P. Xenos. 1990. Education, occupational prestige, and income of Asian-Americans. *Sociology of Education* 631:27–43.

Barrow, C. 1990. *Universities and the capitalist state: Corporate liberalism and the reconstruction of American higher education, 1894–1928.* Madison: University of Wisconsin Press.

Basic Books, Inc., Harper and Row Publishers, Inc., John Wiley & Sons, Inc., McGraw-Hill, Inc., Penguin Books USA, Inc., Prentice-Hall, Inc, Richard D. Irwin, Inc., and William Morrow & Co., Inc. v. Kinko's Graphics Corporation. 1991. No. 89 Civ. 2807CBM, United States District Court for the Southern District of New York, March 28.

Basinger, J. 2003a. Closing in on $1–million. *Chronicle of Higher Education* 50(12): S1.

———. 2003b. Soaring pay, big questions. *Chronicle of Higher Education* 50(12): A9.

Basinger, J., and S. H. Henderson. 2003. Hidden costs of high public pay. *Chronicle of Higher Education* 50(12): A3.

Bearby, S., and B. Siegal. 2002. From the stadium parking lot to the information superhighway: How to protect your trademarks from infringement. *Journal of College and University Law* 28:633–62.

Beck, H. P. 1947. *Men who control our universities: The economic and social composition of governing boards of thirty leading American universities.* New York: Kings Crown Press.

Becker, G. S. 1964. *Human capital: A theoretical and empirical analysis, with special reference to education.* National Bureau of Economic Research, General Series, no. 80. New York: Columbia University Press.

Bell, D. 1973. *The coming of post-industrial society: A venture in social forecasting.* New York: Basic.

Berdahl, R. 1971. *Statewide coordination of higher education.* Washington, DC: American Council on Education.

Berle, A. A., and G. C. Means. 1932. *The modern corporation and private property.* Reprint, New York: Harcourt, Brace & World, 1968.

Ben-David, J. 1984. *The scientist's role in society: A comparative study.* Chicago: University of Chicago Press.

Benjamin, E. 2002. How over-reliance on contingent appointments diminishes faculty involvement in student learning. *Peer Review* Fall 5(1): 4–10.

Bickerstaff, S. 1999. Shackles on the giant: How the federal government created Microsoft, personal computers, and the internet. *Texas Law Review* 78:1.

Bijker, W. 1995. *Of bicycles, bakelites, and bulbs: Toward a theory of sociotechnical change.* Cambridge: MIT Press.

Bijker, W., T. Pinch, and T. Hughes, eds. 1989. *The social construction of technological systems.* Cambridge: MIT Press.

Birnbaum, R. 2000. *Management fads in higher education: Where they come from, what they do, why they fail.* San Francisco: Jossey-Bass.

Bledstein, B. J. 1977. *The culture of professionalism: The middle class and the development of higher education in America.* New York: Norton.

Blumenthal, D., M. Gluck, K. S. Louis, M. Stoto, and D. Wise. 1986a. University-industry research relationships in biotechnology: Implications for the university. *Science* 232:1361–66.

Blumenthal, D., M. Gluck, K. S. Louis, and D. Wise. 1986b. Industrial support of university research in biotechnology. *Science* 231:242–46.

Board of Regents of the University of Wisconsin System & Reebok International Ltd. 1996. Agreement between Reebok International Ltd. and Board of Regents of the University of Wisconsin system on behalf of the University of Wisconsin–Madison and its Division of Intercollegiate Athletics. Available from the University of Wisconsin–Madison.

Bok, D. 2002. Are huge presidential salaries bad for colleges? [Editorial] *Chronicle of Higher Education,* November 22.

———. 2003. *Universities in the marketplace: The commercialization of higher education.* Princeton: Princeton University Press.

Bollier, D. 2002a. The enclosure of the academic commons. *Academe* 88(5): 19.

———. 2002b. *Silent theft: The private plunder of our common wealth.* New York: Routledge.

Borow, T. A. 1998. Copyright ownership of scholarly works created by university faculty and posted on school-provided web pages. *University of Miami Business Law Review* 7:149–90.

Bowen, H. R., and J. H. Schuster. 1986. *American professors: A national resource imperiled.* New York: Oxford University Press.

Bowie, N. E. 1994. *University-industry partnerships: An assessment.* Lanham, MD: Rowman and Littlefield.

Bowles S., and H. Gintis. 1976. *Schooling in capitalist America: Educational reform and the contradictions of economic life.* New York: Basic Books.

———. 2002. Schooling in capitalist America revisited. *Sociology of Education* 751:1–18.

Boyer, E. L. 1987. *College: The undergraduate experience in America.* New York: Harper and Row.

Branscomb, L., et al. 1997a. Technology politics to technology policy. *Issues in Science and Technology* 13 (Spring): 41–48.

———. 1997b. *Investing in innovation, toward a consensus strategy for federal technology policy.* Cambridge: Harvard University, Center for Science and International Affairs.

Brigham Young University. 2002. Intellectual property policy. www.ipsinfo.byu.edu /ippolicy.htm (accessed June 18, 2002).

Brint, S. 1994. *In the age of experts: The changing role of professionals in politics and public life.* Princeton: Princeton University Press.

Brint, S., and J. Karabel. 1989. *The diverted dream: Community colleges and the promise of educational opportunity in America, 1980–1985.* New York: Oxford University Press.

Brown, J. S., and P. Duguid. 2000. *The social life of information.* Cambridge: Harvard Business School Press.

Burris, B. H. 1993. *Technocracy at work.* Albany: SUNY Press.

Busch, L. 2000. *The eclipse of morality: Science, state and the market.* New York: Aldine De Gruyter.

Busch, L., S. Lacy, J. Burkhardt, and L. Lacy. 1991. *Plants, power, and profit: Social, economic, and ethical consequences of the new biotechnologies.* Cambridge: Basil Blackwell.

Bush, V. 1945. *Science—the endless frontier: A report to the president on a program for postwar scientific research.* Reprint, Washington, DC: National Science Foundation, 1990.

California State Colleges and Universities. 1998. Collective bargaining agreement. Available through Higher Education Contract Analysis System, 1997–98. Washington, DC: National Education Association.

Callon, M. 1986. The sociology of an actor-network: The case of the electric vehicle. In *Mapping the dynamics of science and technology,* ed. M. Callon, J. Law, and A. Rip. Basingstoke, UK: Macmillan.

Campbell, T. 1995. *Protecting the public's trust: A search for balance among benefits and conflicts in university-industry relationships.* PhD dissertation, University of Arizona.

———. 1997. Public policy for the 21st century: Addressing potential conflicts in university-industry collaboration. *Review of Higher Education* 204:357–79.

Campbell, T., and S. Slaughter. 1996. Steps toward resolving ambiguities in university-industry relationships. National Science Foundation grant SBR9529216.

———. 1999a. Faculty and administrators' attitudes toward potential conflicts of interest, commitment, and equity in university-industry relations. *Journal of Higher Education* 70(3): 309–32.

———. 1999b. Scientific misconduct and university-industry partnerships. In *Scientific misconduct,* ed. J. M. Braxton. Nashville: Vanderbilt University Press.

Carlson, S. 2003. After losing millions, Columbia U. will close on-line learning venture. *Chronicle of Higher Education,* January 17.

Carnegie Commission on Higher Education. 1971. *New students, new places.* New York: McGraw-Hill.

Carnoy, M. 1993. Multinationals in a changing world economy: Whither the nation state? In *The new global economy in the information age: Reflections on our changing world,* ed. M. Carnoy et al. University Park: Pennsylvania State University Press.

Carr, S. 2000. As distance education comes of age, the challenge is keeping the students. *Chronicle of Higher Education,* February 11.

Castells, M. 1993. The informational economy and the new international division of labor. In *The new global economy in the information age: Reflections on our changing world,* ed. M. Carnoy et al. University Park: Pennsylvania State University Press.

———. 1996. *The information age: Economy, society, and culture.* Vol. 1, *The rise of the network society.* Oxford: Blackwell.

———. 1997. *The information age: Economy, society, and culture.* Vol. 2, *The power of identity.* Oxford: Blackwell.

———. 1998. *The information age: Economy, society, and culture.* Vol. 3, *End of millennium.* Oxford: Blackwell.

———. 2000. *The information age: Economy, society, and culture.* Vol. 3, *End of millennium.* 2d ed. Malden, MA: Blackwell.

Chait, R. 1992. The growing hucksterism of college admission. *Chronicle of Higher Education,* May 20, B1–2.

Chait, R., T. Holland, and B. Taylor. 1991. *The effective board of trustees.* New York: MacMillan.

Chase, R. 1997. *The new unionism: A course for school quality.* Speech presented at the National Press Club, February 5, Washington, DC.

Chemeketa Community College. 2003. Collective bargaining agreement. Available through Higher Education Contract Analysis System, 2003. Washington, DC: National Education Association.

Chew, P. K. 1992. Faculty-generated invention: Who owns the golden egg? *Wisconsin Law Review* 259:38.

Chinoy, B., and T. Salo. 2002. *Internet exchanges: Policy driven evolution.* www.ksg.harvard.edu/iip/cai/chinsal.html (accessed March 1, 2003).

Chomsky, N. 1994. *World Orders Old and New.* New York: Columbia University Press.

Chronicle of Higher Education. 2002a. *The Chronicle Almanac 2002–3: California,* August 30.

———. 2002b. Advertisement for Blackboard, November 1, 13.

Chung, J. 1997. The Digital Performance Right in Sound Recordings Act and its failure to address the issue of digital music's new form of distribution. *Arizona Law Review* 39 (Winter): 1361–89.

City University of New York (CUNY). 1972. Copyright, policy no. 520. Available from City University of New York.

——— 1985. Intellectual property policy. www.portalsearch.cuny.edu/cms/id/documents (accessed spring 2002).

Clark, B. 1970. *The distinctive college: Reed, Antioch, and Swarthmore.* Chicago: Aldine.

———. 1983. *The higher education system: Academic organization in cross-national perspective.* Los Angeles: University of California Press.
———. 1987. *Academic life: Small worlds, different worlds.* Princeton: Carnegie Foundation for the Advancement of Teaching.
———. 1998. *Creating entrepreneurial universities: Organizational pathways of transformation.* Oxford: IAU Press and Pergamon.
Clark, J. 2003. Illegal art: Freedom of expression in the corporate age. *In These Times,* February 17, 37.
Clarke, A. E., and J. H. Fujimura. 1992. *The right tools for the job: At work in twentieth-century life sciences.* Princeton: Princeton University Press.
Cloud County Community College. 2001. Collective bargaining agreement. Available through Higher Education Contract Analysis System, 2003. Washington, DC: National Education Association.
Cockburn C., and S. Ormrod. 1993. *Gender and technology in the making.* London: Sage.
Cohen, S. 1993. Geo-economics: Lessons from America's mistakes. In *The new global economy in the information age: Reflections on our changing world,* ed. M. Carnoy et. al. University Park: Pennsylvania State University Press.
Cohen, W., R. Florida, and W. R. Coe. 1994. *University-industry research centers in the United States.* Pittsburgh: Carnegie Mellon University, Center for Economic Development.
College Board. 2001. Trends in student aid 2001. www.Collegeboard.com (accessed March 2002).
Collison, M. N.-K. 1989. In buyer's market, colleges turn to posh dorms and fast food to lure students. *Chronicle of Higher Education,* September 20.
Committee for Economic Development (CED). 1973. *The management and financing of colleges.* New York: CED.
Conrad, C., J. G. Haworth, and S. B. Millar. 1993. *A silent success: Master's education in the United States.* Baltimore: Johns Hopkins University Press.
Coombe, R. 1998. *The cultural life of intellectual properties: Authorship, appropriation and the law.* Durham: Duke University Press.
———. 1999. Sports trademarks and somatic politics: Locating the law in a critical cultural studies. In *SportCult,* ed. R. Martin and T. Miller. Minneapolis: University of Minnesota Press.
Coriat, B., and F. Orsi. 2002. Establishing a new intellectual property rights regime in the United States: Origins, content, and problems. *Research Policy* 31(8–9): 1491–1507.
Council on Competitiveness. 1996. *Endless frontier, limited resources: U.S. R&D policy for competitiveness.* Washington, DC: Council on Competitiveness.
Council on Governmental Relations (COGR). 1999. A tutorial on technology transfer in U.S. colleges and universities. www.cogr.edu/techtransfertutorial.htm (accessed fall 2002).
Covi, L. 1996. *Material mastery: How university researchers use digital libraries for scholarly communication.* PhD dissertation, University of California, Irvine.
Crenshaw, A. B. 2002. Price wars on campus: Colleges use discounts to draw best mix of top students, paying customers. *Washington Post,* October 5, A1.
Crew, K. D. 2002. New Copyright law for distance education: The meaning and importance of the TEACH Act. www.copyright.iupui.edu/dist_learning.htm (accessed March 1, 2003).

Croissant, J., and K. Ackerman. 1997. *To bean or not to bean: The ironic political economy of vanilla production.* Presented at the Annual Meeting of the Society for Social Studies of Science, Tucson, Arizona, October 14.

Croissant, J., and S. Restivo, eds. 2001. *Degrees of compromise: Industrial interests and academic values.* Albany: SUNY Press.

Croissant, J., G. Rhoades, and A. Hoplight Tapia, eds. Forthcoming. *Social dimensions of information technology.* Albany: SUNY Press.

Cumberland County College. 2003. Collective bargaining agreement. Available through Higher Education Contract Analysis System, 2003. Washington, DC: National Education Association.

Cummings, A. D. G. 1999. "Lions and tigers and bears, oh my," or "Redskins and braves and Indians, oh why?" Ruminations on *McBride v. Utah State Tax Commission,* political correctness and the reasonable person. *California Western Law Review* 36:11.

Currie, J., and J. Newsom, eds. 1998. *Universities and globalization: Critical perspectives.* London: Sage.

Daehn, V. 2000. Professors, regents, rise against selling lecture notes on-line. *Daily Nebraskan* (on-line edition), September 15.

Daniel, P. T. K., and P. D. Pauken. 1999. The impact of the electronic media on instructor creativity and institutional ownership within copyright law. *Education Law Reporter* 164:1–43.

Dasgupta, P., and P. David. 1987. Information disclosure and the economics of science and technology. In *Arrow and the ascent of modern economic theory,* ed. G. Feiwel. New York: New York University Press.

Davis, G. F. 1996. The significance of board interlocks for corporate governance. *Corporate Governance* 43:154–59.

Davis, G. F., M. Yoo, and W. E. Baker. 2003. The network topography of the American corporate elite, 1982–2001. *Strategic Organizations* 1:301–26.

Delucchi, M. 1997. "Liberal arts" colleges and the myth of uniqueness. *Journal of Higher Education* 684:414–26.

Demchak, C. C. 1995. Coping, copying and concentrating: Organizational learning and modernization in militaries. *Journal of Public Administration Research and Theory* 53:345–77.

———. 1996. Numbers or networks: Social construction of technology and organizational dilemmas in IDF modernization. *Armed Forces and Society* 232:179–209.

Diaz, V. 2004. *The digitization and control of intellectual property: Individual and institutional patterns of distributed learning behavior and policy response.* PhD dissertation, University of Arizona.

Dickson, D. 1984. *The new politics of science.* New York: Pantheon.

DiMaggio, P. J., and W. W. Powell. 1983. The iron cage revisited: Institutional isomorphism and collective rationality in organizational fields. *American Sociological Review* 48:147–60.

Dodge City Community College. 2000. Collective bargaining agreement. Available through Higher Education Contract Analysis System, 2003. Washington, DC: National Education Association.

Domhoff, G. W. 1967. *Who rules America?* Englewood Cliffs, NJ: Prentice-Hall.

———. 1990. *The power elite and the state: How policy is made in America.* New York: Aldine de Gruyter.

———. 1996. *State autonomy or class dominance: Case studies on policy making in America.* New York: Aldine de Gruyter.

———, ed. 1980. *Power structure research.* Beverly Hills: Sage.

Domhoff, G. W., and T. R. Dye. 1987. *Power elites and organizations.* Newbury Park, CA: Sage.

Dooris, M. J., and J. J. Fairweather. 1994. Structure and culture in faculty work: Implications for technology transfer. *Review of Higher Education* 121:161–77.

Dougherty, K. 1992. Community colleges and baccalaureate attainment. *Journal of Higher Education* 632:188–214.

———. 1994. *The contradictory college: The conflicting origins, impacts, and futures of the community college.* Albany: SUNY Press.

DuBoff, L. 1985. An academic's copyright: Publish and perish. *Journal of the Copyright Society of the U.S.A.* 32:17–38.

Duderstadt, J. 2000. *Intercollegiate athletics and the American university: A university president's perspective.* Ann Arbor: University of Michigan Press.

Duffy, E. A. 1998. *Crafting a class: College admissions and financial aid: 1955–1994.* Princeton: Princeton University Press.

Dugan, R. E., and J. F. Trump. 1999. Internet2: Separate and unequal. *Journal of Academic Libraries* 25(2): 127–31.

Dundar, H., and D. Lewis. 1995. Departmental productivity in American universities: Economies of scale and scope. *Economics of Education Review* 142:119–44.

Ehrenberg, R. G. 2000. *Tuition rising: Why college costs so much.* Cambridge: Harvard University Press.

———. 2003. Reaching for the brass ring: The *U.S. News & World Report* rankings and competition. *Review of Higher Education* 26(2): 145–62.

Ehrenberg, R. G., J. Cheslock, and J. Epifantseva. 2001. Paying our presidents: What do trustees value? *Review of Higher Education* 25(1): 15–38.

Ehrenberg, R. G., and D. S. Rothstein. 1994. Do historically black institutions of higher education confer unique advantages on black students: An initial analysis. In *Choices and consequences: Contemporary policy issues in education,* ed. R. G. Ehrenberg. Ithaca, NY: IRL Press.

Eisinger, P. K. 1988. *The rise of the entrepreneurial state: State and local economic development policy in the United States.* Madison: University of Wisconsin Press.

Elgin Community College. 2002. Collective bargaining agreement. Available through Higher Education Contract Analysis System, 2003. Washington, DC: National Education Association.

Enloe, C. 1995. The Globetrotting sneaker. *Ms.* 5(5): 10–15

Etzkowitz, H. 1994. Academic-industry relations: A sociological paradigm for economic development. In *Evolutionary economics and chaos theory: New directions in technology studies?* ed. L. Leydesdorff and P. Van den Besselaar. London: Pinter.

Etzkowitz, H., and M. Gulbrandsen. 1999. Public entrepreneur: The trajectory of United States science, technology and industrial policy. *Science and Public Policy* 26(1): 53–62.

Etzkowitz, H., and L. Leydesdorff. 1996. The triple helix: University-industry-government relations. A laboratory for knowledge-based economic development. Presented at the Triple Helix Conference, Amsterdam, January 6.

Etzkowitz, H., A. Webster, and P. Healey. 1998. *Capitalizing knowledge: New interactions of industry and academe.* Albany: SUNY Press.

Evans, F. 1991. To 'informate' or 'automate': The new information technologies and democratization in the workplace. *Social Theory and Practice* 17:409–39.

Evans, P. B., D. Rueschemeyer, and T. Skocpol, eds. 1985. *Bringing the state back in.* New York: Cambridge University Press.

Ewen, S. 1988. *The politics of style in contemporary culture.* New York: Basic Books.

———. 2001. *Captains of consciousness: Advertising and the social roots of the consumer culture.* New York: Basic Books.

Feldman, M., I. Feller, J. Bercovitz, and R. Burton. 2002a. Equity and the technology transfer strategies of American research universities. *Management Science* 48(1): 105–21.

Feldman, M., Feller, I., Ailes, C. P., & Roessner, J. D. 2002b. Impacts of research universities on technological innovation in industry: Evidence from engineering research centers. *Research Policy* 31(3): 457–75.

Feller, I. 1986. Universities as engines of economic development: They think they can. *Research Policy* 19:335–48.

———. 1997. Technology transfer from universities. In *Higher education: Handbook of theory and research,* ed. J. C. Smart. New York: Agathon.

Finkelstein, M. J., R. K. Seal, and J. H. Schuster. 1998. *The new academic generation: A profession in transformation.* Baltimore: Johns Hopkins University Press.

Fligstein, N. 1990. *The transformation of corporate control.* Cambridge: Harvard University Press.

Flores, C. 2002. U. of North Carolina at Chapel Hill drops early-decision admissions. *Chronicle of Higher Education,* May 3, A38.

Foreman, P. 1987. Behind quantum electronics: National security as a basis for physical research in the United States, 1940–1960. Part 1. *Historical Studies in the Physical and Biological Sciences* 18:149–229.

Forsythe, D. E. 1996. New bottles, old wine: Hidden cultural assumptions in a computerized explanation system for migraine sufferers. *Medical Anthropology Quarterly* 10(4): 551– 74.

Foster, A. L. 2001a. Government will seek dismissal of professor's challenge to Digital-Copyright Act. *Chronicle of Higher Education,* October 26, 38.

———. 2001b. 2 scholars face off in copyright clash. *Chronicle of Higher Education,* August 10, 45.

Foucault, M. 1977. *Discipline and punish: The birth of the prison.* Trans. A. Sheridan. New York: Vintage.

———. 1980. *Power/knowledge: Selected interviews & other writings 1972–1977.* Trans. and ed. C. Gordon. New York: Pantheon.

Francis, J. G., and M. C. Hampton. 1999. Resourceful responses: The adaptive research university and the drive to market. *Journal of Higher Education* 70(6): 625–41.

Frank, T. 1997. *The conquest of cool.* Chicago: University of Chicago Press.

Frischmann, B. 2001. Privatization and commercialization of the internet infrastructure: Rethinking market intervention into government and government intervention into market. *Columbia Science and Technology Law Review* 2 (June 8). www.stlr.org /cite.cgi?volume=2&article=/ (accessed December 2, 2003).

Fry, R. 2002. *Latinos in higher education: Many enroll, too few graduate.* Washington, DC: Pew Hispanic Center.

Furner, M. O. 1975. *Advocacy and objectivity: A crisis in the professionalization of American social science, 1865–1905.* Lexington: University of Kentucky Press.

Gatz, L. B., and J. B. Hirt. 2000. Academic and social integration in cyberspace: Students and e-mail. *Review of Higher Education* 23(3): 299–318.

GDA Integrated Services. 2003. Homepage. www.gdais.com (accessed November 2003).

Geiger, R. 1990. Organized research units: Their role in the development of university research. *Journal of Higher Education* 611(1): 1–19.

———. 1993. *Research and relevant knowledge: American universities since World War II.* New York: Oxford University Press.

———. 2002. The competition for high-ability students: Universities in a key marketplace. In *The future of the city of intellect: The changing American university,* ed. S. G. Brint. Stanford: Stanford University Press.

Genetic Savings and Clone. 2003. www.savingsandclone.com (accessed December 2, 2003).

George, J. F., and J. L. King. 1991. Examining the computing and centralization debate. *Communications of the ACM* 34(7): 63–71.

Gibbons, M., et al. 1994. *The new production of knowledge: The dynamics of science and research in contemporary societies.* London: Sage.

Gladieux, L. E., and T. R. Wolanin. 1976. *Congress and the colleges: The national politics of higher education.* Lexington, MA: Lexington Books.

Glen Oaks Community College. 1997. Collective bargaining agreement. Available through Higher Education Contract Analysis System, 1997–98. Washington, DC: National Education Association.

Golden, D. 2001a. Glass floor colleges reject top applicants, accepting only the students likely to enroll. *Wall Street Journal,* May 29, A1.

———. 2001b. Some schools shun top grads; It's done to boost their "yield rates" weeding out those least likely to enroll. *Chicago Sun Times,* October 29, 5.

———. 2002. Foreign students' high tuition spurs eager junior colleges to fudge facts. *International Higher Education* 29 (Fall): 7–8; reprinted from the *Wall Street Journal,* April 2, B1.

Goldman, R., and S. Papson. 1996. *Sign wars: The cluttered landscape of advertising.* New York: Guilford Press.

Goldschmidt, N. P., and J. H. Finkelstein. 2001. Academics on board: University presidents as corporate directors. *Academe: Bulletin of the American Association of University Professors* (September-October): 33–37.

Gose, B. 1998. Yeshiva U. criticized for letting American Express pay for mailing about tuition. *Chronicle of Higher Education,* May 20, A44.

Government-University-Industry Research Roundtable. 1992. *Fateful choices: The future of the U.S. academic research enterprise.* Washington, DC: National Academy Press.

Graham, H. D., and N. A. Diamond. 1997. *The rise of American research universities: Elites and challengers in the postwar era.* Baltimore: Johns Hopkins University Press.

Gramsci, A. 1971. *Selections from the prison notebooks.* Trans. and ed. Q. Hoare and G. Nowell-Smith. New York: International Publishers.

Granstrand, O. 2000. The shift towards intellectual capitalism: The role of infocom technologies. *Research Policy* 29(9): 1061–80.

Gray, M. J., A. W. Astin, and F. Ayala. 1987. *College student outcomes assessment: A talent development perspective.* ASHE-ERIC Higher Education Report, no. 7. College Station, TX: Association for the Study of Higher Education.

Green, K. C. 1995. Paying the digital piper. *Change* 27(2): 53–54.

Greenberg, D. 1967. *The politics of pure science.* New York: New American Library.

———. 2001. *Science, money and politics: Political triumph and ethical erosion.* Chicago: University of Chicago Press.

Greenstein, S. 2000. The evolving structure of commercial internet markets. In *Understanding the digital economy,* ed. E. Brynjolfsson and B. Kahin. Cambridge: MIT Press.

Greider, W. 1997. *One world, ready or not: The manic logic of global capitalism.* New York: Simon & Schuster.

Griswold, C. P., and G. M. Marine. 1996. Political influences on state policy: Higher tuition, higher aid, and the real world. *Review of Higher Education* 19(4): 361–90.

Gumport, P. 1993. The contested terrain of academic program reduction. *Journal of Higher Education* 64(3): 283–311.

Gumport, P., and B. Pusser. 1995. A case of bureaucratic accretion: Context and consequences. *Journal of Higher Education* 66(5): 493–520.

Guston, D. H., and K. Kenniston. 1994. *The fragile contract: University science and the federal government.* Cambridge: MIT Press.

Hackett, E. J., J. Croissant, and B. Schneider. 1992. Industry, academe, and the values of undergraduate engineers. *Research in Higher Education* 33(3): 275–95.

Hannah, S. B. 1996. The Higher Education Act of 1992: Skills, constraints and the politics of higher education. *Journal of Higher Education* 67(5): 498–527.

Haraway, D. 1990. *Primate visions: Gender, race and nature in the world of modern science.* New York: Routledge.

———. 1996. *Modest-witness@second-millennium. FemaleMan-meets-oncomouse: Feminism and technoscience.* New York: Routledge.

Harrison, B., and B. Bluestone. 1990. *The great U-turn: Corporate restructuring and the polarizing of America.* New York: Basic.

Haskell, T. L. 1977. *The emergence of professional social science: The American Social Science Association and the nineteenth century crisis of authority.* Urbana: University of Illinois Press.

Haunschild, P. R. 1993. Interorganizational imitation: The impact of interlocks on corporate acquisition activity. *Administrative Science Quarterly* 38:564–92.

Haunschild, P. R., and C. M. Beckman. 1998. When do interlocks matter? Alternate sources of information and interlock influence. *Administrative Science Quarterly* 43(3): 815–44.

Hearn, J. C. 1991. Academic and nonacademic influences on the college destinations of 1980 high school graduates. *Sociology of Education* 64(3): 158–71.

———. 1998. The growing loan orientation in federal financial-aid policy: A historical perspective. In *Condemning Students to Debt: College Loans and Public Policy,* ed. R. Fossey and M. Bateman. New York: Teachers College Press. Reprinted in *The ASHE Reader on Finance in Higher Education,* ed. J. L Yeager, G. M. Nelson, E. A. Potter, J. C. Weidman, and T. G. Zullo. Boston: Pearson Custom Publishing, 2001.

Hebel, S. 2002. A new look for CUNY: Tough admissions policies have drawn good students, but turned some immigrants away. *Chronicle of Higher Education,* March 1, A20–21.

Heckscher, C. C. 1988. *The new unionism: Employee involvement in the changing corporation.* New York: Basic Books.

Heeger, G. A. 2001. President's testimony to the Maryland general assembly, February 8–9, 2001. www.umuc.edu/president/testimony/2001/testimony.html (accessed March 1, 2003).

Heller, D. E. 2000. *The states and public higher education policy: Affordability, access and accountability.* Baltimore: Johns Hopkins University Press.

Heller, M. A., and R. S. Eisenberg. 1998. Can patents deter innovation? The anticommons in biomedical research. *Science* 280(5364): 698–701.

Henke, A. 2000. ASUI considers reinstating lecture notes service. *UI Argonaut,* September 8. www.argonaut.uidaho.edu (accessed March 1, 2003).

Herken, G. 1992. *Cardinal choices: Presidential science advising from the atomic bomb to SDI.* New York: Oxford University Press.

Hill, B., M. Green, and P. Eckel. 2001. *What governing boards need to know and do about institutional change.* Project on Leadership and Institutional Transformation. Washington, DC: American Council on Education.

Holbrook, D. 1999. UC sues to oust note firm. *Contra Costa Times,* June 15, A1.

———. 2000. Note-taker services gets boot at UC. *West County Times,* February 25, A6.

Hoover, E. 2002. Instant gratification: On-site admissions programs let applicants know immediately whether they have been accepted. *Chronicle of Higher Education,* April 12, A39.

Hopkins, D. S. P. 1990. The higher education production function: Theoretical foundations and empirical findings. In *The economics of American universities,* ed. S. A. Hoenack and E. K. Collins. Albany: SUNY Press.

Hoxby, C. 1997. How the changing market structure of U.S. higher education explains college tuition. Working Paper 6323. Cambridge, MA: National Bureau of Economic Research.

Hundt, R. E. 2000. *You say you want a revolution: A story of information age politics.* New Haven: Yale University Press.

Indiana Higher Education Telecommunications System (IHETS). 2003. About us. www.ihets.org (accessed October).

Institute of International Education (IIE). 2002. *Open doors 2002.* New York: Institute of International Education.

In re Cronyn. 1989. 890 F.2d 1158 U.S. Court of Appeals for the Federal Circuit.

Internet2. 2002a. Intellectual property FAQs. www.internet2.edu/members/html/intellectualproperty-faq.html (accessed fall 2002).

Internet2. 2002b. The Internet commons white paper. www.internet2.edu/html/working-groups.html (accessed fall 2002).

Internet2. 2002c. Pilot intellectual property framework. www.internet2.edu/members/html/intellectualproperty-methods.html (accessed fall 2002).

Internet2. 2002d. Abilene project FAQs. www.internet2.edu/abilene/html/faq-general.html (accessed March 1, 2003).

Internet2. 2002e. Intellectual property framework. http://members.internet2.edu/intellectualproperty.html (accessed March 1, 2003).

Internet2. 2002f. The Internet2 commons. http://commons.internet2.edu (accessed March 1, 2003).

Isserman, A. M. 1994. State economic development policy and practice in the United States: A survey article. *International Regional Science Review* 16(1, 2): 49–100.

Jackson Community College. 2003. Collective bargaining agreement. Available through Higher Education Contract Analysis System, 2003. Washington, DC: National Education Association.

Jacobs, J. A. 1995. Gender and academic specialties: Trends among recipients of college degrees in the 1980s. *Sociology of Education* 68:42–53.

Jaffe, A. B. 2000. The U.S. patent system in transition: Policy innovation and the innovation process. *Research Policy* 29(4, 5): 5331–57.

James, E. 1998. Commercialism among nonprofits: Objectives, opportunities and constraints. In *To profit or not to profit: The commercial transformation of the nonprofit sector,* ed. B. A. Weisbrod. Cambridge: Cambridge University Press.

Jencks, C., and D. Riesman. 1968. *The academic revolution.* New York: Doubleday.

Jessop, B. 1993. Towards a Schumpeterian workfare state? Preliminary remarks on post-Fordist political economy. *Studies in Political Economy* 40 (Spring): 7–39.

J. Moore v. The Regents of the University of California. 1990. 51 Cal. 3d. 120.

Johns Hopkins University v. Cellpro, Inc. 1998. 152 F.3d 1342 U.S. Court of Appeals for the Federal Circuit.

Johns, R. 2000. Interview: Charlene Teters on Native American symbols as mascots. *Thought and Action: The NEA Higher Education Journal* (Summer): 121–30.

Johnson County Community College. 2003. Collective bargaining agreement. Available through Higher Education Contract Analysis System, 2003. Washington, DC: National Education Association.

Johnson, D. 1999. Conflicts of interest and industry-funded research: Chasing norms for professional practice. In *Degrees of compromise: Industrial interests and academic values,* ed. J. Croissant and S. Restivo. Albany: SUNY Press.

Kahn, R. E. 1995. *Revolution in the U.S. information infrastructure.* Washington, DC: National Academy Press.

Kane, T. J. 1999. *The price of admission: Rethinking how Americans pay for college.* Washington, DC: Brookings Institution Press.

Kane, T. J., and C. E. Rouse. 1999. The community college: Educating students at the margin between college and work. *Journal of Economic Perspectives* 13(1): 63–84.

Karabel, J., and A. Astin. 1975. Social class, ability and college "quality." *Social Forces* 53:381– 98.

Karen, D. 2002. Changes in access to higher education in the United States: 1980–1992. *Sociology of Education* 75(3): 191–210.

Keller, G. 1983. *Academic strategy: The management revolution in American higher education.* Baltimore: Johns Hopkins University Press.

Kenney, M. 1986. *Biotechnology: The university-industry complex.* New Haven: Yale University Press.

Kepner-Tregoe, Inc. v. Victor Vroom. 1999. No. 98–7258, 1 86 F.3d 283. August 9. U.S. Court of Appeals for the Second Circuit.

Kerr, C., and M. Gade. 1989. *The guardians: Boards of trustees of American colleges and universities.* Washington, DC: Association of Governing Boards.

Kevles, D. J. 1978. *The physicists.* New York: Knopf.

Kevles, D. J., and L. E. Hood. 1992. *The code of codes: Science and social issues in the human genome project.* Cambridge: Harvard University Press.

Kezar, A., and P. Eckel. 2002. The effect of institutional culture on change strategies in higher education: Universal principles or culturally responsive concepts? *Journal of Higher Education* 73(4): 435–60.

Kimberling, C. R. 1995. Federal student aid: A history and critical analysis. In *The academy in crisis: The political economy of higher education*, ed. J. W. Sommer. New Brunswick: Transaction.

King, L. 1975. *The Washington lobbyists for higher education*. Lexington, MA: Lexington Books.

King, R. C. 1998. *Colonial discourses, collective memories and the exhibition of native American cultures and histories in the contemporary United States*. New York: Garland.

King, R. C., and C. F. Springwood. 2001. *Beyond the cheers: Race as spectacle in college sport*. Albany: SUNY Press.

Kingston, P. W., and L. S. Lewis. 1990. *The high status track: Studies of elite schools and stratification*. Albany: SUNY Press.

Kistner, A. 2000. Web site maneuvering to post lecture notes. *Kansas State eCollegian*, February 22. www.kstatecollegian.com (accessed February 28, 2003).

Klein, N. 2002. *No logo*. New York: Picador.

Kleinman, D. L. 1995. *Politics on the endless frontier: Postwar research policy in the United States*. Durham: Duke University Press.

———. 1998. Untangling context: Understanding a university laboratory in the commercial world. *Science, Technology, & Human Values* 23:3.

Knight, R. D. 1987. Science, space and scholarship: University research and the strategic defense initiative. *Educational Policy* 1(4): 499–512.

Knorr-Cetina, K. D. 1981. *The manufacture of knowledge*. Oxford: Pergamon.

Knowledge Universe 2003. About KU. www.knowledgeu.com/about.html (accessed July 17, 2003).

Kohlberg, L. 1981. *Essays in moral development*. San Francisco: Harper.

Kolko, G. 1963. *The triumph of conservatism: A reinterpretation of American history, 1900–1916*. New York: Free Press of Glencoe.

Korzeniewicz, M., and G. Gereffi. 1994. *Commodity chains and global capitalism*. Westport, CT: Greenwood.

Kraatz, M., and E. Zajac. 1996. Exploring the limits of the new institutionalism: The causes and consequences of illegitimate organizational change. *American Sociological Review* 61(5): 812–36.

Kraut, R., J. Galegher, and C. Egido, eds. 1990. *Intellectual teamwork*. Hillsdale, NJ: Lawrence Erlbaum.

Krieger, Lisa M. 2001. Missyplicity: Pet-cloning effort begins at home. *Extension Foundation: Daily News*. www.lef.org/newsarchive/aging/2001/07/01 (accessed spring 2003).

Krimsky, S. 2003. *Science in the private interest*. Lanham, MD: Rowman and Littlefield.

Kuttner, R. 1997. *Everything for sale: The virtues and limits of markets*. New York: Alfred A. Knopf.

Kyng, M. 1991. Design for cooperation: Cooperating in design. *Communications of the ACM* 34:64–73.

Lape, L. 1992. Ownership of copyrightable works of university professors: The interplay between the copyright act and university copyright policies. *Villanova Law Review* 37:223–71.

Larsen, K., and S. Vincent-Lacrin. 2002. International trade in educational services: Good or bad? *Higher Education Management and Policy* 14(3): 9–46.

Larson, M. S. 1977. *The rise of professionalism: A sociological analysis.* Berkeley: University of California Press.

Latour, B. 1987. *Science in action: How to follow scientists and engineers through society.* Milton Keynes, UK: Open University Press.

Latour B., and S. Woolgar. 1979. *Laboratory life: The social construction of scientific facts.* Beverly Hills: Sage.

Lattinville, R. 1996. Logo Cops: The law and business of collegiate licensing. *The Kansas Journal of Law and Public Policy* 5(3): 81–124.

Lavin, D. E. 1996. *Changing the odds: Open admissions and the life changes of the disadvantaged.* New Haven: Yale University Press.

Law, J., and M. Callon. 1992. The life and death of an aircraft: A network analysis of technological change. In *Shaping technology, building society,* ed. W. Bijker and J. Law. Cambridge: MIT Press.

Leadbeater, C. 1999. *Living on thin air: The new economy.* London: Viking.

Legal Information Institute. 2003. *The Bayh-Dole Act.* Title 35, part II, chap. 18, sec. 200. www4.law.cornell.edu/uscode/35/200.html (accessed November 2003).

Lerman, S., and S. Miyagawa. 2002. OpenCourseWare: A case study in institutional decision-making. *Academe* 88(5): 23–27.

Leslie, D., and E. K. Fretwell. 1996. *Wise moves in hard times: Creating and managing resilient colleges and universities.* San Francisco: Jossey-Bass.

Leslie, L., and P. Brinkman. 1988. *The economic value of higher education.* New York: ACE/Macmillan.

Leslie, L., and G. Johnson. 1974. The market model and higher education. *Journal of Higher Education* 45:1–20.

Leslie, L., R. Oaxaca, and G. Rhoades. 1996. The effects of research related activities on undergraduate education in public research universities. NSF grant SBR9628325.

Leslie, L., and G. Rhoades. 1995. Rising administrative costs: Seeking explanations. *Journal of Higher Education* 66(2): 187–212.

Leslie, L., G. Rhoades, and R. Oaxaca. 1999. Effects of changing revenue patterns on public research universities. Report to the National Science Foundation, grant SBR9628325.

Leslie, S. 1993. *The cold war and American science: The military-industrial-academic complex at MIT and Stanford.* New York: Columbia University Press.

Lessig, L. 1999. *Code and other laws of cyberspace.* New York: Basic Books.

Levin, J. 2001. *Globalizing the community college: Strategies for change in the twenty-first century.* New York: Palgrave.

Lewis, L., E. Farris, K. Snow, and D. Levin. 1999. *Distance education at postsecondary education institutions: 1997–98.* Washington, DC: National Center for Education Statistics.

Louis, K. S., D. Blumenthal, M. Gluck, and M. Soto. 1989. Entrepreneurs in academe: An exploration of behaviors among life scientists. *Administrative Science Quarterly* 34:110– 31.

Low, Michael. 2002. Personal communication to Samantha King. March.

Luker, M., ed. 2000. *Educause leadership strategies.* Vol. 1, *Preparing your campus for a networked future,* 29–40. San Francisco: Jossey Bass.

Lund, K. In progress. *Multiple case study of re-design and restructuring of studio arts schools and departments in the research university environment.* PhD dissertation, University of Arizona.

Lyotard, J. 1984. *The postmodern condition: A report on knowledge.* Trans. G. Bennington and B. Massumi. Minneapolis: University of Minnesota Press.

Lynch, R., J. C. Palmer, and W. N. Grubb. 1991. *Community college involvement in contract training and other economic development activities.* Berkeley, CA: National Center for Research in Vocational Education.

Madsen, H. 1997. *Composition of governing boards of public colleges and universities.* Occasional paper, no. 37. Washington, DC: Association of Governing Boards of Universities and Colleges.

Mann, Michael. 1986. *The sources of social power.* Cambridge: Cambridge University Press.

Marchese, T. 1998. Not-so-distant competitors: How new providers are remaking the postsecondary marketplace. *AAHE Bulletin,* May/June.

Marginson, S., and M. Considine. 2000. *The enterprise university: Power, governance, and reinvention in Australia.* Cambridge: Cambridge University Press.

Marginson, S., and G. Rhoades. 2002. Beyond national states, markets, and systems of higher education: A glonacal agency heuristic. *Higher Education* 43(3): 281–309.

Markusen, A., and J. Yudken. 1992. *Dismantling the cold war economy.* New York: Basic Books.

Maskus, K. E. 2000. *Intellectual property rights in the global economy.* Washington, DC: Institute for International Economics.

McBride v. Motor Vehicle Division of Utah State Tax Commission. 1999. 977. P.2d, 473. Supreme Court of Utah.

McCarthy, Cameron. 1993. After the canon: Knowledge and ideological representation in the multicultural discourse on curriculum reform. In *Race, identity and representations in education,* ed. C. McCarthy and W. Crichlow. New York: Routledge.

McCarthy, Charles. 1912. *The Wisconsin Idea.* Madison: University of Wisconsin Press.

McDonough, P. M. 1997. *Choosing colleges: How social class and schools structure opportunity.* Albany: SUNY Press.

McPherson, M. S., and M. O. Schapiro. 1998. *The student aid game: Meeting need and rewarding talent in American higher education.* Princeton: Princeton University Press.

McSherry, C. 2001. *Who owns academic work? Battling for control of intellectual property.* Cambridge: Harvard University Press.

Media Center North Carolina (MCNC). 2003. Homepage. www.mcnc.org (accessed November 2003).

Melman, S. 1982. *Profits without production.* New York: Knopf.

Merton, R.K. 1942. The normative structure of science. *The sociology of science: Theoretical and empirical investigations.* Reprint, Chicago: University of Chicago Press, 1973.

Metcalfe, A. 2004. *Intermediating associations and the university-industry relationships.* PhD dissertation, University of Arizona.

Metcalfe, A., V. Diaz, and R. Wagoner. 2003. Academe, technology, society, and the market: Four frames of reference for copyright and fair use. *Portal: Libraries and the academy* 3 (2): 191–206.

Middlesex County College. 2003. Collective bargaining agreement. Available through

Higher Education Contract Analysis System, 2003. Washington, DC: National Education Association.

Mills, C. W. 1956. *The power elite.* New York: Oxford University Press.

Minnesota State Colleges and Universities. 1997. Collective bargaining agreement. Available through Higher Education Contract Analysis System, 1997–98. Washington, DC: National Education Association.

Mintzberg, H. 1994. *The rise and fall of strategic planning: Reconceiving roles for planning, plans, planners.* New York: Free Press.

Mizruchi, M. S. 1989. Similarity of political behavior among large American corporations. *American Journal of Sociology* 95:401–24.

———. 1990. Determinants of political opposition among large American corporations. *Social Forces* 68:1065–88.

———. 1996. What do interlocks do? An analysis, critique, and assessment of research on interlocking directorates. *Annual Review of Sociology* 22:271–98.

Monks, J., and R. G. Ehrenberg. 1999. *U.S. News & World Report* rankings: Why they do matter? *Change* 31(6): 43–51.

Monro, Neil. 2002. The new patent puzzle. *The National Journal,* March 2. www.nr.c.org/Killing_Embryos/patentpuzzle030202.html (accessed spring 2003).

Moore v. The Regents of the University of California. 1988. 215 Cal. App. 3d. 709.

Mortenson, T. 1995. Educational attainment by family income, 1970 to 1994. *Postsecondary Education OPPORTUNITY* 41:1–8.

———. 1997. Educational attainment of young adults 1940 to 1955. *Postsecondary Education OPPORTUNITY* 56:1–5.

Moses, H., III, and J. B. Martin. 2001. Academic relationships with industry: A new model of biomedical research. *Journal of the American Medical Association* 285:933.

Mowery, D. C., and A. A. Ziedonis. 2002. Academic patent quality and quantity before and after the Bayh-Dole act in the United States. *Research Policy* 31:399–418.

Mukerji, C. 1989. *A fragile power: Scientists and the state.* Princeton: Princeton University Press.

Mulcahy, D. 1999. (Actor-net) working bodies and representations: Tales from a training field. *Science, Technology, and Human Values* 24(1): 80–104.

Mulkay, M. 1979. *Science and the sociology of knowledge.* London: George Allen and Unwin.

National Association of College Admission Counseling (NACAC). 1998. *Guidelines for the recruitment, admission and support of international students.* Alexandria, VA: NACAC.

———. 2001. *Changes to the statement of principles of good practice and the admission decision options document.* Alexandria, VA: NACAC.

———. 2002. NACAC surveys provide insight into the state of college admission, 2002. *NACAC Bulletin* 40(10): 1, 5, 7.

National Center for Education Statistics (NCES). 2000a. *1999–2000 national postsecondary student aid study.* Washington, DC: U.S. Department of Education, NCES.

———. 2000b. *Distance education at postsecondary education institutions, 1997–1998.* Washington, DC: U.S. Department of Education, NCES.

———. 2001. *Digest of educational statistics, 2001.* Washington, DC: U.S. Department of Education.

National Center for Public Policy and Higher Education (NCPPHE). 2003. College affordability in jeopardy: A special supplement to National Crosstalk. *National Crosstalk* 11(1): 1A–12A.

National Coordination Office for Information Technology Research and Development. 2002. Interagency working group on IT R&D. www.hpcc/.wg/program.html (accessed November 2003).

National Education Association (NEA). 2000a. Campus support for technology. *NEA Higher Education Research Center Update* 6(1): 1–4.

———. 2000b. Distance education at postsecondary education institutions: 1997–98. *NEA Higher Education Research Center Update* 6(2): 1–5.

———. 2003. NEA policy statements. 13. Distance education. www.nea.org/he/policy13.html (accessed December 2003).

National Academy of Sciences, National Research Council. 1995. *Allocating federal funds for science and technology.* Washington, DC: National Academy Press.

National Research Development Corporation v. Varian Associates. 1994. 17 F.3d 1444. U.S. Court of Appeals for the Federal Circuit.

National Science Board (NSB). 2002. *Science and engineering indicators: 2002.* Arlington, VA: National Science Foundation.

National Science Foundation (NSF). 1989. *Industrial participation in NSF programs and activities.* Washington, DC: U.S. Government Printing Office.

———. 2003. Academic research and development expenditures: Fiscal year 2003. Arlington, VA: National Science Foundation.

National Science Foundation and the United States Department of Commerce. 1999. *U.S. Corporate R&D.* Vol. 1, *Top 500 firms in R&D by industry category.* By C. Shepherd and S. Payson. NSF 00–301. Arlington, VA: National Science Foundation/Division of Science Resources Studies.

National Science Foundation, Division of Science Resources Studies. 1999. *U.S. Corporate R&D.* Vol. 2, *Company information on top 500 firms in R&D.* By C. Shepherd and S. Payson. NSF 00–302. Arlington, VA: National Science Foundation.

Nelsen, B., and S. Barley. 1997. For love or money?: Commodification and the construction of an occupational mandate. *Administrative Science Quarterly* 42:619–53.

New York University (NYU). 1988. Policy on computer software copyrights. Available from New York University.

Next Generation Internet Initiative. 1998. Legislation: Next generation internet research act of 1998. Summary. www.ngi.gov/testimony/pl_h_105–305.html (accessed March 1, 2003).

Nimmer, M. 1985. *Cases and materials on copyright and other aspects of entertainment litigation illustrated including unfair competition, defamation, privacy.* St. Paul, MN: West Publishing Company.

Noble, D. F. 1976. *America by design: Science, technology and the rise of corporate capitalism.* New York: Knopf.

———. 1998a. Digital diploma mills: The automation of higher education. *First Monday* 3(1). www.firstmonday.dk/issues/issue3_1/noble/index.html (accessed March 2, 2003).

———. 1998b. Digital diploma mills, Part 2: The coming battle over online instruction. www.communication.ucsd.edu/dl/ddm2.html (accessed March 2, 2003).

———. 1998c. Digital diploma mills, Part 3. The bloom is off the rose. www.vpaa.uillinois.edu/reports_retreats/tid/resources/noble.html (accessed March 2, 2003).

———. 2001. *Digital diploma mills: The automation of higher education.* New York: Monthly Review Press.

Oakton Community College. 2002. Collective bargaining agreement. Available through Higher Education Contract Analysis System, 2003. Washington, DC: National Education Association.

O'Banion, T. 1997. *A learning college for the twenty-first century.* Phoenix, AZ: Oryx Press.

O'Connor, J. 1973. *The fiscal crisis of the state.* New York: St. Martin's Press.

Office of the Vice President for Research, University of Michigan. 1996. Remarks of Charles Vest. *The future of government/university partnership: Proceedings of the 1996 Jerome B. Wiesner symposium.* Ann Arbor: University of Michigan.

Olsen, F. 2002. MIT's open window. *Chronicle of Higher Education,* December 6.

Orgera, J. 2003. Academic capitalism in academic support services: A valued educational resource or another consumable product? Working paper. Center for the Study of Higher Education, University of Arizona, Tuscon.

Ousley, M. D. 2003. *Coffee pots and clocks: Cultural challenges to organizational change in higher education.* PhD dissertation, University of Arizona.

Packard, A. 2002. Copyright or copy wrong: An analysis of university claims to faculty work. *Communication Law and Policy* 7:275–315.

Palmer, D. A., P. D. Jennings, and X. Zhou. 1993. Late adoption of the multidivisional form by large U.S. corporations: Institutional, political and economic accounts. *Administrative Science Quarterly* 38:100–131.

Paulson, K. 2002. Reconfiguring faculty roles for virtual settings. *Journal of Higher Education* 73(1): 123–40.

Peret, A. 2003. The anticybersquatting consumer protection act. www.mbf-law.com/pubs/articles/366.cfm (accessed March 1, 2003).

Perkin, H. J. 1989. *The rise of professional society in England since 1880.* London: Routledge.

Peterson, I. 1985. Bits of ownership. *Science News* 128:188–90.

Phipps, R., and J. Merisotis. 1999. *What's the difference? A review of contemporary research on the effectiveness of distance learning in higher education.* Washington, DC: Institute for Higher Education Policy.

Polse, J. 2001. COMMENT: Holding the sovereign's universities accountable for patent infringement after Florida Prepaid and College Saving Bank. *California Law Review* (March): 507–42.

Powell, W. W. 1990. Neither market nor hierarchy: Network forms of organization. In *Research in organizational behavior, 12,* ed. B. M. Staw and L. L. Cummings. Greenwich, CT: JAI Press.

Powell, W. W., K. Koput, and L. Smith-Doerr. 1996. Interorganizational collaboration and the locus of innovation: Networks of learning in biotechnology. *Administrative Science Quarterly* 41(1): 116–45.

Priest, D. M., W. E. Becker, D. Hossler, and E. St. John, eds. 2002. *Incentive-based budgeting systems in public universities.* Northampton, MA: Edward Elgar.

Pusser, B. 2000. The role of the state in the provision of higher education in the United States. *Australian Universities Review* 13(1): 24–35.

———. 2004. *Burning down the house: Politics, governance and affirmative action at the University of California.* Albany: SUNY Press.

Pusser, B., S. Slaughter, and S. L. Thomas. 2002. Playing the board game: An empirical analysis of university trustee and corporate board interlocks. Paper presented at Association for the Study of Higher Education, November 21, Sacramento.

Regents of the University of Michigan and Nike USA, Inc. 2001. *University of Michigan multi-sport agreement.* Available from the University of Michigan.

Reich, R. B. 1991. *The work of nations: Preparing ourselves for twenty-first century capitalism.* New York: Knopf.

Revoyr, J. 1998. Non-definitive history of collegiate licensing. *Trademark Reporter* (July–August): 370–98.

Rhoades, G. 1995. Rising, stratified administrative costs: Student services' place. In *Budgeting as a tool for policy in student affairs,* ed. D. B. Woodard Jr. New Directions for Student Affairs, no. 70. San Francisco: Jossey-Bass.

———. 1996. Reorganizing the faculty workforce for flexibility: Part-time, professional labor. *Journal of Higher Education* 67(6): 624–59.

———. 1998a. *Managed professionals: Unionized faculty and restructuring academic labor.* Albany: SUNY Press.

———. 1998b. Reviewing and rethinking administrative costs. In *Higher education: Handbook of theory and research,* ed. J. Smart. New York: Agathon.

———. 1998c. *Entrepreneurialism in U.S. public research universities: Strategic incentives and departmental responses.* Paper presented at the European Association for Institutional Research meetings, September, San Sebastian, Spain.

———. 1999. Technology and the changing campus workforce. *Thought & Action* 15(1): 127–38.

———. 2000a. New unionism and over-managed professors. *Thought & Action* 16(1): 83–98.

———. 2000b. Who's doing it right?: Strategic activity in public research universities. *Review of Higher Education* 24(1): 41–66.

———. 2001. Managing productivity in an academic institution: Rethinking the whom, which, what, and whose of productivity. *Research in Higher Education* 42(5): 619–32.

———. 2002a. Whose property is it? *Academe* 87(5): 38–43.

———. 2002b. National implications of local union activity. *Thought & Action* 18(1, 2): 103–14.

Rhoades, G., and C. Maitland. 2000. Innovative approaches to bargaining. *The NEA 2000 Almanac of Higher Education.* Washington, DC: National Education Association.

Rhoades, G., and R. Rhoads. 2003. The public discourse of U.S. graduate employee unions: Social movement identities, ideologies, and strategies. *Review of Higher Education* 262:163–86.

Rhoades, G., and S. Slaughter. 1991a. Professors, administrators, and patents: The negotiation of technology transfer. *Sociology of Education* 64(2): 65–77.

———. 1991b. The public interest and professional labor: Research universities. In *Culture and ideology in higher education: Advancing a critical agenda,* ed. W. Tierney. New York: Praeger.

———. 1997. Academic capitalism, managed professionals and supply-side higher education. *Social Text* 51(2): 9–38.

Rhoades, G., and B. Sporn. 2002. New models of management and shifting modes and costs of production: Europe and the United States. *Tertiary Education and Management,* August 1, 3–28.

Rice University. 1999. Patent and software policies. www.ruf.rice.edu/~presiden/Policies/Research/333–99.html (accessed 13 March, 2002).

Riesman, D. 1958. *Constraint and variety in American education.* Garden City, NY: Doubleday Anchor.

Ritzer, G. 1998. *The McDonaldization thesis: Explorations and extensions.* Thousand Oaks, CA: Sage.

———. 2001. *Explorations in the sociology of consumption: Fast food, credit cards, and casinos.* Thousand Oaks, CA: Sage.

Robinson, J. G., and J. S. McIlwee. 1992. *Women in engineering: Gender, power, and workplace culture.* Albany: SUNY Press.

Rogers, E. M. 1995. *Diffusion of innovations.* New York: Free Press.

Ross, A., ed. 1997. *No sweat: Fashion, free-trade, and the rights of garment workers.* London: Verso.

Ross, D. 1991. *The origins of American social science.* Cambridge: Cambridge University Press.

Root, D. 1996. *Cannibal culture: Art, appropriation, and the commodification of difference.* Boulder, CO: Westview.

Roth, A. E., and X. Xiaolin. 1994. Jumping the gun: Imperfections and institutions relating to the timing of market transactions. *American Economic Review* 84:992–1044.

Rothschild, M., and L. J. White. 1995. The analytics of the pricing of higher education and other services in which the customers are inputs. *Journal of Political Economy* 103(3): 573–86.

Rybarczyk, T. 2002. Tuition hike won't affect all equally. *Daily Illini.* www.dailyillini.com/jan31/news/stories/news_story02.html (accessed fall 2002).

San Diego State university. 1999. Copyright, trademarks, and trade secrets policy. http://gra.sdsu.edu/dra/Intell_Property_5–9–00_Final.htm (accessed June 7, 2002).

Sassen, S. 1991. *The global city: New York, London, Tokyo.* Princeton: Princeton University Press.

Sauve, P. 2002. Trade, education, and the GATS: What's in, what's out, what's all the fuss about? *Higher Education Management and Policy* 14(3): 47–76.

Savan, L. 1994. *The sponsored life: Ads, TV, and American culture.* Philadelphia: Temple University Press.

Schiller, D. 1998. *Digital capitalism.* Cambridge: MIT Press.

Schiller, H. 1989. *Culture, Inc.: The corporate takeover of public expression.* New York: Oxford University Press.

———. 1992. The context of our work. *Societe Francaise des Sciences de l'Information et de la Communication,* 1–6. Huitieme Congres National, Lille, May 21.

Schmidt, P. 2002. States push public universities to commercialize research. *Chronicle of Higher Education,* March 29, A26–27.

Schuster, J. H., D. G. Smith, K. A. Corak, and M. M. Yamada. 1994. *Strategic governance: How to make big decisions better.* American Council on Education. Phoenix, AZ: Oryx Press.

Scott, P., ed. 2000. *Higher education re-formed.* London: Falmer Press.

Selingo, J. 2002. Mission creep?: More regional state colleges start honors programs to raise their profiles and draw better students. *Chronicle of Higher Education,* May 31, A19.

Senge, P. M. 1990. *The fifth discipline: The art and practice of the learning organization.* New York: Doubleday.

Shaw, K. M., and H. London. 2001. Culture and ideology in keeping transfer commitment: Three community colleges. *Review of Higher Education* 25(1): 91–114.

Shulman, J., and W. Bowen. 2001. *The game of life: College sports and educational values.* Princeton: Princeton University Press.

Silva, E. T., and S. Slaughter. 1984. *Serving power: The making of the social science expert.* Westport, CT: Greenwood Press.

Simon, B. 1996. *Beefing up the backstage: Information communication and computers.* With Chandra Mukerji. Presented at the Annual Meeting of the American Sociological Association, August 5, New York.

Simon, T. 1983. Faculty writings: Are they "works made for hire" under the 1976 copyright act? *Journal of College and University Law* 9:485–513.

Sinclair, U. 1923. *The goosestep, a study of American education.* Pasadena, CA: Published by the author.

Slater, J. 1999. Sneak attack: Exploring the effects of Nike and Reebok sponsorship on two college athletic programs. http://oak.cats.ohiou.edu/~slaterj/sneak.htm (accessed March 6, 2003).

Slaughter, S. (McVey). 1975. Social control of social research: The development of the social scientist as expert, 1875–1916. PhD dissertation, University of Wisconsin, Madison.

———. 1981. Political action, faculty autonomy and retrenchment: A decade of academic freedom, 1970–1980. In *Higher Education in American Society,* ed. Philip G. Altbach and Robert O. Berdahl, 73–100. Buffalo: Prometheus Books.

———. 1988. Academic freedom in the modern university. In *Higher Education in American Society,* ed. Philip G. Altbach and Robert O. Berdahl, 77–105. Revised edition, revised essay. Buffalo: Prometheus Books.

———. 1990. *Higher learning and high technology: Dynamics of higher education policy formation.* Albany: SUNY Press.

———. 1993. Beyond basic science: Research university presidents' narratives of science policy. *Science, Technology, and Human Values* 18(3): 278–302.

———. 1997. Class, race, gender and the construction of post-secondary curricula in the United States: Social movement, professionalization and political economic theories of curricular change. *Journal of Curriculum Studies* 29(1): 1–30.

Slaughter, S., and C. Archerd. Forthcoming. Boundaries and quandaries: Professors negotiate the market. *Review of Higher Education.*

Slaughter, S., T. Campbell, P. Holleman, and E. Morgan. 2002. The traffic in students: Graduate students as tokens of exchange between industry and academe. *Science, Technology and Human Values* 27(2): 282–313.

Slaughter, S., and L. Leslie. 1997. *Academic capitalism: Politics, policies and the entrepreneurial university.* Baltimore: Johns Hopkins University Press.

Slaughter, S., and G. Rhoades. 1990. Renorming the social relations of academic science: Technology transfer. *Educational Policy* 4(4): 341–61.

———. 1993. Changes in intellectual property statutes and policies at a public university: Revising the terms of professional labor. *Higher Education* 26:287–312.
———. 1996. The emergence of a competitiveness research and development policy coalition and the commercialization of academic science and technology. *Science, Technology and Human Values* 21(3): 303–39.
———. Forthcoming. From endless frontier to basic science for use: Social contracts between science and society. *Science, Technology, and Human Values.*
Smith, D. N. 1974. *Who rules the universities.* New York: Monthly Review Press.
Smith, V. 2003. The post-baccalaureate online teacher preparation program: A case study of academic capitalism. Unpublished paper. Center for the Study of Higher Education, University of Arizona, Tucson.
Soley, L. 1995. *Leasing the ivory tower: The corporate takeover of academia.* Boston: South End Press.
Southeast Missouri State University. 1983. Patent and copyright policy. Available from Southeast Missouri State University.
Sperber, M. 1990. *College sports Inc. The athletic department vs the university.* New York: Henry Holt.
———. 2001. *Beer and circus: How big-time college sports is crippling undergraduate education.* New York: Henry Holt.
Sperling, J., and R. W. Tucker. 1997. *For-profit higher education: Developing a world-class workforce.* New Brunswick: Transaction Publishers.
Sproull, L., and S. Kiesler. 1991. *Connections: New ways of working in the networked organization.* Cambridge: MIT Press.
Stahler, G., and W. Tash. 1994. Centers and institutes in the research university: Issues, problems, and prospects. *Journal of Higher Education* 65(5): 540–54.
Stanford University. 1996. Research policy handbook. Document 2.6. Openness in research. www.stanford.edu/dept/DoR/rph/2–6/html (accessed November 2003).
———. 1998. Copyright policy. Available from Stanford University.
———. 1999. Research policy handbook. Document 5.1. Inventions, patenting, and licensing. www.stanford.edu/dept/DoR/rph/5–1/html (accessed November 2003).
Star, S. L. 1995 *The cultures of computing.* Cambridge: Blackwell.
State of California. 1974. *The State of California Political Reform Act of 1974.*
State University of New York (SUNY). 1998. Computer software policy. Available from State University of New York.
State University System of Florida. 1988. Collective bargaining agreement. Available from the United Faculty of Florida.
Stiglitz, J., et al. 2000. The role of government in a digital age. http://globalchange.gov/policies/role-gov.html (accessed March 1, 2003).
Stokes, D. 1997. *Pasteur's quadrant: Basic science and technological innovation.* Washington, DC: Brookings Institution Press.
Strom, D. 2002. *Intellectual property issues for higher education unions: A primer.* Washington, DC: American Federation of Teachers.
Swenson, C. 1998. Customers and markets: The cuss words of academe. *Change* 30(5): 34–39.
Texas A&M University and Nike USA, Inc. 1997. *Texas A&M University multi-sport agreement.* Available from Texas A&M University.

Thelin, J. R. 1994. *Games colleges play: Scandal and reform in intercollegiate athletics.* Baltimore: Johns Hopkins University Press.

Thelin, J. R., and L. L. Wiseman. 1989. *The old college try: Balancing academics and athletics in higher education.* Washington, DC: George Washington University, School of Education and Human Development.

Thomas, R. J. 1994. *What machines can't do: Politics and technology in the industrial enterprise.* Berkeley: University of California Press.

Thomas, S., B. Pusser, and S. Slaughter, S. Forthcoming. An empirical analysis of trustee interlocks and organizational learning in public and private research universities.

Tierney, W. G., ed. 1998. *The responsive university: Restructuring for high performance.* Baltimore: Johns Hopkins University Press.

———. 1999. *Building the responsive campus: Creating high performance colleges and universities.* Thousand Oaks, CA: Sage.

Tinto, V. 1993. *Leaving college: Rethinking the causes and cures of student attrition.* Chicago: University of Chicago Press.

Toffler, A. 1970. *Future Shock.* New York: Random House.

Touraine, A. 1974. *The post-industrial society: Tomorrow's social history: Classes, conflicts and culture in the programmed society.* London: Wildwood House.

Triton College. 2000. Collective bargaining agreement. Available through Higher Education Contract Analysis System, 2003. Washington, DC: National Education Association.

Trow, M. 1973. *Problems in the transition from elite to mass education.* Berkeley: Carnegie Commission on Higher Education.

———. 1984. The analysis of status. In *Perspectives on higher education: Eight disciplinary and disciplinary views,* ed. B. Clark. Berkeley: University of California Press.

Troy, L. 1994. *The new unionism in the new society: Public sector unions in the redistributive state.* Fairfax, VA: George Mason University Press.

Twigg, C. 1999. *Improving learning and reducing costs: Redesigning large enrollment courses.* Troy, NY: Pew Learning and Technology Program.

Twitchell, J. 1996. *Adcult USA: The triumph of advertising in American culture.* New York: Columbia University Press.

2003 UA football signees. 2003. *Arizona Daily Star,* February 6, D1.

Ukman, L. 1997. Assertions. *IEG Sponsorship Report* 22:2.

UNext 2003. About UNext: Academic consortium. www.unext.com/company_overview/academiccons.htm (accessed July 17, 2003).

University of California. 1985. University of California patent policy. www.ucop.edu/ott/patentpolicy/patentp1.html (accessed March 1, 2003).

———. 1989. University guidelines on university-industry relations. www.ucop.edu/raohome/cgmemos/89–20.html (accessed March 1, 2003).

———. 1990a. Revision of the University of California patent policy. Available from the University of California.

———. 1990b. University policy on integrity in research. www.ucop.edu/raohome/cgmemos/90–01S1.html (accessed March 1, 2003).

———. 1992. University of California policy on copyright ownership. www.ucop.edu/ucophome/uwnews/copyr.html (accessed March 1, 2003).

———. 1996. Policy on accepting equity when licensing university technology. www.ucop.edu/ott/equi-pol.html (accessed March 1, 2003).

———. 1997a. University of California patent policy. www.ucop.edu/ott/patentpolicy/patentpo.html#pol (accessed March 1, 2003).

———. 1997b. Summary of changes to the patent policy. Available from the University of California.

———. 2002a. Business and finance bulletin G-44 on accepting equity. http://patron.ucop.edu/ottmemos/docs/ott02–01.html (accessed March 1, 2003).

———. 2002b. Policy on ownership of course materials. Available from University of California.

University of Florida v. KPB, Inc. 1996. No. 94–2157. July. United States Court of Appeals for the Eleventh Circuit.

University of Florida. 1993a. Intellectual Property Policy. Available from University of Florida.

———. 1993b. University of Florida patent policy. Available from the University of Florida.

University of Illinois News. 2001. The Cheil controversy. http://www.news.uiuc.edu/ii/01/0419chief.html (accessed fall 2002).

University of Kentucky and Nike USA, Inc. 2001. University of Kentucky all sport product supply agreement. Available from the University of Kentucky.

University of Maryland University College (UMUC). 2003a. The UMUC News Page: UMUC awarded tri-services education contract for Europe. www.umuc.edu/events/press/news143.html (accessed 2003).

———. 2003b. About us. www.umuc.edu/gen/about.html (accessed February 28, 2003).

University of Miami. 1976. Patent and copyright policy. Available from University of Miami.

University of Missouri–Columbia. 1984. Copyright regulations. Available from University of Missouri–Columbia.

———. 2002. Copyright Regulations. Available from University of Missouri–Columbia.

University of North Texas. 2000. Distributed learning. www.unt.edu/legalaffairs/distributed_learning.html (accessed March 4, 2002).

University of South Florida. 1997. Statement of policy and procedures for inventions and works. Available from University of South Florida.

University of Texas at Austin. 2002. Original handbook of operating procedures. www.utexas.edu/policies/hoppm/h0511.html (accessed March 1, 2003).

University of Texas System. 1985. The University of Texas System history of board of regents' rules and regulations and other policies on intellectual property rules, 1985–present. www.utsystem.edu/OGC/Intellectualproperty/contract/IPhistory.htm (accessed March 1, 2003).

———. 1987. The University of Texas System history of board of regents' rules and regulations and other policies on intellectual property rules, 1985–present. www.utsystem.edu/OGC/Intellectualproperty/contract/IPhist-RR1.htm (accessed March 1, 2003).

———. 1992. The University of Texas System history of board of regents' rules and regulations and other policies on intellectual property rules, 1985–present. www.utsystem.edu/ogc/intellectualproperty/contract/iphist-rr7.htm (accessed March 1, 2003).

———. 1998. Management and marketing of copyrighted works. www.utsystem.edu/bor/regentalpolicies/copyrightedworks.htm (accessed March 1, 2003).

———. 2002a. Copyright crash course. The Teach Act finally becomes law. www.utsystem.edu/ogc/IntellectualProperty/teachact.htm (accessed March 1, 2003).

———. 2002b. Regents' rules and regulations. Part two, chapter XII, intellectual property. www.utsystem.edu/OGC/Intellectualproperty/contract/IPhist-RR16.htm (accessed March 1, 2003).

University of Utah. 1970. Patent, inventions and copyrights policy. www.admin.utah.edu/ppmanual.html (accessed March 2001).

———. 1984. Patent, inventions, and copyright policy. www.admin.utah.edu/ppmanual.html (accessed March 2001).

———. 1999a. Patents and inventions, policy #6-4. www.admin.utah.edu/ppmanual/6/6-4.html (accessed March 1, 2003).

———. 1999b. Remunerative consultation and other employment activities. www.admin.utah.edu/ppmanual/2/2–26Rev8 (accessed March 2002).

———. 1999c. University faculty profit-making corporations. www.admin.utah.edu/ppmanual/6/6–3.html (accessed March 2002).

———. 2001. Ownership of copyrightable works and related works. Available from University of Utah.

———. Research handbook. www.osp.utah.edu/Handbook/6–1.html (accessed May 2003).

UNIX System Laboratories, Inc. v. Berkeley Software Design, Inc., the Regents of the University of California. 1993. Civ. No. 92–1667, U.S. District Court for the District of New Jersey.

U.S. Congress, Office of Technology Assessment. 1991. *Biotechnology in a global economy.* BA-494. Washington, DC: U.S. Government Printing Office.

U.S. Copyright Office. 1998. The Digital Millenium Copyright Act of 1998. www.loc.gov/copyright/ (accessed November 2003).

U.S. Department of Defense (DOD). 1994. *Report of the Defense Science Board on antitrust aspects of defense industry consolidation.* Washington, DC: Office of the Undersecretary of Defense for Acquisition and Technology.

U.S. Department of Education. National Center for Educational Statistics. 1998a. *Distance education instruction by postsecondary faculty and staff,* by E. M. Bradburn. Project officer: L. Zimbler. NCES 2002–155. Washington, DC.

———. 1998b. *First-generation: Undergraduates whose parents never enrolled in postsecondary education,* by A. Nunez and S. Cuccaro-Alamin. Project officer: C. D. Carroll. NCES 98–082. Washington, DC.

———. 1999. *Distance education at postsecondary institutions: 1997–98,* by L. Lewis, K. Snow, E. Farris, and D. Levin. Project officer: B. Greene. NCES 2000–013. Washington, DC.

———. 2003. *Distance education at degree granting postsecondary institutions: 2000–2001.* NCES 2003–017. www/nces.gov/ (Web release July 18).

U.S. Department of Education. 1999. *The condition of education.* Washington, DC: U.S. Government Printing Office.

Useem, M. 1979. The social organization of the American business elite and participation of corporate directors in the governance of American institutions. *American Sociology Review* 44: 553–72.

———. 1984. *The inner circle.* New York: Oxford University Press.

Utah State University. 2002. University creative works. http://personnel.usu.edu/policies/327.htm (accessed June 18, 2002).

Vallas, S. 1993. *Power in the workplace: The politics of production at AT&T.* Albany: SUNY Press.

Van Houweling, D. 1998. Building the Internet's future: Internet2, UCAID and NGI *Educom Review* (May/June). www.educause.edu/pub/er/review/reviewArticles/33316.html (accessed December 2, 2003).

———. 2000. Inventing the advanced Internet. In *Preparing your campus for a networked future,* ed. M. A. Luker. Vol. 1 of *Educause leadership strategies.* San Francisco: Jossey Bass.

Varma, R., and R. Worthington. 1995. Immiseration of industrial scientists in corporate laboratories in the United States. *Minerva* 33(4): 325–38.

Veblen, T. 1918. *The higher learning in America: A memorandum on the conduct of universities by business men.* New York: Viking.

Veysey, L. 1965. *The emergence of the American university.* Chicago: University of Chicago Press.

Vice President for Academic Affairs, University of Illinois. 1999. Teaching at an Internet distance: The pedagogy of online teaching and learning. www.vpaa.uillinois.edu/reports_retreats/tid.asp (accessed March 2, 2003).

Volk, C., S. Slaughter, and S. L. Thomas. 2001. Models of institutional resource allocation: Mission, market and gender. *Journal of Higher Education* 72(4): 387–413.

Vonortas, N. S. 2000. Technology policy in the United States and the European Union: Shifting orientation towards technology users. *Science and Public Policy* 27(2): 97–108.

Wade, J., C. O'Reilly, and I. Chandratat. 1990. Golden parachutes: CEOs and the exercise of social influence. *Administrative Science Quarterly* 35: 587–603.

Washington University in St. Louis. 1998a. Intellectual property policy. www.wustl.edu/policies/intelprop.html (accessed February 14, 2003).

———. 1998b. *Conflict of interest.* Center for Technology Management. http://www.wustl.edu (accessed spring 2001).

Watterson, J. 2000. *College football: History, spectacle, controversy.* Baltimore: Johns Hopkins University Press.

Webster, F. 2002. *Theories of the information society.* New York: Routledge.

Webster, J. 1996. *Shaping women's work: Gender, employment, and information technology.* New York: Longman.

Weil, V. 1990. *Owning scientific and technical information: Value and ethical issues.* New Brunswick: Rutgers University Press.

Weisbrod, B. A. 1988. *The nonprofit economy.* Cambridge, MA: Harvard University Press.

———. 1998a. IIT. Serving up ethics for lunch. www.edoc.com/aaas/conduct/iit.htlm (accessed fall 2002).

———. 1998b. The nonprofit mission and its financing: Growing links between nonprofits and the rest of the economy. In *To profit or not to profit: The commercial transformation of the nonprofit sector,* ed. B. A. Weisbrod. Cambridge: Cambridge University Press.

Wertheim, S. M. 2000. Parody and free speech under the anticybersquatting consumer protection act: No laughing matter. *RA&M Newsletter* 4(10).

Western Michigan University. 2003. Collective bargaining agreement. Available through Higher Education Contract Analysis System, 2003. Washington, DC: National Education Association.

Westphal, J. D., R. Gulati, and S. M. Shortell. 1997. Customization or conformity: An institutional and network perspective on the content and consequences of TQM adoption. *Administrative Science Quarterly* 42:366–94.

Westphal, J. D., M. Seidel, and K. Stewart. 2001. Second-order imitation: Uncovering latent effects of board network ties. *Administrative Science Quarterly* 46(4): 717–47.

Wetzel, D., and D. Yaeger. 2000. *Sole influence: Basketball, corporate greed, and the corruption of America's youth.* New York: Warner Books.

Whalen, E. 1991. *Responsibility center budgeting: An approach to decentralized management for institutions of higher education.* Bloomington: Indiana University Press.

Williams, W. A. 1961. *The Contours of American History.* Cleveland: World Publishing.

Williams v. Weisser. 1969. Civ. No. 32615, June 5. Court of Appeal of California, Second Appellate District, Division Five.

Windschitl, M. 1998. The WWW and classroom research: What path should we take? *Educational researcher* 27(1): 28–33.

Winner, L. 1977. *Autonomous technology: Technics-out-of-control as a theme in political thought.* Cambridge: MIT Press.

Winston, G. C. 1999. Subsidies, hierarchy and peers: The awkward economics of higher education. *Journal of Economic Perspectives* 13(1): 13–36.

Worcester Polytechnic Institute. 2002. History of the Internet and Internet2. www.wpi.edu/Admin/IT/Internet2/history.html (accessed March 1, 2003).

World Trade Organization (WTO). 2003. GATS: Fact and fiction. www.wto.org/english/tratop_e/serv_e/gatsfacts1004_e.pdf.

Xie, Y., and Z. Zhou. 2003. Ownership of class notes: Academic freedom or capitalism; Whose freedom, Whose capitalism? Unpublished class paper. Center for the Study of Higher Education, University of Arizona, Tuscon.

Yablon, M. 2001. Test flight: The scam behind SAT bashing. *New Republic,* October 30, 24–25.

Young, J. R. 2003. Early-admission applicants have strong advantage over others applying to elite colleges, new book argues. *Chronicle of Higher Education,* February 21.

Zajac, E. J., and J. D. Westphal. 1996. Director reputation, CEO-board power, and the dynamics of board interlocks. *Administrative science quarterly* 41(3): 507–29.

Zeitlin, M. 1974. Corporate ownership and control: The large corporation and the capitalist class. *American Journal of Sociology* 79:1073–119.

Zimbalist, A. 2001. *Unpaid professionals: Commercialism and conflict in big-time college sports.* Princeton: Princeton University Press.

Zuboff, S. 1988. *In the age of the smart machine: The future of work and power.* New York: Basic Books.

INDEX